PRAISE FOR THE SETH BOOKS

"The Seth books present an alternate map of reality with a new diagram of the psyche . . . useful to all explorers of consciousness."

— Deepak Chopra, author of *The Seven Spiritual Laws of Success*

"Seth was one of my first metaphysical teachers. He remains a constant source of knowledge and inspiration in my life."

— Marianne Williamson, author of *A Return to Love*

"I would like to see the Seth books as required reading for anyone on their spiritual pathway. The amazing in-depth information in the Seth books is as relevant today as it was in the early '70s when Jane Roberts first channeled this material."

— Louise Hay, author of *You Can Heal Your Life*

"Seth's teachings had an important influence on my life and work, and provided one of the initial inspirations for writing *Creative Visualization*."

— Shakti Gawain, author of *Creative Visualization*

"The Seth books were of great benefit to me on my spiritual journey and helped me to see another way of looking at the world."

— Gerald G. Jampolsky, author of *Love Is Letting Go of Fear*

"As you read Seth's words, you will gain more than just new ideas. Seth's energy comes through every page — energy that expands your consciousness and changes your thoughts about the nature of reality."

— Sanaya Roman, author of *Living with Joy*

"Quite simply one of the best books I've ever read."

— Richard Bach, author of *Jonathan Livingston Seagull*

"To my great surprise — and slight annoyance — I found that Seth eloquently and lucidly articulated a view of reality that I had arrived at only after great effort and an extensive study of both paranormal phenomena and quantum physics. . . ."

— Michael Talbot, author of *The Holographic Universe*

BOOKS BY JANE ROBERTS

The Rebellers (1963)

The Coming of Seth (How to Develop Your ESP Power) (1966)

The Seth Material (1970)

Seth Speaks: The Eternal Validity of the Soul, A Seth Book (1972)

The Education of Oversoul Seven (1973)

The Nature of Personal Reality, A Seth Book (1974)

Adventures in Consciousness (1975)

Dialogues of The Soul and Mortal Self in Time (1975)

Psychic Politics: An Aspect Psychology Book (1976)

The World View of Paul Cézanne: A Psychic Interpretation (1977)

The Afterdeath Journal of an American Philosopher: The World View of William James (1978)

The "Unknown" Reality: Vol. 1, A Seth Book (1977)

The "Unknown" Reality: Vol. 2, A Seth Book (1979)

The Further Education of Oversoul Seven (1979)

Emir's Education in the Proper Use of Magical Powers (1979)

The Nature of the Psyche: Its Human Expression, A Seth Book (1979)

The Individual and the Nature of Mass Events, A Seth Book (1981)

The God of Jane: A Psychic Manifesto (1981)

If We Live Again: Or, Public Magic and Private Love (1982)

Oversoul Seven and the Museum of Time (1984)

Dreams, "Evolution," & Value Fulfillment: Vol. 1, A Seth Book (1986)

Dreams, "Evolution," & Value Fulfillment: Vol. 2, A Seth Book (1986)

Seth, Dreams, and Projection of Consciousness (1986)

The Magical Approach, A Seth Book (1995)

The Way Toward Health, A Seth Book (1997)

SETH SPEAKS . . .

If you believe firmly that your consciousness is locked up somewhere inside your skull and is powerless to escape it, if you feel that your consciousness ends at the boundary of your body, then you sell yourself short, and you will think that I am a delusion. I am no more a delusion than you are.

I can say this to each of my readers honestly: I am older than you are, at least in terms of age as you think of it.

If a writer can qualify as any kind of authority on the basis of age, therefore, then I should get a medal. I am an energy personality essence, no longer focused in physical matter. As such, I am aware of some truths that many of you seem to have forgotten.

I hope to remind you of these.

SETH SPEAKS

THE
ETERNAL VALIDITY
OF THE SOUL

A
Seth
BOOK

SETH
SPEAKS

THE
ETERNAL VALIDITY
OF THE SOUL

Jane Roberts
NOTES BY ROBERT F. BUTTS

AMBER-ALLEN PUBLISHING

NEW WORLD LIBRARY

Co-published by Amber-Allen Publishing and New World Library

EDITORIAL OFFICE:
Amber-Allen Publishing
P.O. Box 6657
San Rafael, CA 94903

DISTRIBUTION OFFICE:
New World Library
14 Pamaron Way
Novato, CA 94949

Editorial: Janet Mills
Cover Art: Robert F. Butts
Cover Design: Beth Hansen

Library of Congress Cataloging-in-Publication Data

Seth, (Spirit), 1929–1984
     Seth speaks : the eternal validity of the soul / [channeled by] Jane
     Roberts : notes by Robert F. Butts.
          p.   cm. – (A Seth book)
     Originally published: Englewood Cliffs, N.J. : Prentice-Hall, 1972.
     ISBN 978-1-878424-07-5 (alk. paper) : $18.95
          1. Spirit writings. 2. Reincarnation–Miscellanea. 3. Soul–Miscel-
     lanea. I. Roberts, Jane, 1929–1984   II. Butts, Robert F.   III. Title.
     IV. Series: Seth (Spirit), 1929–1984. Seth book.
     BF1301.S387 1994   94 - 10678
     133.9'3–dc20   CIP

ISBN 978-1-878424-07-5
Printed in Canada on 100% Post-Consumer Waste Recycled Paper
Distributed by Publishers Group West

42   41   40   39   38

CONTENTS

INTRODUCTION

This book was written by a personality called Seth, who speaks of himself as an "energy personality essence" no longer focused in physical form. He has been speaking through me for over seven years now, in twice weekly trance sessions.

My psychic initiation really began one evening in September, 1963, however, as I sat writing poetry. Suddenly my consciousness left my body, and my mind was barraged by ideas that were astonishing and new to me at the time. On return to my body, I discovered that my hands had produced an automatic script, explaining many of the concepts that I'd been given. The notes were even titled — *The Physical Universe as Idea Construction.*

Because of that experience, I began doing research into psychic activity, and planned a book on the project. In line with this, my husband, Rob, and I experimented with a Ouija board late in 1963. After the first few sessions, the pointer spelled out messages that claimed to come from a personality called Seth.

Neither Rob or I had any psychic background, and when I began to anticipate the board's replies, I took it for granted that they were coming from my subconscious. Not long after, however, I felt impelled to say the words aloud, and within a month I was speaking for Seth while in a trance state.

The messages seemed to begin where *Idea Construction* left off, and later Seth said that my expansion of consciousness experience had represented his first attempt at contact: Since then, Seth has delivered a continuing manuscript that now totals over six thousand typewritten pages. We call it the Seth material, and it deals with such topics as the nature of physical matter, time, and reality, the god concept, probable universes, health, and reincarnation. From the beginning, the obvious quality of the material intrigued us, and it was for this reason that we continued.

Following the publication of my first book in this field, letters came from strangers asking for Seth's help. We held sessions for those most in need. Many of the people involved couldn't attend, since they lived in other parts of the country, yet Seth's advice helped them, and the information he gave by mail concerning individual backgrounds was correct.

Rob has always taken verbatim notes of the Seth sessions, using his own shorthand system. Later in the week he types them and adds them to our collection of Seth material. Rob's excellent notes point up the living framework in which the sessions take place. His support and encouragement have been invaluable.

To our way of thinking, we have kept over six hundred appointments with the universe — though Rob would never describe it that way himself. These appointments are kept in our well-lighted, large living room, but in deeper terms they take place within the spaceless area of human personality.

I do not mean to imply that we have any cornerstone on truth, or give the impression that we wait breathlessly for the undistorted secrets of the ages to gush forth. I do know that each individual has access to intuitional knowledge and can gain glimpses of inner reality. The universe speaks to each of us in this regard. In our case, the Seth sessions are the framework in which this kind of communication takes place.

In *The Seth Material,* published in 1970, I explained these events and gave Seth's views on a variety of subjects with excerpts from the sessions. I also described our encounters with psychologists and parapsychologists, as we tried to understand our experiences and place them within the context of normal life. The tests we conducted to verify Seth's clairvoyant abilities were also described. As far as we are concerned, he came through with flying colors.

It was extremely difficult to choose a few excerpts on any given topic from Seth's growing body of work. As a result, *The Seth Material* necessarily left many questions unanswered and many topics unexplored. Two weeks after it was finished, however, Seth dictated the outline for this present manuscript, in which he would be free to state his ideas in his own way, in book form.

Here is a copy of that outline, which was given to us in Session 510, January 19, 1970. As you'll see here, Seth calls me Ruburt, and Rob, Joseph. These names represent our entire personalities as distinguished from our present physically oriented selves.

I am working on some other material just now that you will be given, and so you must bear with me for a few moments. For example, I would like to give you some idea of the contents of my own book. Many issues will be involved. The book will include a description of the way in which it is being written, and the procedures necessary so that my own ideas can be spoken by Ruburt, or for that matter translated at all, in vocal terms.

I do not have a physical body, and yet I will be writing a book. The first chapter will explain how and why.

(By now [Rob wrote in his notes] Jane's pace had slowed considerably, and her eyes were often closed. She took many pauses, some of them long.)

The next chapter will describe what you may call my present environment; my present "characteristics," and my associates. By this I mean those others with whom I come in contact.

The next chapter will describe my work, and those dimensions of reality into which it takes me, for as I travel into your reality I also travel into others, to fulfill that purpose which is mine to fill.

The next chapter will deal with my past in your terms, and some of those personalities that I have been and have known. At the same time I will make it clear that there is no past, present, or future, and explain that there is no contradiction even though I may speak in terms of past existences. This may possibly run two chapters.

The next chapter will give the story of our meeting — you *(to me)*, Ruburt and I, from my viewpoint of course, and the ways in which I contacted Ruburt's inner awareness long before either of you knew anything about psychic phenomena, or my existence.

The next chapter will deal with the experience of any personality at the point of death, and with the many variations on this basic adventure. I will use some of my own deaths as examples.

The next chapter will deal with existence after death, with its many variations. Both of these chapters will bear on reincarnation as it applies to death, and some emphasis will also be given to death *at the end of* the last incarnation.

The next chapter will deal with the emotional realities of love and kinship between personalities — with what happens to these during succeeding incarnations, for some fall by the wayside and some are retained.

The next chapter will deal with your physical reality as it appears to me and others like me. This chapter will contain some rather fascinating points, for not only do you form the physical reality that you know, but you are also forming other quite valid environments in other realities by your present thoughts, desires and emotions.

The next chapter will deal with the eternal validity of dreams as gateways into these other realities, and as open areas through which the "inner self" glimpses the many facets of its experience and communicates with other levels of its reality.

The next chapter will deal further with this subject, as I relate the various ways that I have entered the dreams of others, both as an instructor and as a guide.

The next chapter will deal with the basic methods of communication that are used by any consciousness, according to its degree, whether or not it is physical. This will lead up to the basic communication used by human personalities as you understand them, and point out these inner communications as existing independently of the physical senses, which are merely physical extensions of inner perception.

I will tell the reader how he sees what he sees, or hears what he hears, and why. I hope to show through the entire book that the reader himself is independent of his physical image, and I hope, myself, to give him some methods that will prove my thesis to him.

The next chapter will relate what experience I have had in all my existences with those "pyramid gestalts" of which I speak in the material, and about my own relationship with the personality you call Seth

Two, and with multidimensional consciousnesses far more evolved than I.

My message to the reader will be: "Basically, you are no more of a physical personality than I am, and in telling you of my reality I tell you of your own."

There will be a chapter on the religions of the world, on the distortions and truths within them; the three Christs; and some data concerning a lost religion, belonging to a people of which you have no information. These people lived on a planet in the same space that your earth now occupies, "before" your planet existed. They destroyed it through their own error, and were reincarnated when your planet was prepared. Their memories became the basis for the birth of religion as you now think of it.

There will be a chapter on probable gods and probable systems.

There will be a question and answer chapter.

There will be a final chapter in which I will ask the reader to close his eyes and become aware of the reality in which I exist, and of his own inner reality. I will give the methods. In this chapter I will invite the reader to use his "inner senses," to see me in his own way.

While my communications will come exclusively through Ruburt at all times, to protect the integrity of the material, I will invite the reader to become aware of me as a personality, so that he may then realize that communication from other realities is possible, and that he himself is therefore open to perception that is not physical.

Now this is my outline for the book, but it contains merely a sketch of my intentions. I am not giving a fuller outline, for I do not want Ruburt to anticipate me. The difficulties involved in such communications will be given thoroughly. It will be made clear that so-called paranormal communications come from various levels of reality, and that those communications describe the reality in which they exist. So I will describe mine, and others of which I have knowledge.

This is not to say that other dimensions do not exist of which I am ignorant. I will dictate the book during our sessions.

This is the title for our book *(smile): Seth Speaks: The Eternal Validity of the Soul.*

I am using the term soul, for it will have instant meaning to most readers. I suggest you equip yourself with some good pens.

Precisely because I am acquainted with the effort involved in writing a book, I was cautious when Seth spoke of writing his own. Though I knew perfectly well that he could do it, a nagging part of me questioned. "Granted, the Seth material is really significant, but what does Seth know about writing books? About the organization required? Or about directing himself to the public?"

Rob kept telling me not to worry about it. Friends and students seemed astonished that of all people, I should have any doubts, but I thought — of all people, who else *should* have doubts? Here was a stated intent. Could Seth follow through?

Seth began dictating the book in our next Session 511, January 21, 1970, and finished it in Session 591, August 11, 1971. The intervening sessions did not all involve book dictation, however. Some were devoted to personal matters, some given for specific people who needed help, and some were in answer to philosophical questions not connected with the book. I also took several "little vacations." Despite such layoffs, Seth always picked right up, precisely where he left off dictation.

During the time that he was working on his book, I was writing four hours a day on a book of my own, conducting my weekly ESP class, and finding myself swamped by the correspondence that followed publication of *The Seth Material*. I also began holding a weekly class in creative writing.

Out of curiosity, I looked over a few of the early chapters of Seth's book, then stayed away from it. Occasionally Rob told me about a few passages that he thought my students might be particularly interested in. Otherwise I paid no attention to the book, being content to let Seth do it. Generally speaking, I put his work out of my mind, and didn't even see the manuscript for months at a time.

Reading the finished book was a delightful experience. As a whole it was completely new to me, though each word had been spoken through my lips, and I had devoted many evenings in trance to its production. This was particularly strange to me since I am a writer myself, used to organizing my own material, keeping track of it, and hovering over it like a mother hen.

Because of my own writing experience, I'm also well aware of the process involved in translating unconscious material into conscious reality. It's particularly obvious when I'm working on poetry. Whatever else is involved in Seth's book, certainly some kind of unconscious activity is operating at high gear. It was only natural, then, that I found myself comparing my own conscious creative experience with the trance procedure involved in Seth's book. I wanted to discover why I felt that Seth's book was *his*, as divorced from mine. If both were coming from the same unconscious, then why the subjective differences in my feelings?

These differences were obvious from the first. When I'm caught up in inspiration, writing a poem, then I'm "turned on," excited, filled with a sense of urgency, and discovery. Just before this happens, however, an idea comes out of nowhere, it seems. It is "given." It simply appears, and from it new creative connections spring.

I'm alert, yet open and receptive — suspended in a strange psychic elasticity between poised attention and passivity. The particular poem or idea is the only thing in the world for me at that point. The highly personal involvement, the work and play involved in helping the idea "out," all make the poem mine.

This kind of experience has been familiar to me since early childhood. It is the cornerstone of my existence. Without it, or when I am not working generally within that framework, I become listless and sad. To some degree, I have that same sense of personal creativity now, as I write this introduction. It is "mine."

I was not connected in this way with Seth's book, and had no awareness of the creative processes involved. I went into trance as I do for our regular sessions. Seth dictated the book through me, speaking through my lips. The creative work was so distant from me, that in this respect I could not call the product my own. I am, instead, given a complete product in Seth's book — an excellent one — for which I am, of course, exceedingly grateful.

I've found that only my own writing gives me the particular kind of creative satisfaction that I need, however — the conscious involvement with unconscious material, the "excitement of the chase." Because Seth does his thing, I am not absolved from doing mine. I would feel deprived if I did not continue with my own work.

Anyone can say, of course, that in Seth's book the hidden processes are so separate from my normal consciousness that the final product only *seems* to come from another personality. I can only state my own feelings and emphasize that Seth's book, and the whole six-thousand-page manuscript of Seth material, don't take care of my own creative expression or responsibility. If both came from the same unconscious, it seems that there would be no slack to take up.

Despite this, I'm aware of the fact that I was necessary to the production of Seth's book. He needs my ability with words; even, I think, my turn of mind. Certainly my writing training aids in the translation of his material and helps give it form, no matter how unconsciously this is done. Certain personality characteristics are important too, I imagine — the agility with which I can switch the focus of my consciousness, for example.

Seth intimates as much in Chapter Four, when he says, "Now the information in this book is being directed to some extent through the inner senses of the woman who is in trance as I write it. Such endeavor is the result of highly organized inner precision, and of training. [She] could not receive the information from me — it could not be translated nor interpreted — while she was focused intensely in the physical environment."

Looked at merely as an example of unconscious production, however, Seth's book clearly shows that organization, discrimination, and reasoning are certainly not qualities of the conscious mind alone, and demonstrates the range and activity of which the inner self is capable. I do not believe that I could get the equivalent of Seth's book on my own. The best I could do would be to hit certain high points, perhaps in isolated poems or essays, and they would lack the overall unity, continuity, and organization that Seth has here provided automatically.

Besides this, I have certain unique experiences during sessions that seem to compensate for my lack of conscious creative involvement. Often I participate in Seth's great energy and humor, for example, enjoying a sense of emotional richness and encountering Seth's personality on a very strange level. I feel his mood and vitality clearly, though they are not directed at me, but to whomever Seth is addressing at the moment. I feel them as they pass through me.

As Rob's notes show, I often have other kinds of experiences, also, while speaking for Seth. Sometimes, for instance, I see inner visions. These may illustrate what Seth is saying, so that I am receiving information in two ways, or they may be completely separate from the script.

I've had several "out-of-body" experiences also during sessions, when I saw events actually happening some thousands of miles away.

This book is Seth's way of demonstrating that human personality is multidimensional, that we exist in many realities at once, that the soul or inner self is not something apart from us, but the very medium in which we exist. He emphasizes that "truth" is not found by going from teacher to teacher, church to church, or discipline to discipline, but by looking within the self. The intimate knowledge of consciousness, the "secrets of the universe," are not esoteric truths to be hidden from the people, then. Such information is as natural to man as air, and as available to those who honestly seek it by looking to the source within.

In my opinion, Seth has written a book that is a classic of its kind. After referring to him cautiously as "a personality," I feel bound to add that Seth is an astute philosopher and psychologist, deeply knowledgeable in the ways of human personality, and well aware of the triumph and plight of human consciousness.

I'm personally intrigued, of course, that this book was written through me, without my conscious mind there at every point, anxiously checking, organizing, and criticizing, as it does in my own work. Then, while my creative and intuitional abilities are given a good deal of freedom, the conscious mind is definitely in control. Yet this book was not written "by itself," in the same way that some poems seem to be. Often a writer will say that a certain book "wrote itself," and I know what that means. In this case, however, the book came from a specific source, not just from "out there," and it is colored by the author's personality, which is not mine.

The whole creative venture may be the initiation of a personality, Seth, who then writes books. Seth may be as much of a creation as his book is. If so, this is an excellent instance of multidimensional art, done at such a rich level of unconsciousness that the "artist" is unaware of her own work and as much intrigued by it as anyone else.

This is an interesting hypothesis. In fact, Seth speaks about multidimensional art in his book. But Seth does more than write books. He is a fully developed personality with a variety of interests: writing, teaching, helping others. His sense of humor is quite individualistic and unlike mine. He is shrewd; in his manner more earthy than ethereal. He knows how to explain complex theories simply, in person-to-person contact. Perhaps more important, he is able to relate these ideas to ordinary living.

Seth also appears frequently in the dreams of my students, giving them instructions that work — either involving methods of using their abilities or of achieving certain goals. Almost all of my students have frequent "class dreams," also, in which Seth addresses them as a group and initiates dream experiments. Sometimes they see him as he appears in the portrait Rob painted of him. On occasion he speaks through my image, as in normal sessions. I have awakened many times, when such dream sessions were taking place, hearing Seth's words still lingering in my mind.

It's not unusual that students should dream of Seth, of course, or that they should dream of me. But certainly Seth has achieved independent status in their eyes and has become a vehicle of instruction even in the dream state. In other words, besides producing the continuing Seth material and this book, Seth has entered the minds and consciousness of many people.

This is a good deal of accomplishment in seven years for any personality, regardless of its status. For a nonphysical personality, it is astonishing indeed. To ascribe all of this activity to a figment of the unconscious seems rather much. (In the same amount of time I've published two books, finished another, and begun a fourth. I mention this to show that Seth hasn't been absorbing any of my own creativity.)

Rob and I don't refer to Seth as a spirit; we dislike the connotations of the term. Actually what we object to is the conventional idea of a spirit, which is an extension of quite limited ideas of human personality, only projected more or less intact into an afterlife. You can say that Seth is a dramatization of the unconscious or an independent personality. Personally, I don't see why the statements have to be contradictory. Seth may be a dramatization playing a very real role — explaining his greater reality in the only terms we can understand. This is my opinion at this time.

First of all, to me the term "unconscious" is a poor one, barely hinting at an actual open psychic system, with deep intertwining roots uniting all kinds of consciousness; a network in which we are all connected. Our individuality rises out of it, but also helps form it. This source contains past, present, and future information; only the ego experiencing time as we know it. I also believe that this open system contains other kinds of consciousness beside our own.

Because of my own experiences, particularly with out-of-body states, I'm convinced that consciousness is not dependent upon physical matter. Certainly physical expression is *my* main mode of existence right now, but I don't take this to infer that all consciousness must be so oriented. Only the most blind egotism, it seems to me, would dare define reality in its own terms or project its own limitations and experience upon the rest of existence.

I accept Seth's idea of multidimensional personality as described in this book because my experiences, and those of my students seem to confirm it. I also think that in that open system of consciousness and unlimited source, there is an independent Seth who operates in quite different terms than we do.

In what terms? Quite honestly, I don't know. The closest I've come to explaining my own views was in a short intuitive statement I wrote for my ESP class, as I tried to clear my ideas for myself and my students as well. Rob had told me about the "Speakers", as Seth calls them in this book — personalities who continually speak to man through the ages, reminding him of inner knowledge so that it is never really forgotten. This evocative idea inspired me to write the small piece which I am including here. It points up the framework in which I think Seth and others like him may exist.

"We come together in ways that we do not understand. We're composed of elements, chemicals, and atoms, and yet we speak and call ourselves by name. We organize about our inner stuff the outer stuff that coagulates into flesh and bone. Our identities or personalities spring from sources we do not know.

"Perhaps what we are has always waited, hidden in the possibilities of creation, dispersed and unknowing — in the rain and wind that swept across Europe in the thirteenth century — in the heaving mountain ranges — in the clouds that rushed through the skies of other times and places. As dust particles, we may have blown past Greek doorways. We may have been sparked on and off into consciousness and unconsciousness a million times, touched by desire, by yearnings toward creativity and perfection we barely understood.

"And so there may be others now (like Seth), also without images, but knowing — others who have been what we are and more — others who remember what we have forgotten. They may have discovered through some acceleration of consciousness other forms of being, or dimensions of reality of which we are also part.

"So we give them names who are nameless, as basically we are nameless. And we listen, but usually we try to squeeze their messages into concepts that we can understand, cloaking them in worn stereotyped images. Yet they are all about us, in the wind and trees, formed and unformed, more alive in many ways perhaps than we are — the speakers.

"Through these voices, these intuitions, these flashes of insights and messages, the universe speaks to us, to each of us personally. You are being addressed, and so am I. Learn to hear your own messages, not to distort what you hear or translate it into old alphabets.

"In class (and in life, generally,) I think we are responding to such messages, sometimes acting them out with almost childlike wisdom, forming them into dramas that are original and individualistic — dramas that arouse within us meanings that cannot be put into words.

"This may be the kind of play in which the 'gods' indulge, from which creations grow, sprawling out in all directions. We may be responding to the gods in ourselves — those inner sparks of knowing that defy our own three-dimensional knowledge.

"Seth may be leading us out of our usual limitations, into another realm that is ours by right — elemental whether we are in flesh or out of it. He may be the voice of our combined selves, saying, 'While you are conscious bodies, remember what it was like and will be like to be bodiless, to be freewheeling energy without a name but with a voice that does not need tongue, with a creativity that does not need flesh. We are yourselves, turned inside out.'"

Regardless of my ideas about Seth or the nature of reality, however, this manuscript must stand on its own as a book. It bears the mark of Seth's personality, as any book carries indelibly within it the stamp of its author, no more and no less. The ideas within it deserve a hearing, despite their source, and conversely, because of it.

When our sessions first began, I thought of publishing the material as my own, so that it could be accepted for its value, without introducing questions about its source. This did not seem just, however, because the way the Seth material is produced is part of the message and reinforces it.

Seth's dictation is given as we received it, in order, with no paragraphs added or deleted. He certainly knows the difference between spoken and written language. His class sessions are less formal, with a good amount of give and take. This book, though, is much more like our own private sessions in which the body of the material is delivered. The emphasis is more definitely on content, the stress on the written rather than the spoken word.

Seth's sentence structure has not been changed either, except in occasional instances. (A few times I made two sentences out of one long one, for example.) Much of the punctuation was indicated by Seth. In such cases, we just inserted the hyphens, semicolons, and parentheses as he suggested, and deleted the directions themselves to avoid distracting the reader. Where Seth asked for quotes, we have used double quotes; otherwise, where the meaning seems to call for them, single quotation marks are used. Seth also instructed us to underline certain words.

Seth's sentences are often long, particularly for verbal delivery, yet he never gets lost or loses touch with syntax or meaning. Whenever a difficulty seemed to exist in this respect, we checked the original session and saw that somewhere along the line an error in copying had been made. (I noticed this particularly, since I have tried dictating letters into a recorder, with noted lack of success. After the first few sentences, I had great difficulty in remembering what I'd said, or how I expressed it.)

Proofreading involved work on Rob's notes mainly, as he made them more presentable. In some cases, material not a part of the book was included if it seemed relevant, cast sidelights on the method of presentation, or gave insights into Seth himself. As Rob's notes also show, Seth began dictating the Appendix as soon as the book was finished. Rather amusingly, I didn't realize that Seth had already begun the Appendix, and I spent several days wondering just who was supposed to take care of it — and if Seth was, when he would begin.

Here is another note of interest along these lines. I write three drafts of my own work, and sometimes still wind up dissatisfied. This book was dictated in its final draft. Seth also followed his outline far more faithfully than I've ever followed mine. He also deviated from it in some cases, however, as is every author's right.

From here on, Seth speaks for himself.

Jane Roberts
Elmira, New York
September 27, 1971

SETH
SPEAKS

THE
ETERNAL VALIDITY
OF THE SOUL

PART ONE

CHAPTER 1

I Do Not Have a Physical Body,
Yet I Am Writing This Book

SESSION 511, JANUARY 21, 1970,
9:10 P.M. WEDNESDAY

(*In beginning these notes, let me mention that there are certain definite changes in Jane when she is in trance and speaking for Seth.*

(*Usually Jane goes in and out of trance with remarkable speed. Her eyes aren't closed during sessions, except for relatively brief periods — but they can be barely open, say, or half open, or wide open and much darker than usual. She sits for sessions in her Kennedy rocker, but on occasion she gets up and moves about. She smokes in trance and sips a little wine, beer, or coffee. Sometimes, when her trance has been very deep, it takes her a few minutes "to really come out of it," as she puts it. Almost always she joins me in a snack after the session, no matter how late it is.*

(*Jane's voice in trance can be almost conversational in tone, volume, and pace, but is subject to a wide range of these qualities. Usually it's somewhat deeper and stronger than her "own" voice. Once in a while her "Seth voice" is very loud indeed, much more powerful, with definite masculine overtones and with an obvious, tremendous energy behind it. Most of our sessions however are fairly quiet.*

(*Seth speaks with an accent that's hard to pinpoint. It's been called Russian, Irish, German, Dutch, Italian, and even French. Seth once humorously commented that his way of speaking was actually due to his own "cosmopolitan background," acquired through many lifetimes. Jane and I think it is simply individual, and that it invokes various responses in people according to their own ethnic and emotional backgrounds.*

(There are two more effects that Jane always manifests while she is in trance. One is a more angular quality in her mannerisms. The other is a rearrangement of her facial muscles; a tautness resulting, I believe, from an infusion of energy — or of consciousness. At times this effect is quite pronounced, and I can easily sense the immediacy of Seth's presence.

(I think these changes in Jane during sessions are caused by her creative reception of a portion of an entity, an essence, that we call Seth, and by her own ideas of what this certain segment is like as she casts it in the masculine gender. Her transformation as Seth is original, and absorbing to watch and participate in. Regardless of degree, Seth is uniquely and kindly present. I am listening to, and exchanging dialogue with, another personality.

(Before the session, Jane said she felt rather nervous; she thought Seth would start his own book this evening. Her feeling of nervousness is quite unusual in these sessions. I offered reassurances, telling her to forget the whole thing and let the book come out in its own way.)

Now: I bid you, Joseph, a good evening.

("Good evening, Seth.")

Our friend Ruburt does indeed have stage fright, and to some extent this is understandable, so I bear with him.

However, let us begin with Chapter One. *(Smile.)* Ruburt may write an introduction if he likes. *(Pause.)*

Chapter One

Now: You have heard of ghost hunters. I can quite literally be called a ghost writer, though I do not approve of the term "ghost." It is true that I am usually not seen in physical terms. I do not like the word "spirit," either; and yet if your definition of that word implies the idea of a personality without a physical body, then I would have to agree that the description fits me.

I address an unseen audience. However, I know that my readers exist, and therefore I shall ask each of them, now, to grant me the same privilege.

I write this book through the auspices of a woman of whom I have become quite fond. To others it seems strange that I address her as "Ruburt," and "him," but the fact is that I have known her in other times and places, by other names. She has been both a man and a woman, and the entire identity who has lived these separate lives can be designated by the name of Ruburt.

Names are not important, however. My name is Seth. Names are simply designations, symbols; and yet since you must use them, I shall also. I write this book with the cooperation of Ruburt, who speaks the words for me. In this life Ruburt is called Jane, and her husband, Robert Butts, takes down the words that Jane speaks. I call him Joseph.

My readers may suppose that they are physical creatures, bound within physical bodies, imprisoned within bone, flesh, and skin. If you believe that your existence is dependent upon this corporeal image, then you feel in danger of extinction, for no physical form lasts, and no body, however beautiful in youth, retains the same vigor and enchantment in old age. If you identify with your own youth, or beauty, or intellect, or accomplishments, then there is the constant gnawing knowledge that these attributes can and will vanish.

I am writing this book to assure you that this is not the case. Basically you are no more of a physical being than I am, and I have donned and discarded more bodies than I care to tell. Personalities who do not exist do not write books. I am quite independent of a physical image, and so are you.

Consciousness creates form. It is not the other way around. All personalities are not physical. It is only because you are so busily concerned with daily matters that you do not realize that there is a portion of you who knows that its own powers are far superior to those shown by the ordinary self.

You have each lived other existences, and that knowledge is within you though you are not consciously aware of it. I hope that this book will serve to release the deeply intuitive self within each of my readers, and to bring to the foreground of consciousness whatever particular insights will serve you most.

As I begin this book it is late January, in your time, 1970. Ruburt is a slim, dark-haired, quick woman now, who sits in a rocker and speaks these words for me.

(*Long pause at 9:35.*) My consciousness is fairly well focused within Ruburt's body. It is a cold night. This is our first experience in writing a complete book in trance, and Ruburt was somewhat nervous before the session began. It is not just a simple matter of having this woman speak for me. There are many manipulations necessary, and psychological

· 4 ·

adjustments. We have established what I refer to as a psychological bridge between us — that is, between Ruburt and myself.

I do not speak through Ruburt as one might through a telephone. Instead there is a psychological extension, a projection of characteristics on both of our parts, and this I use for our communications. Later I will explain how this psychological framework is created and maintained, for it is like a road that must be kept clear of debris. You would be much better off in reading this book if you asked yourself who you are, rather than asked who I am, for you cannot understand what I am unless you understand the nature of personality and the characteristics of consciousness.

If you believe firmly that your consciousness is locked up somewhere inside your skull and is powerless to escape it, if you feel that your consciousness ends at the boundary of your body, then you sell yourself short, and you will think that I am a delusion. I am no more a delusion than you are, and that may be a loaded sentence.

I can say this to each of my readers honestly *(smile)*: I am older than you are, at least in terms of age as you think of it.

If a writer can qualify as any kind of authority on the basis of age, therefore, then I should get a medal. I am an energy personality essence, no longer focused in physical matter. As such, I am aware of some truths that many of you seem to have forgotten.

I hope to remind you of these. I do not speak so much to the part of you that you think of as yourself as to that part of you that you do not know, that you have to some extent denied and to some extent forgotten. That part of you reads this book, [even] as "you" read it.

I speak to those who believe in a god, and those who do not, to those who believe that science will find all answers as to the nature of reality, and to those who do not. I hope to give you clues that will enable you to study the nature of reality for yourself as you have never studied it before.

There are several things that I shall ask you to understand. You are not stuck in time like a fly in a closed bottle, whose wings are therefore useless. You cannot trust your physical senses to give you a true picture of reality. They are lovely liars, with such a fantastic tale to tell that you believe it without question. You are sometimes wiser, more creative, and far more knowledgeable when you are dreaming than when you are awake.

These statements may seem highly dubious to you now, but when we are finished I hope that you will see that they are plain statements of fact.

What I will tell you has been told before throughout the centuries, and given again when it was forgotten. I hope to clarify many points that have been distorted through the years. And I offer my original interpretation of others, for no knowledge exists in a vacuum, and all information must be interpreted and colored by the personality who holds it and passes it on. Therefore I describe reality as I know it, and my experience in many layers and dimensions.

This is not to say that other realities do not exist. I have been conscious before your earth was formed. To write this book — and in most of my communications with Ruburt — I adopt from my own bank of past personalities those characteristics that seem appropriate. There are many of us, personalities like myself, unfocused in physical matter or time. Our existence seems strange to you only because you do not realize the true potentials of personality, and you are hypnotized by your own limited concepts.

(Pause, then humorously): You may take a break.

("Thank you.")

(10:18. Jane left trance rather easily, although it had been a good one. She was quite surprised that so much time had passed. She was also much relieved that Seth had started the book, while keeping her well under. "Oh, he's smart," she laughed. "Somebody's pretty tricky.")

(Seth resumed his book at 10:34.)

I am primarily a teacher, but I have not been a man of letters *per se*. I am primarily a personality with a message: You create the world that you know. You have been given perhaps the most awesome gift of all: the ability to project your thoughts outward into physical form.

The gift brings a responsibility, and many of you are tempted to congratulate yourselves on the successes of your lives, and blame God, fate, and society for your failures. In like manner, mankind has a tendency to project his own guilt and his own errors upon a father-god image, who it seems must grow weary of so many complaints.

The fact is that each of you create your own physical reality; and *en masse*, you create both the glories and the terrors that exist within your earthly experience. Until you realize that you are the creators, you will refuse to accept this responsibility. Nor can you blame a devil for the world's misfortunes. You have grown sophisticated enough to realize that the Devil is a projection of your own psyche, but you have not grown wise enough to learn how to use your creativity constructively.

Most of my readers are familiar with the term, "muscle bound." As a species you have grown "ego bound" instead, held in a spiritual rigidity, with the intuitive portions of the self either denied or distorted beyond any recognition.

(Pause at 10:45.) The hour is growing late. Both of my friends must get up early in the morning. Ruburt is working on two books of his own and must get his sleep. Before I end this session I ask you to imagine our setting, for Ruburt has told me that a writer must be careful to set the scene. *(Humorously.)*

I speak through Ruburt twice a week, on Mondays and Wednesdays, in this same large *(living)* room. The lights are always lit. This evening it is enjoyable for me to look out through Ruburt's eyes at the wintry corner beyond.

Physical reality has always been refreshing to me, and through Ruburt's cooperation and as I write this book, I see that I was correct in appreciating its unique charms. There is one other character to be mentioned here: Willy, the cat, a beloved monster who is now sleeping.

(Willy was sleeping — snoring, actually — on top of our old-fashioned TV set. His position put him just in back of Jane's head as she sat in her rocker.)

The nature of animal consciousness in itself is a highly interesting subject, and one that we will later consider. The cat is aware of my presence, and has on several occasions reacted rather noticeably to it. In this book I hope to show the constant interactions that occur between all units of consciousness, the communication that leaps beyond the barriers of species; and in some of these discussions, we will use Willy as a case in point.

You may take a break or end the session as you prefer.

("Okay, then we'll end it, I guess.")

My heartiest wishes to you both.

("It's very interesting."

(Pause, and smile.) I hope you enjoy it.

("Good night, Seth."

(11:00 P.M. Jane was out of trance quickly. Her pace had been good

throughout the session. She said she was glad Seth had begun work on his book. "For ages in the past," she said, "whenever I thought Seth wanted to start the book, I was afraid to let him do it."

(Jane wondered now about reading the book as Seth produced it. It might be impressive to say that she didn't see the script until it was finished. We decided that it didn't matter whether she did or not, though, so she will read this material when I finish typing it up.)

SESSION 512, JANUARY 27, 1970,
9:02 P.M. TUESDAY

(Monday night's regularly scheduled session was postponed until tonight.

(Jane's pace was quite slow, with many long pauses. A few are indicated in the material. Her voice was average; her eyes were open often.)

Good evening.

("Good evening, Seth.")

Now, let us return to our new manuscript.

Since we have mentioned animals, let me say here that they do possess a kind of consciousness that does not allow them as many freedoms as your own. Yet at the same time, they are not hampered in its use by certain characteristics that often impede the practical potential of human consciousness.

Consciousness is a way of perceiving the various dimensions of reality. Consciousness as you know it is highly specialized. The physical senses allow you to perceive the three-dimensional world, and yet by their very nature they can inhibit the perception of other equally valid dimensions. Most of you identify with your daily physically oriented self. You would not think of identifying with one portion of your body and ignoring all other parts, and yet you are doing the same thing *(smile)* when you imagine that the egotistical self carries the burden of your identity.

I am telling you that you are not a cosmic bag of bones and flesh, thrown together through some mixture of chemicals and elements. I am telling you that your consciousness is not some fiery product, formed merely accidentally through the interworkings of chemical components.

You are not a forsaken offshoot of physical matter, nor is your consciousness meant to vanish like a puff of smoke. Instead, you form the physical body that you know at a deeply unconscious level with great discrimination, miraculous clarity, and intimate unconscious knowledge of each minute cell that composes it. This is not meant symbolically.

Now because your conscious mind, as you think of it, is not aware of these activities, you do not identify with this inner portion of yourselves. You prefer to identify with the part of you who watches television or cooks or works — the part you think knows what it is doing. But this seemingly unconscious portion of yourself is far more knowledgeable, and upon its smooth functioning your entire physical existence depends.

This portion is conscious, aware, alert. It is you, so focused in physical reality, who do not listen to its voice, who do not understand that it is the great psychological strength from which your physically oriented self springs.

I call this seemingly unconscious the "inner ego," for it directs inner activities. It correlates information that is perceived not through the physical senses, but through other inner channels. It is the inner perceiver of reality that exists beyond the three-dimensional. It carries within it the memory of each of your past existences. It looks into subjective dimensions that are literally infinite, and from these subjective dimensions all objective realities flow. *(Long pause.)*

All necessary information is given to you through these inner channels, and unbelievable inner activities take place before you can so much as lift a finger, flicker an eyelid, or read this sentence upon the page. This portion of your identity is quite natively clairvoyant and telepathic, so that you are warned of disasters before they occur, whether or not you consciously accept the message, and all communication takes place long before a word is spoken.

(Quietly): I may pause now and then to give you a rest.

("I'm okay.")

The "outer ego" and the inner ego operate together, the one to enable you to manipulate in the world that you know, the other to bring you those delicate inner perceptions without which physical existence could not be maintained.

There is however a portion of you, the deeper identity who forms both the inner ego and the outer ego, who decided that you would be a physical being in this place and in this time. This is the core of your identity, the psychic seed from which you sprang, the multidimensional personality of which you are part.

For those of you who wonder where I place the subconscious, as psychologists think of it, you can imagine it as a meeting place, so to speak, between the outer and inner egos. You must understand that there are no real divisions to the self, however, so we speak of various portions only to make the basic idea clear.

Since we are addressing individuals who do identify with the "normally conscious self," I bring such matters up in this first chapter because I will be using the terms later in the book, and because I want to state the fact of multidimensional personality as soon as possible.

You cannot understand yourselves, and you cannot accept my independent existence, until you rid yourself of the notion that personality is a "here and now" attribute of consciousness. Now some of the things that I may say about physical reality in this book may startle you, but remember that I am viewing it from an entirely different standpoint.

(Jane paused frequently here as she spoke for Seth. Her eyes were closed often.) You are presently focused entirely within it, wondering perhaps what else if anything there may be outside. I am outside, returning momentarily to a dimension that I know and loved. I am not in your terms a resident, however. While I have a psychic "passport," there are still some problems of translation, inconveniences of entry that I must contend with.

Many people, I hear, have lived for years within New York City and never taken a tour through the Empire State Building, while many foreigners are well acquainted with it. And so while you have a physical address, I may still be able to point out some very strange and miraculous psychic and psychological structures within your own system of reality that you have ignored.

I hope, quite frankly, to do far more than this. I hope to take you on a tour through the levels of reality that are available to you, and to guide you on a journey through the dimensions of your own psychological structure — to open up whole areas of your own consciousness of which you have been relatively unaware. I hope, therefore, not only to explain the multidimensional aspects of personality, but to give each reader some glimpse of that greater identity that is his own.

(Quietly): You may take your break.

(10:07. Jane was out of trance easily and quickly. She had no idea, she said,

of her pace, fast or slow, or of the passage of time per se. She said she had the impression that the material from Seth was highly condensed and directed, aimed at the reader, that he was trying to get the ideas across as clearly and concisely as possible.

(Jane now told me she had been very tired before the session. She resumed in the same manner at 10:29.)

The self that you know is but one fragment of your entire identity. These fragment selves are not strung together, however, like beads of a string. They are more like the various skins of an onion, or segments of an orange, all connected through the one vitality and growing out into various realities while springing from the same source.

I am not comparing personality to an orange or an onion, but I want to emphasize that as these things grow from within outward, so does each fragment of the entire self. You observe the outside aspect of objects. Your physical senses permit you to perceive the exterior forms to which you then react, but your physical senses to some extent force you to perceive reality in this manner, and the inside vitality within matter and form is not so apparent.

I can tell you, for example, that there is consciousness even within a nail, but few of my readers will take me seriously enough to stop in midsentence, and say good morning or good afternoon to the nearest nail they can find, stuck in a piece of wood.

Nevertheless, the atoms and molecules within the nail do possess their own kind of consciousness. The atoms and molecules that make up the pages of this book are also, within their own level, aware. Nothing exists — neither rock, mineral, plant, animal, or air — that is not filled with consciousness of its own kind. So you stand amid a constant vital commotion, a gestalt of aware energy, and you are yourselves physically composed of conscious cells that carry within themselves the realization of their own identity, that cooperate willingly to form the corporeal structure that is your physical body.

I am saying, of course, that there is no such thing as dead matter. There is no object that was not formed by consciousness, and each consciousness, regardless of its degree, rejoices in sensation and creativity. You cannot understand what you are unless you understand such matters.

For convenience's sake, you close out the multitudinous inner communications that leap between the tiniest parts of your flesh, yet even as physical creatures, you are to some extent a portion of other consciousnesses. There are no limitations to the self. There are no limitations to its potentials. *(Pause.)* You can adopt artificial limitations through your own ignorance, however. You can identify, for example, with your outer ego alone, and cut yourself off from abilities that are a part of you. You can deny, but you cannot change, the facts. The personality is multidimensional, even though many people hide their heads, figuratively speaking, in the sand of three-dimensional existence and pretend there is nothing more.

(Humorously): In this book I hope to pull some heads out of the sand. *(Long pause.)* You may break or end the session as you prefer.

("We'll take the break." 10:59 to 11:10.)

Now: We will shortly be finished with our Chapter One, with very little more to go. *(Amused)*: That is not for the book.

I do not mean to underestimate the outer ego. You have simply overestimated it. Nor has its true nature been recognized.

We will have more to say concerning this point, but for now it is enough to realize that your sense of identity and continuity is not dependent upon the ego.

Now at times I will be using the term "camouflage," referring to the physical world to which the outer ego relates, for physical form is one of the camouflages that reality adopts. The camouflage is real, and yet there is a much greater reality within it — the vitality that gave it form. Your physical senses then allow you to perceive this camouflage, for they are attuned to it in a highly specialized manner. But to sense the reality within the form requires a different sort of attention, and more delicate manipulations than the physical senses provide.

The ego is a jealous god, and it wants its interests served. It does not want to admit the reality of any dimensions except those within which it feels comfortable and can understand. It was meant to be an aid but it has been allowed to become a tyrant. Even so, it is much more resilient and eager to learn than is generally supposed. It is not natively as rigid as it seems. Its curiosity can be of great value.

If you have a limited conception of the nature of reality, then your ego will do its best to keep you in the small enclosed area of your accepted reality. If, on the other hand, your intuitions and creative instincts are allowed freedom, then they communicate some knowledge of greater dimensions to this most physically oriented portion of your personality.

(11:35 P.M. The session was interrupted because Rooney, one of our two cats, wanted to go out for the night. Seth had been doing well. Jane left trance quickly. After I let the cat out she waited briefly, then decided to call it an evening before Seth could return. It doesn't seem that Chapter One is quite finished.)

SESSION 513, FEBRUARY 5, 1970,
9:10 P.M. THURSDAY

(Ordinarily this session would have been held yesterday, but Jane wanted to try it on a Thursday for variety. Before the session she said, "I still get stage fright when I think of Seth doing this book on his own." And when the session began, Seth did at once resume work on "his" book.)

Good evening.

("Good evening, Seth.")

Now: We will continue.

The fact of this book is proof that the ego does not have the whole kettle of personality to itself, for there is no doubt that it is being produced by some other personality than that of the writer known as Jane Roberts. Since that Jane Roberts has no abilities that are not inherent in the species as a whole, then at the very least it must be admitted that human personality has many more attributes than those usually ascribed to it. I hope to explain what these abilities are, and point out the ways that each individual can use to release these potentials.

Personality is a gestalt of ever-changing perception. It is the part of the identity which perceives. I do not force my perceptions upon the woman through whom I speak, nor is her consciousness blotted out during our communications. Instead there is an expansion of her consciousness and a projection of energy that is directed away from three-dimensional reality.

This concentration <u>away</u> from the physical system may make it appear as if her consciousness is blotted out. Instead, more is added to it. Now from my own field of reality I focus my attention toward the woman, but the words that she speaks — these words upon the pages — are not initially verbal at all.

In the first place, language as you know it is a slow affair: letter by letter strung out to make a word, and words to make a sentence, the result of a linear thought pattern. Language, as you know it, is partially and grammatically the end product of your physical time sequences. You can only focus upon so many things at one time, and your language structure is not given to the communication of intricate, simultaneous experience.

I am aware of a different kind of experience, not linear, and can focus upon and react to an infinite variety of simultaneous events. Ruburt could not express them, and so they must be leveled out into linear expression if they are to be communicated. This ability to perceive and react to unlimited simultaneous events is a basic characteristic of each whole self or entity. Therefore, I do not claim it as some feat that is exclusively my own.

Each reader, being presently ensconced within a physical form, I presume (humorously), knows only a small portion of himself — as I mentioned earlier. The entity is the overall identity of which his personality is one manifestation — an independent and eternally valid portion. In these communications, therefore, Ruburt's consciousness expands, and yet focuses in a different dimension, a dimension between his reality and mine, a field relatively free of distraction. Here I impress certain concepts upon him, with his permission and assent. They are not neutral, in that all knowledge or information bears the stamp of the personality who holds it or passes it on.

Ruburt makes his verbal knowledge available for our use, and quite automatically the two of us together cause the various words that will be spoken. Distractions can occur, as any information can be distorted. We are used to working together now, however, and the distortions are very few.

Some of my energy is also projected through Ruburt, and his energy and mine both activate his physical form during our sessions, and now as I speak these sentences. There are many other ramifications that I will discuss later.

You may take your break.

(9:46 to 9:55.)

I am not, therefore, a product of Ruburt's subconscious, any more than he is a product of my subconscious mind. Nor am I a secondary personality, cleverly trying to undermine a precarious ego. I have seen to it in fact that all portions of Ruburt's personality are benefited, and their integrity maintained and honored.

There is within his personality a rather unique facility that makes our communications possible. I will try to put this as simply as possible: There is within his psyche what amounts to a transparent dimensional warp that serves almost like an open window through which other realities can be perceived, a multidimensional opening that has to some extent escaped being clouded over by the shade of physical focus.

The physical senses usually blind you to these open channels, for they perceive reality only in their own image. To some extent, then, I enter your reality through a psychological warp in your space and time. In a manner of speaking, such an open channel serves much as a pathway between Ruburt's personality and my own, so that communication is possible between. Such psychological and psychic warps between dimensions of existence are not infrequent. They are merely recognized as such infrequently and utilized even less so.

(Long pause, one of many. But overall Jane's pace was faster and more confident than in the first two sessions dealing with Seth's book. She also liked what Seth had done on his book so far.)

I will try to give you some idea of my own nonphysical existence. Let it serve to remind you that your own basic identity is as nonphysical as my own.

That is the end of Chapter One.

("Okay.")

CHAPTER 2

My Present Environment,
Work, and Activities

(*It was 10:16. Jane paused, rubbing her closed eyes.*)
We will begin Chapter Two.

While my environment differs in rather important respects *(humorously)* from that of my readers, I can assure you, with ironic understatement, that it is as vivid, varied, and vital as physical existence. It is more pleasurable — though my ideas of pleasure have changed some since I was a physical being — being more rewarding and offering far greater opportunities for creative achievement.

My present existence is the most challenging one that I have known, and I have known many, both physical and nonphysical. There is not just one dimension in which nonphysical consciousness resides, any more than there is only one country on your planet or planet within your solar system.

My environment, now, is not the one in which you will find yourself immediately after death. I cannot help speaking humorously, but you must die many times before you enter this particular plane of existence. (Birth is much more of a shock than death. Sometimes when you die you do not realize it, but birth almost always implies a sharp and sudden recognition. So there is no need to fear death. And I, who have died more times than I care to tell, write this book to tell you so.)

My work in this environment provides far more challenge than any of you know, and it also necessitates the manipulation of creative materials that are nearly beyond your present comprehension. I will say more of this shortly. First of all, you must understand that no objective reality exists but that which is created by consciousness. Consciousness always creates form, and not the other way around. So my environment is a reality of existence created by myself and others like me, and it represents the manifestation of our development.

We do not use permanent structures. There is not a city or a town, for example, in which I dwell. I do not mean to imply that we are off in empty space. For one thing we do not think of space as you do, and we form whatever particular images we want to surround us.

They are created by our mental patterns, [just] as your own physical reality is created in perfect replica of your inner desires and thoughts. You think that objects exist independently of you, not realizing that they are instead the manifestations of your own psychological and psychic selves. We realize that we form our own reality, and therefore we do so with considerable joy and creative abandon. In my environment you would be highly disoriented, for it would seem to you as if it lacked coherency.

We are aware of the inner laws that govern all "materializations," however. I can have it night or day, in your terms, as I prefer — or any period, say, of your history. These changing forms would in no way bother my associates, for they would take them as immediate clues as to my mood, feelings, and ideas.

(While delivering this paragraph Jane walked into the kitchen, still in trance, to rummage for a book of matches; she wanted to light a cigarette.)

Permanency and stability basically have nothing to do with form, but with the integration of pleasure, purpose, accomplishment, and identity. I "travel" to many other levels of existence in order to fulfill my duties, which are primarily those of a teacher and educator, and I use whatever aids and techniques serve me best within those systems.

In other words, I may teach the same lesson in many different ways, according to the abilities and assumptions that are inherent in any given system in which I must operate. I use one portion of myself from many personalities that are available to my identity in these communications, and in this book. In other systems of reality, this particular Seth personality that I, the larger Seth identity adopt here, would not be understood.

All systems of reality are not physically oriented, you see, and some are entirely unacquainted with physical form. Nor is sex, as you understand it, natural to them. Therefore I would not communicate as a male personality who has lived many physical existences, though this is a legitimate and valid portion of my identity.

Are your fingers tired?

(*"No, I'm okay." 10:54.*)

Now: In my home environment I assume whatever shape I please, and it may vary, and does, with the nature of my thoughts. You, however, form your own physical image at an unconscious level in more or less the same manner, but with some important differences. You usually do not realize that your physical body is created by you at each moment as a direct result of your inner conception of what you are, or that it changes in important chemical and electromagnetic ways with the ever-moving pace of your own thought.

Having long ago recognized the dependence of form upon consciousness, we have simply been able to change our forms entirely so that they more faithfully follow each nuance of our inner experience.

You may take a break or end the session as you prefer.

(*"We'll take the break."*

(*11:00. Jane's trance had been good, although she appeared to come out of it quickly enough. She said she knew each word as she delivered it during the session, but forgot it almost at once. By 11:05, though, she realized she hadn't really "completely come out of it" at break after all. Resume at 11:07.*)

Now: This ability to change form is an inherent characteristic of any consciousness. Only the degree of proficiency and actualization varies. You can see this in your own system, in a slowed-down version, when you observe the changing forms taken by living matter through its "evolutionary" history.

Now, we can also take several forms at one time, so to speak, but you can also do this although you do not generally realize it. Your physical form can lie sleeping and inert upon the bed while your consciousness travels in a dream form to places quite distant. Simultaneously you may create a "thought-form" of yourself, identical in every respect, and this may appear in the room of a friend quite without your conscious awareness. So consciousness is not limited as to the forms it can create at any given time.

Practically speaking, we are rather more advanced along these lines than you, and when we create such forms we do so with complete awareness. I share my field of existence with others who have more or less the same challenges to meet, the same overall pattern of development. Some I have known and others I have not. We communicate telepathically, but then again, telepathy is the basis for your languages, without which their symbolism would be meaningless.

Because we <u>do</u> communicate in this manner, this does not necessarily mean that we use mental words, for we do not. We communicate instead through what I can only call thermal and electromagnetic images that are capable of supporting much more meaning in one "sequence." The intensity of the communication is dependent upon the emotional intensity behind it, although the phrase "emotional intensity" may be misleading.

We do feel an equivalent of what you call emotions, though these are not the love or hate or anger that you know. Your feelings can best be described as the three-dimensional materializations of far greater psychological events and experiences that are related to the "inner senses."

I will explain these inner senses to you later, at the end of this chapter. Suffice it here to say that we have strong emotional experience, although it differs in a large measure from your own. It is far less limited and far more expansive in that we are also aware and responsive to the emotional "climate" as a whole. We are much freer to feel and experience, because we are not so afraid of being swept away by feeling.

Our identities do not feel threatened, for example, by the strong emotions of another. We are able to travel <u>through</u> emotions in a way that is not now natural to you, and to translate them into other facets of creativity than those with which you are familiar. We do not feel the need to conceal emotions, for we know it is basically impossible and undesirable. Within your system they can appear troublesome because you have not yet learned how to use them. We are only now learning their full potential, and the powers of creativity with which they are connected.

We will end our session.

(*"Okay."*)

My heartiest regards to you both, and a fond good evening.

(*"Good evening, Seth. It's been very good."*)

(Still as Seth, Jane leaned forward humorously): You are the first to read it.

("Yes. It's a pleasure."

(11:37 P.M. Jane had been really out, she said later. She knew only that Seth had talked about emotion.)

SESSION 514, FEBRUARY 9, 1970,
9:35 P.M. MONDAY

(This session was witnessed by Carl and Sue Watkins and their infant son Sean. Carl and Sue are members of Jane's ESP class.)

Good evening.

("Good evening, Seth.")

Good evening to our friends. You have come to see an author at work, and so we shall continue, if you will bear with us, with Chapter Two.

Now: Since we realize that our identity is not dependent upon form, therefore, of course, we do not fear changing it, knowing that we can adopt any form we desire.

We do not know death in your terms. Our existence takes us into many other environments, and we blend *(gesture)* into these. We follow what rules of form exist within these environments. All of us here are teachers, and we therefore adapt our methods, also, so that they will make sense to personalities with varying ideas of reality.

Consciousness is not dependent upon form, as I have said, and yet it always seeks to create form. We do not exist in any time framework as you know it. Minutes, hours, or years have lost both their meaning and their fascination. We are quite aware of the time situations within other systems, however, and we must take them into account in our communications. Otherwise what we say would not be understood.

There are no real barriers to separate the systems of which I speak. The only separation is brought about by the varying abilities of personalities to perceive and manipulate. You exist in the midst of many other systems of reality, for example, but you do not perceive them. And even when some event intrudes from these systems into your own three-dimensional existence, you are not able to interpret it, for it is distorted by the very fact of entry.

I told you that we do not experience your time sequence. We travel through various intensities. Our work, development, and experience all takes place within what I term the "moment point." Here, within the moment point, the smallest thought is brought to fruition, the slightest possibility explored, the probabilities thoroughly examined, the least or the most forceful feeling entertained. It is difficult to explain this clearly, and yet the moment point is the framework within which we have our psychological experience. Within it, simultaneous actions follow "freely" through associative patterns. For example, pretend that I think of you, Joseph. In so doing I immediately experience — and fully — your past, present, and future (in your terms), and all of those strong or determining emotions and motivations that have ruled you. I can travel through those experiences with you, if I choose. We can follow a consciousness through all of its forms, for example, and in your terms, within the flicker of an eye.

Now it takes study, development, and experience before an identity can learn to hold its own stability in the face of such constant stimuli; and many of us have gotten lost, even forgetting who we were until we once more awakened to ourselves. Much of this is quite automatic to us now. In the infinite varieties of consciousness, we are still aware of a small percentage of the entire banks of personalities that exist. For our "vacations" we visit amid quite simple life forms, and blend with them.

To this extent we indulge in relaxation and sleep, for we can spend a century as a tree or as an uncomplicated life form in another reality. We delight our consciousness with the enjoyment of simple existence. We may create, you see, the forest in which we grow. Usually however we are highly active, our full energies focused in our work and in new challenges.

We can form from ourselves, from our own psychological entireties, other personalities whenever we wish. These, however, must then develop according to their own merit, using the creative abilities inherent in them. They are free to go their own way. We do not do this lightly, however.

Now you may take your first break, and we shall continue.

(*10:02. Jane's trance had been a deep one. She said she'd been exhausted before the session. We'd spent the afternoon moving furniture. Nothing seemed to bother Seth this evening once he started, however; not even Sean nursing. Resume at the same fast pace at 10:20.*)

Now: Each reader is a portion of his or her own entity, and is developing toward the same kind of existence that I know. In childhood and in the dream state, each personality is aware to some extent of the true freedom that belongs to its own inner consciousness. These abilities of which I speak, therefore, are inherent characteristics of consciousness as a whole and of each personality.

My environment, as I told you, changes constantly, but then, so does your own. You rationalize away quite legitimate intuitive perception at such times. For example, if a room suddenly appears small and cramped to you, you take it for granted that this change of dimension is imaginative, and that the room has not changed regardless of your feelings.

The fact is that the room under such conditions will have changed quite definitely, and in very major respects, even though the physical dimensions will still measure the same. The entire psychological impact of the room will have altered. Its effect will be felt by others beside yourself. It will attract certain kinds of events rather than others, and it will alter your own psychological structure and hormonal output. You will react to the altered state of the room even in quite physical ways, though its width or length, in inches or feet, may not seem to vary.

I told our good friend Joseph to underline the word "seem" because your instruments would show no physical alteration — since the instruments within such a room would themselves have already altered to the same degree.

You are constantly changing the form, the shape, the contour, and the meaning of your physical body and most intimate environment, although you do your best to ignore these constant alterations. On the other hand, we allow them full rein, knowing that we are motivated by an inner stability that can well afford spontaneity and creation, and realizing that spiritual and psychological identity are dependent upon creative change.

Our environment therefore is composed of exquisite imbalances, where change is allowed full play. Your own time structure misleads you into your ideas of the relative permanency of physical matter, and you close your eyes to the constant alterations within it. Your physical senses confine you as best they can to the perception of a highly formalized reality. Only through the use of the intuitions and in sleep and dream states, as a rule, can you perceive the joyfully changing nature of your own, and any, consciousness.

One of my duties is to enlighten you on such matters. We must use concepts that are at least fairly familiar to you. In doing so, we therefore use portions of our own personalities, with whom you can to some extent relate.

There is no end to our environment. In your terms there would be no lack of space or time in which to operate. Now this would put tremendous pressure on any consciousness without proper background and development. We do not have one simple, cozy universe in which to hide. We are still alert to other quite alien systems of reality that flash on the very outskirts of consciousness as we know it. There are far more various kinds of consciousness than there are physical forms, each with its own patterns of perception, dwelling within its own camouflage system. Yet all of these have inner knowledge of the reality that exists within all camouflage and that composes any reality, by whatever name it is called.

Now you may take your break.

(10:44 to 10:56.)

Now, many of these freedoms are quite natural to you in the dream state, and you form dream environments often to exercise such potentials. Later I will have at least some remarks to make concerning the ways that you can learn to recognize your own feats, to compare them with your proficiency in daily physical life.

You can learn to change your physical environment, therefore, by learning to change and manipulate your dream environment. You can also suggest specific dreams in which a desired change is seen, and under certain conditions these will then appear in your physical reality. Now often you do this without realizing it.

Whole consciousness adopts various forms. It need not always be within a form. All forms are not physical ones. Some personalities, therefore, have never been physical. They have evolved along different lines, and their psychological structures would be alien to your own.

To some extent I also travel through such environments. Consciousness must show itself, however. It cannot unbe. It is not physical, it must therefore show its activation in other ways. In some systems for example, it forms highly integrated mathematical and musical patterns that are themselves stimuli for other universal systems. I am not very well acquainted with these, however, and cannot speak of them with any great familiarity.

If my environment is not a permanently structured one, then as I have told you, neither is your own. If I am aware of communicating now through Ruburt, in different ways each of you telepathically communicates to and through other personalities, though with little knowledge of your accomplishment.

Now I will end our session. I would sing a lullaby — this is not for the book — for our small friend here *(Sean Watkins, who was nursing again)*. But I am not in voice for it.

My heartiest wishes to you all. A fond good evening. *(Amused and emphatic):* And this is indeed [a] first and final draft.

("Good night, Seth. Thank you — it's been very interesting.")

(11:08 P.M. Seth's parting remark was in answer to a question Sue had raised earlier in the evening, about how much revision his book would require. Jane's opinion, so far, was that the book wouldn't need any work except for the re-arranging of an occasional awkward phrase, etc.)

SESSION 515, FEBRUARY 11, 1970, 9:20 P.M. WEDNESDAY

Good evening.

("Good evening, Seth.")

We will return to our Chapter Two.

Now: The senses that you use, in a very real manner, create the environment that you perceive. Your physical senses necessitate the perception of a three-dimensional reality. Consciousness is equipped with inner perceptors, however. These are inherent within all consciousness, regardless of its development. These perceptors operate quite independently from those that might be assumed when a given consciousness adopts a specialized form, such as a physical body, in order to operate in a particular system.

Each reader, therefore, has inner senses, and to some extent uses them constantly, though he is not aware of doing so at an egotistical level. Now, we use the inner senses quite freely and consciously. If you were to do so, then you would perceive the same kind of environment in which I have my existence. You would see an uncamouflaged situation, in which events and form were free and not stuck in a jellylike mold of time. You could see, for example, your present living room not only as a conglomeration of permanent-appearing furniture, but switch your focus and see the immense and constant dance of molecules and other particles that compose the various objects.

You could see a phosphorescentlike glow, the aura of electromagnetic "structures" that compose the molecules themselves. You could, if you wished, condense your consciousness until it was small enough to travel through a single molecule, and from the molecule's own world look out and survey the universe of the room and the gigantic galaxy of interrelated, ever-moving starlike shapes. Now all of these possibilities represent a legitimate reality. Yours is no more legitimate than any other, but it is the only one that you perceive.

Using the inner senses, we become conscious creators, cocreators. But you are unconscious cocreators whether you know it or not. If our environment seems unstructured to you, it is only because you do not understand the true nature of order, which has nothing to do with permanent form, but only appears to have form from your perspective.

There is no four o'clock in the afternoon or nine o'clock in the evening in my environment. By this I mean that I am not restricted to a time sequence. There is nothing preventing me from experiencing such sequences if I choose. We experience time, or what you would call its equivalent nature, in terms of intensities of experience — a psychological time with its own peaks and valleys.

This is somewhat similar to your own emotional feelings when time seems speeded up or slowed down, but it is vastly different in important ways. Our psychological time could be compared in terms of environment to the walls of a room, but in our case the walls would be constantly changing in color, size, height, depth and width.

Our psychological structures are different, practically speaking, in that we consciously utilize a multidimensional psychological reality that you inherently possess, but are unfamiliar with at an egotistical level. It is natural, then, that our environment would have multidimensional qualities that the physical senses would never perceive.

Now, I project a portion of my reality as I dictate this book to an undifferentiated level between systems that is relatively clear of camouflage. It is an inactive area, comparatively speaking. If you were thinking in terms of physical reality, then this area could be likened to one immediately above the atmosphere of your earth. However I am speaking of psychological and psychic atmospheres, and this area is sufficiently distant from Ruburt's physically oriented self so that the communications can be relatively understood.

It is also in a way distant from my own environment, for in my own environment I would have some difficulties in relating information in physically oriented terms. You must understand that by distance I do not refer to space.

You may take your break.

(9:56. Jane's trance has been good, but she was out of it almost at once. Resume at 10:22.)

Creation and perception are far more intimately connected than any of your scientists realize.

It is quite true that your physical senses create the reality that they perceive. A tree is something far different to a microbe, a bird, an insect, and a man who stands beneath it. I am not saying that the tree only appears to be different. It is different. You perceive its reality through one set of highly specialized senses. This does not mean that its reality exists in that form in any more basic way than it exists in the form perceived by the microbe, insect, or bird. You cannot perceive the quite valid reality of that tree in any context but your own. This applies to anything within the physical system that you know.

It is not that physical reality is false. It is that the physical picture is simply one of an infinite number of ways of perceiving the various guises through which consciousness expresses itself. The physical senses force you to translate experience into physical perceptions. The inner senses open your range of perception, allow you to interpret experience in a far freer manner and to create new forms and new channels through which you, or any consciousness, can know itself.

Consciousness is, among other things, a spontaneous exercise in creativity. You are learning now, in a three-dimensional context, the ways in which your emotional and psychic existence can create varieties of physical form. You manipulate within the psychic environment, and these manipulations are then automatically impressed upon the physical mold. Now our environment is in itself creative in a different manner than yours. Your environment is creative in that trees bear fruit, that there is a self-sustaining principle, that the earth feeds its own, for

· 26 ·

example. The naturally creative aspects are the materializations of the deepest psychic, spiritual, and physical inclinations of the species, set up in your terms eons ago, and a part of the racial bank of psychic knowledge.

We endow the elements of our environment with an even greater creativity that is difficult to explain. We do not have flowers that grow, for example. But the intensity, the condensed psychic strength of our psychological natures forms new dimensions of activity. If you paint a picture within three-dimensional existence, then the painting must be on a flat surface, merely hinting at the complete three-dimensional experience that you cannot insert into it. In our environment, however, we could actually create whatever dimensional effects we desired. All of these abilities are not ours alone. They are your heritage. As you will see later in this book, you exercise your own inner senses, and multidimensional abilities, more frequently than it might seem, in other states of consciousness than the normal, waking one.

Since my own environment does not have easily defined physical elements, you will be able to understand its nature by inference, as I explain some related topics throughout this book.

Your own physical environment appears as it does to you because of your own psychological structure. If you gained your sense of personal continuity through associative processes primarily, rather than as a result of the familiarity of self moving through time, then you would experience physical reality in an entirely different fashion. Objects from past and present could be perceived at once, their presence justified through associative connections. Say that your father throughout his lifetime has eight favorite chairs. If your perceptive mechanisms were primarily set up as a result of intuitive association rather than time sequence, then you would perceive all of these chairs at one time; or seeing one, you would be aware of the others. So environment is not a separate thing in itself, but the result of perceptive patterns, and these are determined by psychological structure.

So if you want to know what my environment is like, you will have to understand what I am. In order to explain, I shall have to speak about the nature of consciousness in general. In doing so I shall end up telling you much about yourself. The inner portions of your identity are already aware of much that I will tell you. Part of my purpose is to acquaint your egotistical self with knowledge that is already known to a larger portion of your own consciousness, that you have long ignored.

You look out into the physical universe, and interpret reality according to the information received from your "outer senses." I will stand, figuratively speaking, in physical reality and look inward for you, and describe those realities of consciousness and experience that you are presently too fascinated to see. For you are fascinated with physical reality, and you are in as deep a trance now as the woman is through whom I write this book.

All of your attention is focused in a highly specialized way upon one shining, bright point that you call reality. There are other realities all about you, but you ignore their existence, and you blot out all stimuli that come from them. There is a reason for such a trance, as you will discover, but little by little you must wake up. My purpose is to open your inner eyes.

And I end our session. We are close to the end of Chapter Two. Now I wish you good evening.

("Good night, Seth. It's been very good."

(11:12 P.M. Jane was quickly out of a deep trance. "I don't remember anything.")

SESSION 518, MARCH 18, 1970,
9:25 P.M. WEDNESDAY

(Jane has been taking something of a rest for the last month or so. She's had but two regular sessions — one for friends, and a personal one for us — and only one for her weekly ESP class. [Class sessions aren't numbered.] Occasionally Jane has wondered what effect, if any, the break would have on Seth's book. However, after giving me some very astute data about my painting, Seth resumed book dictation very smoothly at 9:33 — just as though there hadn't been any time lapse from February 11 to March 18.

(A note: I thought it would be of interest to show, by periodically recording the time, how long Seth takes to deliver a certain amount of finished material for his book.)

Give us a moment, then. I will give you the very last of Chapter Two, and begin the following chapter.

My environment includes, of course, those other personalities with whom I come in contact. Communication, perception, and environment can hardly be separated. Therefore the kind of communication that is carried on by myself and my associates is extremely important in any discussion of our environment.

In the following chapter I hope to give you an idea, quite simply, of our existence, the work in which we are involved, the dimension in which we exist, the purposes that we hold dear; and most of all, of those concerns that make up our experience.

CHAPTER 3

MY WORK AND THOSE DIMENSIONS OF REALITY INTO WHICH IT TAKES ME

(9:43.) Now I have friends even as you do, though my friends may be of longer standing. You must understand that we experience our own reality in quite a different manner than you do. We are aware of what you would call our past selves, those personalities we have adopted in various other existences.

Because we use telepathy we can hide little from each other, even if we wished to. This, I am sure, seems an invasion of privacy to you, and yet I assure you that even now none of your thoughts are hidden, but are known quite clearly to your family and friends — and I may add, unfortunately, to those you consider enemies as well. You are simply not aware of this fact.

This does not mean that each of us is like an open book to the other. Quite the contrary. There is such a thing as mental etiquette, mental manners. We are much more aware of our own thoughts than you are. We realize our freedom to choose our thoughts, and we choose them with some discrimination and finesse.

(Pause at 9:49.) The power of our thoughts has been made clear to us, through trial and error in other existences. We have discovered that no one can escape the vast creativity of the mental image, or of emotion. This does not mean that we are not spontaneous, or that we must deliberate between one thought or another, in anxious concern that one might be negative or destructive. That, in your terms, is behind us.

Our psychological structure does mean that we can communicate in far more various forms than those with which you are familiar, however. Pretend, for example, that you meet a childhood friend whom you have long forgotten. Now you may have little in common. Yet you may have a fine afternoon's discussion centered about old teachers and classmates, and establish a certain rapport.

So, when I "meet" another, I may be able to relate to him much better on the basis of a particular past life experience, even though in my "now" we have little in common. We may have known each other, for example, as entirely different people in the fourteenth century, and we may communicate very nicely by discussing those experiences, much as you and your hypothetical childhood friend established rapport by remembering your past.

We will be quite aware that we are ourselves, however — the multidimensional personalities who shared a more or less common environment at one level of our existence. As you will see, this analogy is a rather simple one that will do only for now, because past, present, and future do not really exist in those terms.

Our experience, however, does not include the time divisions with which you are familiar. We have far more friends and associates than you do, simply because we are aware of varying connections in what we call for now "past" incarnations.

(10:00.) We have of course therefore more knowledge at our fingertips, so to speak. There is no period of time, in your terms, that you can mention, but some of us have been from there, and carry within our memories the indelible experience that was gained in that particular context.

We do not feel the need to hide our emotions or thoughts from others, because all of us by now well recognize the cooperative nature of all consciousness and reality, and our part in it. We are highly motivated. *(Humorously):* Could spirits be anything else?

("I guess not.")

Simply because we have at our command the full use of our energy, it is not diverted into conflicts. We do not fritter it away, but utilize it for those unique and individual purposes that are a basic part of our psychological experience.

Now, each whole self, or multidimensional personality, has its own

· 31 ·

purposes, missions, and creative endeavors that are initial and basic parts of itself and that determine those qualities that make it eternally valid and eternally seeking. We are finally free to utilize our energy in those directions. We face many challenges of quite momentous nature, and we realize that our purposes are not only important in themselves, but for the surprising offshoots that develop in our efforts to pursue them. In working for our purposes, we realize we are blazing trails that can also be used by others.

We also suspect — certainly I do — that the purposes themselves will have surprising results, astounding consequences that we have never realized, and that they will merely lead to new avenues. Realizing this helps us keep a sense of humor.

(10:11.) When one has been born and has died many times, expecting extinction with each death, and when this experience is followed by the realization that existence still continues, then a sense of the divine comedy enters in.

We are beginning to learn the creative joy of play. I believe, for example, that all creativity and consciousness is born in the quality of play, as opposed to work, in the quickened intuitional spontaneity that I see as a constant through all my own existences, and in the experience of those I know.

I communicate with your dimension, for example, not by willing myself to your level of reality, but by imagining myself there. All of my deaths would have been adventures had I realized what I know now. On the one hand you take life too seriously, and on the other, you do not take playful existence seriously enough.

We enjoy a sense of play that is highly spontaneous, and yet I suppose you would call it responsible play. Certainly it is creative play. We play, for example, with the mobility of our consciousness, seeing how "far" one can send it. We are constantly surprised at the products of our own consciousness, of the dimensions of reality through which we can hopscotch. It might seem that we use our consciousness idly in such play, and yet again, the pathways we make continue to exist and can be used by others. We leave messages to any who come by, mental signposts.

I suggest your break.

(10:25. Jane was out of her trance easily. She had delivered the material smoothly and without long pauses, in an average voice. She was quite surprised

to learn that an hour had passed, however. Jane had no images or visions, as far as she recalled, when dictating material. Resume at a slower pace at 10:35.)

We can be highly motivated therefore, and yet use and understand the creative use of play, both as a method of attaining our goals and purposes and as a surprising and creative endeavor in itself.

Now, in my work as a teacher I travel into many dimensions of existence, even as a traveling professor might give lectures in various states or countries. Here, however, the resemblance ends, largely, since before I can begin to work I must set up preliminary psychological structures and learn to know my pupils before teaching can even begin.

(Jane's delivery was quite a bit slower now.)

I must have a thorough knowledge of the particular system of reality in which my pupil operates, of his or her system of thought, of the symbols that are meaningful. The stability of the pupil's personality must be correctly gauged by me. The needs of that personality cannot be ignored but must be taken into consideration.

The pupil must be encouraged, but not overly extended while development continues. My material must be presented in such a way that it makes sense in the context in which the pupil understands reality, particularly in the early stages. Great care must be utilized, even before serious learning can begin, that all levels of the personality develop at a more or less constant rate.

Often the material I present will initially be given without any sign of my presence, seemingly as a startling revelation. For no matter how carefully I present the material, it is still bound to change past ideas that are strongly a part of the pupil's personality. What I say is one thing, but the pupil of course is thrust into psychological and psychic behavior and experience that may seem quite alien to him on a conscious level.

(Pause at 10:51.) The problems vary according to the system in which my pupil has his or her existence. In your system, for example, and in connection with the woman through whom I now write this book, initial contact on my part was made long before our sessions began.

The personality was never consciously aware of the initial meeting. She simply experienced sudden new thoughts, and since she is a poet, these appeared as poetic inspirations. At one time some years ago, at a writers' conference, she became involved in circumstances that could have led to her psychic development before she was ready. The psychological climate at that time, of those involved, initiated the conditions, and without realizing what she was about our friend [Jane] went into a trance.

(Long pause at 11:01. In 1957, after Jane had sold her first few short stories, she was invited to a conference of science fiction writers at Milford, Pennsylvania. I couldn't go because of my own work, so Jane attended the conference with Cyril Kornbluth [now deceased], a friend and a well-known writer who lived near our home in Sayre, Pennsylvania.

(Jane went into a trance one evening during a discussion. Out of this episode — which we did not understand was a trance for several years afterward — evolved a group of writers, Jane among them, who called themselves "The Five." Long and involved letters were exchanged among the members of The Five by a round-robin technique. The four other writers in the group were much better known than Jane was.)

I had known of her psychic gifts since her childhood, but the insights necessary were channeled through the poetry until the personality attained the necessary background that was needed in this particular case. In the affair just mentioned, therefore, I was informed and saw to it that the episode ended and was not pursued.

It was hardly an accidental performance, however. Quite without knowing it, the personality decided to try its wings, figuratively speaking. As a part of my work, therefore, I have been coaching the young woman in one way or another since her childhood — and all of this as a preliminary to the serious work that began with our sessions.

This is a normal part of my activity in many levels of existence. It is highly diversified work, for the personality structures vary. While within the systems in which I work there are certain basic similarities, in some dimensions I would not be equipped to be a teacher simply because the basic concepts of experience would be alien to my nature, and the learning processes themselves outside of my own experience.

You may take your break.

(11:09. Jane's trance had been good. "I haven't the slightest idea what that was all about." Her pace had picked up a bit. Resume at 11:20.)

Now: We will continue our book at our next session.

(Seth dictated a few paragraphs of material for a woman who had recently lost her husband; she had requested a session.)

And now I bid you good evening.

("Good night, Seth.")

My heartiest regards — and if you did not have to take notes, I would talk with you longer.

("Thank you." End at 11:30 P.M.)

SESSION 519, MARCH 23, 1970,
9:10 P.M. MONDAY

Good evening.

("Good evening, Seth.")

Now your ideas of space are highly erroneous. So in my contacts with your sphere of activity, I do not sweep through bright golden skies like some spiritual superman into your physical domain.

I will go into this in a later chapter, but in a very real manner, space as you perceive it simply does not exist. Not only is the illusion of space caused by your own physical perceptive mechanisms, but it is also caused by mental patterns that you have accepted — patterns that are adopted by consciousness when it reaches a certain stage of "evolution" within your system.

(9:16. As in last session, I will indicate the time periodically to show the rate at which Seth delivers material.)

When you arrive, or emerge, into physical life, not only is your mind not a blank slate, waiting for the scrolls that experience will write upon it, but you are already equipped with a memory bank far surpassing that of any computer. You face your first day upon the planet with skills and abilities already built in, though they may or may not be used; and they are not merely the result of heredity as you think of it.

You may think of your soul or entity — though only briefly and for the sake of this analogy — as some conscious and living, divinely inspired computer who programs its own existences and lifetimes. But this computer is so highly endowed with creativity that each of the various personalities it programs spring into consciousness and song, and in turn create realities that may have been undreamed of by the computer itself.

(9:25.) Each such personality, however, comes with a built-in idea of the reality in which it will operate, and its mental equipment is highly tailored to meet very specialized environments. It has full freedom, but it must operate within the context of existence to which it has been

programmed. Within the personality, however, in the most secret recesses, is the condensed knowledge that resides in the computer as a whole. I must emphasize that I am not saying that the soul or entity is a computer, but only asking you to look at the matter in this light in order to make several points clear.

Each personality has within it the ability not only to gain a new type of existence in the environment — in your case in physical reality — but to add creatively to the very quality of its own consciousness, and in so doing to work its way through the specialized system, breaking the barriers of reality as it knows it.

(9:30.) Now, there is a purpose in all this that will also be discussed later. I mention this whole subject here, however, because I want you to see that your environment is not real in the terms that you imagine it to be. When you are born, then, you are already "conditioned" to perceive reality in a particular manner, and to interpret experience in a very limited but intense range.

I must explain this before I can clearly give you an idea of my environment, or of those other systems of reality in which I operate. There is no space between my environment and yours, for example, no physical boundaries that separate us. In a very real way of speaking, your concept of reality as seen through your physical senses, scientific instruments, or arrived at through deduction, bears little resemblance to the facts — and the facts are difficult to explain.

(9:34. Seth-Jane leaned forward for emphasis, gesturing, eyes dark and wide.)
Your planetary systems exist at once, simultaneously, both in time and in space. The universe that you seem to perceive, either visually or through instruments, appears to be composed of galaxies, stars, and planets, at various distances from you. Basically, however, this is an illusion. Your senses and your very existence as physical creatures program you to perceive the universe in such a way. The universe as you know it is your interpretation of events as they intrude upon your three-dimensional reality. The events are mental. This does not mean that you cannot travel to other planets, for example, within that physical universe, any more than it means that you cannot use tables to hold books, glasses, and oranges (*as our coffee table did at that moment*), although the table has no solid qualities of its own.

(9:42. Jane's pace was now slowing considerably after a fast start.)

When I enter your system, I move through a series of mental and psychic events. You would <u>interpret</u> these events as space and time, and so often I must use the terms, for I must use your language rather than my own.

Root assumptions are those built-in ideas of reality of which I spoke — those agreements upon which you base your ideas of existence. Space and time, for example, are root assumptions. Each system of reality has its own set of such agreements. When I communicate within your system, I must use and understand the root assumptions upon which it is based. As a teacher it is part of my job to understand and use these, and I have had existences in many such systems as a part of what you may call my basic training; though in your terms my associates and I had other names for them.

You may take your break.

(9:52. Jane was out of trance almost immediately. "I feel like someone on that TV show," she said, referring to a popular science fiction program we'd seen earlier this evening. She tried to describe an image she'd had just before Seth began speaking, while saying it couldn't really be put into words: "I saw . . . a field of something like stars. An idea would be projected out there by us against this field so that it seemed to explode. Yet really the idea's right here," she said, nodding toward her cupped hands, which she held just below her chin.

(During break Jane got a brief but clear message from Seth: We should turn our bed back so that its head pointed north again, instead of to the west as it does now.

(Resume at a slow pace at 10:02.)

The entity, or the soul, has a far more creative and complicated nature than even your religions have ever granted it.

It utilizes numberless methods of perception, and it has at its command many other kinds of consciousness. Your idea of the soul is indeed limited by your three-dimensional concepts. The soul can change the focus of its consciousness, and uses consciousness as you use the eyes in your head. Now in my level of existence I am simply aware of the fact, strange as it may seem, that I am not my consciousness. My consciousness is an attribute to be used by me. This applies to each of the readers of this book, even though the knowledge may be hidden. Soul or entity, then, is more than consciousness.

When I enter your environment, I turn my consciousness in your direction, therefore. In one way, I translate what I am into an event that you can understand to some extent. In a much more limited manner, any artist does the same thing when he translates what he is, or a portion of it, into a painting. There is at least an evocative analogy there.

When I enter your system, I intrude into three-dimensional reality, and you must interpret what happens in the light of your own root assumptions. Now whether or not you realize it, each of you intrudes into other systems of reality in your dream states without the full participation of your normally conscious self. In subjective experience you leave behind physical existence and act, at times, with strong purpose and creative validity within dreams that you forget the instant you awaken.

When you think of the purpose of your existence, you think in terms of daily waking life, but you also work at your purpose in these other dream dimensions, and you are then in communication with other portions of your own entity, at work at endeavors quite as valid as those you are about in waking life.

(10:17.) When I contact your reality, therefore, it is as if I were entering one of your dreams. I can be aware of myself as I dictate this book through Jane Roberts, and yet also be aware of myself in my own environment; for I send only a portion of myself here, as you perhaps send out a portion of your consciousness as you write a letter to a friend, and yet are aware of the room in which you sit. I send out much more than you do in a letter, for a portion of my consciousness is now within the entranced woman as I dictate, but the analogy is close enough.

My environment, as I mentioned earlier, is not one of a personality recently dead in your terms, but later I will describe what you can expect under those conditions. One large difference between your environment and mine is that you must physically materialize mental acts as physical matter. We understand the reality of mental acts and recognize their brilliant validity. We accept them for what they are, and therefore we are beyond the necessity to materialize them and interpret them in such a rigid manner.

Your earth was very dear to me. I can now turn the focus of my consciousness toward it, and if I choose, experience it as you do; but I can also perceive it in many ways that you cannot in your time.

Now some of you who read this book will immediately and intuitively grasp what I am saying, for you will have already suspected that you are viewing experience through highly distorted, though colorful, figurative lenses. Remember also that if physical reality <u>is</u> in a larger sense an illusion, it is an illusion caused by a greater reality. The illusion itself has a purpose and a meaning.

You may take your break.

(10:31. Jane was again out of trance very quickly, yet she couldn't remember any of the material.

(Without necessarily expecting an answer this evening, I asked a question I thought Jane might want to consider if and when she wrote an introduction for this book: Could she dictate the whole book for Seth in, say, a month's worth of daily sessions, or did she need a certain amount of day-by-day living and experience, over a period of months, perhaps, in order to be able to let the book come through?

(Resume at the same slow pace at 10:45.)

Perhaps it is better to say that physical reality is <u>one form</u> that reality takes. In your system, however, you are focused much more intensely upon one relatively small aspect of experience.

We can travel freely through varying numbers of such realities. Our experience at this point includes our work in each. I do not mean to minimize the importance of your present personalities, nor of physical existence. To the contrary.

Three-dimensional experience is an invaluable place of training. Your personality as you now know it will indeed persevere, and with its memories, but it is only a part of your entire identity, even as your childhood in this life is an extremely important part of your present personality, though now you are far more than a child.

You will continue to grow and develop, and you will become aware of other environments, even as you left your childhood home. But environments are not objective <u>things</u>, conglomerations of objects that exist independently of you. Instead you form them and they are quite literally extensions of yourself; materialized mental acts that extend outward from your consciousness.

I will tell you exactly how you form your environment. I form mine following the same rules, though you end up with physical objects and I do not.

Now I will begin, there, on our book at our next session.

("All right.")

(Pause at 10:56.) To your question: The book could be written on consecutive evenings, as well as with our present method. A certain leeway is always left for spontaneity and surprises, so that anything in your experience can be used as an example or as a point about which I can build a discussion that I had already intended in any case.

I suggest, merely, that Ruburt try the bed arrangement for a week, and then see what he thinks.

("Okay." Our bedroom is small and it's difficult to have the bed lined up north-south; besides, Jane can't see out the single window then. We didn't turn the bed as Seth suggested.)

My heartiest wishes to you both, and a fond good evening.

("Good night, Seth. Thank you."

(11:00 P.M. "I have funny feelings," Jane said when she was out of trance. "I feel as though not much time has really passed since Seth started the book. But subjectively I think there's a vast amount of information in it so far — that somehow I'm expressing an accumulated amount, or a richness, of experience. Maybe I'm looking for some crazy expression like condensed richness. . . ."

(Jane then used the analogy of a library, without implying that she was getting the data "from a library somewhere.")

SESSION 520, MARCH 25, 1970,
9:09 P.M. WEDNESDAY

(As far as we knew, Seth would resume dictation on Chapter Three of his book this evening. A minute or two before the session began Jane told me that she had a "glimmer" from Seth — a few sentences. "Then," she said, "I settle down and wait for the session to start. But I still can't tell you just how I do it.")

Good evening.

("Good evening, Seth.")

Back to our book.

(With pauses): Your scientists are finally learning what philosophers have known for centuries — that mind can influence matter. They still have to discover the fact that mind creates and forms matter.

Now your closest environment, physically speaking, is your body. It is not like some manikin-shape in which you are imprisoned, that exists apart from you like a casing. Your body is not beautiful or ugly, healthy or deformed, swift or slow simply because this is the kind of body that was thrust upon you indiscriminately at birth. Instead your physical form, your corporeal personal environment, is the physical materialization of your own thoughts, emotions, and interpretations.

Quite literally, the "inner self" forms the body by magically transforming thoughts and emotions into physical counterparts. You grow the body. Its condition perfectly mirrors your subjective state at any given time. Using atoms and molecules, you build your body, forming basic elements into a form that you call your own.

You are intuitively aware that you form your image, and that you are independent of it. You do not realize that you create your larger environment and the physical world as you know it by propelling your thoughts and emotions into matter — a breakthrough into three-dimensional life. The inner self, therefore, individually and *en masse*, sends its psychic energy out, forming tentacles that coalesce into form.

(9:23.) Each emotion and thought has its own electromagnetic reality, completely unique. It is highly equipped to combine with certain others, according to the various ranges of intensity that you may include. In a manner of speaking, three-dimensional objects are formed in somewhat the same way that the images you see on your television screen are formed, but with a large difference. And if you are not tuned into that particular frequency, you will not perceive the physical objects at all.

(As Seth, Jane leaned forward for emphasis while speaking. Her delivery was somewhat different this evening. I thought she was reacting to our own environment. Sounds seemed to carry through above and below us. Jane would deliver a sentence, then pause longer than usual, so that her accustomed rhythm was a little off.)

Each of you act as transformers, unconsciously, automatically transforming highly sophisticated electromagnetic units into physical objects. You are in the middle of a "matter-concentrated system," surrounded, so to speak, by weaker areas in which what you would call "pseudo-matter" persists. Each thought and emotion spontaneously exists as a simple or complex electromagnetic unit — unperceived, incidentally, as yet by your scientists.

(9:27.) The intensity determines both the strength and the permanency of the physical image into which the thought or emotion will be materialized. In my own material I am explaining this in depth. Here,

I merely want you to understand that the world that you know is the reflection of an inner reality.

You are made basically of the same ingredients as a chair, a stone, a head of lettuce, a bird. In a gigantic cooperative endeavor, all consciousness joins together to make the forms that you perceive. Now, because this is known to us, we can change our environments and our own physical forms as we wish, and without confusion, for we perceive the reality that lies beneath.

We also realize that permanency of form is an illusion, since all consciousness must be in a state of change. We can be, in your terms, in several places at once because we realize the true mobility of consciousness. Now whenever you think emotionally of another person, you send out a counterpart of yourself, beneath the intensity of matter, but a definite form. This form, projecting outward from your own consciousness, completely escapes your egotistical attention. When I think emotionally of someone else, I do the same thing, except that a portion of my consciousness is within the image, and can communicate.

You may take your break.

(9:37. Jane was out of her trance quickly. The noises in the house continued. She had been bothered by them during her delivery, and they had interfered with my note taking. Nevertheless, she was surprised that almost half an hour had passed.

(At 9:56, though, as she sat waiting to go back into trance, Jane said, "Either I'm tired tonight, or the house is getting to me, but now it's harder to get going. . . ." Resume at 9:58.)

Environments are primarily mental creations of consciousness thrust out into many forms. I have a fourteenth-century study, my favorite, with which I am very pleased, for example. In your physical terms it does not exist, and I know quite well it is my mental production. Yet I enjoy it, and often take a physical form in order to sit at the desk and look out the window at the countryside.

Now you do the same thing when you sit in your living room, but you do not realize what you are doing; and presently you are somewhat restricted. When my associates and I meet, we often translate each other's thoughts into various shapes and forms out of pure enjoyment in the practice. We have what you might call a game, demanding some expertise, where for our own amusement we see which of us can translate any given thought into the most numerous forms. *(Pause.)*

There are such subtle qualities affecting the nature of all thought, such emotional gradations, that no one is ever identical — *(smile)* and incidentally, no physical object in your system is an exact duplicate of any other. The atoms and molecules that compose it — any object — have their own identities that color and qualify any object that they form.

You accept and perceive and focus upon continuities and similarities as you perceive physical objects of any kind, and in a very important manner you shut out and ignore dissimilarities out of a given field of actuality. Therefore you are very highly discriminating, accepting certain qualities and ignoring others. Your bodies not only change completely every seven years, for example. They change constantly with each breath.

(10:12.) Within the flesh, atoms and molecules constantly die and are replaced. The hormones are in a constant state of motion and alteration. Electromagnetic properties of skin and cell continually leap and change, and even reverse themselves. The physical matter that composed your body a moment ago is different in important ways from the matter that forms your body in this instant.

If you perceived the constant change within your body with as much persistence as you attend to its seemingly permanent nature, then you would be amazed that you ever considered the body as one more or less constant, more or less cohesive, entity. Even subjectively you focus upon and indeed manufacture the idea of a relatively stable, relatively permanent conscious self. You stress those ideas and thoughts and attitudes that you recall from "past" experience as your own, completely ignoring those that once were "characteristic" and now are vanished — ignoring the fact also that you cannot hold thought. The thought of a moment before, in your terms, vanishes away.

You try to maintain a constant, relatively permanent physical and subjective self in order to maintain a relatively constant, relatively permanent environment. So you are always in a position of ignoring such changes. Those that you refuse to acknowledge are precisely those that would give you a much better understanding of the true nature of reality, individual subjectivity, and the physical environment that seems to surround you.

(10:23. The above paragraphs were given at a much faster pace.)

What happens to a thought when it leaves your conscious mind? It does not simply disappear. You can learn to follow it, but you are usually frightened of turning your attention away from its intense focus in three-dimensional existence. Therefore, it seems that the thought disappears. It seems also that your subjectivity has a mysterious unknown quality about it, and that even your mental life has a sort of insidious dropping-off point, a subjective cliff over which thoughts and memories fall, to disappear into nothingness. Therefore to protect yourself, to protect your subjectivity from drifting, you erect various psychological barriers at what you suppose to be the danger points. Instead, you see, you can follow these thoughts and emotions simply by realizing that your own reality continues in another direction, beside the one with which you mainly identify. For these thoughts and emotions that have left your conscious mind will lead you into other environments.

(10:29.) These subjective openings through which thoughts seem to disappear are in fact like psychic warps, connecting the self that you know with other universes of experience — realities where symbols come to life and thoughts are not denied their potential.

There is communication between these other realities and your own in your dream states, and a constant interaction between both systems. If there is any point where your own consciousness seems to elude you or escape you, or if there is any point where your consciousness seems to end, then these are the points where you have yourselves set up psychological and psychic barriers, and these are precisely those areas that you should explore. Otherwise you feel as if your consciousness is enclosed within your skull, immobile and constricted, and every lost thought or forgotten memory at least symbolically seems like a small death. And such is not the case.

I suggest your break.

(10:36. Jane's trance had been deeper this time; she hadn't been bothered by any kind of noise. Resume at 10:52.)

Now: That is the end of dictation for this evening.

(Now Seth briefly discussed some out-of-body episodes that Jane had experienced yesterday afternoon.)

I will, then, end our session with my heartiest regards to you both; and may I remind Ruburt again of the suggestion I made concerning his bed.

Now good evening.

("Good night, Seth."

(11:05 P.M. See the 519th session, in which Seth suggests that Jane try turning our bed to a north-south position. We haven't done this yet.

(Jane still reads Seth's material on his book. I can tell that her concern about it is much diminished, but also that her interest in it is as lively as ever.)

CHAPTER 4

Reincarnational Dramas

SESSION 521, MARCH 30, 1970, 9:08 P.M. MONDAY

(Jane began speaking in an average voice, at a good pace with few pauses.)
Now, good evening.

("Good evening, Seth.")

We will now begin our next chapter. It is, I believe, Chapter Four.

("Yes.")

Your own environment includes far more than you may have supposed. Earlier I referred to your environment in terms of the daily physical existence and surroundings with which you are currently connected. In actuality, you are aware of very little of your larger, more extensive environment. Consider your present self as an actor in a play; hardly a new analogy, but a suitable one. The scene is set in the twentieth century. You create the props, the settings, the themes; in fact you write, produce, and act in the entire production — you and every other individual who takes part.

You are so focused in your roles, however; so intrigued by the reality that you have created, so entranced by the problems, challenges, hopes, and sorrows of your particular roles that you have forgotten they are of your own creation. This intensely moving drama, with all its joys and tragedies, can be compared with your present life, your present environment, both individually and *en masse.*

But there are other plays going on simultaneously, in which you also have a part to play. These have their own scenery, their own props. They take place in different periods of time. One may be called "Life in the twelfth century A.D." One may be called "Life in the eighteenth century," or "in 500 B.C.," or "in A.D. 3000." You also create these plays and act in them. These settings also represent your environment, the environment that surrounds your entire personality.

I am speaking of the portion of you who is taking part in this particular period piece, however; and that particular portion of your entire personality is so focused within this drama that you are not aware of the others in which you also play a role. You do not understand your own multidimensional reality; therefore it seems strange or unbelievable when I tell you that you live many existences at one time. It is difficult for you to imagine being in two places at once, much less in two or more times, or centuries.

(Pause at 9:24.) Now stated simply, time is not a series of moments. The words that you speak, the acts that you perform, appear to take place in time, as a chair or table appears to take up space. These appearances however are a part of the complicated props that you have set up "beforehand," and within the play you must accept these as real.

Four o'clock in the afternoon is a very handy reference. You can say to a friend, "I will meet you at four o'clock at the corner," or at a restaurant, for a drink or a chat or a meal, and your friend will know precisely where and when he will find you. This will happen despite the fact that four o'clock in the afternoon has no basic meaning, but is an agreed-upon designation — a gentlemen's agreement, if you prefer. If you attend the theatre at nine o'clock in the evening, but the actions of the play take place within the morning hours, and the actors are shown eating breakfast, you accept the time as given within the theatre's play. You also pretend that it is morning.

Each of you are now involved in a much larger production, in which you all agree on certain basic assumptions that serve as a framework within which the play can occur. The assumptions are that time is a series of moments one after another; that an objective world exists quite independently of your own creation and perception of it; that you are bound within the physical bodies that you have donned; and that you are limited by time and space.

(9:35.) Other assumptions accepted for the same reason include the

idea that all perception comes through your physical senses; in other words, that all information comes from without, and that no information can come from within. You therefore are forced to focus intensely upon the actions of the play. Now these various plays, these creative period pieces represent what you would call reincarnational lives.

They all exist basically at one time. Those who are still involved in these highly complicated passion-play seminars called reincarnational existences, find it difficult to see beyond them. Some, resting between productions, as it were, try to communicate with those who are still taking part; but they themselves are merely in the wings, so to speak, and can only see so far.

The plays seem to be taking place one before the other, and so these communications seem to intensify the false idea that time is a series of moments, passing in a single line from some inconceivable beginning to some equally inconceivable end.

Are your fingers tired?

(*"No." It was 9:42.*)

This leads you to think in terms of a very limited progress, both in individual terms and in terms of your species as a whole. You think, those of you who have even considered reincarnation, "Well, certainly the race must have progressed from the time of the Middle Ages," although you greatly fear it has not; or you turn to technological progress and say, "At least we have come a long way in that direction."

You may smile and think to yourself that it is quite difficult to imagine a Roman senator addressing the multitudes through a microphone, for example; his children, watching his performance on television. But all of this is highly misleading. Progress does not exist in the terms that you consider it to, any more than time does.

In each play, both individually and *en masse*, different problems are set up. Progress can be measured in terms of the particular ways in which those problems were solved or not solved. Great advances have been made in certain periods. For example, great offshoots appeared that from your viewpoint you might not consider progress at all.

You may take your break.

(*9:51. Jane left trance quickly. "Wow," she said, "Seth's going to have an awful lot to say about that — I can feel it up here." She touched her forehead. "Every so often I get a huge sweep of something that I can't put into words; do you know what I mean? But he's going to break it down for us.*

("It's funny," she continued, "I didn't feel particularly psychic tonight but the material's good. That's happened before, too. When there's someone here that I don't like, or they turn me off for some reason, then we won't have a session — the material won't come through. But I don't need to feel psychic when we're here alone; the material just comes through no matter what, and it's always good."

(Jane resumed at a slower pace at 10:15.)

Now: Incidentally *(humorously)*, you need not record this. My "now's," beginning a sentence, are often simply cues to you, and need not necessarily go along with our script.

("Okay, I understand.")

<u>Now</u> *(humorously louder)*: in some plays, generally speaking, the actors are each working on a seemingly minute portion of a larger problem that the play itself is to resolve.

Though I use the analogy here of a drama, these "plays" are highly spontaneous affairs in which the actors have full freedom <u>within</u> the play's framework. And granting these assumptions that have been stated, there are no rehearsals. There are observers, as you will see later in our book. As in any good theatre production, there is an overall theme within each play. The great artists, for example, did not emerge out of a particular time simply because they were born into it, or (because) the conditions were favorable.

(According to Seth, each individual chooses the time and place of every "life" in his reincarnational cycle.)

The play itself was concerned with the actualization of intuitive truth into what you would call artistic form, with a creativity of such vast and sweeping results that it would serve to awaken latent abilities within each actor and to serve as a model of behavior.

Periods of renaissance — spiritual, artistic, or psychic — occur because the intense inner focus of those involved in the drama are directed toward those ends. The challenge may be different in each play, but the great themes are beacons to all consciousness. They serve as models.

(10:17.) Progress has nothing to do with time, you see, but with psychic and spiritual focus. Each play is entirely different from any other. It is not correct, therefore, to suppose that your actions in this life are

caused by a previous existence, or that you are being punished in this life for crimes in a past one. The lives are simultaneous.

Your own multidimensional personality is so endowed that it can have these experiences and still retain its identity. It is, of course, affected by the various plays in which it takes part. There is instant communication and an instant, if you prefer, feedback system.

These plays are hardly without purpose. In them the multidimensional personality learns through its own actions. It tries out an endless variety of poses, behavior patterns, attitudes, and changes others as a result.

The word "result," you see, automatically infers cause and effect — the cause happening before the effect, and this is simply one small example of the strength of such distortions, and of the inherent difficulties involved with verbal thought, for it always implies a single-line delineation.

(10:26.) You are the multidimensional self who has these existences, who creates and takes part in these cosmic passion plays, so to speak. It is only because you focus in this particular role now that you identify your entire being with it. You have set these rules for yourself for a reason. And consciousness is in a state of becoming, and so this multidimensional self of which I speak is not a psychological structure completed and done with. It is also in a state of becoming.

It is learning the art of actualization. It has within it infinite sources of creativity, unlimited possibilities of development. But it has yet to learn the means of actualization, and must find within itself ways to bring into existence those untold creations that are within it.

(10:32.) Therefore it creates varieties of conditions in which to operate, and sets itself challenges, some doomed to failure in your terms, at least initially, because it must first create the conditions which will bring new creations about. And all of this is done with great spontaneity and unbounded joy. *(Pause.)*

You therefore create far more environments than you realize. Now, each actor, going about the role, focused within the play, has an inner guideline. He is not left, therefore, abandoned within a play that he has forgotten in his own creation. He has knowledge and information that comes to him through what I call the inner senses.

(10:39. Long pause.) He has other sources of information, therefore,

than those strictly given within the confines of the production. Each actor knows this instinctively, and there are periods set and allowed for within the play itself in which each actor retires in order to refresh himself. In these he is informed through the inner senses of his other roles, and he realizes that he is far more than the self appearing in any given play.

In these periods he understands that he had his hand in the writing of the play, and he is freed from those assumptions that bind him while he is actively concerned with the drama's activities. These periods, of course, coincide with your sleep states and dreaming conditions; but there are also other times when each actor sees quite clearly that he is surrounded by props, and when his vision suddenly pierces the seeming reality of the production.

(10:44.) This does not mean that the play is not real, or that it should not be taken seriously. It does mean playing a role — an important one. Each actor must of himself realize, however, the nature of the production and his part in it. He must actualize himself out of the three-dimensional confines of the play's setting.

There is great cooperation behind such momentous productions, and in playing his role, each actor first actualizes himself within three-dimensional reality. The multidimensional self cannot act within three-dimensional reality until it materializes a portion of itself within it. Do you follow me?

("Yes.")

Within this reality, it then brings about all kinds of creativity and development that could not appear otherwise. It must then propel itself from this system however, through another act, another actualization on the part of itself that is three-dimensional.

During its three-dimensional existence it has helped others in ways that they could not otherwise be helped, and it has been itself benefited and developed in ways that would be impossible otherwise.

I suggest your break.

(10:55. Jane's trance had been deep. Resume at 11:02.)

Now: The meaning of the play is within you, therefore. It is only the conscious portion of you that acts so well, and that is focused so securely within the props of the production.

The purpose of any given life is available to you, the knowledge beneath the surface of the conscious self you know. All kinds of hints and clues are also available. You have the knowledge of your entire multidimensional personality at your fingertips. When you realize that you do, this knowledge allows you to solve the problems or meet the challenges you have set, quicker, in your terms; and also opens further areas of creativity by which the entire play or production can be enriched.

(11:08.) To the extent, therefore, that you allow the intuitions and knowledge of the multidimensional self to flow through the conscious self, to that extent not only do you perform your role in the play more effectively, but also you add new energy, insights, and creativity to the entire dimension.

Now it seems to you, of course, that you are the only conscious part of yourself, for you are identifying with the actor in this particular production. The other portions of your multidimensional personality, in these other reincarnational plays, are also conscious, however. And because you are a multidimensional consciousness, "you" are also conscious in other realities beside these.

Your multidimensional personality, your true identity, the real you, is conscious of itself, as itself, in any of these roles.

End of dictation. Now give us a moment.

(After a pause Seth went on to give us both some answers to personal questions.)

Do you have further questions?

("No, I guess not. It's getting late.")

Then I will indeed bring our session to a close, with my heartiest regards to you both.

("Good night, Seth, and thank you.")

(11:24 P.M. Seth's production of his book had come to be a natural part of the framework by now. He was also beginning to deviate somewhat from the outline he'd given in the 510th session on January 10, 1970, but we had expected this. Seth was on his own, Jane said. Many people knew about his book by now.

(A note, added later: Except for one instance, Seth was to give many more chapters after this session before Jane looked at the book again. . . .)

SESSION 522, APRIL 8, 1970,
9:13 P.M. WEDNESDAY

Now, good evening.

("Good evening, Seth.")

We will continue.

These "period pieces," overall, have a particular purpose. By the very nature of consciousness, it seeks to materialize itself in as many dimensions as possible — to create from itself new levels of awareness, new offshoots. In doing so it creates all reality. Reality, therefore, is always in a state of becoming. The thoughts that you think, for example, in your actor's roles, are still completely unique and lead to new creativity. Certain aspects of your own consciousness could be fulfilled in no other way.

When you think of reincarnation, you suppose a series of progressions. Instead the various lives grow out of what your inner self is. They are not thrust upon you by some outside agency. They are a material development, as your consciousness opens up and expresses itself in as many ways as possible. It is not restricted to one three-dimensional lifetime, nor is it restricted to three-dimensional existence alone.

Your consciousness then takes many forms, and these forms need not be alike any more, say, than a caterpillar is like a butterfly. The soul or entity has complete freedom of expression. It changes its form to suit its expression, and it forms environments like stage settings, and worlds to suit its purposes. Each setting brings forth new developments.

(*Jane was taking many more pauses.*) The soul or entity is highly individualized spiritual energy. It forms whatever body you now wear, and is the motive power behind your physical survival, for from it you derive your vitality. Consciousness can never be still, but seeks further creativity.

(*9:28.*) The soul, therefore, or entity, endows three-dimensional reality, and the three-dimensional self with its own properties. The abilities of the entity lie within the three-dimensional self. The three-dimensional self, the actor, has access to this information and to these potentials. In learning to use these potentials, in learning to rediscover its relationship with the entity, the three-dimensional self raises still further the level of achievement, comprehension, and creativity. The three-dimensional self becomes more than it knows.

Not only is the entity strengthened, but portions of it, having been actualized in three-dimensional existence, now add to the very quality and nature of that existence. Without this creativity, planetary life in your terms would always be sterile. The soul or entity then gives breath to the body, and to the three-dimensional self within it. The three-dimensional self then goes about its purpose of opening up new areas of creativity.

Entities or souls, in other words, send out portions of themselves to open up avenues of reality that would not exist otherwise. *(Long pause at 9:39.)* The three-dimensional selves, in existing within these realities, must focus their attention there completely. An inner awareness gives them a source of energy and strength. They must, however, come to understand their roles as actors, "finally" from their roles, and through another act of comprehension, return to the entity.

There are those who appear within these plays fully aware. These personalities willingly take roles, knowing that they are roles, in order to lead the others toward the necessary realization and development. They lead the actors to see beyond the selves and settings they have created. These personalities from other levels of existence oversee the play, so to speak, and appear among the actors. Their purpose is to open up within the three-dimensional selves those psychological doorways that will release the three-dimensional self for further development in another system of reality.

Now you may take your break and we shall continue.

(9:50. Jane's trance had been relatively light. Resume at 9:58.)

Now: You are learning to be cocreators. You are learning to be gods as you now understand the term. You are learning responsibility — the responsibility of any individualized consciousness. You are learning to handle the energy that is yourself, for creative purposes.

You will be bound to those you love and those you hate, though you will learn to release and lose and dissipate the hatred. You will learn to use even hatred creatively and to turn it to the higher ends, to transform it finally into love. I will make this clearer in later chapters.

The settings in your physical environment, the sometimes lovely paraphernalia, the physical aspects of life as you know it, are all camouflages, and so I call your physical reality a camouflage. Yet these camouflages are composed of the vitality of the universe. The rocks and stones and mountains and earth are living camouflage, interlocking psychic webs formed by minute consciousnesses that you cannot perceive as such. The atoms and molecules within them have their own consciousness, as do the atoms and molecules with your body.

(10:07.) Since you all have a hand in forming this physical setting, and since you are ensconced yourself in a physical form, then using the physical senses you will only perceive this fantastic setting. The reality that exists both within it and beyond it will elude you. Even the actor is not entirely three-dimensional, however. He is a part of a multidimensional self.

Within him there are methods of perception that allow him to see through the camouflage settings, to see beyond the stage. He uses these inner senses constantly, though the actor part of himself is so intent upon the play that this escapes him. In a large manner, the physical senses actually form the physical reality they seem to only perceive. They are themselves part of the camouflage, but they are like lenses over your natural inner perceptions that force you to "see" an available field of activity as physical matter; and so they can be relied upon only to tell you what is happening in a superficial manner. You can tell the position of the other actors for example, or time by clock, but these physical senses will not tell you that time is itself a camouflage, or that consciousness forms the other actors, or that realities that you cannot see exist over and beyond the physical matter that is so apparent.

You can, however, using your inner senses, perceive reality as it exists apart from the play and your role in it. In order to do this you must, of course, momentarily at least turn your attention away from the constant activity that is taking place — turn off the physical senses, as it were — and switch your attention to those events that have escaped you earlier.

(10:20.) Highly simplified indeed, the effect would be something like changing one set of glasses for another, for the physical senses are as artificial, basically speaking, to the inner self, as a set of glasses or a hearing aid is to the physical self. The inner senses, therefore, are but rarely used completely consciously.

You would be more than disoriented, for example, but quite terrified, if between one moment and the next your familiar environment as you knew it disappeared to be replaced by other sets of data that you were not ready to understand, so much information from the inner senses must be translated in terms that you can comprehend. Such information must somehow make sense to you as three-dimensional selves, in other words.

Your particular set of camouflages is not the only set, you see. Other realities have entirely different systems, but all personalities have inner senses that are attributes of consciousness, and through these inner senses communications are maintained about which the normally conscious self knows little. Part of my purpose is to make some of these communications known.

(10:29.) The soul or entity, then, is not the self that reads this book. Your environment is not simply the world about you as you know it, but also consists of past-life environments upon which you are not now focusing. Your real environment is composed of your thoughts and emotions, for from these you form not only this reality but each reality in which you take part. *(Long pause.)*

Your real environment is innocent of space and time as you know them. In your real environment you have no need for words, for communication is instantaneous. In your real environment you form the physical world that you know.

The inner senses will allow you to perceive the reality that is independent of physical form. I will ask you all to momentarily forsake your roles therefore, and to try this simple exercise.

Now you may take your break.

(10:36. Jane's trance had been deeper this time. "I know I wasn't in as deep the first time," she said, "because I heard that siren." A fire engine had passed a couple of blocks away from our house at about 9:30; only now did Jane remember to tell me she'd heard it. "I worry when I hear things like that while Seth's writing his book. I don't want to mess anything up. . . ."

(Resume at 10:53.)

Now, pretend that you are on a lighted stage, the stage being the room in which you now sit. Close your eyes and pretend that the lights have gone out, the setting has disappeared and you are alone.

Everything is dark. Be quiet. Imagine as vividly as you can the existence of inner senses. For now pretend that they correspond to your physical ones. Clear from your mind all thoughts and worries. Be receptive. Very gently listen, not to physical sounds but to sounds that come through the inner senses.

Images may begin to appear. Accept them as sights quite as valid as those you see physically. Pretend that there is an inner world, and that it will be revealed to you as you learn to perceive it with these inner senses.

(10:58.) Pretend that you have been blind to this world all your life, and are now slowly gaining sight within it. Do not judge the whole inner world by the disjointed images that you may at first perceive, or by the sounds that you may at first hear, for you will still be using your inner senses quite imperfectly.

Do this simple exercise for a few moments before sleep or in the resting state. It may also be done even in the midst of an ordinary task that does not take all of your attention.

You will simply be learning to focus in a new dimension of awareness, taking quick snapshots, as it were, in a strange environment. Remember that you will only be perceiving snatches. Simply accept them, but do not attempt to make any overall judgments or interpretations at this stage.

Ten minutes a day to begin with is quite sufficient. Now the information in this book is being directed to some extent through the inner senses of the woman who is in trance as I write it. Such endeavor is the result of highly organized inner precision, and of training. Ruburt could not receive the information from me, it could not be translated nor interpreted while she was focused intensely in the physical environment. So the inner senses are channels that provide communication between various dimensions of existence. Yet even here the information must be distorted to some extent as it is translated into physical terms. Otherwise it would not be perceived at all.

End of dictation. Do you have questions?

("Nothing in particular, I guess.")

Whenever you want a less formal session, or have questions, then let me know.

("I will.")

(Humorously): I am willing to take time out from my writing chores.

("I know it.")

My heartiest good wishes then, and a fond good evening.

("Good evening, Seth. Thank you very much." 11:10 P.M.)

SESSION 523, APRIL 13, 1970,
9:13 P.M. MONDAY

Good evening.

("Good evening, Seth.")

We will finish Chapter Four.

(*"All right."*)

Now: I have spent some time emphasizing the fact that each of us forms our own environment, because I want you to realize that the responsibility for your life and your environment is your own.

If you believe otherwise, then you are limited; your environment then represents the sum total of knowledge and experience. As long as you believe your environment to be objective and independent of yourself, then to a large extent you feel powerless to change it, to see beyond it, or to imagine other alternatives that may be less apparent. Later in the book I will explain various methods that will allow you to change your environment beneficially and drastically.

(*9:23. Note the semicolon in the first sentence of the above paragraph. Seth requested that I punctuate the sentence just that way. He made such requests often while dictating this book.*)

I have also discussed reincarnation in terms of environment because many schools of thought over-emphasize the effects of reincarnational existences, so that often they explain present-life circumstances as a result of rigid and uncompromising patterns determined in a "past" life. You will feel relatively incompetent to handle present physical reality, to alter your environment, to affect and change your world, if you feel that you are at the mercy of conditions over which you have no control.

The reasons given for such subjugations matter little in the long run, for the reasons change with the times and with your culture. You are not under a sentence placed upon you for original sin, by any childhood events, or by past-life experience. Your life, for example, may be far less fulfilling than you think you would prefer. You may be less when you would be more, but you are not under a pall placed upon your psyche, either by original sin, Freud's infancy syndromes, or past-life influences. I will try to explain the past-life influences a bit more clearly here. They affect you as any experience does. Time is not closed, however — it is open. One life is not buried in the past, disconnected from the present self and any future self as well.

(*In this delivery Jane's pace was relatively slow.*)

As I explained earlier, the lives or the plays are happening at once. Creativity and consciousness are never linear achievements. In each life you choose and create your own settings or environments; and in this one you chose your parents and whatever childhood incidents that came within your experience. You wrote the script.

(9:35.) Like a true absent-minded professor, the conscious self forgets all this, however, so when tragedy appears in the script, difficulty or challenges, the conscious self looks for someone or something to blame. Before this book is done I hope to show you precisely how you create each <u>minute</u> of your experience so that you can begin to exert your true creative responsibility on a conscious level — or nearly so.

As you read this book, now and then look about you at the room in which you sit. Chairs and tables, the ceilings and the floors, may seem very real and solid — quite permanent — while you by contrast may feel yourself to be highly vulnerable, caught in a moment between birth and extinction. You may even feel jealous when you think of it, imagining that the physical universe will continue to exist long after you are gone. By the end of our book, however, I hope you will realize the eternal validity of your own consciousness, and the <u>impermanence</u> of those physical aspects of your environment, and of your universe, that now seem so secure. Do you have that?

("Yes.")

That is the end of Chapter Four. You may take your break.

(9:44 to 10:02.)

CHAPTER 5

HOW THOUGHTS FORM MATTER —
COORDINATION POINTS

G ive us a moment.
(A two-minute pause followed, ending at 10:04.)

Chapter Five: As you read the words upon this page, you realize that the information that you are receiving is not an attribute of the letters of the words themselves. The printed line does not <u>contain</u> information. It transmits information. Where <u>is</u> the information that is being transmitted then, if it is not upon the page? *(Pause.)*

The same question of course applies when you read a newspaper, and when you speak to another person. Your actual words convey information, feelings, or thoughts. Obviously the thoughts or the feelings, and the words, are not the same thing. The letters upon the page are symbols, and you have agreed upon various meanings connected with them. You take it for granted without even thinking of it that the symbols — the letters — are not the reality — the information or thoughts — which they attempt to convey.

Now in the same way, I am telling you that objects are also symbols that stand for a reality whose meaning the objects, like the letters, transmit. The true information is not in the objects any more than the thought is <u>in</u> the letters or in words. Words are methods of expression. So are physical objects in a different kind of medium. You are used to the idea that you express yourselves directly through words. You can hear yourself speak them. You can feel the muscles in your throat move, and if you are aware, you can perceive multitudinous reactions within your own body — actions that all accompany your speech.

(10:29.) Physical objects are the result of another kind of expression. You create them as surely as you create words. I do not mean that you create them with your hands alone, or through manufacture. I mean that objects are natural by-products of the evolution of your species, even as words are. Examine for a moment your knowledge of your own speech, however. Though you hear the words and recognize their appropriateness, and though they may more or less approximate an expression of your feeling, they are not your feeling, and there must be a gap between your thought and your expression of it.

The familiarity of speech begins to vanish when you realize that you, yourself, when you begin a sentence do not know precisely how you will end it, or even how you form the words. You do not consciously know how you manipulate a staggering pyramid of symbols, picking from them precisely those you need to express a given thought. For that matter, you do not know how you think.

You do not know how you translate these symbols upon this page into thoughts, and then store them, or make them your own. Since the mechanisms of normal speech are so little known to you on a conscious level, then it is not surprising that you are equally unaware of more complicated tasks that you also perform — such as the constant creation of your physical environment as a method of communication and expression.

It is only from this viewpoint that the true nature of physical matter can be understood. It is only by comprehending the nature of this constant translation of thoughts and desires — not into words now, but into physical objects — that you can realize your true independence from circumstance, time, and environment.

Now you may take a break. *(Smile, at 10:36.)* A note: I am very pleased. . . .

("At what, Seth?")

I am pleased with the beginning of my chapter, for I think I have hit upon an analogy, and a true one, that will release the reader from the artificial bondage of physical form. When he sees it as a method of his own expression, he will realize his own creativeness.

(10:38. Jane's trance had been good, her pace rather slow. She said the two-minute pause at the start of the delivery took place because she was consciously

"hung up" over how Seth was going to begin Chapter Five. She also realized that if she "just sat there," Seth would do okay on his own.

(Jane had a lot of images while Seth was speaking. He had the idea for this chapter very clearly in mind, she said; and, with extraordinary vividness, he was "impressing" her with his idea of matter being used as a means of communication. Yet she couldn't describe the images she had seen.

(While telling me this, Jane abruptly remembered that during part of the delivery she seemed to be standing beside the long, floor-to-ceiling bookcase that divides our living room from her workroom. This would be a distance of about six feet from the rocker she always uses for sessions.

(Jane had a "memory," now, of giving part of Seth's data from the bookcase area, of seeing the living room from a different viewpoint. She didn't remember going out of her body. "It came back like a dream," she said. Nor could she remember any more about the episode. She didn't remember seeing herself in her chair, for instance, nor did she see me as I sat on the couch taking notes. She was much intrigued by the idea of being out-of-body, and able to watch herself give material for Seth.

(Resume at 10:56.)

Now, it is easy to see that you translate feelings into words or bodily expressions and gestures, but not quite as easy to realize that you <u>form</u> your physical body as effortlessly and unselfconsciously as you translate feelings into symbols that become words.

(Long pause at 11:01.) You have heard the expression before, I am sure, that the environment expresses a particular individual's personality. I am telling you that this is a literal and not symbolic truth. The letters upon the page have the reality only of ink and paper. The information they convey is invisible. As an object, this book itself is only paper and ink. It is a carrier of information.

You may perhaps argue that the book was manufactured physically, and did not suddenly erupt through Ruburt's skull, already printed and bound. You in turn had to borrow or purchase the book, so you may think, "Surely, I did not create the book, as I created my words." But before we are finished we will see that basically speaking, each of you create the book you hold in your hands, and that your entire physical environment comes as naturally out of your inner mind as words come out of your mouths, and that man forms physical objects as unselfconsciously and as automatically as he forms his own breath.

End of dictation for this evening. *(Smile.)*

("Good night, Seth, and thank you." 11:14 P.M.)

(Jane didn't feel particularly well this evening, but decided to sit for a session to see what developed. When she began speaking her pace was quite slow and her eyes were closed most of the time.)

Good evening.

("Good evening, Seth.")

Now, for our book. The peculiar, particular aspects of your physical world are dependent upon your existence and focus within it. The physical universe does not contain physical objects of solidity, width and depth, for example, to those whose existence is not within it.

Other kinds of consciousness coexist within the same "space" that your world inhabits. They do not perceive your physical objects, for their reality is composed of a different camouflage structure. You do not perceive them, and generally speaking they do not perceive you. This is a general statement, however, for various points of your realities can and do coincide, so to speak.

These points are not recognized as such, but they are points of what you could call double reality, containing great energy potential; coordinate points, indeed, where realities merge. There are main coordinate points, pure mathematically, sources of fantastic energy, and subordinate coordinate points, vast in number.

(Long pause at 9:29.) There are four absolute coordinate points that intersect all realities. These coordinate points also act as channels through which energy flows, and as warps or invisible paths from one reality to another. They also act as transformers, and provide much of the generating energy that makes creation continuous in your terms. *(Many pauses.)*

Your space is filled with these subordinate points, and as you will see later, these are important in allowing you to transform thoughts and emotions into physical matter. When a thought or emotion attains a certain intensity, it automatically attracts the power of one of these subordinate points, and is therefore highly charged, and in one way magnified, though not in size.

These points impinge upon what you call time, as well as space. There are certain points in time and space, therefore, (again in your terms), that are more conducive than others, where both ideas and matter will be more highly charged. Practically speaking, this means that buildings will last longer; in your context, that ideas wedded to form will be relatively eternal. The pyramids, for example, are a case in point.

(Slow at 9:43.) These coordinate points — absolute, main, or subordinate — represent accumulations or traces of pure energy, minute to an extreme if you are thinking in terms of size — smaller than any particle of which your scientists know for example, but composed of pure energy. And yet this energy must be activated. It is dormant until then — and it cannot be activated physically.

(9:50.) Now: A few clues here that might help you, or mathematicians. There is an ever-so-minute alteration of gravity forces in the neighborhood of all of these points, even of the subordinate ones, and all the so-called physical laws to some extent or another will be found to have a wavering effect in these neighborhoods. The subordinate points also serve in a way as supports, as structural intensifications within the unseen fabric of energy that forms all realities and manifestations. While they are traces or accumulations of pure energy, there is a great difference between the amount of energy available in the various subordinate points, and between the main and the absolute points.

You may take your break.

(9:57. Jane felt better now. She was surprised when I told her the delivery had been so slow. In trance she is unaware of her pauses, or of their number. "I haven't any sense of time then," she said. "My space is filled. I don't know how else to put it. . . . "

(Resume in the same manner at 10:17.)

These are points, therefore, of concentrated energy. The subordinate points are far more common, and practically speaking, affect your daily concerns. There are better places than others to build houses or structures — points where health and vitality are strengthened, where, other things being equal, plants will grow and flourish and where all beneficial conditions seem to meet.

Some people can sense such neighborhoods instinctively. They occur within certain angles made by coordinate points. The points obviously are not themselves physical — that is, they are not visible, though they may be mathematically deduced. They are felt, however, as intensified energy.

(10:23.) In a given room, plants will grow more effectively in a particular area than in other areas, providing that both areas contain such necessary requirements as light. All of your space is permeated by these coordination points, so that certain invisible angles are formed.

(10:26.) This is highly simplified, but some angles will be more "on the outskirts" than others, and will be less favorable for all conditions of growth and activity. In speaking of these angles we will treat them as three-dimensional, though they are of course multidimensional. Since the nature of these angles is not the main topic of my book, it is not possible to explain them thoroughly here. They will seem to be stronger during certain times than other times, though these differences have nothing to do with either the nature of the coordinate points or with the nature of time. Other elements affect them, but we need not be concerned with these now.

(10:31.) The concentrated energy points are activated by emotional intensities that are well within your normal range. Your own emotions or feelings will activate these coordinates whether you know of them or not. Greater energy will therefore be added to the original thought or feeling, and its projection into physical matter accelerated. Now this applies regardless of the nature of the feeling; only its intensity is involved here.

These points are like invisible power plants, in other words, activated when any emotional feeling or thought of sufficient intensity comes into contact. The points themselves intensify whatever activates them in a quite neutral manner.

We are rather slow with this material, since it is new, but mainly because I would like it translated into as precise terms as possible; and without a scientific background on Ruburt's part, I must use ingenuity.

You may take a break.

(10:39 to 11:14.)

Now: This is highly simplified, but the subjective experience of any consciousness is automatically expressed as electromagnetic energy units. These exist "beneath" the range of physical matter. They are, if you prefer, incipient particles that have not yet emerged into matter.

These units are natural emanations from all kinds of consciousness.

They are the invisible formations resulting from reaction to any kind of stimuli. They very seldom exist in isolation, but unite under certain laws. They change both their form and their pulsation. Their relative "duration" depends upon the original intensity behind them — that is, behind the original thought, emotion, stimuli, or reaction that brought them into being.

(11:21.) Again, highly simplified here, under certain conditions these coagulate into matter. Those electromagnetic units of high enough intensity automatically activate the subordinate coordinate points of which I have spoken. They are, therefore, accelerated and propelled into matter far more quickly, in your terms, than units of lesser intensity. Molecules would appear as large as planets to these units. Atoms and molecules and planets and these electromagnetic energy units are simply different manifestations of the same principles that bring the units themselves into being. It is only your relative position, your focus within an apparent space and time, that makes this seem so unlikely.

Each thought or emotion therefore exists as an electromagnetic energy unit or as a combination of these under certain conditions, and often with the help of coordinate points, they emerge into the building blocks of physical matter. This emergence into matter occurs as a neutral "result" regardless of the nature of any given thought or emotion. Mental images, accompanied by strong emotion, are blueprints therefore upon which a corresponding physical object, or condition or event, will in your terms appear.

Now: End of dictation. Do you have questions?

("No.")

We are doing very well with our Chapter Five. My heartiest regards and a fond good evening.

("Good night, Seth, and thank you very much." 11:32 P.M.)

SESSION 525, APRIL 22, 1970,
9:14 P.M. WEDNESDAY

(Seth's dictation on his book tonight was preceded by four pages of personal material that we have deleted. Resume after break at 10:03.)

The intensity of a feeling or thought or mental image is, therefore, the important element in determining its subsequent physical materialization.

The intensity is the core about which the electromagnetic energy units form. In your terms, the more intense the core, the sooner the physical materialization. This would apply whether the mental image was a fearful one or a joyful one. Now there is a very important problem here: If your turn of mind is highly intense and you think in vivid mental emotional images, these will be swiftly formed into physical events. If you are also of a highly pessimistic nature, given to thoughts and feelings of potential disaster, then these thoughts will be quite faithfully reproduced in experience.

The more intense your imagination and inner experience, therefore, the more important it is that you realize the methods by which this inner experience becomes physically real. Your thoughts and emotions begin their journey into physical actualization at the moment of conception. If you happen to live in an area where the coordinate environment is strong, one of those areas I have spoken of as unusually conducive, then it will seem that you are deluged by illnesses or disasters, if these are the nature of your thoughts, because all thought is so fertile in this environment. If, on the other hand, your feelings and subjective experience are fairly well balanced, fairly optimistic and creative in a constructive manner, then it will seem to you that you have been blessed with unusual luck, for your pleasant suppositions will come to pass so quickly.

Briefly, in your own country, the West Coast, portions of the East Coast, Utah, the Great Lakes, the Chicago area, the Minneapolis area, and some other southwestern areas, are in those neighborhoods of excellent coordinate activity, for the reasons given. Materialization will quickly appear, and potentials therefore for both constructive and destructive elements are high.

(10:20.) Give us a moment. These coordinate points themselves activate the behavior of atoms and molecules as, say for example, the sun aids the growth of plants. The coordinates activate the generating behavior of atoms and molecules, and greatly encourage their cooperative abilities; their tendency to swarm, so to speak, into organizations and structural groupings.

The coordinate points magnify or intensify the behavior, the latent spontaneity inherent within the properties of physical matter. They act as psychic generators, propelling what is not yet physical into physical form.

Now you may take your break.

(10:25 to 10:38.)

Now, this is not to be a technical book, so this is not the time nor place to discuss thoroughly the action, behavior or effects of these coordinate points; nor of the electromagnetic energy units — those natural emanations of consciousness of which I spoke. I want it known, however, that thoughts and emotions are formed into physical matter by very definite methods and through laws quite valid, though they may be presently unknown.

In other portions of the Seth material these processes will be made very clear for those of you who desire to pursue the question further, or those who may be interested from a scientific point of view. Here, we are discussing such issues only because they touch upon the multidimensional aspect of personality. They allow you to materialize certain subjective experiences into three-dimensional reality. Before I leave the subject, however, let me remind you that these emanations in varying degrees rise from all consciousness, not simply your own. This includes cellular consciousness as well, so that an invisible network of electromagnetic units pervades your entire atmosphere; and upon this webwork and from it, the particles of physical matter are then formed.

Now: A whole book could easily be written upon this subject. Information regarding the "locations" of main and absolute coordinate points could be highly advantageous, for example. You pride yourselves on your technology, and the production of durable goods, buildings and roads, yet many of these are insignificant when compared to other structures within the "past."

A true understanding of the way in which an idea becomes physical matter would result in a complete revamping of your so-called modern technology, and in buildings, roads, and other structures that would far outlast those you now have. While the psychic reality behind physical matter is ignored, then you cannot use those methods effectively that do exist, nor can you take advantage of them. You cannot understand the psychic reality that is the true impetus for your physical existence unless you first realize your own psychic reality, and independence from physical laws.

My first purpose, therefore, is to make you aware of the inner identity of which you are part, and to clear away some of the intellectual and superstitious debris that prevents you from recognizing your own potentialities and freedom. Then perhaps you can begin to learn the many ways in which that freedom can be used.

That is the end of dictation. It may well be the end of Chapter Five. You may end the session or take a break if you prefer.

("We'll take the break, then."

(10:58 P.M. It developed that this was the end of the session. We were both tired. Jane's pace had been considerably faster than last session, her eyes closed much of the time.)

CHAPTER 6

THE SOUL AND THE NATURE
OF ITS PERCEPTION

SESSION 526, MAY 4, 1970,
10:00 P.M. MONDAY

(*T*he session began late this evening because of my own distractions with *painting; I worked late, and needed a short rest. Jane felt well. Her pace was quite rapid — as fast as it's been, I believe, since Seth started his book. Jane's manner was easy and relaxed, her voice average, her eyes closed often.*)

Good evening.

(*"Good evening, Seth."*)

Now: We will have a short session, and begin to dictate the next chapter.

With the little background given so far, we can at least begin to discuss the subject of this book: The eternal validity of the soul. Even when we are exploring other issues, we will be trying to illustrate the multidimensional aspect of this inner self. There are many misconceptions connected with it, and first of all we shall try to dismiss these.

First of all, a soul is not something that you have. It is what you are. I usually use the term "entity" in preference to the term "soul," simply because those particular misconceptions are not so connected with the word "entity," and its connotations are less religious in an organizational sense.

The trouble is that you frequently consider the soul or entity as a finished, static "thing" that belongs to you but is not you. The soul or entity — in other words, your most intimate powerful inner identity —

is and must be forever changing. It is not, therefore, something like a cherished heirloom. It is alive, responsive, curious. It forms the flesh and the world that you know, and it is in a state of becoming.

Now, in the three-dimensional reality in which your ego has its main focus, becoming presupposes arrival, or a destination — an ending to that which has been in a state of becoming. But the soul or entity has its existence basically in other dimensions, and in these, fulfillment is not dependent upon arrivals at any points, spiritual or otherwise.

The soul or entity is always in a state of flux, or learning, and of developments that have to do with subjective experience rather than with time or space. This is not nearly as mysterious as it might sound. Each of my readers plays a game in which the egotistical conscious self pretends not to know what the whole self definitely does know. Since the ego is definitely a part of the whole self, then it must necessarily be basically aware of such knowledge. In its intense focus in physical reality, however, it pretends not to know, until it feels able to utilize the information in physical terms.

You do have access to the inner self, therefore. You are hardly cut off from your own soul or entity. The ego prefers to consider itself the captain at the helm, so to speak, since it is the ego who most directly deals with the sometimes tumultuous seas of physical reality, and it does not want to be distracted from this task.

Channels, psychological and psychic, always exist, sending communications back and forth through the various levels of the self, and the ego accepts necessary information and data from inner portions of the personality without question. Its position in fact depends in a large manner upon this unquestioning acceptance of inner data. The ego, in other words, the "exterior" self that you think of as your self — that portion of you maintains its safety and its seeming command precisely because inner layers of your own personality constantly uphold it, keep the physical body operating, and maintain communications with the multitudinous stimuli that come both from outside conditions and inside conditions. The soul or entity is not diminished but expanded through reincarnations, through existence and experience in probable realities — something that I will explain later.

(10:19. Note the amount of material given since 10:00.)

It is only because you have a highly limited conception of your own

· 71 ·

entity that you insist upon its being almost sterile in its singularity. There are millions of cells within your body, but you call your body a unit, and consider it your own. You do form it, from the inside out, and yet you form it from living substance, and each smallest particle has its own living consciousness. There are clumps of matter, and in that respect there are clumps of consciousness, each individual, with their own destiny and abilities and potentials. There are no limitations to your own entity: therefore, how can your entity or soul have boundaries, for boundaries would enclose it and deny it freedom.

You may take your break.

(10:24. Jane resumed at the same fast pace at 10:33.)

Now: Often it seems that the soul is thought of as a precious stone, to be finally presented as a gift to God, or considered as some women used to consider their virginity — something highly prized that must be lost; the losing of it being signified as a fine gift to the receiver.

In many philosophies this sort of idea is retained — the soul being returned to a primal giver, or being dissolved in a nebulous state somewhere between being and nonbeing. The soul is, however, first of all creative. It can be discussed from many viewpoints. Its characteristics can be given to some degree, and indeed most of my readers could find out these characteristics for themselves if they were highly enough motivated, and if this was their main concern. The soul or entity is itself the most highly motivated, most highly energized, and most potent consciousness-unit known in any universe.

It is energy concentrated to a degree quite unbelievable to you. It contains potentials unlimited, but it must work out its own identity and form its own worlds. It carries within it the burden of all being. Within it are personality potentials beyond your comprehension. Remember, this is your own soul or entity I am speaking of, as well as soul or entity in general. You are one manifestation of your own soul. How many of you would want to limit your reality, your entire reality, to the experience you now know? You do this when you imagine that your present self is your entire personality, or insist that your identity be maintained unchanged through an endless eternity.

(10:43.) Such an eternity would be dead indeed. In many ways the soul is an incipient god, and later in this book we will discuss the "god concept." For now, however, we will simply be concerned with the entity

or soul, the larger self that whispers even now in the hidden recesses of each reader's experience. I hope in this book not only to assure you of the eternal validity of your soul or entity, but to help you sense its vital reality within yourself. First of all, however, you must have some idea of your own psychological and psychic structure. When you understand to some extent who and what you are, then I can explain more clearly who and what I am. I hope to acquaint you with those deeply creative aspects of your own being, so that you can use these to extend and expand your entire experience.

(Somewhat humorously): That is the end of dictation. Now give me a moment. *(Pause.)*

I wanted to begin this chapter. It always makes Ruburt feel better. It ends the suspense *(smiling)* as to what the next chapter will be. But give me a moment here. *(Pause.)*

Now: Remember in your portrait the sense of play, and a light hand. Otherwise you lose your sparkling colors and end up with a murkiness that you do not intend. Remember that the soul is plain behind the facade that you see — that even the body is in a constant state of almost magical activity, even though as you paint it in its chair, it is physically motionless.

(Here, unexpectedly, Seth referred to a large portrait I've been working on for the last month and the one that gave me so much trouble today. The painting is of a patient in the hospital where my father stays. The subject sits mute and quite rigid in his wheelchair. Everything went well until I ran into difficulties with the color of his clothing. I found this so irritating, finally, that I ended up doing the whole thing over.

(As usual, Seth's observations about painting are excellent; I've said this many times before. Nor have I ever heard Jane discuss painting in Seth's manner. The two personalities approach the subject from widely divergent viewpoints.)

You want the feeling, within that apparent state of motionlessness, of highly accelerated contained activity that cannot be physically expressed — that must radiate from the painting despite the obvious and illusionary appearance of your figure.

You are stressing perhaps too strongly the aspects of the chair, as the binding elements that hold your figure more or less stationary. He, of course also creates the chair, as you know, and therefore the limitations. I believe there is some difficulty, or was *(there was!)* with the lower right-hand corner, a matter perhaps of needing more transparent lights — not too obviously applied however. You are working these matters out. Do you have questions?

(*"I guess not. I'm too bleary to think."*)

I will then close our session. My heartiest regards and a fond good evening.

(*"Thank you, Seth. It's been very good."*)

Thank you for taking dictation when you were weary.

(*"Well, I wasn't that badly off."*

(*10:58 P.M. Jane's pace had been good right up until the end of the session.*)

SESSION 527, MAY 11, 1970,
9:12 P.M. MONDAY

Good evening.

(*"Good evening, Seth."*)

Now: We will continue with the chapter we began.

Many individuals imagine the soul to be an immortalized ego, forgetting that the ego as you know it is only a small portion of the self; so this section of the personality is simply projected onward, ad infinitum, so to speak. Because the dimensions of your reality are so little understood, your concepts are bound to be limited. In considering "immortality," mankind seems to hope for further egotistical development, and yet he objects to the idea that such development might involve change. He says through his religions that he has a soul indeed, without even asking what a soul is, and often he seems to regard it, again, as an object in his possession.

Now personality, even as you know it, constantly changes, and not always in ways that are anticipated — most often, in fact, in unpredictable ways. You insist upon focusing your attention upon the similarities that are woven through your own behavior; and upon these you build a theory that the self follows a pattern that you, instead, have transposed upon it. And the transposed pattern prevents you from seeing the self as it really is. Therefore, you also project this distorted viewpoint upon your conception of the reality of the soul. You think of the soul, therefore, in the light of erroneous conceptions that you hold regarding even the nature of your mortal selves.

(*9:25.*) Even the mortal self, you see, is far more miraculous and wondrous than you perceive, and possesses far more abilities than you ascribe to it. You do not understand as yet the true nature of perception, even as far as the mortal self is concerned, and therefore you can hardly understand the perceptions of the soul. For the soul, above all, perceives and creates. Remember again that you are a soul now. The soul within you, therefore, is now perceiving. Its methods of perception are the same now as they were before your physical birth, and as they will be after your physical death. So basically the inner portion of you, the soul-stuff, will not suddenly change its methods of perception nor its characteristics after physical death.

You can find out what the soul is now, therefore. It is not something waiting for you at your death, nor is it something you must save or redeem, and it is also something that you cannot lose. The term, "to lose or save your soul", has been grossly misinterpreted and distorted, for it is the part of you that is indeed indestructible. We will go into this particular matter in a portion of the book dealing with religion and the god concept.

Your own personality as you know it, that portion of you that you consider most precious, most uniquely you, will also never be destroyed or lost. It is a portion of the soul. It will not be gobbled by the soul, nor erased by it, nor subjugated by it; nor on the other hand can it ever be separated. It is, nevertheless, only one aspect of your soul. Your individuality, in whatever way you want to think of it, continues to exist in your terms.

It continues to grow and develop, but its growth and development are highly dependent upon its realization that while it is distinct and individual, it is also but one manifestation of the soul. To the extent that it realizes this, it learns to unfold in creativity, and to use those abilities that lie inherent within it.

Now unfortunately, it would be much easier simply to tell you that your individuality continues to exist, and let it go at that. While this would make a fairly reasonable parable, it has been told in that particular way before, and there are dangers in the very simplicity of the tale. The truth is that the personality you are now and the personality that you have been and will be — in the terms in which you understand time — all of these personalities are manifestations of the soul, of your soul.

(9:42.) Your soul therefore — the soul that you are — the soul that

you are part of — that soul is a far more creative and miraculous phenomenon than you previously supposed. And when this is not clearly understood, and when the concept is watered down for simplicity's sake, as mentioned earlier, then the intense vitality of the soul can never be understood. Your soul, therefore, possesses the wisdom, information, and knowledge that is part of the experience of all these other personalities; and you have within yourselves access to this information, but only if you realize the true nature of your reality. Let me emphasize again that these personalities exist independently within and are a part of the soul, and each of them is free to create and develop.

There is however an inner communication, and the knowledge of one is available to any — not after physical death, but now in your present moment. Now the soul itself, as mentioned earlier, is not static. It grows and develops even through the experience of those personalities that compose it, and it is, to put it as simply as possible, more than the sum of its parts.

(9:50.) Now, there are no closed systems in reality. In your physical system the nature of your perceptions limits your idea of reality to some extent, because you purposely decide to focus within a given "locale." But basically speaking, consciousness can never be a closed system, and all barriers of such a nature are illusion. Therefore the soul itself is not a closed system. When you consider the soul, however, you usually think of it in such a light — unchanging, a psychic or spiritual citadel. But citadels not only keep out invaders, they also prevent expansion and development.

There are many matters here very difficult to express in words, for you are so afraid for your sense of identity that you resist the idea that the soul, for example, is an open spiritual system, a powerhouse of creativity that shoots out in all directions — and yet this is indeed the case.

I tell you this, and at the same time remind you that your present personality is never lost. Now another word for the soul is entity. You see it is not a simple matter of giving you a definition of a soul or entity, for even to have a glimpse in logical terms you would have to understand it in spiritual, psychic, and electromagnetic terms, and understand the basic nature of consciousness and action as well. But you can intuitively discover the nature of the soul or entity, and in many ways intuitive knowledge is superior to any other kind.

One prerequisite for such an intuitive understanding of the soul is the desire to achieve it. If the desire is strong enough, then you will be automatically led to experiences that will result in vivid, unmistakable subjective knowledge. There are methods that will enable you to do this, and I will give you some toward the end of this book.

(10:02.) For now, here is one quite effective but simple exercise. Close your eyes after having read this chapter to this point, and try to sense within yourself the source of power from which your own breathing and life forces come. Some of you will do this successfully at your first try. Others may take longer. When you feel within yourself this source, then try to sense this power flow outward through your entire physical being, through the fingertips and toes, through the pores of your body, all directions, with yourself as center. Imagine the rays undiminished, reaching then through the foliage and clouds above, through the center of the earth below, extending even to the farthest reaches of the universe.

Now I do not mean this to be merely a symbolic exercise, for though it may begin with imagination, it is based upon fact, and emanations from your consciousness and the creativity of your soul do indeed reach outward in that manner. The exercise will give you some idea of the true nature, creativity, and vitality of the soul from which you can draw your own energy and of which you are an individual and unique portion.

(Humorously): You may take your break.

("Thank you."

(10:10. Jane had been in a deep trance; her pace had been fast, with few pauses. Seth, she said, could have cheerfully continued unabated. He called a break only because I deliberately let my weary right hand flop down on the couch. Jane felt well. She had no sense of an hour's having passed. Note the amount of material delivered.

(As is often the case, Jane said she had no memory of the first portion of the chapter, given on May 4. Resume in the same fast manner at 10:27.)

Now: This discussion is not meant to be an esoteric presentation with little practical meaning in your daily lives. The fact is that while you hold limited concepts of your own reality, then you cannot practically take advantage of many abilities that are your own; and while you have a limited concept of the soul, then to some extent you cut yourself off from the source of your own being and creativity.

Now these abilities operate whether you know it or not, but often they operate in spite of you rather than with your conscious cooperation; and often when you do find yourself using them, you become frightened, disoriented, or confused. No matter what you have been taught, you must understand, for example, that basically speaking, perceptions are not physical in the way the term is usually used. If you catch yourself perceiving information through other than your physical senses, then you must accept the fact that this is the way perception works.

What often happens is that your conception of reality is so limited that you take fright whenever you perceive any experience that does not fit into your conception. Now I am not speaking merely of abilities loosely called "extrasensory perception." These experiences seem extraordinary to you only because you have for so long denied the existence of any perception that did not come through the physical senses.

So-called extrasensory perception gives you but a crude and distorted idea of the basic ways in which the inner self receives information, but the concepts built around extrasensory perception are at least nearer the truth, and as such represent an improvement over the idea that all perception is basically physical.

Now it is nearly impossible to separate a discussion of the nature of the soul from a discussion of the nature of perception. Very briefly let us review a few points: You form physical matter and the physical world that you know. The physical senses actually can be said to create the physical world, in that they force you to perceive an available field of energy in physical terms, and impose a highly specialized pattern upon this field of reality. Using the physical senses, you can perceive reality in no other way.

(10:44.) This physical perception in no way alters the native, basic, unfettered perception that is characteristic of the inner self, the inner self being the portion of the soul that is within you. The inner self knows its relationship with the soul. It is a portion of the self that acts, you might say, as a messenger between the soul and the present personality. You must also realize that while I use terms like "soul" or "entity," "inner self," and "present personality," I do so only for the sake of convenience, for one is a part of the other; there is no point where one begins and another ends.

You can see this easily for yourself if you consider the way in which psychologists use the terms "ego," "subconscious," and even "unconscious." What seems subconscious in one instant may be conscious the next. An unconscious motive may also be conscious at one point. Even in these terms your experience should tell you that the words themselves make divisions that do not exist in your own experience.

You seem to perceive exclusively through your physical senses, and yet you have only to extend your egotistical idea of reality, and you will find even your egotistical self accepting quite readily the existence of nonphysical information.

(Pause at 10:53.) As it does, so its own ideas of its own nature will automatically change and expand, for you will have removed limitations to its growth. Now any act of perception changes the perceiver, and so the soul, considered as a perceiver, must also change. There are no real divisions between the perceiver and the thing seemingly perceived. In many ways the thing perceived is an extension of the perceiver. This may seem strange, but all acts are mental, or if you prefer, psychic acts. This is an extremely simple explanation; but the thought creates the reality. Then the creator of the thought perceives the object, and he does not understand the connection between him and this seemingly separate thing.

This characteristic of materializing thoughts and emotions into physical realities is an attribute of the soul. Now in your reality, these thoughts are made physical. In other realities, they may be "constructed" in an entirely different fashion. So your soul, that which you are, constructs your physical daily reality for you from the nature of your thoughts and expectations.

You can readily see, therefore, how important your subjective feelings really are. This knowledge — that your universe is idea construction — can immediately give you clues that enable you to change your environment and circumstances beneficially. When you do not understand the nature of the soul, and do not realize that your thoughts and feelings form physical reality, then you feel powerless to change it. In later chapters of this book, I hope to give you some practical information that will enable you to alter practically the very nature and structure of daily life.

(Jane, as Seth, leaned forward, smiling.) Do you grow weary?

("I could use a break. A short one." Still in trance and quite amused, Jane

continued to stare at me. Her eyes were very dark. "I'm okay," I said. "Do you want to continue? I'm all right.")

I would not have it on my conscience. Now what we need is an extra set of fingers for you. By all means take your break. *(Humorously):* I do not mean to keep you overlong.

("It's all right."

(Suddenly loud and powerful): I could dictate all night, one night, and then you could take three sessions off.

("I believe you could."

(11:09. Again Jane's trance had been deep, and again I had writer's cramp. I had no doubts that Seth could speak all night; the only limitations here were our own. Jane felt a very strong energy.

(This break marked the end of dictation on his book for the evening, Seth announced when he returned at 11:28. He then delivered a page or so of personal material for Jane and me, and ended the session in a jovial mood at 11:35 P.M.)

SESSION 528, MAY 13, 1970, ·9:03 P.M. WEDNESDAY

Now: Good evening.

("Good evening, Seth.")

(Smile.) It is the writer's hour, and we will resume dictation.

The soul perceives all experience directly. Most experiences of which you are aware come packaged in physical wrapping, and you take the wrapping for the experience itself, and do not think of looking inside. The world that you know is one of the infinite materializations taken by consciousness, and as such it is valid.

The soul, however, does not need to follow the laws and principles that are a part of the physical reality, and it does not depend upon physical perception. The soul's perceptions are of acts and events that are mental, that lie, so to speak, beneath physical events as you know them. The soul's perceptions are not dependent upon time, because time is a physical camouflage and does not apply to nonphysical reality.

Now it is difficult to explain to you how direct experience actually works, for it exists — a total field of perception, innocent of the physical clues such as color, size, weight, and sense, with which your physical perceptions are clothed.

(9:19.) Words are used to tell of an experience, but they obviously are not the experience that they attempt to describe. Your physical subjective experience is so involved with word thinking, however, that it is almost impossible for you to conceive of an experience that is not thought-word oriented.

Now, each event of which you are aware is already a translation of an inner event, a psychic or mental event that is perceived by the soul directly, but translated by the physically oriented portions of the self into physical sense terms.

It goes without saying then that the soul does not require a physical body for purposes of perception; that perception is not dependent upon physical senses; that experience continues whether or not you are in this life or another; and also that the soul's basic methods of perception are also operating within you now even as you read this book. It also follows that your experience within the physical system is dependent upon a physical form and physical senses — again, because these interpret reality and translate it into physical data. It also follows that some hints of the soul's direct experience can be gained by momentarily switching the physical senses off — by refusing to use them as perceptors, and falling back upon other methods. Now you do this to some extent in the dream state, but even then in many dreams you still tend to translate experience into hallucinatory physical terms. Most of the dreams that you recall are of this nature.

At certain depths of sleep, however, the soul's perception operates relatively unhampered. You drink, so to speak, from the pure well of perception. You communicate with the depths of your own being, and the source of your creativity. These experiences, not being translated physically, do not remain in the morning. You do not remember them as dreams. Dreams, however, may later the same evening be formed from the information gained during what I will call the "depth experience." These will not be exact or near translations of the experience, but rather of the nature of dream parables — an entirely different thing, you see.

(9:35.) Now this particular level of consciousness, occurring in the sleep state, has not been pinpointed by your scientists. During it, energy is generated that makes the dream state itself possible. It is true that dreams allow the physically oriented self to digest current experience, but it is also true that the experience is then returned to its initial

components. It breaks apart, so to speak. Portions of it are retained as "past" physical sense data, but the whole experience returns to its initial direct state.

It exists then, "eternally," separated from the physical clothing that you need in order to understand it. Physical existence is one way in which the soul chooses to experience its own actuality. The soul, in other words, has created a world for you to inhabit, to change — a complete sphere of activity in which new developments and indeed new forms of consciousness can emerge.

In a manner of speaking, you continually create your soul as it continually creates you.

You may take your break.

(9:43. At times Jane's delivery had approached the speed of the last session. Resume more slowly at 10:05.)

Now, the soul is never diminished, nor basically are any portions of the self.

The soul can be considered as an electromagnetic energy field, of which you are part. It is a field of concentrated action when you consider it in this light — a powerhouse of probabilities or probable actions, seeking to be expressed; a grouping of nonphysical consciousnesses that nevertheless knows itself as an identity. Look at it this way: The young woman through whom I speak once stated in a poem, and I quote: "These atoms speak, and call themselves my name."

Now your physical body is a field of energy with a certain form, however, and when someone asks you your name, your lips speak it — and yet the name does not belong to the atoms and molecules in the lips that utter the syllables. The name has meaning only to you. Within your body you cannot put your finger upon your own identity. If you could travel within your body, you could not find where your identity resides, yet you say, "This is my body," and, "This is my name."

(10:14.) If you cannot be found, even by yourself, within your body, then where is this identity of yours that claims to hold the cells and organs as its own? Your identity obviously has some connection with your body, since you have no trouble distinguishing your body from someone else's, and you certainly have no trouble distinguishing between your body and the chair, say, upon which you may sit.

In a larger manner, the identity of the soul can be seen from the

· 82 ·

same viewpoint. It knows who it is, and is far more certain of its identity, indeed, than your physical self is of its identity. And yet now where in this electromagnetic energy field can the identity of the soul as such be found?

It regenerates all other portions of itself, and gives you the identity that is your own. And when it should be asked, "Who are you?" it would simply answer, "I am I," and be answering for you also.

(Pause at 10:20.) Now in terms of psychology as you understand it, the soul could be considered as a prime identity that is in itself a gestalt of many other individual consciousnesses — an unlimited self that is yet able to express itself in many ways and forms and yet maintain its own identity, its own "I am-ness," even while it is aware that its I am-ness may be part of another I am-ness. Now I am sure it may seem inconceivable to you, but the fact is that this I am-ness is retained even though it may, figuratively speaking, now merge with and travel through other such energy fields. There is, in other words, a give and take between souls or entities, and no end of possibilities, both of development and expansion. Again, the soul is not a closed system.

It is only because your present existence is so highly focused in one narrow area that you put such stern limits upon your definitions and the self, and then project these upon your concepts of the soul. You worry for your physical identity and limit the extent of your perceptions for fear you cannot handle more and retain your selfhood.

The soul is not frightened for its identity. It is sure of itself. It ever seeks. It is not afraid of being overwhelmed by experience or perception. If you had a more thorough understanding of the nature of identity you would not, for example, fear telepathy, for behind this concern is the worry that your identity will be swept away by the suggestions or thoughts of others.

No psychological system is closed, no consciousness is closed, regardless of any appearances to the contrary within your own system. The soul is a traveler, as has been said so often; but it is also the creator of all experience, and of all destinations in your terms. It creates worlds as it goes, so to speak.

Now this is the true nature of the psychological being of which you are part. As mentioned earlier, later in the book I will give you some practical suggestions that will allow you to recognize some of your own deeper abilities, and utilize them for your own development, pleasure, and education.

Consciousness is not basically built upon those precepts of good and evil that so presently concern you. By inference, neither is a soul. This does not mean that in your system, and in some others, these problems do not exist and that good is not preferable to the evil. It simply means that the soul knows that good and evil are but different manifestations of a far greater reality.

Now you may take your break.

(10:37 to 10:44.)

Now: I want to emphasize again that while all this sounds difficult in the telling, it becomes much more clear intuitively when you learn to experience what you are, for if you cannot travel inside your physical body to find your identity, you can travel through your psychological self.

There are far more wonders to perceive through this inward exploration than you can possibly believe until you begin such a journey for yourself. You are a soul; you are a particular manifestation of a soul, and it is sheer nonsense to think that you must remain ignorant of the nature of your own being. You may not be able to put your knowledge clearly into words, but this will in no way negate the value or the validity of the experience that will be yours once you begin to look inward.

Now you may call this a spiritual or psychological or psychic exploration, as you prefer. You will not be trying to find your soul. In that respect there is nothing to find. It is not lost, and you are not lost. The words you use may make no difference, but your intent does indeed.

End of dictation. And now give us a moment, if you please.

(Pause at 10:51. As in the last session, Seth closed the evening's work by delivering a page of personal material for Jane and me. End at 11:01 P.M.

(Jane hasn't been reading Seth's book lately. After listening to my description of this session, however, she asked me to give her a copy of a couple of pages after I typed them. She wants to read them to her ESP class.)

CHAPTER 7

THE POTENTIALS OF THE SOUL

SESSION 530, MAY 20, 1970,
9:19 P.M. WEDNESDAY

Good evening.

("Good evening, Seth.")

Now: We will resume dictation, and we are beginning Chapter Eight. *(Note: This was apparently a slip of the tongue.)*

It seems to you that you have only one form, the physical one that you perceive, and no other. It also seems that your form can only be in one place at one time. You have indeed other forms that you do not perceive, and you also create various kinds of forms for various purposes, although you do not perceive these physically either.

Your main sense of identity is involved with your physical body, so that it is, for example, extremely difficult for you to imagine yourself without it, or outside it, or in any way disconnected from it. Form is the result of concentrated energy, the pattern for it caused by vividly directed emotional or psychic idea images. The intensity is all important. If you have, for example, a highly vivid desire to be somewhere else, then without realizing it consciously a pseudophysical form, identical with your own, may appear in that very spot. The desire will carry the imprint of your personality and image, even though you remain unaware of the image or its appearance in the other location.

Though this thought-image usually is not seen by others, it is quite possible that in the future scientific instruments may perceive it. As it is, such an image may be perceived by those who have developed use of the inner senses. Any intense mental act — thought or emotion — will not only be constructed in some physical or pseudophysical manner, but will also bear to some extent the imprint of the personality who originally conceived it.

(9:30.) There are many such incipient or latent forms. To help you imagine what I am speaking of, you might think of them as ghost images, or shadow images, though this is only for the sake of analogy — forms, for example, just beneath, that have not emerged completely into physical reality as you know it, but are nevertheless vivid enough to be constructed. You would think them quite real indeed, if you could see them.

Each individual actually sends such replica images of himself out frequently, though the degree of the materialization may differ, some forms, for example, being more or less shadowy than others. However, these forms are not mere projections — "flat" images. They have a definite effect upon the atmosphere. They "make room" for themselves in ways that are rather difficult to explain, although they may coexist at times with physical objects or shapes, or may even be superimposed upon these. In this case there is a definite interaction — an interchange that is, again, beneath physical perception.

You may suddenly strongly wish that you were standing by a beloved but distant, familiar seashore, for example. This intense desire would then act something like a core of energy projected outward from your own mind, given a form, your form. The place that you had envisioned would then attract the form, and it would instantaneously stand there. This happens with great frequency.

It would not be seen under usual circumstances. On the other hand, if the desire were still more intense, the energy core would be greater, and a portion of your own flow of consciousness would be imparted to the form, so that for a moment you in your room might suddenly smell the salt air, or in some other way perceive the environment in which this pseudoimage stands.

(9:44.) The extent of perception will vary here to a great degree. To begin with, your physical form is the result of great emotional focus. The fantastic energy of your psyche not only created your physical body, but maintains it. It is not one continuous thing, although to you it seems permanent enough while it lasts. It is nevertheless in a constant state of pulsation, and because of the nature of energy and its construction, the body is actually blinking off and on.

Now: This is difficult to explain, and for our present purposes it is not entirely necessary that you understand the reasons for this pulsing; but even physically, you are "not here" as often as you are. Your emotional intensity and focus create forms beside your physical body, however their duration and degree are dependent upon the intensity of any given emotional origin.

Your space is therefore filled with incipient forms, quite vivid, but beneath the regular structure of matter that you perceive.

(*Jane, as Seth, reached across the coffee table between us, to take my half-full glass of beer. I note this because of the following*):

Ruburt thanks you. You need not note this down. We slow down now and then to choose the particular word, for some of this material is rather difficult.

(*"Very interesting." I had noticed the nearly regular variations in the speed of Jane's delivery not long after the session began. Each segment of this fast, then slow, tempo seemed to cover a few paragraphs at the most. The effect was much more apparent tonight than usual.*)

These projections, then, actually are sent out constantly. Some more sophisticated scientific instruments than you now have would clearly show not only the existence of these forms, but also vibrations in varying waves of intensity surrounding those physical objects that you do perceive.

(*9:57.*) To make this clearer, look at any table in the room before you. It is physical, solid, and you perceive it easily. Now for an analogy, imagine if you can that behind the table is another just like it, but not quite as physical, and behind that one another, and another behind that — each one more difficult to perceive, fading into invisibility. And in front of the table is a table just like it, only a bit less physical appearing than the "real" table — it also having a succession of even less physical tables extending outward. And the same for each side of the table.

Now anything that appears in physical terms also exists in other terms that you do not perceive. You only perceive realities when they achieve a certain "pitch," when they seem to coalesce into matter. But they actually exist, and quite validly at other levels.

Now you may take your break, and relax at another level.

(10:02 to 10:20.) There are also realities *(pause)*, that are "relatively more valid" than your own; in comparison, strictly for an analogy, for example, your physical table would appear as shadowy in contrast, as [like] those very shadowy tables we imagine. You would have a sort of "supertable" in those terms. Yours is not a system of reality formed by the most intense concentration of energy, therefore. It is simply the one you are tuned into, part and parcel of. You perceive it simply for this reason.

Other portions of yourself, therefore, of which you are not consciously aware, do inhabit what you could call a supersystem of reality in which consciousness learns to handle and perceive much stronger concentrations of energy, and to construct "forms" of a different nature indeed.

Your idea of space is then highly distorted, since space to you is simply where nothing is perceived. It is obviously filled with all kinds of phenomena *(pause)*, that make no impression at all upon your perceptive mechanisms. Now in various ways and on occasion, you can tune into these other realities to some degree — and you do so spasmodically, though in many cases the experience is lost because it does not register physically.

(Pause at 10:30.) Think again about this form that you sent to the oceanside. Though it was not equipped with your own physical senses, it was of itself to some extent able to perceive. You projected it unknowingly, but through quite natural laws. The form built up from intense emotional desire. *(Pause.)* The image then follows its own laws of reality, and to <u>some</u> extent, and to a lesser degree than you, has a consciousness. *(Pause.)*

Now: You are, using an analogy again, sent out by a superself who strongly desired existence in physical form. You are no puppet of this superself. You will follow your own lines of development, and through means far too difficult to explain here, you add to the experience of the superself and also then extend the nature of its reality. You also insure your own development, and you are able to draw upon the abilities of the superself.

Nor will you ever be swallowed by the self that in these terms seems so superior. Because you exist, you send out like projections of your own, as mentioned earlier. There is no end to the reality of consciousness, nor the means of its materialization. Nor is there any end to the developments possible for each identity.

Now: I wanted to begin this chapter this evening so that we would have a good start. I will give you an easy, short session, however.

("I'm okay.")

You yawned frequently.

("That hardly matters. I feel pretty good right now.")

Take a very brief break then and we shall continue.

(10:43. Jane's trance had been good. The regular rhythm of the session had continued. Resume at a slower rate at 10:54.)

Now: Let me make it clear once again: Your present personality as you think of it is indeed "indelible," and continues after death to grow and develop.

I mention this again in the middle of our present discussion so that you do not feel lost, or negated, or insignificant. There are obviously an infinite number of gradations in the types and kinds of forms of which we have been speaking. That energy which is projected from our "superself," that spark of intense identity that resulted in your physical birth, that unique impetus, in the one way has many similarities to the old concept of the soul — except that it contains only a part of the story.

(Long pause at 11:01. Jane was now pausing very noticeably between many phrases as she delivered this material.)

While you continue to exist and develop as an individual, your whole self, or soul, has such vast potential, that it can never be expressed fully through one personality, as somewhat explained in one previous chapter.

Now, through very intense emotional focus you can create a form, and project it to another person who may then perceive it. This may be done consciously or unconsciously; and that is rather important. This discussion does not concern the so-called astral form, which is something entirely different. The physical body is the materialization of the astral form.

(11:05.) It does not desert the body for any length of time, however, and it is not this that is projected in cases like the seaside analogy used earlier. You are presently focused not only in your physical body, but within a particular frequency of events that you interpret as time. Other

historical periods exist simultaneously, in forms quite as valid; and other reincarnational selves. Again, you simply are not tuned to those frequencies.

You can know what happened in the past and have histories, because according to the rules of the game that you accepted, you believe that the past, but not the future, can be perceived. You could have histories of the future in the present, if the rules of the game were different. Do you follow me?

("Yes.")

(Long pause at 11:11.) In other levels of reality, the rules of the game change. After death in your terms, you are quite free perceptively. The future appears as clearly as the past. Even this is highly complicated, however, for there is not just one past. You accept as real only certain classifications of events and ignore others. We have mentioned events. There are also probable pasts therefore, that exist quite outside your comprehension. You choose one particular group of these, and latch upon this group of events as the only ones possible, not realizing that you have selected from an infinite variety of past events.

There are then, obviously, probable futures and probable presents. I am trying to discuss this in your terms, since basically, you must understand, the words "past," "present," and "future" are no more meaningful as far as true experience is concerned than are the words "ego," "conscious," or "unconscious."

I will end dictation for this evening. In this probable evening *(humorously)* I select that probable alternative. My fondest wishes to you both.

(11:20. Following this, Seth gave two very interesting pages of material concerning a psychic investigator-writer and his wife; they had witnessed the deleted 529th session for last Monday, May 18. Tonight's session actually ended, then, at 11:35 P.M.)

SESSION 531, MAY 25, 1970, 9:22 P.M. MONDAY

Good evening.

("Good evening, Seth.")

Now: We will resume our dictation.

Not only are you part of other independent selves, each one focused in its own reality, but there is a sympathetic relationship that exists. For example, because of this relationship, your experience need not be limited by the physical perceptive mechanisms. You can draw upon knowledge that belongs to these other independent selves. You can learn to focus your attention away from physical reality, to learn new methods of perception that will enable you to enlarge your concept of reality and greatly expand your own experience.

(9:28. Jane's delivery gradually began to speed up.)

It is only because you believe that physical existence is the only valid one, that it does not occur to you to look for other realities. Such things as telepathy and clairvoyance can give you hints of other kinds of perception, but you are also involved in quite definite experiences both while you are normally waking and while you are asleep.

The so-called stream of consciousness is simply that — one small stream of thoughts, images, and impressions — that is part of a much deeper river of consciousness that represents your own far greater existence and experience. You spend all your time examining this one small stream, so that you become hypnotized by its flow, and entranced by its motion. Simultaneously these other streams of perception and consciousness go by without your notice, yet they are very much a part of you, and they represent quite valid aspects, events, actions, emotions with which you are also involved in other layers of reality.

(9:35.) You are as actively and vividly concerned in these realities as you are in the one in which your main attention is now focused. Now, as you are merely concerned with your physical body and physical self as a rule, you give your attention to the stream of consciousness that seems to deal with it. These other streams of consciousness, however, are connected with other self-forms that you do not perceive. The body, in other words, is simply one manifestation of what you are in one reality, but in these other realities you have other forms.

"You" are not divorced from these other streams of consciousness in any basic way; only your focus of attention closes you off from them, and from the events in which they are involved. If you think of your stream of consciousness as transparent, however, then you can learn to look through and beneath it to others that lie in other beds of reality. You can also learn to rise above your present stream of consciousness and perceive others that run, for analogy's sake, parallel. The point is that you are only limited to the self you know if you think that you are, and if you do not realize that that self is far from your entire identity.

Now often you tune into these other streams of consciousness without realizing that you have done so — for again, they are a part of the same river of your identity. All are therefore connected.

Any creative work involves you in a cooperative process in which you learn to dip into these other streams of consciousness, and come up with a perception that has far more dimensions than one arising from the one narrow, usual stream of consciousness that you know. Great creativity is then multidimensional for this reason. Its origin is not from one reality, but from many, and it is tinged with the multiplicity of that origin.

(9:49.) Great creativity always seems greater than its pure physical dimension and reality. By contrast with the so-called usual, it appears almost as an intrusion. It takes the breath away. Such creativity automatically reminds each man of his own multidimensional reality. The words "know thyself," therefore, mean far more than most people ever suppose.

Now in moments of solitude you may become aware of some of these other streams of consciousness. You may at times for example, hear words, or see images that appear out of context with your own thoughts. According to your education, beliefs, and background you may interpret these in any number of ways. For that matter, they may originate from several sources. On many occasions, however, you have inadvertently tuned in on one of your other streams of consciousness, opened momentarily a channel to those other levels of reality in which other portions of you dwell.

Some of these may involve the thoughts of what you would call a reincarnational self, focused in another period of history as you know it. You may instead, "pick up" an event in which a probable self is involved, according to your inclination, your psychic suppleness, your curiosity, your desire for knowledge. In other words, you may become aware of a far greater reality than you now know, use abilities that you do not realize you possess, know beyond all doubt that your own consciousness and identity is independent of the world in which you now focus your primary attention. If all of that were not true, I would not be writing this book and you would not be reading it.

(Gentle humor): Now you may take your break.

("Thank you." 10:01 to 10:10.)

Now: These other existences of yours go on quite merrily whether you are waking or sleeping, but while you are awake ordinarily you block them out. In the dream state you are much more aware of them, although there is a final process of dreaming that often masks intense psychological and psychic experience, and unfortunately what you usually recall is this final dream version.

In this final version the basic experience is converted as nearly as possible into physical terms. It is therefore distorted. This final touching-up process is not done by deeper layers of the self however, but is much more <u>nearly</u> a conscious process than you realize.

One small point might explain what I mean here. If you do not want to remember a particular dream, you yourself censor the memory on levels quite close to consciousness. Often you can even catch yourself in the act of purposely dropping the memory of a dream. The touching-up process occurs <u>almost</u> at this same level, though not quite.

Here the basic experience is hastily dressed up as much as possible in physical clothes. This is not because you want to understand the experience, but because you refuse to accept it as basically nonphysical. All dreams are not of this nature. Some dreams themselves do take place in psychic or mental areas connected with your daily activities, in which case no dressing-up process is necessary. But in the very deep reaches of sleep experience — those, incidentally, not yet touched upon by scientists in so-called dream laboratories — you are in communication with other portions of your own identity, and with the other realities in which they exist.

(10:20.) In this state you also pursue works and endeavors that may or may not be connected with your interests as you know of them. You are learning, studying, playing; you are anything but asleep *(smile)* as you think of the term. You are highly active. *(Humorously):* You are involved in the underground work, in the real nitty-gritty of existence.

Now let me emphasize here that you are simply not unconscious. It only seems that you are, because as a rule you remember none of this in the morning. To some extent, however, some people are aware of these activities, and there are also methods that will enable you to recall them to some degree.

I do not want to minimize the importance of your state of

consciousness; as, for example, you read this book. Presumably you are awake, but in many ways when you are awake, you are resting far more than you are in your so-called unconscious nightly state. Then to a larger extent you realize your own reality, and are free to use abilities that in the daytime you ignore or deny.

(10:26.) At a very simple level, for example, your consciousness leaves your body often in the sleep state. You communicate with people in other levels of reality that you have known, but far beyond this, you creatively maintain and revitalize your physical image. You process daily experience, project it into what you think of as the future, choose from an infinity of probable events those you will make physical, and begin the mental and psychic processes that will bring them into the world of substance.

At the same time, you make this information available to all these other portions of your identity, who dwell in entirely different realities, and you receive from them comparable information. You do not lose contact with your ordinary waking self. You simply do not focus upon it. You turn your attention away. In the daytime you simply reverse the process. If you were looking at your daily normal self from the other viewpoint, you see, using an analogy here, you might find that physically waking self as strange as you now find the sleeping self. The analogy will not hold however, simply because this sleeping self of yours is far more knowledgeable than the waking self of which you are so proud.

(10:35.) The seeming division is not arbitrary, or forced upon you. It is simply caused by your present stage of development, and it does vary. Many people take excursions into other realities — swim, so to speak, through other streams of consciousness as a part of their normal waking lives. Sometimes strange fish pop up in those waters!

Now I am obviously such a one in your terms, swimming up through other dimensions of reality and observing a dimension of existence that is yours rather than my own. There are, therefore, channels that exist between all these streams of consciousness, all these symbolic rivers of psychological and psychic experience, and there are journeys that can be made from my dimension as well as yours.

Now initially Ruburt and Joseph and I were a part of the same entity, or overall identity, and so symbolically speaking, there are psychic currents that unite us. All of these merge into what has often been compared to as an ocean of consciousness, a well from which all actuality springs. Start with any one consciousness, and theoretically you will find all others.

(*Pause at 10:43.*) Now often the ego acts as a dam, to hold back other perceptions — not because it was meant to, or because it is in the nature of an ego to behave in such a fashion, or even because it is a main function of an ego, but simply because you have been taught that the purpose of an ego is restrictive rather than expanding. You actually imagine that the ego is a very weak portion of the self, that it must defend itself against other areas of the self that are far stronger and more persuasive and indeed more dangerous; and so you have trained it to wear blinders, and quite against its natural inclinations.

The ego does want to understand and interpret physical reality, and to relate to it. It wants to help you survive within physical existence, but by putting blinders upon it, you hamper its perception and native flexibility. Then because it is inflexible you say that this is the natural function and characteristic of the ego.

It cannot relate to a reality that you will not allow it to perceive. It can poorly help you to survive when you do not allow it to use its abilities to discover those true conditions in which it must manipulate. You put blinders upon it, and then say that it cannot see.

You may take your break.

(*10:49. Jane had been well dissociated. "I've really been out tonight, I can tell you that. . . ." Her pace had been good, with short pauses occasionally. Resume at 11:02.*)

That was the end of dictation. Now give us a moment.

(*Following his pattern of late, Seth wound up the session with a couple of pages of other material. This time the data concerned the reasons behind Jane's years of training in writing poetry and fiction. It was very astute, I thought. Seth explained how Jane's poetry had always been "a creative offshoot of her desire to understand the nature of existence and reality, her way of probing psychically . . . into other realms . . . a method of investigation and a method of exploring the results."*

(*Her fiction, Seth added, was Jane's "way of probing probabilities and of trying to understand other people. All of her [writing] is a part of her creative life, but now she is investigating the nature of reality far more directly. . . . There is a great unity in the personality's main interests. Nothing will be left behind. The creative self is operating, you see — going exactly where it wants to go."*)

(Jane's psychic experiences, Seth said, would themselves initiate other creative endeavors, leading her to delve into deeper, literally unending, universal pools of creativity. . . .

(End at 11:21 P.M.)

CHAPTER 8

SLEEP, DREAMS, AND CONSCIOUSNESS

SESSION 532, MAY 27, 1970, 9:24 P.M. WEDNESDAY

Good evening.

("Good evening, Seth.")

Persons vary in the amount of sleep they need, and no pill will ever allow them to dispense with sleep entirely, for too much work is done in that state. However, this could be done far more effectively with two, rather than one, sleep periods of lesser duration.

Two periods of three hours apiece would be quite sufficient for most people, if the proper suggestions were given before sleep — suggestions that would insure the body's complete recuperation. In many cases ten hours sleep, for example, is actually disadvantageous, resulting in a sluggishness both of mind and body. In this case the spirit has simply been away from the body for too long a time, resulting in a loss of muscular flexibility.

(Jane's delivery was quite fast, and remained so throughout the session.)

As many light snacks would actually be much better than three large meals a day, so short naps rather than such an extended period would also be more effective. There would be other benefits. The conscious self would recall more of its dream adventures as a matter of course, and gradually these would be added to the totality of experience as the ego thinks of it.

As a result of more frequent, briefer sleep periods, there would also

· 97 ·

be higher peaks of conscious focus, and a more steady renewal of both physical and psychic activity. There would not be such a definite division between the various areas or levels of the self. A more economical use of energy would result, and also a more effective use of nutrients. Consciousness as you know it would also become more flexible and mobile.

This would not lead to a blurring of consciousness or focus. Instead the greater flexibility would result in a perfection of conscious focus. The seeming great division between the waking and the sleeping self is largely a result of the division in function, the two being largely separated — a block of time being allotted to the one, and a larger block of time to the other. They are kept apart, then, because of your use of time.

(9:36.) Initially, your conscious life followed the light of day. Now with artificial light this need not be the case. There are opportunities here, then, to be gained from your technology that you are not presently taking advantage of. To sleep all day and work all night is hardly the answer; it is simply the inversion of your present habits. But it would be far more effective and efficient to divide the twenty-four-hour period in a different way.

There are many variations, in fact, that would be better than your present system. Ideally, sleeping five hours at a time, you gain the maximum benefit, and anything else over this time is not nearly as helpful. Those who require more sleep would then take, say, a two-hour nap. For others a four-hour block sleep session and two naps would be highly beneficial. With suggestion properly given, the body can recuperate in half the time now given to sleep. In any case it is much more bracing and efficient to have the physical body active rather than inactive for, say, eight to ten hours.

You have trained your consciousness to follow certain patterns that are not necessarily natural for it, and these patterns increase the sense of alienation between the waking and dreaming self. To some extent you drug the body with suggestion, so that it believes it must sleep away a certain amount of hours in one block. Animals sleep when they are tired, and awaken in a much more natural fashion.

You would retain a far greater memory of your subjective experiences, and your body would be healthier, if these sleeping patterns were changed. Six to eight hours of sleep in all would be sufficient with the nap patterns outlined. And even those who think they now need more sleep than this would find that they did not, if all the time was not spent in one block. The entire system, physical, mental, and psychic, would benefit.

The divisions between the self would not be nearly as severe. Physical and mental work would be easier, and the body itself would gain steady periods of refreshment and rest. Now, as a rule, it must wait, regardless of its condition, at least for some sixteen hours. For other reasons having to do with the chemical reactions during the dream state, bodily health would be improved; and this particular schedule would also be of help in schizophrenia, and generally aid persons with problems of depression, or those with mental instability.

(9:52.) Your sense of time would also be less rigorous and rigid. Creative abilities would be quickened, and the great problem of insomnia that exists for many people would be largely conquered — for what they fear is often the long period of time in which consciousness, as they think of it, seems to be extinguished.

Small meals or snacks would then be taken upon rising. This method of eating and sleeping would greatly help various metabolic difficulties, and also aid in the development of spiritual and psychic ability. For many reasons, physical activity at night has a different effect upon the body than physical activity during the day, and ideally, both effects are necessary.

At certain times during the night the negative ions in the air are much stronger, or numerous, than in the daytime, for example; and activity during this time, particularly a walk or outside activity, would be highly beneficial from a health standpoint.

Now the period just before dawn often represents a crisis point for persons severely ill. Consciousness has been away from the body for too long a period, and such a returning consciousness then has difficulty dealing with the sick body mechanism. The practice in hospitals of giving drugs to patients so that they will sleep entirely throughout the night is detrimental for this reason. In many cases it is too great a strain on the part of the returning consciousness to take over again the ailing mechanism.

Such medications also often prevent certain necessary dream cycles that can help the body recuperate, and the consciousness then becomes highly disoriented. Some of the divisions between different portions of the self, therefore, are not basically necessary but are the result of custom and convenience.

In earlier periods of time, even though there were no electric lights for example, sleep was not long and continuous at night, for sleeping quarters were not as secure. The caveman, for example, while sleeping was on the alert for predators. The mysterious aspects of the natural night in outside surroundings kept him partially alert. He awakened often, and surveyed the nearby land and his own place of shelter.

(10:04.) He did not sleep in long blocks as you do. His sleeping periods were instead for two or three hours, stretched through the nighttime from dusk to dawn, but alternated by periods of high wakefulness and alert activity. He also crept out to seek food when he hoped his predators were sleeping.

This resulted in a mobility of consciousness that indeed insured his physical survival, and those intuitions that appeared to him in the dream state were remembered and taken advantage of in the waking state.

Now, many diseases are simply caused by this division of yours and this long period of bodily inactivity, and this extended focus of attention in either waking or dreaming reality. Your normal consciousness can benefit by excursions and rest in those other fields of actuality that are entered when you sleep, and the so-called sleeping consciousness will also benefit by frequent excursions into the waking state.

Now you may take your break.

(10:10. Jane's trance had been deep, her pace fast throughout. Yet she remembered some of the material, which usually isn't the case. She hadn't been reading about sleep recently. "The whole bit is far out to me," she said. "I haven't been entertaining any ideas like these, at least consciously." Resume in the same manner at 10:22.)

Now: I bring up these matters here because such changes in habitual patterns would definitely result in greater understanding of the nature of the self. The inner dreaming portions of the personality seem strange to you not only because of a basic difference of focus, but because you clearly devote opposite portions of a twenty-four hour cycle to these areas of the self.

You separate them as much as possible. In doing so you divide your intuitive, creative, and psychic abilities quite neatly from your physical, manipulative, objective abilities. It makes no difference how many hours of sleep you think you need. You would be much better off sleeping in several shorter periods, and you would actually then require less time. The largest sleep unit should be at night. But again, the efficiency of sleep is lessened and disadvantages set in after six to eight hours of physical inactivity.

The functions of hormones and chemicals, and of adrenal processes in particular, would function with far greater effectiveness with these alternating periods of activities as I have mentioned. The wear and tear upon the body would be minimized, while at the same time all regenerative powers would be used to the maximum. Both those with a high and low metabolism would benefit.

The psychic centers would be activated more frequently, and the entire identity of the personality would be better strengthened and maintained. The resulting mobility and flexibility of consciousness would cause an added dividend in increased conscious concentration, and fatigue levels would always remain below danger points. A greater equalization, both physical and mental, would result.

Now such schedules could be adopted quite easily. Those who work the American working hours, for example, could sleep between four to six hours an evening, according to individual variations, and nap after supper. I want to make it plain, however, that anything over a six- to eight-hour continuous sleeping period works against you, and a ten-hour period for example can be quite disadvantageous. On awakening often then you do not feel rested, but drained of energy. You have not been minding the store.

If you do not understand that in periods of sleep your consciousness actually does leave your body, then what I have said will be meaningless. Now your consciousness does return at times, to check upon the physical mechanisms, and the simple consciousness of atom and cell — the body consciousness — is always with the body, so it is not vacant. But the largely creative portions of the self do leave the body, and for large periods of time when you sleep.

(10:39.) Some cases of strong neurotic behavior result from your present sleeping habits. Sleepwalking to some degree is also connected here. Consciousness wants to return to the body, but it has been hypnotized into the idea that the body must not awaken. Excess nervous energy takes over, and rouses the muscles to activity, because the body knows it has been inactive for too long and otherwise severe muscular cramps would result.

The same applies to your eating habits. By turn you overstuff and then starve the tissues. This has definite effects upon the nature of your consciousness, your creativity, your degree of concentration. Along these lines, for example, you do literally starve your bodies at night, and add to the aging of your bodies by denying them food throughout those long hours. All of this reflects upon the strength and nature of your consciousness.

Your food should be divided within the twenty-four hour period, and not just during the times of wakefulness — that is, if the sleep patterns were changed as I suggest, you would also be eating during some night hours. You would eat far less at any given "mealtime," however. Small amounts of food much more frequently taken would be much more beneficial than your present practice in physical, mental, and psychic terms.

Changing the sleep patterns would automatically change the eating patterns. You would find you were a much more united identity. You would become aware of your clairvoyant and telepathic abilities, for example, to a far greater degree, and you would not feel the deep separation that you now feel between the dreaming and waking self. To a large degree this sense of alienation would vanish.

Your enjoyment of nature would also increase, for as a rule you are largely unacquainted with the nighttime. You could take much better advantage of the intuitional knowledge that occurs in the dream state, and the cycle of your moods would not swing so definitely as it often does. You would feel much safer and more secure in all areas of existence.

The problems of senility would also be reduced, for stimuli would not be minimized for so long a time. And consciousness, with a greater flexibility, would know more of its own sense of joy.

You may take a break. *(Suddenly louder):* And if you do not try this, how can you expect others to?

(Jokingly: "I don't know.")

Your own periods of creative work would also be more effective and efficient if you followed the advice given here.

("Well, we'll see what we can do."

(10:53 P.M. Jane's trance had again been deep, her pace rapid. Indeed, her speed left my writing hand almost numb. This break proved to be the end of the recorded session.

(Now, for the second time recently, Seth and I enjoyed a chat without my taking notes. He explained in more detail how an altered sleep pattern would considerably improve my painting. After it was over I wished I had recorded the conversation, since it contained much information that could be applied generally. Jane ended the evening by saying she "wasn't even in a session mood tonight."

(Since this session — it is June 1 as I type this — Jane and I have been experimenting somewhat with altered sleep patterns, and we can say that Seth's ideas seem eminently workable. After a shorter nighttime sleep period, we have no difficulty waking up easily, alert and ready to go. We supplement this pattern with one or two rest periods during the daylight hours. The system adds an unaccustomed sharpness of appreciation to all of our activities.)

SESSION 533, JUNE 1, 1970,
9:20 P.M. MONDAY

(Previous to the material given below, Seth delivered five pages of personal data for Jane and me. He resumed dictation on Chapter Eight of his own book after a break at 10:10.

(Humorously): Dictation.

("All right.")

Now: It is well known that fluctuations of consciousness and alertness exist in the sleep state. Some periods of dream activity do indeed supersede those of some waking states. But there are also fluctuations in normal waking consciousness, rhythms of intense activity followed by a much less active period of consciousness.

Some waking states, of course, come very close to sleep states. These blend one into the other so that the rhythm often goes unnoticed. These gradations of consciousness are accompanied by changes in the physical organism. In the more sluggish periods of waking consciousness there is a lack of concentration, a cutting off of stimuli to varying degrees, an increase in accidents, and generally a lower body tone.

(10:28.) Because of your habits of an extended sleep period, followed

by an extended waking period, you do not take advantage of these rhythms of consciousness. The high peaks are to some extent smothered, or even go unnoticed. The sharp contrasts and the high efficiency of the natural waking consciousness is barely utilized.

Now I am giving all of this material here because it will help you understand and use your present abilities. You are asking too much of normal waking consciousness, smoothing out the valleys and peaks of its activity, demanding in some cases that it go full blast ahead when it is actually at a minimal period, denying yourself the great mobility of consciousness that is possible.

(10:33.) The suggestions given earlier in this chapter, concerning sleeping habits, will result in a natural use of these rhythms. The peaks will be experienced more frequently. Concentration will be increased, problems seen more clearly, and learning capacities better utilized.

(Earlier in the day I had remarked to Jane that it seemed the adverb "far" was showing up in the material quite often. Now Seth-Jane leaned forward, smiling with mock emphasis.)

I was going to say, "far better utilized."

("Yes.")

Now: This extended period, given to waking consciousness without rest periods, builds up chemicals in the blood that are discharged in sleep. But in the meantime they make the body sluggish and retard conscious concentration. The long sleep period to which you are accustomed then does become necessary. A vicious circle then is formed. This forces overstimulations during the night, increasing the body's work, making it perform continuously over an extended time physical purifications that ideally would be taken care of in briefer periods of rest. The ego feels threatened by the extended "leave of absence" it must take, becomes wary of sleep, and sets up barriers against the dream state. Many of these are highly artificial.

(10:42.) A seeming duality is the result and a mistrust on one part of the self toward the other. Much creative material of quite practical value is lost in the process. The procedures mentioned would allow much greater access to such information, and the waking self would be more refreshed. The symbolism in dreams would appear with greater

clarity, not, for example, be lost through the many hours you now give to sleep.

Muscular strength would benefit. The blood would be cleansed more effectively than when the body lies prone for such a time. Most of all, there would be far — if you will excuse me — better communication between the subjective layers of the self, an increased sense of security, and, particularly with children, an earlier kindling of creative abilities.

Now you may take a break or end the session as you prefer.

("We'll take the break." 10:50 to 11:04.)

A clear, uncluttered, bright, and powerful consciousness needs frequent rest periods if its efficiency is to be maintained, and if it is to correctly interpret reality. Otherwise it distorts what is perceived.

Rest or sleep cures — very extended sleep periods — have been helpful for therapy in some cases, not because extended sleep is in itself beneficial, but because so many toxins had built up that such extended periods were required. Learning processes are definitely hampered through your present habits, for there are certain periods when consciousness is attuned to learning, and yet you try to force learning during unrecognized minimal periods. Creative and psychic abilities are thrust into the background simply because of this artificial division. Dualities result that affect all of your activities.

In some cases you literally force yourselves to sleep when your consciousness could be at one of its maximum points. This is, incidentally, in the predawn period. In certain afternoon hours consciousness is lowered, and needs refreshment that is instead denied.

If the stages of waking consciousness were examined as sleep stages are presently being examined, for example, you would find a much greater range of activity than is suspected. Certain transition stages are completely ignored. In many ways it can be said that consciousness does indeed flicker, and varies in intensities. It is not like a steady beam of light, for instance.

Now I will end our dictation. My heartiest regards to you both.

("The same to you, Seth. Thank you."

(11:15 P.M. Jane, out of trance, was surprised by the quick ending of the session.)

· 105 ·

SESSION 534, JUNE 8, 1970,
9:05 P.M. MONDAY

(No session was held last Wednesday, June 3.

(At 8:30 tonight Jane and I discussed Seth's progress on his book. Jane was somewhat concerned. She wasn't reading the book now, but she realized Seth wasn't following, literally, the outline he'd given for it before he began dictating it chapter by chapter. I told her I thought Seth was presenting it just as he wanted it done; she agreed that she might as well relax and just let it come out.

(I would now like to describe two effects, one of Jane's and one of mine, that took place almost simultaneously some few minutes before the session began. In addition, my experience blended into another one after the session started — but more about that later.

(1. As we sat waiting for the session to begin, Jane told me that the face of Joseph, in my oil painting of Ruburt and Joseph, smiled down at her from its spot on the living room wall. When Jane became aware of the smiling effect she looked away from the painting, then quickly back at it. The effect was still there, she said; it lasted for perhaps two minutes, until just before session time at 9.*

(Jane faced the painting as she sat in her Kennedy rocker, but my back was to it because of my position on the couch. During the several times I turned to look at it I noticed nothing out of the ordinary. Jane told me that Joseph, representing my own entity, smiled broadly at her in a way the painting actually doesn't. The expression in the eyes changed first, the smile spreading from them down to the mouth. The forehead didn't move. It was as though the painting became abruptly alive, although the painted head of Ruburt did not change.

(Jane doesn't particularly like the painting, and has never seen this change in it before.

(2. My effect concerns an interference in my vision, without an actual loss of sight. It produced no aftereffects this evening, nor had it ever in earlier years beyond a very slight headache. Tonight I didn't get the headache. Strangely I've never been alarmed by this phenomenon. With my somewhat secretive nature I'd had no urge, even as a child, to tell my parents about it, or to see a doctor. The absence of aftereffects, and the continued clarity of my mental processes, may have been reassuring.

(The effect, which always reminded me of a mirage, began with a smallish, bright sawtooth pattern of light just to the right of my direct line of vision. Now,

---

*For illustrations of this painting, see *The Seth Material*, Prentice Hall, Inc., 1970.

with memory of almost-forgotten episodes returning, I knew that this brilliant, shimmering pattern could spread so that as I looked at an object it would be obliterated, even while I still had peripheral vision.

(At times the interference had covered a wide enough area so that I had a difficult time seeing the drawing paper before me, for instance, or the pencil I felt in my hand. The shimmering varied in intensity. On one occasion I lay down and closed my eyes simply because it was easier to do this than anything else. Such effects lasted half an hour at the most, usually less.

(Now, I wondered once again at my calm response to this as I grew up — to something whose origins were so completely outside any kind of knowledge I possessed. When the interference had been strong, covering most of the field of vision, I had experienced a peculiar sense of both darkness and light, with the objective world indistinguishable within what I can only describe as a field of patterned, alternating lightness and darkness that possessed a velvety depth.

(Tonight's experience wasn't that intense. I first realized its onset at about 8:50, and at once began to give myself suggestions to minimize it because I didn't want to alarm Jane by delaying the session. At the same time Jane began to describe the smile she perceived in the painting; I could see the painting well enough when she asked me to check it, although my vision effect was still building. My suggestions were very beneficial, though, and by session time at 9:05 I realized that not only had my experience gone as "far" as it was going to go, but also that it was on the retreat. By 9:15 the last traces of it were gone and my vision was clear.

(There is more to follow; for as this experience waned it was replaced, or led into, an event of a different kind. This one was new to me, and most interesting. Subsequent notes, and Seth himself, explain what transpired as the session progressed. I'll say here that the new effect involved the gradual loss of my ability first to spell, and then to write. . . .

(Jane began to speak for Seth at quite a slow pace, in contrast to her faster rate of recent sessions. As the session began I had to make a little bit of an effort to see the page clearly in order to write.)

Good evening.

("Good evening, Seth.")

(Just before the session I had commented on the peaceful evening, which was very warm.)

I hope I do not shatter your peace.

("No.")

We will resume dictation. *(Pause; one of many.)* Consciousness has many characteristics, some of course known to you. Many of the characteristics of consciousness, however, are not so apparent, since presently you largely use your own consciousness in such a way that its perceptions appear in quite other than "natural" guises. You are aware of your own consciousness, in other words, through the medium of your own physical mechanism. You are not nearly as aware of your own consciousness when it is not operating primarily through the mediumship of the body, as it does in out-of-body states and some dissociated conditions.

(By the time I wrote the last sentence I was aware — again, without being upset — that it was taking me just a little longer than usual to come up with my abbreviations or symbols for such common words as "does," "as," and "even." This action of course should have been automatic. But visual interference was now lifting considerably.

(By 9:12 I began to spell an occasional word incorrectly. To show what was happening I'm including, in parentheses after the corrected word, some of the mistakes my notes contain.)

The characteristics of consciousness are the same *(seme)* whether you are in a body or outside of one. The peaks and valleys of consciousness that I mentioned exist to some degree in all consciousness despite the form adopted *(adepted)* after death *(deth)*. The nature of your consciousness is no different basically *(bascially)* than it is now, though you may not be aware of many of its characteristics.

(I caught myself omitting the word "not" from the last sentence, and was quite aware by now that something was up. More and more I had to make a deliberate effort to get the notes down correctly. In the material below, I couldn't think of some of the symbols I used and had to write the words out.)

Now your consciousness is telepathic and clairvoyant, for example, even though you may not realize it. In sleep when *(whene)* you often presume yourself to be unconscious *(unconsious)* you may be far more conscious than you are now, but simply using abilities of consciousness that you do not accept as real or valid *(valed)* in waking *(waping)* life. You therefore shut *(shup)* them out of your conscious experience *(experiencl)*. Consciousness, yours and mine, is quite independent of both *(poth)* time and space. And after death you are simply aware of the greater powers of consciousness that exist within you all the time.

(9:21. I had a lot of trouble getting the following sentences down. Many of the words were misspelled, some so much so that I crossed them out and quickly

tried again — with the humorous result that the corrections also contained errors. My vision was by now very clear.

(For the first time I conceded to myself that perhaps I ought to ask Seth to slow down, while realizing his pace was slow to begin with. I didn't ask him what was happening. That worthy stared at me through Jane's eyes without a sign that anything unusual might be taking place in the session. . . .)

Since they do, of course, you can discover them now and learn to use them. This will directly *(dreactly)* assist you in after-death *(agter)* experience. You will not be nearly so startled by the nature of your own reactions *(reactone)* if you understand beforehand for example that your consciousness not only is not imprisoned by your physical body, but *(bud)* can create other portions at will. Those who "overidentify" their consciousness with their body can suffer self-created torment *(tortment)* for no reason, lingering about the body. Indeed, quite the forlorn soul, thinking it has no other place to go.

(For "beforehand" in the paragraph above, I wrote "byeborehoune," then crossed that out and tried twice more. I now made a determined effort to spell correctly and write clearly. It helped. It was something like coming out of a deep sleep and immediately making a strong effort to focus in physical reality.)

You are, as I said earlier, a spirit now; and that spirit has a consciousness. The consciousness belongs to the spirit then, but the two are not the same. The spirit may turn its consciousness off and on. By its nature consciousness may flicker and fluctuate, but the spirit does not.

I do not particularly like the word "spirit" because of several implications attached to it, but it *(ot)* suits our purposes in that the word does imply an independence from physical form.

Consciousness does not refresh itself in sleep. It is merely turned in another direction. Consciousness does not sleep then in those terms and while it may be turned off it is not like a light.

(9:28. The difficulty I had been experiencing with my spelling abruptly returned to an even greater degree. Along with the misspellings and the crossing out of words, I now had to worry about simply keeping up with Seth's rather slow pace. For the first time I thought of asking for a break, yet I still wasn't alarmed. I had trouble with the whole paragraph.)

Turning it off does not extinguish *(expetnrise)* it in the way that a light *(like)* disappears *(disappeares)* when a switch is turned. Following the analogy *(aneleogy)*, if consciousness were *(werse)* like *(light)* a light that belonged *(belenge)* to you, even when you switched it off, there would be a sort of twilight, but not darkness *(darkners)*.

(By now I was sitting tensely on the edge of our couch, bending over the notebook as it lay on the coffee table before me. This is a position I seldom use — perhaps I thought it would help me really grapple with this experience. I asked Seth to wait a minute.)

The spirit, therefore, is never in a state of nothingness, with its consciousness extinguished. It is very important therefore that such be realized, for there . . .

(The rest of the sentence is unintelligible in my notes. Here is the way I actually wrote it: "The spirit tre is never n a state of nethigness, with its conscescness x x extenigly. It os very important tre thanch be realize, fr thre if ech expct if a sctich it is . . ."

(In considerable surprise I asked Seth to wait once more. I missed a couple of sentences here, and very nearly gave up trying to take notes. I thought of one more try, however. Jane, as Seth, sat waiting rather noncommittally, eyes open.)

It is very important to understand that consciousness is never extinguished. . . .

(9:35. Again I quickly fell way behind. When I found myself writing "ich-stantale" for "extinguished," I gave up and asked Seth for a break. It came at once. I was nonplussed. I was clearheaded but unable, literally, to continue taking notes. Still I wasn't alarmed.

(When I started to explain to Jane why I had to stop, I discovered that on top of everything else I was having trouble speaking coherently. Seth then returned briefly, with a broad smile. From memory I recall his saying:)

You have been acting out the material this evening, Joseph. . . .

(With those words understanding came quickly, although the effects didn't lift that easily. I made many errors talking to Jane, but the vocal difficulty never matched that of the spelling or writing. At first Jane was very concerned at my experiences before and during the session; she told me later that at this point she almost decided not to continue the session. She finally believed my reassurances, however, and realized that I was all right physically.

(Seth suspended dictation on his book at my request, but during a brief interlude suggested that I have Jane turn on the rest of the lights in the room when she came out of trance. Then, I was to imagine my consciousness growing brighter and brighter, filling the room like light; I would find that all of my abilities would soon return. I wasn't able to remember some subsequent information.

(Thus, I had experienced altered states of seeing, writing, spelling, and speaking this evening — all facets of course of my physical means of communication. Sitting in the glare of the brilliantly lit room, I described everything in detail to Jane, including the vision effects of earlier years. She wondered if my loss of communicative abilities was also related to my father's senility and his own physical retreat. I didn't know. I hadn't experienced anything unusual involving him recently.

(Slowly I resumed work on my notes. I was most anxious that Seth explain all. And he was right: by 10:30 I was much better. I caught up on the notes finally and told Jane I was ready for the session to continue. Now we received the most interesting data of all — that pertaining to my curious lack of alarm at the events of the evening. Resume at a faster pace at 10:47.)

Now: In the demonstration in which Joseph so kindly assisted us, several points were made to implement the material just given.

Earlier I said that you are only familiar with those characteristics of your own consciousness that you use through the mediumship of the body. You rely upon the body to express the perceptions of your consciousness. You tend, again, to identify the expression of your consciousness with the body.

In our demonstration, to which of course Joseph gave his permission, he allowed his consciousness to retreat, and to some degree began to cut off its physical expression. He was not aware consciously of his permission, simply because this kind of demonstration could not be held if the normal waking consciousness knew. It would automatically be frightened. As I spoke about the dimming of consciousness, Joseph then experienced it.

(10:55. This may be a tricky point, and it may not. Seth used the word "dimming." Certainly some of my abilities for physical expression had withdrawn considerably, yet I had remained clearheaded and alert, and, out of habit, thoroughly occupied with trying to use them. . . . Nor had I become aware of any kind of heightened consciousness, or sudden telepathic or clairvoyant powers.

(Now, I was having no trouble taking notes.)

Give us a moment. This was an exercise, actually, in the manipulation of consciousness. Close to death, this same sort of thing happens in varying degrees when the consciousness realizes that it can no longer express itself through the mediumship of the body. If the dying person overidentifies with the body then he can easily panic, thinking that all expression is therefore cut off, and for that matter that his consciousness is about to be extinguished.

Such a belief in extinction, such a certainty that identity is about to be blotted out in the next moment, is a severe psychological experience, that in itself can bring about unfortunate reactions. What happens instead is that you find consciousness quite intact, and its expression far less limited than it was before. Joseph chose subconsciously to interrupt those methods of expression he was using at the time simply so that their interference would claim due notice.

We will be dealing now, after what I hope is suitable background material, with some chapters on the nature of existence after physical death, at the point of death, and involving the final physical death at the end of the reincarnational cycle. It was important that you understand something about the nature and behavior of your own consciousness before we could begin.

You may take a break.

(11:06. Jane's pace had been considerably faster this time. In the last paragraph, I had a bit of difficulty spelling just two words. Resume more slowly at 11:20.)

Now: You also drew upon some knowledge, Joseph, from past experience in our demonstration, when in your final illness motor function was impaired. This was in Denmark. The last note is an aside, rather than strict dictation.

(According to Seth, the three of us were involved in Denmark in the 1600's. I was a landowner, Jane was my son, and Seth was a spice merchant. See Chapter Twenty-two.)

Now I am ending this chapter, and with it I am ending Part One of my book. Give us a moment now — and end of dictation.

(But Seth wasn't through work on his book yet. The following material shows the relationship between my vision effects and the events in the session itself. It's very interesting that I would choose tonight, of all nights, to try for visual data, although in recent days I've been inquiring mentally about subjects for my next oil painting. I haven't said anything about this to Jane.)

The earlier vision experiences were unsuccessful preliminary attempts on an unconscious level to pick up images of models for your paintings. In the blurred dark portion, the models would have appeared. Do you follow me?

("Yes.")

The blurred areas represented a confusion of vibrations. You could not get the material visually in physical terms, though you were trying to, but you could not receive it as internal vision either at that point. Instead you ended up almost with a displacement. There was always a sense of motion in the background that was interpreted visually as an unsteadiness, a massing of blurs.

Now you acquiesced in our experiment earlier this evening, when Ruburt and you spoke at the [supper] table. Ruburt was telepathically aware of the arrangement, though not at a conscious level. The smiling portrait that Jane saw was your work in a way. Ruburt was aware of the arrangement for the demonstration, but was also somewhat alarmed at the particular way you would choose to interpret the experience. The smiling portrait was to reassure her — Jane now rather than Ruburt. You sent the reassurance. Ruburt picked it up from Joseph. Do you follow me?

("Yes." And a very effective method, I thought.)

Now: I will close for this evening.

("It's been very interesting.")

I thank you for your assistance. A hearty good evening to you both.

(11:36 P.M. "Good night, Seth." Again, I had minor trouble spelling a few words after the last break. That was all.)

PART TWO

CHAPTER 9

THE "DEATH" EXPERIENCE

SESSION 535, JUNE 17, 1970,
9:00 P.M. WEDNESDAY

(*The regularly scheduled sessions for June 10 and 15 were not held, so that Jane could rest. We did conduct one quite successful experiment on our own, however, involving hypnosis during my trip to the dentist. Jane held her ESP class last night, but had no session.*)

Good evening.

(*"Good evening, Seth."*)

We will begin Part Two, Chapter Nine, and we will title this, "The Death Experience."

What happens at the point of death? The question is much more easily asked than answered. Basically there is not any particular point of death in those terms, even in the case of a sudden accident. I will attempt to give you a practical answer to what you think of as this practical question, however. What the question really means to most people is this: What will happen when I am not alive in physical terms any longer? What will I feel? Will I still be myself? Will the emotions that propelled me in life continue to do so? Is there a heaven or a hell? Will I be greeted by gods or demons, enemies, or beloved ones? Most of all the question means: When I am dead, will I still be who I am now, and will I remember those who are dear to me now?

I will answer the questions in those terms also, then; but before I do so, there are several seemingly impractical considerations concerning the nature of life and death, with which we must deal.

First of all, let us consider the fact just mentioned. There is no separate, indivisible, specific point of death. Life is a state of becoming, and death is a part of this process of becoming. You are alive now, a consciousness knowing itself, sparkling with cognition amid a debris of dead and dying cells; alive while the atoms and molecules of your body die and are reborn. You are alive, therefore, in the midst of small deaths; portions of your own image crumble away moment by moment and are replaced, and you scarcely give the matter a thought. So you are to some extent now alive in the midst of the death of yourself — alive despite, and yet because of, the multitudinous deaths and rebirths that occur within your body in physical terms.

If the cells did not die and were not replenished, the physical image would not continue to exist, so now in the present, as you know it, your consciousness flickers about your ever-changing corporeal image.

In many ways you can compare your consciousness as you know it now to a firefly, for while it seems to you that your consciousness is continuous, this is not so. It also flickers off and on, though as we mentioned earlier, it is never completely extinguished. Its focus is not nearly as constant as you suppose, however. So as you are alive in the midst of your own multitudinous small deaths, so though you do not realize it, you are often "dead," even amid the sparkling life of your own consciousness.

I am using your own terms here. By "dead," therefore, I mean completely unfocused in physical reality. Now your consciousness, quite simply, is not physically alive, physically oriented, for exactly the same amount of time as it is physically alive and oriented. *(Typing this on June 22, I wondered if I transcribed what Seth had said correctly. Jane and I decided that I had — and it does make sense.)* This may sound confusing, but hopefully we shall make it clearer. There are pulsations of consciousness, though again you may not be aware of them.

Consider this analogy. For one instant your consciousness is "alive," focused in physical reality. Now for the next instant it is focused somewhere else entirely, in a different system of reality. It is unalive, or "dead" to your way of thinking. The next instant it is "alive" again, focused in your reality, but you are not aware of the intervening instant of unaliveness.

Your sense of continuity therefore is built up entirely on every other pulsation of consciousness. Is that clear to you?

("Yes." Pause at 9:25.)

Remember this is an analogy, so that the word "instant" should not be taken too literally. There is, then, what we can call an underside of consciousness. Now, in the same way, atoms and molecules exist so that they are "dead," or inactive within your system, then alive or active, but you cannot perceive the instant in which they do not exist. Since your bodies and your entire physical universe are composed of atoms and molecules, then I am telling you that the entire structure exists in the same manner. It flickers off and on, in other words, and in a certain rhythm, as, say, the rhythm of breath.

There are overall rhythms, and within them an infinity of individual variations — almost like cosmic metabolism. In these terms, what you call death is simply the insertion of a longer duration of that pulsation of which you are not aware, a long pause in that other dimension, so to speak.

The death, say, of physical tissue, is merely a part of the process of life as you know it in your system, a part of the process of becoming. And from those tissues, as you know, new life will spring.

Consciousness — human consciousness — is not dependent upon the tissues, and yet there is no physical matter that is not brought into being by some portion of consciousness. For example, when your individual consciousness has left the body in a way that I will shortly explain, then the simple consciousnesses of atoms and molecules remain, and are not annihilated.

You may take a break and we shall continue.

("Do you have a title for Part One of your book?")

I do not yet. The title I gave you is only for Chapter Nine. Since we are getting down to specifics, I will title the chapters individually.

(9:40. Jane was well dissociated. Resume at 9:57.)

Now: In your present situation you arbitrarily consider yourselves to be dependent upon one given physical image: You identify yourself with your body.

As mentioned earlier, all through your lifetime, portions of that body die, and the body that you have now does not contain one particle of physical matter that "it" had, say ten years ago. Your body is completely different now, then, than it was ten years ago. The body that you had ten years ago, my dear readers, is dead. Yet obviously you do not feel that you are dead, and you are quite able to read this book with the eyes that are composed of completely new matter. The pupils, the "identical" pupils that you have now, did not exist ten years ago, and yet there seems to be no great gap in your vision.

This process, you see, continues so smoothly that you are not aware of it. The pulses mentioned earlier are so short in duration that your consciousness skips over them merrily, yet your <u>physical</u> perception cannot seem to bridge the gap when the longer rhythm of pulsation occurs. And so this is the time that you perceive as death. What you want to know, therefore, is what happens when your consciousness is directed away from physical reality, and when momentarily it seems to have no image to wear.

Quite practically speaking, there is no one answer, for each of you is an individual. Generally speaking, of course, there is an answer that will serve to cover main issues of this experience, but the kinds of deaths have much to do with the experience that consciousness undergoes. Also involved is the development of the consciousness itself, and its overall characteristic method of handling experience.

The ideas that you have involving the nature of reality will strongly color your experiences, for you will interpret them in the light of your beliefs, even as now you interpret daily life according to your ideas of what is possible or not possible. Your consciousness may withdraw from your body slowly or quickly, according to many variables.

(Pause at 10:11.) In many cases of senility, for example, the strongly organized portions of personality have already left the body, and are meeting the new circumstances. The fear of death itself can cause such a psychological panic that out of a sense of self-preservation and defense you lower your consciousness so that you are in a state of coma, and you may take some time to recover.

A belief in hell fires can cause you to hallucinate Hades' conditions. A belief in a stereotyped heaven can result in a hallucination of heavenly conditions. You always form your own reality according to your ideas and expectations. This is the nature of consciousness in whatever reality it finds itself. Such hallucinations, I assure you, are temporary.

Consciousness must use its abilities. The boredom and stagnation of a stereotyped heaven will not for long content the striving consciousness. There are teachers to explain the conditions and circumstances. You are not left alone, therefore, lost in mazes of hallucination. You may or may not realize immediately that you are dead in physical terms.

(10:20.) You will find yourself in another form, an image that will appear physical to you to a large degree, as long as you do not try to manipulate within the physical system with it. Then the differences between it and the physical body will become obvious.

If you firmly believe that your consciousness is a product of your physical body, then you may attempt to cling to it. There is an order of personalities, an honorary guard, so to speak, who are ever ready to lend assistance and aid, however.

Now this honorary guard is made up of people in your terms both living and dead. Those who are living in your system of reality perform these activities in an "out-of-body" experience while the physical body sleeps. They are familiar with the projection of consciousness, with the sensations involved, and they help orient those who will not be returning to the physical body.

(10:26.) These people are particularly helpful because they are still involved with physical reality, and have a more immediate understanding of the feelings and emotions involved at your end. Such persons may or may not have a memory of their nightly activities. Experiences with projection of consciousness and knowledge of the mobility of consciousness, are therefore very helpful as preparations for death. You can experience the after-death environment beforehand, so to speak, and learn the conditions that will be encountered.

This is not, incidentally, necessarily any kind of somber endeavor, nor are the after-death environments somber at all. To the contrary, they are generally far more intense and joyful than the reality you now know.

You will simply be learning to operate in a new environment in which different laws apply, and the laws are far less limiting than the physical ones with which you now operate. In other words, you must learn to understand and use new freedoms.

Even these experiences will vary, however, and even this state is a state of becoming, for many will continue into other physical lives. Some will exist and develop their abilities in different systems of reality altogether, and so for a time will remain in this "intermediary" state.

Now you may take your break

(10:35 to 10:48.)

(Mildly humorous): Now: For those of you who are lazy I can offer no hope: Death will not bring you an eternal resting place. You may rest, if this is your wish, for a while. Not only must you use your abilities after death, however, but you must face up to yourself for those that you did not use during your previous existence.

Those of you who had faith in life after death will find it much easier to accustom yourself to the new conditions. Those of you who do not have such faith may gain it in a different way, by following through in the exercises I will give you later in this book; for these will enable you to extend your perceptions to these other layers of reality if you are persistent, expectant, and determined.

Now consciousness as you know it is used to these brief gaps of physical nonexistence mentioned earlier. Longer gaps disorient it to varying degrees, but these are not unusual. When the physical body sleeps, consciousness often leaves the physical system for fairly long periods, in your terms. But because the consciousness is not in the normally physically awake state, it is not aware of these gaps and is relatively unconcerned.

(10:50.) If consciousness vacated the body for the same amount of time from a normally physically awake state, it would consider itself dead, for it could not rationalize the gap of dimension and experience. Therefore in the sleep state, each of you have undergone — to some degree — the same kind of absence of consciousness from physical reality that you experience during death.

In these cases, you return to the body, but you have passed over the threshold into these other existences many many times, so it will not be as unfamiliar to you as you may now suppose. Dream-recall experiments and other mental disciplines to be mentioned later will make these points quite clear to all of you who embark upon the suggested exercises.

Now, you may or may not be greeted by friends or relatives immediately following death. This is a personal matter, as always. Overall, you may be far more interested in people that you have known in past lives than those close to you in the present one, for example.

(11:03.) Your true feeling toward relatives who are also dead will be

known to you and to them. There is no hypocrisy. You do not pretend to love a parent who did little to earn your respect or love. Telepathy operates without distortion in this after-death period, so you must deal with the true relationships that exist between yourself and all relatives and friends who await you.

You may find that someone you considered merely an enemy actually deserved your love and respect, for example, and you will then treat him accordingly. Your own motives will be crystal clear. You will react to this clearness, however, in your own way. You will not be automatically wise if you were not so before, but neither will there be a way to hide from your own feelings, emotions, or motives. Whether or not you accept inferior motives in yourself or learn from them is still up to you. The opportunities for growth and development are very rich, however, and the learning methods at your disposal very effective.

You examine the fabric of the existence you have left, and you learn to understand how your experiences were the result of your own thoughts and emotions and how these affected others. Until this examination is through, you are not yet aware of the larger portions of your own identity. When you realize the significance and meaning of the life you have just left, then you are ready for conscious knowledge of your other existences.

You become aware, then, of an expanded awareness. What you are begins to include what you have been in other lives, and you begin to make plans for your next physical existence, if you decide upon one. You can instead enter another level of reality, and then return to a physical existence if you choose.

(11:15.) Now this is the end of dictation. You may ask me questions or end the session as you prefer.

(I was ready with questions about painting, so the session didn't end until 11:26 P.M.)

SESSION 536, JUNE 22, 1970,
9:18 P.M. MONDAY

Good evening.

("Good evening, Seth.")

Now: We will continue dictation.

Your consciousness, as you think of it, may of course leave your body entirely before physical death. (As mentioned earlier, there is no precise point of death, but I am speaking as if there is for the sake of your convenience.)

Your conscious self — You may take a break and tend to your chores. . . .

(Already I was putting my notebook aside. Our black cat, Rooney, was scratching at the door of our living room. Jane sat waiting half in trance — a feeling she later described as "weird" — while I followed the cat down the hall. Before I got back inside the apartment our paperboy arrived; by the time I finished paying him Jane was out of trance. Resume finally at 9:27.)

Now: Your consciousness leaves the physical organism in various ways, according to the conditions. In some cases the organism itself is still able to function to some degree, although without the leadership or organization that existed previously. The simple consciousness of atoms, cells, and organs continues to exist, after the main consciousness has left, for some time.

There may or may not be disorientation on your part, according to your beliefs and development. Now I do not necessarily mean intellectual development. The intellect should go hand in hand with the emotions and intuitions, but if it pulls against these too strongly, difficulties can arise when the newly freed consciousness seizes upon its ideas about reality after death, rather than facing the particular reality in which it finds itself. It can deny feeling, in other words, and even attempt to argue itself out of its present independence from the body.

(9:32.) Again, as mentioned earlier, an individual can be so certain that death is the end of all, that oblivion, though temporary, results. In many cases, immediately on leaving the body there is, of course, amazement and a recognition of the situation. The body itself may be viewed, for example, and many funerals have a guest of honor amidst the company — and no one gazes into the face of the corpse with as much curiosity and wonder.

At this point many variations in behavior emerge, each the result of individual background, knowledge, and habit. The surroundings in which the dead find themselves will often vary. Vivid hallucinations may form experience quite as real as any in mortal life. Now, I have told you that thoughts and emotions form physical reality, and they form after-death experience. This does not mean that the experiences are not valid, any more than it means that physical life is not valid.

Certain images have been used to symbolize such a transition from one existence to another, and many of these are extremely valuable in that they provide a framework with understandable references. The crossing of the River Styx is such a one. The dying expected certain procedures to occur in a more or less orderly fashion. The maps were known beforehand. At death, the consciousness hallucinated the river vividly. Relatives and friends already dead entered into the ritual, which was a profound ceremony also on their parts. The river was as real as any that you know, as treacherous to a traveler alone without proper knowledge. Guides were always at the river to help such travelers across.

It does not do to say that such a river is illusion. The symbol is reality, you see. The way was planned. Now, that particular map is no longer generally in use. The living do not know how to read it. Christianity has believed in a heaven and a hell, a purgatory, and reckoning; and so, at death, to those who so believe in these symbols, another ceremony is enacted, and the guides take on the guises of those beloved figures of Christian saints and heroes.

(Pause at 9:48.) Then with this as framework, and in terms that they can understand, such individuals are told the true situation. Mass religious movements have for centuries fulfilled that purpose, in giving man some plan to be followed. It little mattered that later the plan was seen as a child's primer, a book of instructions complete with colorful tales, for the main purpose was served and there was little disorientation.

In periods where no such mass ideas are held, there is more disorientation, and when life after death is completely denied, the problem is somewhat magnified. Many, of course, are overjoyed to find themselves still conscious. Others have to learn all over again about certain laws of behavior, for they do not realize the creative potency of their thoughts or emotions.

Such an individual may find himself in ten different environments within the flicker of an eyelash, for example, with no idea of the reason behind the situation. He will see no continuity at all, and feel himself flung without rhyme or reason from one experience to another, never realizing that his own thoughts are propelling him quite literally.

(9:55.) I am speaking now of the events immediately following death, for there are other stages. Guides will helpfully become a part of your

· 124 ·

hallucinations, in order to help you out of them, but they must first of all get your trust.

At one time — in your terms — I myself acted as such a guide; as in a sleep state Ruburt now follows the same road. The situation is rather tricky from the guide's viewpoint, for psychologically utmost discretion must be used. One man's Moses, as I discovered, may not be another man's Moses. I have served as a rather creditable Moses on several occasions — and once, though this is hard to believe, to an Arab.

(10:00.) The Arab was a very interesting character, by the way, and to illustrate some of the difficulties involved, I will tell you about him. He hated the Jews, but somehow he was obsessed with the idea that Moses was more powerful than Allah, and for years this was the secret sin upon his conscience. He spent some time in Constantinople at the time of the Crusades. He was captured, and ended up with a group of Turks, all to be executed by the Christians, in this case very horribly so. They forced his mouth open and stuffed it with burning coals, as a starter. He cried to Allah, and then in greater desperation to Moses, and as his consciousness left his body, Moses was there.

He believed in Moses more than he did Allah, and I did not know until the last moment which form I was to assume. He was a very likable chap, and under the circumstances I did not mind when he seemed to expect a battle for his soul. Moses and Allah were to fight for him. He could not rid himself of the idea of force, though he had died by force, and nothing could persuade him to accept any kind of peace or contentment, or any rest, until some kind of battle was wrought.

A friend and I, with some others, staged the ceremony, and from opposite clouds in the sky Allah and I shouted out our claims upon his soul — while he, poor man, cowered on the ground between us. Now while I tell this story humorously, you must understand that the man's belief brought it about, and so to set him free, we worked it through.

I called upon Jehovah, but to no avail, because our Arab did not know of Jehovah — only of Moses — and it was in Moses he put his faith. Allah drew a cosmic sword and I set it afire so that he dropped it. It fell to the ground and set the land aflame. Our Arab cried out again. He saw leagues of followers behind Allah, and so leagues of followers appeared behind me. Our friend was convinced that one of the three of us must be destroyed, and he feared mightily that he would be the victim.

Finally the opposing clouds in which we appeared came closer. In my hand I held a tablet that said: "Thou shalt not kill." Allah held a sword. As we came closer we exchanged these items, and our followers merged. We came together, forming the image of a s-u-n *(spelled out)*, and we said: "We are one."

The two diametrically opposed ideas had to merge or the man would have had no peace, and only when these opposites were united could we begin to explain his situation.

You may take your break.

(10:20. Jane's trance had been deep, although she recalled parts of Seth's adventure. She said she had a series of images which paralleled the material, yet she couldn't describe them now.

(The Crusades consisted of a series of military expeditions sent out by the Christian powers in the eleventh, twelfth, and thirteenth centuries, to recover the Holy Land from the Moslems. While Seth was giving the data, Jane said, she wondered what an Arab would be doing in Turkish Constantinople in those days. I explained the geography of the region. Presumably, such a traveler could have reached Constantinople [now Istanbul], by an overland journey across Turkey, which lay north of the Arab lands, or by sailing the eastern Mediterranean around Turkey, through the Dardanelles and so into the city. Distances in the Middle East are comparatively short.

(Jane literally has no sense of geography or of distance, facts that have unwittingly worked to her advantage in sessions. On the other hand, she has an unerring sense of direction in local surroundings, and can indicate the points of the compass far better than I can. Resume at 10:43.)

Now: To be such a guide requires great discipline and training.

Before the event just mentioned, for example, I had spent many life-times acting as a guide under the tutorship of another in my daily sleep states.

It is possible for example to lose yourself momentarily in the hallucinations that are being formed, and in such cases another teacher must bail you out. Delicate probing of the psychological processes is necessary, and the variety of hallucinations in which you may become involved is endless. You may, for example, take the form of an individual's dearly beloved dead pet.

All of these hallucinatory activities take place usually some short time immediately following death. Some individuals are fully aware of their circumstances, however, because of previous training and development, and they are ready after a rest, if they desire to progress to other stages.

They may, for example, become aware of their own reincarnational selves, recognizing quite readily personalities they knew in other lives, if those personalities are not otherwise engaged. They may deliberately now hallucinate, or they may "relive" certain portions of past lives if they choose. Then there is a period of self-examination, a rendering of accounts, so to speak, in which they are able to view their entire performance, their abilities and weak points and to decide whether or not they will return to physical existence.

(10:55.) Any given individual may experience any of these stages, you see; except for the self-examination, many may be sidestepped entirely. Since the emotions are so important, it is of great benefit if friends are waiting for you. In many instances, however, these friends have progressed to other stages of activity, and often a guide will take the guise of a friend for a while, so that you will feel more confident.

Of course, it is only because most people believe that you cannot leave your body that you do not consciously have out-of-body experiences with any frequency, generally speaking, in your lifetimes. Such experiences would acquaint you far better than words with some understanding of the conditions that will be encountered.

Remember that in one way, your physical existence is the result of mass hallucination. Vast gulfs exist between one man's reality and another's. After death, experience has as much organization, highly intricate and involved, as you know now. You have your private hallucinations now, only you do not realize what they are. Such hallucinations as I have been speaking of, intense symbolistic encounters, can also occur in your sleep states, when the personality is at a time of great change, or when opposing ideas must be unified, or if one must give way to another. These are highly charged, significant psychological and psychic events, whether they happen before or after death.

(11:05.) Occurring in the dream state, they can change the course of a civilization. After death, an individual may visualize his (immediately previous physical) life as an animal with which he must come to terms, and such a battle or encounter has far-reaching consequences, for the man must come to terms with all portions of himself. In this case, whether the hallucination ends with him riding the animal, making friends with it, domesticating it, killing it or being killed by it, each alternative . . . *(Jane coughed, then paused and took a sip of beer)* is carefully weighed, and the results will have much to do with his future development.

You had better take a break for Ruburt's sake.

("All right." Jane's voice was now quite hoarse and weak; I believe she would have been forced to stop in a few more moments. This is one of the very few times, in seven years of sessions, that she has had any voice interference.

(At 11:11 I read the last two paragraphs of the material to her, but she couldn't make any emotional connections that might explain the voice difficulty, nor could I. Jane is inordinately fond of animals. Perhaps Seth's example had caused the reaction, I thought, but she didn't seem to respond here either. Resume at 11:20, in a voice stronger but rougher than usual.)

Now: We will shortly end the session.

This "life-symbolization" may be adopted by those who gave little thought to self-examination during their lifetime. It is a part of the self-examination process, therefore, in which an individual forms his life into an image and then deals with it. Such a method is not used by all. Sometimes a series of such episodes are necessary. . . .

That is the end of dictation, and my heartiest regards to you both, and to the beloved monster beside you.

("Good night, Seth, and thank you." Our cat, Willy, lay snoozing beside me on the couch. 11:25 P.M. Jane soon recovered her usual voice.)

SESSION 537, JUNE 24, 1970,
9:24 P.M. WEDNESDAY

(John Barclay, an out-of-town businessman, witnessed the session. John brought a tape with him, as he had promised. Upon it he had summarized the data Seth had given him about his professional life over a period of several years, and the ways in which it had, or had not, worked out. The results were good.

(As she often does when witnesses are present, Jane began her delivery at a fast and animated pace. Her eyes were wide open and very dark, her voice stronger than usual. It was as though she drew extra energy from John and put it to immediate use.)

Now: Good evening.

(John and I: "Good evening, Seth.")

Good evening to our friend here. I hope you will forgive me if I do some dictation on my book. I have to get him *(pointing to me)* when I can get him, if I want to get my book done.

(In high good humor): Now: We are writing some saga. Resume dictation, then.

One of Ruburt's students wondered whether or not there was any kind of organization in the immediate after-death experiences. Since this is a question that will come into many minds, I will deal with it here.

First of all, it should be obvious from what I have said so far that there is no one after-death reality, but [that] each experience is different. Generally speaking, however, there are dimensions into which these individual experiences will fall. For example, there is an initial stage for those who are still focused strongly in physical reality, and for those who need a period of recuperation and rest. On this level there will be hospitals and rest homes. The patients do not yet realize that there is nothing wrong with them at all.

In some cases, the idea of illness is so strong that they have built their earthly years about this psychological center. They project ill conditions upon the new body as they did upon the old one. They are given various kinds of treatment of a psychic nature, and told that the condition of that body is being brought about by the nature of their own beliefs.

(9:32.) Now, many individuals do not need to pass through this particular period. It goes without saying that the hospitals and training centers are not physical in your terms. They are often, in fact, maintained *en masse* by the guides who carry out the necessary plans. Now you may call this mass hallucination if you will. The fact is that to those encountering that reality, the events are quite real.

There are also training centers. In these the nature of reality is explained in accordance with an individual's ability to understand and perceive it. The familiar parables, for some, will still be used at least initially, and then these individuals will be gradually weaned away from them. In these centers there are certain classes in which instruction is given for the benefit of those who chose to return to the physical environment.

They are taught, in other words, the methods that allow them to translate emotion and thought into physical actuality. There is no time lag, as there must be in the three-dimensional system, between the initiation of such thoughts and their materialization.

All of this occurs more or less at one level, though you must understand that I am simplifying the issues here to some extent. For example, some individuals do not undergo any such periods, but because of development and progress during their past lives, they are ready to begin more ambitious programs.

Now I have spoken of such development earlier. Some of my readers, not being perhaps aware of any psychic ability of their own, might think then that they are in for a long and protracted period of after-death training. Let me hasten to tell you that all such ability is not necessarily conscious, and that much of it takes place during the sleep state when you are simply not aware of it.

Now I suggest your break, and we will return.

("I hope so," I said, joking.)

I always do. Like a bad penny, you cannot get rid of me.

("All right." 9:42 to 9:58.) Now: You may after death utterly refuse to believe that you are dead, and continue to focus your emotional energy toward those you have known in life.

If you have been obsessed with a particular project, for example, you may try to complete it. There are always guides to help you understand your situation, but you may be so engrossed that you pay them no heed.

Now: I will cover the subject of ghosts separately, rather than in this chapter. Suffice it to say that large fields of emotional focus toward physical reality can hold you back from further development.

When consciousness leaves the body and is away for some time then the connection is, of course, broken. In out-of-body states the connection still holds. Now it is possible for an individual who has died to completely misinterpret the experience and attempt to reenter the corpse. This can happen when the personality identified himself almost exclusively with the physical image.

It is not common. But nevertheless, under various circumstances, such individuals will attempt to reactivate the physical mechanism, becoming more panicstricken when they discover the body's condition. Some, for example, have wept over the corpse long after the mourners

have left, not realizing that they themselves are completely whole —
where, for example, the body may have been ill or the organs beyond
repair.

They are like a dog worrying a bone. Those who have not identified their consciousness with the body completely, find it much easier
to leave it. Those who have hated the body find, strangely enough, that
immediately after death they are quite drawn to it.

(10:07.) All of these circumstances then may or may not occur according to the individual involved. However, after leaving the physical
body, you will immediately find yourself in another. This is the same kind
of form in which you travel in out-of-body projections, and again let me
remind my readers that each of them leaves the body for some time
each night during sleep.

This form will seem physical. It will not be seen by those still in the
physical body however, generally speaking. It can do anything that you
do now in your dreams. Therefore it flies, goes through solid objects,
and is moved directly by your will, taking you, say, from one location
to another as you may think of these locations.

If you wonder what Aunt Sally is doing in, say, Poughkeepsie, New
York, then you will find yourself there. However, you cannot as a rule
manipulate physical objects. You cannot pick up a lamp or throw a dish.
This body is yours instantly, but it is not the only form that you will have.
For that matter, this image is not a new one. It is interwound with your
physical body now, but you do not perceive it. Following death, it will
be the only body you are aware of for some time.

(Pause at 10:15.) Much later and on many levels you will finally learn
to take many forms, as you choose, consciously. In one manner of speaking you do this now, you see, translating your psychological experience
— your thoughts and emotions — quite literally but unconsciously into
physical objects. You may find that when you imagine yourself as a child
— after death — that you suddenly have the form of the child that you
were. For a certain period of time, therefore, you can manipulate this
form so that it takes any appearance that it had when it was connected
with your physical form in the immediately previous physical life. You
may die at eighty and after death think of the youth and vitality that you
had at twenty, and find then that your form changes to correspond with
this inner image.

Most individuals after death choose a more mature image that usually corresponds to the peak physical abilities, regardless of the age when the physical peak was reached. Others choose instead to take the form they had at the particular point when the greatest mental or emotional heights were achieved, regardless of the beauty or age that characterized the form. Do you follow me?

("Yes.")

You will feel comfortable with the form that you choose, therefore, and you will usually use it when you want to communicate with others you have known; though for such communications with the living, you may instead adopt the form you had when you were known to the individual you want to contact.

Now you may take a break, and I will contact you again.

(As Seth, Jane pointed to John Barclay, sitting beside me on the couch. In connection with his business, John had attended a gathering this afternoon at which champagne had been served; he was now sleepy. . . .)

He is in the dream state.

("He looks it."

(John, smiling: "Just trying to follow you, Seth. Slowly."

(10:25 to 10:37. Seth finally broke into a long conversation Jane, John, and I were having during our break.)

Now: May I continue dictation?

These after-death environments do not exist necessarily on other planets. They do not take up space, so the question, "Where does all this happen?" is meaningless in basic terms.

It is the result of your own misinterpretations of the nature of reality. There is no one place therefore, no specific location. These environments exist unperceived by you amid the physical world that you know. Your perceptive mechanisms simply do not allow you to tune in to their ranges. You react to a highly specific but limited field. As I mentioned earlier, other realities coexist with your own at death, for example. You simply divest yourself of physical paraphernalia, tune into different fields, and react to other sets of assumptions.

(10:43.) From this other viewpoint, you can to some extent perceive physical reality. However, there are energy fields that do separate them. Your entire concept of space is so distorted that any true explanation is highly difficult. Give us a moment. *(Pause.)*

As your perceptive mechanisms insist that objects are solid, for example, so they insist that such a thing as space exists. Now what your senses tell you about the nature of matter is entirely erroneous, and what they tell you about space is equally wrong — wrong in terms of basic reality, but quite in keeping of course with three-dimensional concepts. *(Humorously):* In out-of-body experiences from the living state, many of the problems are encountered, in terms of space, that will be met after death. And in such episodes, therefore, the true nature of time and space becomes more apparent. After death it does not take time to go through space, for example. Space does not exist in terms of distance. This is illusion. There are barriers, but they are mental or psychic barriers. For example, there are intensities of experience that are interpreted in your reality as distance in miles.

After death you may find yourself in a training center. Now theoretically, this center could be in the middle of your present living room, in physical space, but the distance between you and the members of your family still living — sitting perhaps, thinking of you or reading a paper — would have nothing to do with space as you know it. You would be more separated from them than if you were, say, on the moon.

You could perhaps change your own focus of attention away from the center, and theoretically see the room and its inhabitants; and yet still this distance that has nothing to do with miles would be between you.

(10:55.) End of dictation. I am afraid I would put my friend to sleep over here. *(Jane, as Seth, pointed to John. He laughed.*

(John: "Sorry I've given you that impression, Seth.")

It was a true impression.

(John: "I'm gonna catch it tonight.")

Now: Do you have any questions?

(John: "Just generally. Nothing specific. . . ." John and Seth then engaged in a brief conversation, and the session ended at 11:04 P.M.

(My original notes for this session included Seth's long delivery in Jane's ESP class last night, June 23, 1970. Seth dealt with organization in that session also — but organization within our own reality as well as in others. Since that session answers questions Jane and I are often asked, we've included it in the Appendix almost in its entirety.)

CHAPTER 10

"DEATH" CONDITIONS IN LIFE

SESSION 538, JUNE 29, 1970,
9:07 P.M. MONDAY

Good evening.

("Good evening, Seth.")

(Humorously): Now: Chapter Ten: " 'Death' Conditions in Life." *(Seth repeated this chapter heading to make sure I punctuated it correctly.)*

After-death experiences will not seem so alien or incomprehensible if you realize that you encounter similar situations as a normal part of your present existence.

In sleep and dream states you are involved in the same dimension of existence in which you will have your after-death experiences. You do not remember the most important part of these nightly adventures, and so those you do recall seem bizarre or chaotic as a rule. This is simply because in your present state of development you are not able to manipulate consciously within more than one environment.

You do exist consciously in a coherent, purposeful creative state while the physical body sleeps, however, and you carry on many of the activities that I told you would be encountered after death. You simply turn the main focus of your attention in a different dimension of activity, one in which you have indeed continuously operated.

(9:15.) Now, as you have memory of your waking life and as you retain a large body of such memory for daily physical encounters, and as this fount of memory provides you with a sense of daily continuity,

so also does your dreaming self have an equally large body of memory. As there is continuity to your daily life, so there is continuity in your sleeping life.

A portion of you, therefore, is aware of each and every dream encounter and experience. Dreams are no more hallucinatory than your physical life is. Your waking physical self is the dreamer, as far as your dreaming self is concerned: You are the dreamer it sends on its way. Your daily experiences are the dreams that it dreams, so when you look at your dreaming self or consider it, you do so with a highly prejudiced eye, taking it for granted that your "reality" is real, and its reality is illusion.

(9:20.) Its reality is far more native to your being, however. If you do not find coherence in the dream state, it is because you have hypnotized yourselves into believing that none exists. Of course you try to translate your nightly adventures into physical terms upon awakening, and attempt to fit them into your often limited distortion of the nature of reality.

To some extent this is natural. You are focused in a daily life for a reason. You have adopted it as a challenge. But within its framework you are also meant to grow and develop, and to extend the limits of your consciousness. It is very difficult to admit that you are in many ways more effective and creative in the sleep state than the waking state, and somewhat shattering to admit that the dream body can indeed fly, defying both time and space. It is much easier to pretend that all such experiences are symbolic and not literal, to evolve complicated psychological theories, for example, to explain flying dreams.

The simple fact is that when you dream you are flying, you often are. In the dream state you operate under the same conditions, more or less, that are native to a consciousness not focused in physical reality. Many of your experiences, therefore, are precisely those you may meet after death. You may speak with dead friends or relatives, revisit the past, greet old classmates, walk down streets that existed fifty years earlier in physical time, travel through space without taking any physical time to do so, be met by guides, be instructed, teach others, perform meaningful work, solve problems, hallucinate.

In physical life there is a lag between the conception of an idea and its physical construction. In dream reality, this is not so. Therefore, the best way to become acquainted with after-death reality ahead of time, so to speak, is to explore and understand the nature of your own dreaming self. Not very many people want to take the time or energy.

The methods are available, however, and those who do use them will not find themselves alienated when the full focus of their attention is turned in that direction after death.

Now you may take your break.

(9:34 to 9:47.)

Now: Since your conscious memory is connected so strongly with awareness <u>within</u> the body, although you leave the body when it sleeps, the waking consciousness usually has no memory of this.

In the sleeping state, you have memory of everyone you have ever met in your dreams, though you may or may not have met some of these people in your daytime existence. In the sleeping state you may have constant experience through the years with close associates who may live in another portion of the world entirely, and be strangers to you in the waking state.

As your daily endeavors have meaning and purpose, so do your dream adventures, and in these also you attain various goals of your own. These you will continue in the after-death experience. The vitality, force, life, and creativity behind your physical existence is generated in this other dimension. In other words, you are in many ways a fleshy projection of your dreaming self.

The dreaming self as you conceive of it, however, is but a shadow of its own reality, for the dreaming self is a psychological point of reference and, in your terms, [of] continuity, that brings together all portions of your identity. Of its deeper nature, only the most developed are aware. It represents, in other words, one strong uniting facet of your entire identity. Its experiences are as vivid and its "personality" as rich — in fact richer — in context as the physical personality you know.

Pretend for a moment that you are a child, and I am trying to undertake the particular chore of explaining to you what your most developed, adult self will be like — and in my explanation, I say that this adult self is to some extent already a part of you, an outgrowth or projection of what you are. And the child says, "But what will happen to me? Must I die to become this other self? I do not want to change. How can I ever be this adult self when it is not what I am now, <u>without</u> dying as what I am?"

I am in somewhat the same position when I try to explain to you the nature of this inner self, for while you can become aware of it in dreams, you cannot truly appreciate its maturity or abilities; yet they are yours in the same way that the man's abilities belonged to the child. In the dream state you learn, among other things, how to construct your own physical reality day by day, just as after death you learn how to construct your next physical lifetime. ·

(10:07.) In dreams you solve the problems. In the daytime you are (only) consciously aware of the methods of problem solving that you learned in sleep. In dreams you set your goals, as after death you set the goals for another incarnation.

Now, no psychological structure is easy to describe in words. Simply to explain the nature of personality as it is generally known, all kinds of terms are used: id, subconscious, ego, superego; all of these to differentiate the interweaving actions that make up the physical personality. The dreaming self is just as complicated. So you can say that certain portions of it deal with physical reality, physical manipulation, and plans; some with deeper levels of creativity and achievement that insure physical survival; some with communication, with even more extensive elements of the personality now generally unknown; some with the continuing experience and existence of what you may call the soul or overall individual entity, the true multidimensional self.

The soul creates the flesh. The creator hardly looks down upon its creation. The soul creates the flesh for a reason, and physical existence for a reason, so none of this is to lead you to a distaste for physical life, nor toward a lack of appreciation for those sensual joys with which you are surrounded. Any inner journeys should allow you to find greater significance, beauty, and meaning in life as you know it now; but full enjoyment and development also means that you use all of your abilities, that you explore inner dimensions with as much wonder and enthusiasm. With proper understanding, therefore, it is quite possible for you to become quite familiar now with after-death landscapes and environments and experiences. You will find them to be as vivid as any you know. Such explorations will completely alter somber preconceptions about existence after death. It is very important that you divest yourself of as many preconceptions as possible, however, for these will impede your progress.

You may take a short break.

(10:23 to 10:39.)

Generally speaking, if you are fairly content about physical reality, you are in a better position to study these inner environments.

If you see evil all about you in physical life, and if it seems to out-weigh the good, then you are not ready. You should not embark upon an exploration of these nightly adventures if you are depressed, for at this time your own psychic state is predisposed toward depressing experiences, whether awake or asleep. You should not embark upon such a study if you hope to substitute inner experience for physical experience.

If your ideas of good and evil are rigorous, unbending, then you do not have the understanding that is necessary for any conscious manipulation in this other dimension. In other words, you should be as flexible mentally, psychologically, and spiritually as possible, open to new ideas, creative, and not overly dependent upon organizations or dogma.

You should be fairly competent and sympathetic. At the same time you should be outgoing enough in your physical environment so that you are capable of handling your life as it is. You need all your resources. This is to be an active exploration and endeavor, not a passive withdrawal, and certainly not a cowardly retreat. Toward the end of this book, methods will be given for those who are interested so that you can explore these after-death conditions consciously, having some control over your experiences and progress.

Here, however, I want to describe these conditions somewhat more thoroughly. Now, in physical life you see what you want to see. You perceive from the available field of reality certain data — data selected carefully by you in accordance with your ideas of what reality is. You create the data to begin with.

If you believe all men are evil, you simply will not experience the goodness in men. You will be completely closed to it. They in turn will always show you their worst side. You will telepathically see to it that others dislike you, and you will project your dislike upon them.

(10:54.) Your experience, in other words, follows your expectations. Now the same applies to after-death experience and to the dream experience, and to any out-of-body encounters. If you are obsessed with

the idea of evil, then you will meet evil conditions. If you believe in devils, then you will encounter these. As I mentioned earlier, there is greater freedom when consciousness is not physically directed. Thoughts and emotions are constructed, again, into reality without the physical time lapse. So if you believe you will be met by a demon, you will create your own thought-form of one, not realizing that it is of your own creation.

Therefore, if you find yourself concentrating upon the evils of physical existence in such a manner, then you are not ready for such explorations. It is, of course, possible under such conditions to meet a thought-form belonging to someone else, but if you do not believe in demons to begin with, you will always recognize the nature of the phenomena and be unharmed.

If it is your own thought-form, then, in fact, you may learn from it by asking yourself what it represents, what problem that you have so materialized. Now you may hallucinate the same sort of thing after death, use it for a symbol, and undergo a spiritual battle of sorts that would, of course, not be necessary had you more understanding. You will work out your ideas, problems or dilemmas at your own level of understanding.

Now: End of dictation for the evening. Unless you have questions, I will end the session.

(*"Do you know what I said to Jane yesterday — about our going on tour to promote* The Seth Material? *Do you have any thoughts on this?"*)

I will discuss it at a later date.

(*"Okay."*)

Not too late a date. My heartiest wishes then, and a fond good evening.

(*"Good evening, Seth. It's been very interesting."*)

I hope to keep you interested in my saga.

(*11:02 P.M. Jane's trance had been good. "He's got the whole rest of that chapter planned," she said when she came out of it. "I can sense whole blocks of material all ready. But now, it starts to fade, to go. . . ."*

(*As it turned out, we didn't ask Seth about promotion work again, and he didn't bring up the subject himself.* The Seth Material *was published in September, 1970, and we did go on tour.*)

(At the end of the last session, which was held the day before yesterday, Jane told me that Seth had the rest of Chapter Ten planned; tonight, now, she said she didn't have the slightest idea of how Seth would continue his work on the chapter.

(The day had been very hot and sticky. Stormy weather had been building up for some hours. Finally it began to rain hard, with thunder and lightning, at about 9. We wondered whether a session would be held, since Seth had told us some time ago that electrical displays interfered with trance states. Yet the session began as usual; Seth, at least, was apparently not bothered.)

Now: We will resume dictation.

After-death environments exist all about you, now. Period.

It is as if your present situation and all its physical phenomena were projected from within yourself outward, giving you a continuous running motion picture, forcing you to perceive only those images that were being transposed. These seem so real that you find yourself in the position of reacting to them constantly.

(Pause at 9:23. By now the storm was so noisy that Seth increased the volume of his voice.)

They serve to mask other quite valid realities that exist at the same time, however, and actually from these other realities you gain the power and the knowledge to operate the material projections. You can "set the machine on idle," so to speak, stop the apparent motion, and turn your attention to these realities.

First of all, you must realize that they exist. As a preliminary to the methods I will give later, it is a good idea to ask yourself now and then: "What am I actually conscious of at this time?" Do this when your eyes open, and again when they are closed.

When your eyes are open, do not take it for granted that only the immediately perceivable objects exist. Look where space seems empty, and listen in the middle of silence. There are molecular structures in every inch of empty space, but you have taught yourself not to perceive them. There are other voices, but you have conditioned your ears not to hear them. You use your inner senses when you are in the dream state, and ignore them when you are waking.

(Now the lights dimmed a couple of times.)

The inner senses are equipped to perceive data that is not physical. They are not deceived by the images that you project in three-dimensional reality. Now, they can perceive physical objects. Your physical senses are extensions of these inner methods of perception, and after death it is upon these that you will rely. They are used in out-of-body experiences. They operate constantly beneath normal waking consciousness . . .

(There had been an accident, or fire, or both in our section of the city after the storm broke loose. With sirens screeching several cars and trucks sped past on Walnut Street, two doors away. I expected all the racket to break Jane's trance, but it didn't; she paused for a few moments and then continued.)

. . . so that you can even become familiar with the nature of perception after death, now. Period.

In other words, the environment, conditions, and methods of perception will not be alien. You are not suddenly thrust into an unknown; that unknown is a part of you now. It was a part of you before this physical birth, and will be after physical death. These conditions, however, have been blotted out of your consciousness in the main, throughout physical history. Mankind has had various conceptions of his own reality but he has purposely, it seems, turned away from it in the last century. There are many reasons for this, and we will try to cover some of them.

Take your break.

(9:37. Break came early, considering the time the session began. "Things are unsettled," Jane said. "I was bothered at times." She had been aware of the sirens especially. She said her trance had been "pulsating" or wavelike: she would go "in" good, and then swing up closer to her usual state of consciousness. Yet as far as I could tell the material was as good as ever, the manner of her delivery unchanged.

(The rain, thunder and lightning continued unabated, the noise racketing back and forth over the city. It was the kind of a storm in which even this big and solid house shook at times. Jane's voice was still stronger than usual when she resumed, though at a slower pace, at 9:52.)

In many ways then, you are "dead" now — and as dead as you will ever be.

While you go about your daily chores and endeavors, beneath normal waking consciousness you are constantly focused in other realities also, reacting to stimuli of which your physical conscious self is not aware, perceiving conditions through the inner senses, and experiencing events that are not even registered within the physical brain. That whole last portion should be underlined.

After death you are simply aware of these dimensions of activity that you now ignore. Now, physical existence predominates. Then, it will not. Nor, however, will it be lost to you; your memories, for example, will be retained. You will simply step out of a particular framework of reference. Under certain conditions you will even be free to use the years seemingly given to you in different ways.

(10:01.) For example: I told you time does not consist of a series of moments, one before the other, though you do perceive it now in that fashion. Events are not things that happen to you. They are materialized experiences formed by you according to your expectations and beliefs. Inner portions of your personality realize this now. After death you will not concentrate upon the physical forms taken by time and events. You may use the same elements, as a painter might use his colors.

(10:07. We were now having a very heavy, hard rain.)

Perhaps your life span runs for seventy-seven years. After death you may, under certain conditions and if you choose, experience the events of those seventy-seven years at your leisure — but not necessarily in terms of continuity. You may alter the events. You can manipulate within that particular dimension of activity that represented your seventy-seven years.

If you find severe errors of judgment, you may then correct them. You may perfect, in other words, but you cannot again enter into that frame of reference as a completely participating consciousness following, say, the historic trends of the time, joining into the mass-hallucinated existence that resulted from the applied consciousness of your self and your "contemporaries."

Some choose this rather than reincarnating, or rather as a study before a new reincarnation. These people are often perfectionists at heart. They must go back and create. They must right their errors. They use the immediately-past life as a canvas, and with the same "canvas," they attempt a better picture. This is a mental and psychic exercise, undertaken by many, demanding great concentration, and is no more hallucinatory than any existence.

Now you may take your break.

(10:14. Jane's trance had been deeper, but she was surprised at the short delivery; she thought she had been out for a longer time. The rain had tapered off somewhat by now, and it was cooler. "It's still a strange night," she said. Resume at 10:31.)

You may feel that you want to "relive" certain episodes of your life so that you can understand them better. Your life's experience, therefore, is your own. Such conditions certainly are not alien. In ordinary living, you often imagine yourself behaving in a different manner than you did, or in your mind reexperiencing events in order to gain greater understanding from them. Your life is your own personal experience- perspective, and when at death you take it out of the mass physical time context, then you can experience it in many ways. Events and objects are not absolute, remember, but plastic. Events can be changed both before and after their occurrence. They are never stable or permanent, even though within the context of three-dimensional reality they may appear so.

Anything of which you are aware in three-dimensional existence is only a projection of a greater reality into that dimension. The events of which you are conscious are only those fragments of activities that intrude or appear to your normal waking consciousness. Other portions of these events are quite clear to you both in the dreaming state and beneath waking consciousness during the day.

(10:42. Jane's pace was quite slow.) If you want to know what death is like, then become aware of your own consciousness as it is divorced from physical activities. You will find that it is highly active. With practice you will discover that your normal waking consciousness is highly limited, and that what you thought of once as death conditions seem much more like life conditions. End of dictation.

Now there is some instability this evening, resulting from the atmosphere, but we held the session in any case.

("I thought it was good.")

We will end it, however. There is some additional strain on Ruburt in such circumstances, and there is no need prolonging it. A fond good evening.

("The same to you, Seth." 10:46. Jane said she felt all right. Although her trances had varied somewhat tonight, the only "additional strain" she'd been aware of, really, was some trouble going back into trance after breaks.)

(Afterwards we talked over Jane's recent idea — to holding, say, a session per day for six consecutive days, to see how much Seth would get done on the book in such an arbitrary period. It would be interesting to see part of it produced that way. The idea never materialized, however, even though Seth had expressed his willingness to try something like this back in March, when Chapter Three was underway. See the notes for the 10:31 break in the 519th session, and Seth's subsequent remarks. Jane stopped looking at the book in the 521st session for March 30; it's now July 1.)

SESSION 540, JULY 6, 1970,
9:29 P.M. MONDAY

("Good evening, Seth.")

Now: We will resume dictation. *(Pause.)* Such other existences and realities as just described coexist with your own, and in the waking state you are not aware of them. Now, often in your dreams you are able to perceive such other situations, but you often wind them into dream paraphernalia of your own, in which case upon awakening you have little clear memory.

In the same way in the midst of life, you dwell with so-called ghosts and apparitions, and for that matter you yourselves appear as apparitions to others, particularly when you send strong thought-forms of yourself from the sleep state, or even when unconsciously you travel out of your physical body.

There are obviously as many kinds of ghosts and apparitions as there are people. They are as alert or as unalert to their situation as you are to your own. They are not fully focused in physical reality, however, either in personality or in form, and this is their main distinction. Some apparitions are thought-forms sent by survival personalities out of lingering deep anxiety. They portray the same compulsive-type behavior that can be seen in many instances in your ordinary experience.

The same mechanism that causes a disturbed woman, say, to perform repetitive action such as a constant washing and rewashing of hands, also causes a particular kind of apparition to return time and time again to one place. In such cases the behavior is often composed of repetitive action.

For various reasons, such a personality has not learned to assimilate its own experience. The characteristics of such apparitions follow those of a disturbed personality — with some exceptions, however. The whole consciousness is not present. The personality itself seems to be having a nightmare, or a series of recurring dreams, during which it returns to the physical environment. The personality itself is "safe and sound," but certain portions of it work out unresolved problems, and discharge energy in such a fashion.

(9:44.) They are in themselves quite harmless. Only your interpretation of their actions can cause difficulties. Now in the middle of life, of life conditions, you also appear on occasion as ghosts in other levels of reality, where your "pseudoappearance" causes some comment and is the ground for many myths — and you are not even aware of this.

Now I am speaking generally. Again, there are exceptions where memory is retained, but as a rule ghosts and apparitions are not any <u>more</u> aware of their effect upon others than you are when you appear quite unconsciously as ghosts in worlds that would be quite strange to you.

(The combination of) thought, emotion, and desire creates form, possesses energy, (and) is made of energy. It will show itself in as many ways as possible. You only recognize the physical materializations, but as mentioned earlier in this book, you send pseudoforms of yourself out from yourself of which you are not aware; and this is completely aside from the existence of astral travel or projection, which is a much more complicated affair.

You appear in astral form in realities that are comparatively more advanced than your own. You are usually recognized because of your disorientation. You do not know how to manipulate. *(Humorously):* You do not know the customs. But whether you have a physical form or not, if you have emotions or feelings, these will take form. They have a reality. If you think strongly of an object, somewhere it will appear.

If you think strongly of being in another location, a pseudoimage of yourself will be projected out from you to that place, whether or not it is perceived and whether or not you yourself are conscious of it, or con-<u>scious in</u> it. This applies (both) to those who have left your physical system and to those who are in it.

(9:55.) All of these forms are called secondary constructions, for as a rule full consciousness of the personality is not in them. They are automatic projections.

Now, in primary constructions, a consciousness, usually fully aware and alert, adopts a form — not his "native" one — and consciously projects it, often into another level of reality. Even this is a rather complicated endeavor, and one seldom used for purposes of communication.

There are other much easier methods. I have explained to some degree the way images are constructed out of an available field of energy. You perceive only your own constructions. If a "ghost" wants to contact you therefore, he can do so through telepathy, and you can yourself construct the corresponding image if you desire. Or the individual might send you a thought-form at the same time that he telepathically communicates with you. Your rooms are full now of thought-forms that you do not perceive; and again, you are as much a ghostly phenomenon now as you will be after death. You are simply not aware of the fact.

You ignore certain temperature variations and stirrings of air as imagination, that are instead indicative of such thought-forms. You thrust into the background telepathic communications that often accompany such forms, and you turn aside from all clues that other realities exist quite validly with your own, and that in the midst of one existence you are surrounded by intangible but valid evidence. The very words "life" and "death" serve to limit your understanding, to set up barriers where none intrinsically exist.

You may take your break.

(10:07. Jane was easily out of trance. Her delivery this evening was a bit different than usual. Her voice was quiet, almost conversational in manner and pace, although the speed varied at times. Resume in the same way at 10:18.)

Some dead friends and relatives do visit you, projecting from their own level of reality into yours, but you cannot as a rule perceive their forms. They are not more ghostly, or "dead," however, than you are when you project into their reality — as you do, from the sleep state.

As a rule, however, they can perceive you on those occasions. What you often forget is that such individuals are in various stages of development. Some have stronger connections to the physical system than others. The length of time an individual has been dead in your terms has little to do with whether or not you will be so visited, but rather the intensity of the relationship.

As mentioned earlier, however, in the sleep state you may help recently dead persons, complete strangers, to acclimate to after-death conditions, even though this knowledge is not available to you in the morning. So others, strangers, may communicate with you when you are sleeping, and even guide you through various periods of your life.

It is not a simple matter to explain life conditions as you know them, so it is extremely difficult to discuss the complexities of which you are not aware.

The main point I want to make in this chapter is that you are already familiar with all conditions you will meet after death, and you can become consciously aware of these to some extent. *(Pause, smile at 10:29.)* End of chapter.

Now: Give us a moment.

CHAPTER 11

AFTER-DEATH CHOICES AND THE
MECHANICS OF TRANSITION

There are unlimited varieties of experience open to you after death, all possible, but some less probable than others, according to your development. Very generally now, there are three main areas, though exceptions and extraordinary cases can take other roads.

You may decide upon another reincarnation. You may decide to focus instead upon your past life, using it as the stuff of new experience, as mentioned previously creating variations of events as you have known them, making corrections as you choose. Or you may enter another system of probability entirely; and this is quite apart from a reincarnational existence. You will be leaving all thoughts of continuity of time behind you in such a case.

Now some individuals, some personalities, prefer a life organization bound about past, present, and future in a seemingly logical structure, and these persons usually choose reincarnation. Others naively prefer to experience events in an extraordinarily intuitive manner, with the organization being provided by the associative processes. These will choose a system of probabilities for their next main endeavor.

Some simply find the physical system not to their liking, and in such a way take leave of it. This cannot be done, however, until the reincarnational cycle, once chosen, is completed, so the last choice exists for those who have developed their abilities through reincarnation as far as possible within that system.

Some, finished with reincarnation, may choose to reenter the cycle acting as teachers, and in such cases some recognition of higher identity is always present. Now there is an in-between stage of relative indecision, a midplane of existence; a rest area, comparatively speaking, and it is from this area that most communication from relatives occurs. This is usually the level that is visited by the living in projections from the dream state.

Now you may take your break.

(10:45 to 10:54.)

Before the time of choosing, however, there is a period of self-examination, and your full "history" becomes available to you. You understand the nature of the entity, and you are advised by other portions of that entity, more "advanced" than yourself.

You will become aware of your other reincarnational selves, for example. There will be emotional ties with other personalities whom you have known in past lives, and some of these may supersede your relationships in the immediately past life. This is a meeting place for individuals from your own system also, however.

All necessary explanations are given to those who are disoriented. Those who do not realize that they are dead are here told of their true condition, and all efforts are made to refresh the energies and spirits. It is a time of study and comprehension. It is from this area that some disturbed personalities have those dreams of returning to the physical environment.

It is a place of commerce between systems, so to speak. Conditions and development are important, rather than the length an individual stays in this area. It is an intermediary step, but an important one. In your dreams you have been here.

Now: End of dictation. I wanted to end one chapter and begin another. I will close the session unless you have questions.

("I guess not.")

My heartiest wishes to you both, and a fond good evening

("Good night, Seth, and thank you very much." 11:05 P.M.)

SESSION 541, JULY 13, 1970, 8:40 P.M. MONDAY

(No session was held for July 8th, as scheduled. Tam Mossman, Jane's editor at Prentice Hall, called this morning to say that the first copies of her book,

The Seth Material, *have arrived at Prentice Hall from the printer. He's mailing a book to Jane today.*

(This afternoon, I gave myself suggestions that I have a projection experience when I lay down, but I did not succeed. Then, shortly after supper, I had a visual experience like that described in the notes for the 534th session, in Chapter Eight. I told Jane about it as it progressed. Once again she was concerned, but as usual I felt no alarm. The experience lasted for perhaps half an hour.

(In Chapter Eight, Seth had said this was my way of trying to see models for my paintings. I hoped to see something really good this evening now that I was prepared, but nothing developed. The only aftereffect was a slight headache, as before, and this soon passed.

(Maybe, I thought, the experience was a delayed reaction to the projection suggestions. Just before the session I asked my pendulum a few questions — keeping in mind that I wasn't so sure this technique should be used to explore other than physically oriented data. Usually I get excellent results with the pendulum; I learned now that the visual-interference effects had been caused by my unsuccessful attempts to perceive a thought-form sent out by a survival personality. This backed up the reasons given by Seth, then, for the eye phenomenon. Usually we use the pendulum to reach information that is just below normal waking consciousness.

(I also learned that no particular painting of mine was involved, nor were my efforts to project this afternoon; that the survival personality was unknown to me, and that the pendulum couldn't tell me who the personality was.

(With this explanation, I didn't feel it necessary to ask Seth about the experience. I did hope he would comment on it, but he did not. . . . Jane and I were both ready for the session ahead of time, for a change.)

Now, I bid you an early good evening.

("Good evening, Seth.")

Resume dictation: Reincarnation involves far more than a simple decision to undergo another physical existence. In this in-between period of which I am speaking, many issues therefore are considered.

When most people think of reincarnation, they think in terms of a one-line progression in which the soul perfects itself in each succeeding life. This is a gross simplification. There are endless varieties of this one theme, individual variations. The process of reincarnation is used in many ways, therefore, and in this time of rest individuals must decide on the unique way in which reincarnation will be of use.

(8:45.) Some, for example, choose to isolate various characteristics in a given life, and work on these almost exclusively, basing a given existence upon, say, one main theme. As seen from a physical viewpoint, such a personality would appear very one-sided, and far from a well-developed individual.

In one life the intellect may purposely be very high, and those powers of the mind carried as far as the individual can take them. These abilities are then studied thoroughly by the entire personality, both the benefits and the detrimental aspects of the intellect weighed carefully. Through experience in another life this same kind of individual might specialize in emotional development, and purposely underplay intellectual abilities.

Again, the physical picture would not be necessarily that of a well-developed or balanced personality. Specific creative abilities might be specialized in the same manner. If you looked at these lives as a series of progressions in usual terms, then you would be left with many questions unanswered. Nevertheless the development does occur, but the individuals choose the way in which they prefer this development to take place.

(8:51.) Through denying themselves, say, intellectual development in a given life, personalities also learn the value and purpose of that which they do not possess. The desire for it is then born within them — if, for example, earlier they did not understand the purposes of the intellect. So in the time of choosing, personalities decide upon the ways in which they will develop in the following incarnation.

Some will choose progression at an easier rate and in a more balanced manner. They will help keep all the strands of personality working at once, so to speak, and even meet again and again people they have known in other lives. They will work out problems at a rather easy rate, rather than in, say, an explosive way. They will pace themselves as dancers do.

In this time of rest and choosing, all counsel is given. Some personalities do reincarnate before they are advised to, for many reasons. This is usually unfortunate in the short run, for the necessary planning has not taken place. But in the long run great lessons will still be learned from the "error." There is no time schedule, and yet it is very unusual for an individual to wait for anything over three centuries between lives, for this makes the orientation very difficult, and the emotional ties with earth have become weak.

The relationships for the next life have to be settled upon, and this involves telepathic communication with all those who will be involved. This is a time, then, of many projections. There are those who are simply loners, who reincarnate without any great feeling for earth's historical periods. There are others who like to return when their contemporaries from some particular past historical time return again, and therefore there are group patterns that involve reincarnational cycles in which many, but not all, are involved.

(To me, now, at 9:02): You, for example, did not operate within a cycle in those terms. Now: There are personal cycles of course, in which families may reincarnate, taking different relationships to each other, and you have been involved in several of these.

There are different depths to be probed in reincarnational existences. Some choose to "go all the way." These personalities specialize in physical existence, and their knowledge of this system is most comprehensive. For these there is a movement through each of your racial types — a requirement that is not laid upon most. There is intensive preoccupation with historical periods. Many of these personalities live comparatively short lives, but very intense ones, and they experience more lives than most other individuals. They return, in other words, in as many historical times as possible, finally helping to shape the world as you know it.

You may take your break.

(9:08. Jane's pace had been fairly fast most of the time, her voice quiet. As she came out of trance we heard the paperboy coming up the stairs. I paid him.

(Not long after these sessions began, several years ago, Seth told Jane and me that the three of us had experienced lives in Denmark in the 1600's. Ever since then I've thought my interest in the art of Western Europe for that same period, embracing the work of Rembrandt and Vermeer, Van Dyke, and Rubens, et al., more than coincidental. I mentioned to Jane now my curiosity as to whether my artistic career had any connection with my Denmark life. I wanted to know my life span then, also.

(Resume at a slower pace at 9:20.)

Now: Dictation. In one way or another you are all travelers before you begin even your first reincarnational cycle. To make it as simple as

I can, I will say that you do not have the same backgrounds, necessarily, when you enter the physical system of reality. As mentioned earlier, earthly existence is a training period; and yet as far as possible I would like you to forget your ordinary ideas of progression.

Ideas of good, better, best can lead you astray, for example. You are learning to be as completely as possible. In one way you are learning to create yourselves. In so doing during the reincarnational cycle, you are focusing your main abilities in physical life, developing human qualities and characteristics, opening new dimensions of activity. This does not mean that good does not exist, or that in your terms you do not "progress," but your concepts of good and progression are extremely distorted.

Now many personalities have extraordinary talents along specific lines, and these may show up again and again in succeeding existences. They may be tempered, used in various combinations, and yet overall still remain a personality's strongest mark of individuality and uniqueness. While most people adopt different trades, occupations, and interests, for example, throughout the reincarnational cycle, with some there will be a very noticeable line of continuity. It may be broken occasionally, but it is always there. They may be priests or teachers, for example, almost exclusively.

There will be some more material in this book dwelling specifically upon reincarnation, but here I want to point out that in this time of choosing between lives, many more issues are at stake than a simple matter of proposed rebirth.

On occasion, some personalities may be given an exception to the general rule and take a sabbatical (*humorously*) from reincarnations, a side trip so to speak, to another layer of reality, and then return. Such cases are not common, however. Such matters are also decided at this time. Those who choose to leave this system, whose reincarnational cycles are finished, have many more decisions to make.

Entering the field of probabilities can be compared to entering the reincarnational cycle. There will be a sustained focus of awareness and existence in an entirely different sort of reality. Powers latent but barely glimpsed within the multidimensional personality are drawn upon and used when such a choice is made.

The psychological experience varies considerably from that you know, and yet there are hints of it within your own psyche. Here the personality must learn to group events in an entirely different way, and completely without any reliance upon the time structure as you know it.

(9:40.) In this one, as in no other reality, intellectual and intuitive abilities finally work so well together that there is little distinction between them. The self that decides upon reincarnational existence is the same self who chooses experience within the probable system. The structure of personality, however, within the system is quite different. The personality structures with which you are familiar are but one variety of the many forms of awareness available to you.

The probable system, therefore, is as complicated as the reincarnational one. Now I have told you that all action is simultaneous; therefore, on the one hand, you exist in both systems at once. However, to explain to you that decisions are involved, and to separate these events, I must simplify them to some degree. Put it this way: A portion of the whole self focuses in reincarnational cycles and handles developments there. Another portion focuses in probabilities and handles developments there.

In parentheses: (There is also a probable system, of course, in which no reincarnational cycles exist, and a cycle of reincarnations in which no probabilities exist.) The openness and flexibility of the personality is highly important. Doorways to existences can be opened, and the personality can refuse to see them.

On the other hand, all probable existence is open, and consciousness can make a door where there was none in those terms. There are guides and teachers in this time of choosing and decision, to point out alternatives and to explain the nature of existence. All personalities are not at the same level of development. There are therefore advanced teachers and teachers at "lower" levels.

(9:51.) But this is not a time of confusion, but of great illumination, and unbelievable challenge. There will be later material in this book on the god concept that will help you understand some things that remain unsaid in this chapter.

Now for those who choose to recombine, "mix or match," events from the immediately past life — to try it over in new ways for example, lessons must also be given. In many of these cases there is a severe

problem and a certain rigidity coupled with the perfectionist characteristics mentioned earlier.

The earth years will be experienced again, but not necessarily in
continuity. The events may be used in any way the individual chooses;
altered, played back the way they happened for contrast; the way, perhaps, an actor would play an old movie in which he appeared over again
in order to study it. Only in this case, of course, the actor can change
his approach or the ending. He has full freedom with the events within
those years.

The other actors, however, are thought-forms, unless a few contemporaries join in the affair together.

Now you may take your break.

*(10:00. During the last delivery someone began to move into the apartment
above us. Once out of trance, Jane said she had been bothered by the racket over
our heads, but that she "held on to the trance" until break. Resume at the same
slow rate at 10:12.)*

Now: Under these conditions the personality manipulates events
consciously of course, and studies the various effects. The focus demanded is quite intensive.

He is told the nature of those who participate with him. He realizes they are thought-forms, for example, and his own; but again,
thought-forms do possess a certain reality and consciousness. They are
not cardboard actors for him to simply push around at will. He must,
therefore, take them into consideration, and he has a certain responsibility toward them.

They will grow in consciousness and continue their own lines of development on different levels. In one way, we are all thought-forms, and
this will be further explained in the material dealing with the god concept. Understand, however, that I do not mean that we lack our own
initiative for action, individuality or purpose — and remember also here
that you live from the inside out. Then perhaps the statement will have
more meaning for you.

Now in this time of choosing all of these matters are considered, and
suitable preparations made, but the planning itself is all a part of experience and of development. The in-between existence, therefore, is every
bit as important as the period that is chosen. You learn to plan your existences, in other words. You also make friends and acquaintances in these

rest periods whom you meet again and again — and only, perhaps, during in-between existences.

With them you may discuss your experience during reincarnational cycles. These are like old friends. The teachers, for example, are themselves within a cycle. The more advanced ones have already encountered the systems of reincarnation and probabilities, and are themselves deciding upon the "future" nature of their own experience. Their choices, however, are not your choices. While I may mention some other realms of existence open to them in a later chapter, we will not be involved with them here.

Now give us a moment. End of dictation. *(Pause, at 10:27.)*

(I yawned. Amused): Are you awake and alert?

("Yes.")

Then give us a moment. . . . We have two broken-up periods for you. One very brief, 1611 to 1635. This is Denmark. Then 1638 to 1674. In one of these the information is as I gave it (several years ago). I was a spice merchant, and well traveled. I also carried paint pigments, or what ended up as paint pigments. Now give us time. *(Pause.)*

There was a group of three men, painters. We will get what we can. Pronunciation is poor. We are after a name that sounds like *M. A.* then Daimeer *(my phonetic interpretation)*. I do not know if that was called Madaimeer. *(With gestures.)* There is a connection someplace here with music and a Peer Gynt suite. Do you follow me?

("Yes.")

Woods and charcoal. Coal fires. You, I believe, now working on the floor of a hut, involved in the final process of making charcoal. *(Long pause.)*

A connection with Van Elver, though I am not sure of its extent.

(I've painted a portrait of Van Elver, who is the fourteenth-century artist [Danish or Norwegian] from whom Seth receives information on painting techniques.*)

The name Wedoor *(phonetic)* and a Germanic firm who handled artists' supplies then, and was also famous for the dyeing of cloth and clothes.

To assemble this material is difficult. Not to get it.

---

*An illustration of this painting appears in *The Seth Material.* The name Van Elver isn't given in the caption, but the painting is easily identifiable.

Van Elver the younger. (The cities were) clearing houses for country artists, but many more painters did portraits of wealthy farmers and their land and establishments. These were hung of course in places of honor in the homes.

Even the poorer peasants and farmers bought portraits of themselves, however, from perhaps less gifted artists, and many unknowns took payment for portraits in the form of room and board, and painted all the more slowly.

(Jane, as Seth, smiled and leaned forward.) Now, you were a minor artist of that nature for a period. Not, therefore, during your entire life. You did better than room and board, and purchased land where you determined to settle down.

Two friends continued to travel and paint, however, and visited you occasionally, and you envied them to some degree. One became fairly well known at the time. His name was Van Dyck, but not the famous one. You loved your land but blamed it also, thinking that perhaps you might have been well-known as an artist had you not obtained it.

You thought you would settle down and paint on your fine farm, but instead you turned into a farmer, and a lecherous one at that. There is some connection here with your ambiguous feelings about money now, you see, and possessions.

Family name, as close as I can come: Raminkin, or Ra-man-ken *(both my phonetic interpretations)*. The letters *H, E, I, M*. These form either the first name or were tacked onto the name just given. *(Emphatically):* You did my portrait then, too.

("That's interesting." As Seth, Jane pointed to my portrait of Seth; it hung on the wall behind me, so that she faced it as she sat in her rocker.)

You did a better job this time.

("That's good.")

Give us a moment. That was my last full reincarnation, adopted then because I loved the sea, and it served a strong purpose in spreading ideas from one country to another. The men who traveled with me also took part in the seeding of ideas. We spread them about the world as it was then known.

Frank Withers was a fragment personality of mine. He will continue, himself, to reincarnate and go his own way. Many of us leave fragment personalities as you leave children. Do you follow me?

("Yes." Frank Withers was the original name given to us when the sessions began in late 1963.)

And now I wish you a fond good evening.

("Good evening to you, Seth. Thank you very much.")

And you must do me in charcoal sometime.

("Okay.")

I may even appear and sit for you, though briefly.

("All right."

(10:57 P.M. Jane's trance had been deep. We've received little information on our past lives, preferring to wait on this endeavor for various personal reasons. We found the data concerning Denmark intriguing. Jane and I ended up unsure, though, as to whether I lived two short lives, or one longer life divided into two spheres of activity.

(This in turn led me to wonder if tonight's session contradicted one held several years ago, in which Seth stated that I had lived to an old age in the Denmark life. Jane had been my son. Actually there was no contradiction — merely a misinterpretation on our parts. Seth goes into more detail on this in the 595th session, in the Appendix.

(I do a lot of drawing in charcoal in this *life, too.)*

SESSION 546, AUGUST 19, 1970,
9:20 P.M. WEDNESDAY

(Seth has suspended dictation on his book for the last five weeks. Two weeks of this went for our vacation, but otherwise we've been very busy. Of the four regular sessions held in the remaining time, large portions dealt with matters growing out of the September 4th publication of Jane's own book, The Seth Material, *and a projected radio and television tour.*

(Now that we could relax a little, however, we had every confidence that Seth would easily resume work on Chapter Eleven of his book, even though Jane hasn't looked at it for quite a while now. Such was the case.)

Good evening.

("Good evening, Seth.")

Now: We will resume dictation.

The time of choosing is dependent upon the condition and circumstances of the individual following transition from physical life. Some take longer than others to understand the true situation.

Others must be divested of many impeding ideas and symbols, as explained earlier. The time of choosing may happen almost immediately, in your terms, or it may be put off for a much longer period while training is carried on. The main impediments standing in the way of the time of choosing are, of course, the faulty ideas harbored by any given individual.

A belief in heaven or hell, under certain conditions, can be equally disadvantageous. Some will refuse to accept the idea of further work, development, and challenge, believing instead that conventional heaven situations are the only possibility. For some time they may indeed inhabit such an environment, until they learn through their own experience that existence demands development, and that such a heaven would be sterile, boring, and indeed "deadly."

Then they are ready for the time of choosing. Others may insist that because of their transgressions they will be cast into hell, and because of the force of such belief, they may for some time actually encounter such conditions. In either case, however, there are always teachers available. They try to get through these false beliefs.

In the Hades conditions, the individuals come somewhat more quickly to their senses. Their own fears trigger within themselves the answering release. Their need, in other words, more quickly opens up the inner doorways of knowledge. Their state does not usually last as long, therefore, as the heaven state.

Either state, however, puts off the time of choosing and the next existence. There is one point I would like to mention here: In all cases, the individual creates his experience. I say this again at the risk of repeating myself because this is a basic fact of all consciousness and existence. There are no special "places" or situations or conditions set apart after physical death in which any given personality must have experience.

Suicides, as a class, for example, do not have any particular "punishment" meted out to them, nor is their condition any worse a priori. They are treated as individuals. Any problems that were not faced in this life will, however, be faced in another one. This applies not only to suicides, however.

A suicide may bring about his own death because he rejects existence on any but highly specific terms chosen by himself. If this is the case, then of course he will have to learn differently. Many others, however, choose to deny experience while within the physical system, committing suicide quite as effectively while still physically alive.

(9:38.) The conditions connected with an act of suicide are also important, and the inner reality and realization of the individual. I mention this here because many philosophies teach that suicides are met by a sort of special, almost vindictive fate, and such is not the case. However, if a person kills himself, believing that the act will annihilate his consciousness forever, then this false idea may severely impede his progress, for it will be further intensified by guilt.

Again, teachers are available to explain the true situation. Various therapies are used. For example, the personality may be led back to the events prior to the decision. Then the personality is allowed to change the decision. An amnesia effect is induced, so that the suicide itself is forgotten. Only later is the individual informed of the act, when he is better able to face it and understand it.

Obviously, however, these conditions are also impediments to the time of choosing. It goes without saying that an obsession with earthly concerns also acts in the same manner. In such instances, often the personality will insist upon focusing his perceptive abilities and energies toward physical existence. This is a psychic refusal to accept the fact of death. The individual knows quite well that he is dead in your terms, but he refuses to complete the psychic separation.

Now: There are instances of course where the individuals concerned do not realize the fact of death. It is not a matter of refusing to accept it, but a lack of perception. In this state such an individual will also be obsessed with earthly concerns, and wander perhaps bewildered throughout his own home or surroundings. The time of choosing will, of course, necessarily be postponed.

The mechanics of transition therefore are highly variable, as the mechanics of physical life are highly variable. Many of the impediments that I have mentioned impede progress not only after death, but during your own physical existence. This should certainly be taken into consideration. An overly strong identification with the sexual characteristics can also hold back progress. If an individual considers identity strongly in terms of male or female identity, then such a person may refuse to accept the fact of the sexual changes that occur in reincarnational existences. This kind of sexual identification, however, also impedes personality development during physical life.

You may take your break and we will continue.

(9:53. Jane's trance had been good, her pace rather fast, her voice quiet. She wasn't as active or strong as she had been last night, though, when she held a session for her ESP class. Resume at 10:11.)

Now: While, generally speaking, the issues just mentioned operate as impediments, there are always exceptions. A belief in heaven that is not an <u>obsessional</u> belief can be used as a useful framework, as a basis of operation in which an individual will often accept easily then, the new explanations that will be offered.

Even a belief in a time of judgment is a useful framework in many instances, for while there <u>is</u> no punishment meted out in your terms, the individual is then prepared for some kind of spiritual examination and evaluation.

Those who understand thoroughly that reality is self-created will have least difficulty. Those who have learned to understand and operate in the mechanics of the dream state will have great advantage. A belief in demons is highly disadvantageous after death, as it is during physical existence. A systematized theology of opposites is also detrimental. If you believe, for example, that all good must be balanced by evil, then you bind yourself into a system of reality that is highly limiting, and that contains within it the seeds of great torment.

In such a system, even good becomes suspect, because an equal evil is seen to follow it. The god-versus-devil, angels-versus-demons — the gulf between animals and angels — all of these distortions are impediments. In your system of reality now you set up great contrasts and opposing factors. These operate as root assumptions within your reality.

They are extremely superficial and largely the result of misused intellectual abilities. The intellect alone cannot understand what the intuitions most certainly know. In trying to make sense in its terms of physical existence, the intellect has set up these opposing factors. The intellect says, "If there is good, there must be evil," for it wants things explained in neat parcels. If there is an up, there must be a down. There must be balance. The inner self, however, realizes that in much larger terms, evil is simply ignorance, that "up" and "down" are neat terms applied to space which knows no such directions.

(10:25.) A strong belief in such opposing forces is highly detrimental, however, for it prevents an understanding of the facts — the

facts of inner unity and of oneness, of interconnections and of cooperation. A belief, therefore, an obsessional belief in such opposing factors, is perhaps the most detrimental element, not only after death but during any existence.

There are some individuals who have never experienced during physical life that sense of harmony and oneness in which such opposing factors merge. Such individuals have many stages to go through following transition, and usually many other physical lives "ahead" of them.

As you form your physical existence individually and collectively, so after the time of choosing, you join others who have decided upon the same general kind of experience. A strong cooperative venture is then begun as preparations are made. These will vary according to the type of existence chosen. There are general patterns, therefore. No individual's reality is identical with another's, and yet there are overall groupings.

You may take your break.

(10:34. At first I thought the break was announced because our cat, Willy, had jumped up into Jane's lap while she was speaking. She flinched so I thought he interrupted her, but upon coming out of trance Jane said she hardly remembered the incident. Her pace had again been fast. Resume in the same manner at 10:44.)

Quite simply, a belief in the good without a belief in the evil, may seem highly unrealistic to you. This belief, however, is the best kind of insurance that you can have, both during physical life and afterward.

It may outrage your intellect, and the evidence of your physical senses may shout that it is untrue, yet a belief in good without a belief in evil is actually highly realistic, since in physical life it will keep your body healthier, keep you psychologically free of many fears and mental difficulties, and bring you a feeling of ease and spontaneity in which the development of your abilities can be better fulfilled. After death it will release you from the belief in demons and hell, and enforced punishment. You will be better prepared to understand the nature of reality as it is. I understand that the concept does indeed offend your intellect, and that your senses seem to deny it. Yet you should already realize that your senses tell you many things, which are not true; and I tell you that your physical senses perceive a reality that is a result of your beliefs.

Believing in evils, you will of course perceive them. Your world has not tried the experiment as yet which would release you. Christianity was but a distortion of this main truth — that is, organized Christianity as you know it. I am not simply speaking here of the original precepts. They were hardly given a chance, and we will discuss some of this later in the book.

The experiment that would transform your world would operate upon the basic idea that you create your own reality according to the nature of your beliefs, and that all existence was blessed, and that evil did not exist in it. If these ideas were followed individually and collectively, then the evidence of your physical senses would find no contradiction. They would perceive the world and existence as good.

This is the experiment that has not been tried, and these are the truths that you must learn after physical death. Some, after death, understanding these truths, choose to return to physical existence and explain them. Through the centuries this has been the way. In the system of probabilities that originates within physical reality, this is also the case.

There are systems of probability not connected with your own system at all, much more advanced than any you presently imagine, and in these, the truths of which I have been speaking are well known. In them individuals creatively and purposely create realities, knowing how to do so and giving full rein to the creative abilities of consciousness.

(10:59.) I mention this here simply to point out that there are many other after-death conditions not connected with your system. When you have learned to your capacity in this in-between period, you are ready to progress. The in-between period itself, however, has many dimensions of activity and divisions of experience. As you can see, to put it as simply as possible, everyone does not "know" everyone else.

Instead of countries or physical divisions, you have psychological states. To an individual in one, another might seem quite foreign. In many communications with those in these transitional states, messages through mediums can appear as highly contradictory. The experience of the "dead" is not the same. The conditions and situations vary. An individual explaining his reality can only explain what he knows. Again, such material often offends the intellect that demands simple, neat answers and descriptions that tally.

Most individuals from these stages who communicate with "living"

· 163 ·

relatives, have not reached the time of choosing as yet, and have not completed their training.

(11:06.) They may still be perceiving reality in terms of their old beliefs. Almost all communications come from this level, particularly when there is a bond of relationship in an immediately previous life. Even at this level, however, such messages serve a purpose. The communicators can inform living relatives that existence continues and they can do it in terms that the living can understand.

They can relate to the living, since often their beliefs are still the same; in fortunate circumstances they can communicate their knowledge as they learn. Gradually, however, their own interests change. They take up relationships in their new existence.

At the time of choosing, therefore, the personality is already preparing itself to leave for another existence. In your terms of time this in-between period can last for centuries. It can last only a few years. Again, however, there are exceptions. There are cases in which a personality goes very quickly into another physical life, in perhaps a matter of hours. This is usually unfortunate, and is caused by an obsessive desire to return to physical life.

Such a quick return, however, can also be taken by a personality who is charged with a great purpose, who disregards or discards an old physical body, and is reborn almost immediately into a new one in order to finish an important and necessary project already begun.

Now we will end our session unless you have questions.

("I guess not.")

A hearty good evening to you both.

("Good night, Seth.")

You should have been here for last night's ESP class session. You would have enjoyed it —

("I'm going to read it." I had been typing a session in my studio, while class met in our living room. The session had been recorded by a class member, as usual, and we'll have a transcript of it in a few days.)

— and you would not have had to take notes. *(Pause.)* Now I am with you here strongly this evening, and if you give yourself the suggestions, then I will help you out of your body. Tell yourself to remember.

("Okay. I'd like to project.")

Until later, then.

("Good night, Seth, and thank you." 11:18 P.M. Jane's trance had been quite deep, and it took her longer than usual to come out of it. In the latter part of the session I had been able to easily sense the immediacy of Seth's presence.

(Jane told me that "at the tail end of the session," she had picked up this idea from Seth; I could tape a session, and while it was in progress I would be free to do a series of sketches of her speaking for Seth. From the sketches I could then do an oil of her. Jane was sure the idea came from Seth. She'd never thought of it before; and neither had I, for that matter.

(Upon retiring I attempted the suggestions about projection as mentioned by Seth, but I had nothing to report in the morning. If I wait until I go to bed I'll usually have difficulty giving myself suggestions; I fall asleep too quickly. Jane approaches the sleep state in a more leisurely manner.)

SESSION 547, AUGUST 24, 1970, 9:10 P.M. MONDAY

Now: Good evening.

("Good evening, Seth.")

We will resume dictation. *(Jane, as Seth, directed an inquiring look at me.)* Unless you have any preliminary questions . . .

("No.")

There are some points I would like to add here. The time of choosing is somewhat more complicated if the last reincarnational cycle, in your terms, is completed.

First of all you must understand, again, that now you do not realize your true identity. You identify instead with your present ego, so when you think in terms of life after death you really mean a future life of the ego that you know. At the end of the reincarnational cycle you understand quite thoroughly that you, the basic identity, the inner core of your being, is more than the sum of your reincarnational personalities.

You might say that the personalities then are but divisions of your self here. There is no competition between them. There never was any real division, but only a seeming one in which you played various roles, developed different abilities, learned to create in new and diverse ways. These reincarnational personalities continue to develop, but they also understand that their main identity is also yours.

When the cycle is finished, therefore, you have complete knowledge of your past lives. The information, experience, and abilities are

· 165 ·

at your fingertips. This merely means that you understand your multidimensional reality in practical terms. I have used the word multidimensional often, and you see I mean it quite literally, for your reality exists not only in terms of reincarnational existences but also in the probable realities mentioned earlier.

When the time of choosing comes, therefore, the choices available are far more diverse than those offered or possible to personalities who must still reincarnate. There is always the opportunity to teach if you have the inclination and the capabilities, but multidimensional teaching is far different than teaching as you know it now, and it demands rigorous training.

Such a teacher must be able to instruct various portions of one entity, in your terms, at the same time. Say, for example, a particular entity has reincarnations in the fourteenth century, [in] 3 B.C., in the year A.D. 260, and in the time of Atlantis. A teacher would simultaneously be in contact with these various personalities, communicating with them in terms that they could understand. Such communication demands a complete knowledge of the root assumptions of such eras, and of the general philosophical and scientific climate of thought at the time.

(9:26.) The entity might well be exploring several probable systems too, and these personalities would also have to be reached and contacted. The amount of knowledge and training necessary makes such a teaching communicator-career extremely demanding, but it is one of the courses available. The process of learning such information necessarily adds to the development and abilities of the teacher. A delicate manipulation of energy is required, and a constant travel through dimensions. Once such a choice is made, training immediately begins, always under the leadership of a practical expert. The vocation, for it is a vocation, leads such a teacher even into other realms of reality than those he previously knew existed.

Now: Others, finished with reincarnations and of a different overall nature, may begin the long journey leading toward the vocation of a creator. On a much different plane, this can be compared to geniuses in creative fields within your own physical reality.

Instead of paints, pigments, words, musical notes, the creators begin to experiment with dimensions of actuality, imparting knowledge in as many forms as possible — and I do not mean physical forms. What you would call time is manipulated as an artist would manipulate pigment. What you would call space is gathered together in different ways.

Art is created, then, using time — for example — as a structure. In your terms time and space might be mixed. The beauties of various ages, the natural beauties, the paintings and buildings are all recreated as learning methods for these beginners. One of their main preoccupations is to create beauty that impinges itself in as many various dimensions of reality as possible.

Such a work would be perceived in your system as one thing, for example, but would also be perceived in probable realities, though perhaps in an entirely different way — a multidimensional art, you see, so free and elemental that it would appear simultaneously in many realities.

Such an art is impossible to describe in words. The concept has no verbal equivalent. These creators, however, are also involved in inspiring those in all levels of reality available to them. For example, inspiration in your system is often the work of such creators.

You may take your break and we shall continue.

(9:44 to 10:00.)

Now: These "art forms" are often symbolic representations of the nature of reality. They will be interpreted in various ways, according to the abilities of those who perceive them.

In your terms they may be living dramas. They will always be psychic structures, however, existing apart from any given system of reality, but at least partially perceived by many. Some exist in what you might term the astral plane, and you perceive them in visits during the sleep state.

(10:03. Our cat, Willy, suddenly jumped up into Jane's lap — just as he'd done in the last session. Instinctively I spoke to him rather loudly, afraid he'd shock Jane out of trance. Her eyes flickered at the sound of my voice, but she continued speaking. Willy jumped down.)

Others are perceived in glimpses or bits and pieces by your temporal mind while you are half-sleeping and half-waking, or in other periods of dissociation. There are various kinds of multidimensional art, and therefore many levels in which the creators work. The whole Christ story was such a creation.

(Pause at 10:06. I sneezed. This wasn't the first time I had sneezed since the session started.)

There are also those who choose to be healers, and of course this involves far more than healing as you are familiar with it. These healers must be able to work with all levels of the entity's experience, directly helping those personalities that are a part of it. Again, this involves a manipulation through reincarnational patterns, and here again, great diversification. A healer begins with reincarnational selves with various difficulties. . . .

(*I sneezed three times.*) Do you want a break?

(*"I guess not." Although I took a moment to think it over.*)

The healing involved is always psychic and spiritual, and these healers are available to help each personality in your system as you know it, in your present time, and in other systems.

In a larger context, and with greater training, advanced healers deal with the spiritual maladies of vast numbers of personalities. There are those who combine the qualities of teacher, creator, and healer. Others choose lines of development that are particularly suited to their own characteristics.

I suggest your break.

(*10:15. Willy had begun to act up again, so I deposited him in another room and closed the door. Jane said she had been bothered by him, and by my sneezing. She had a vague memory of the near-shout I'd directed at Willy. My own energies, she said, were very scattered this evening; she had picked this up. It was certainly true that I wasn't at my best. I continued to sneeze after she resumed at 10:25.*)

I do not want to discuss the purpose of consciousness's continuous existence or development in this chapter, however. I simply want to make it clear that vast possibilities of progress are possible, and to stress the fact that each personality has full freedom.

The developments of consciousness that take place are natural attributes, natural stages. There is no coercion applied. All of the further developments are inherent in the personality that you know, even as the adult is inherent in the child.

Now these descriptions of after-death events may sound very complicated, particularly if you have been used to a simple tale of heaven or eternal rest. Unfortunately, the words fail to describe many of the basics that I would have you understand. You have within yourself, however, the ability to release your intuitions and to receive inner knowledge.

As you read this book, the words are meant to release your own intuitional abilities. When you are reading it, your own dreams will give you added information and will be in your mind upon awakening if you are alert for them. There is no such simple end to the life that you know, [such] as the story of heaven. There is the freedom to understand your own reality, to develop your abilities further, and to feel more deeply the nature of your own existence as a part of All That Is.

(10:34.) That is the end of the chapter, and the end of our session unless you have questions.

("No, I guess not." I was too tired and uncomfortable.)

My heartiest regards to you both, and a fond good evening.

("Good evening, Seth.")

Now: A small note. A portion of you was earlier projected to the hospital where your father is. Ruburt felt the absence of that part of you. You were simply trying to look in on him. In the very back of your mind you wondered if he knew, now, that he ever had hay fever, and it was that that triggered the unconscious projection.

Your unconscious self is a strong portion of our sessions, and it was for this reason that Ruburt sensed this absence. And now, good evening.

("Good evening, Seth. Thank you.")

(10:39 P.M. The session ended comparatively early, for obvious reasons. Seth's information about my unconscious projection was very interesting. An event of that kind could have easily caused my sneezing. There are strong connections involving my father, myself, and hay fever.

(This is the season for hay fever. Although I'm not bothered much now, in earlier years I suffered with it extensively. I had my first bout when I was three years old. At about the same time my father got rid of his, for good. Seth told me some time ago that my father had given me his hay fever, and that for reasons of my own I had accepted the "gift."

(My symptoms gradually subsided through the balance of the evening.)

CHAPTER 12

REINCARNATIONAL RELATIONSHIPS

SESSION 550, SEPTEMBER 28, 1970,
9:35 P.M. MONDAY

(*From September 7 until 19 Jane and I were on a radio and television tour of seven cities, to publicize Jane's book,* The Seth Material. *We found the experience stimulating and educational; Seth spoke on television in Boston, and was very well received.*

(Two sessions have been held since our return home — to answer questions and handle other matters raised by the tour. Now with this work taken care of, Jane was eager for Seth to resume work on his book.

(Carl and Sue Watkins witnessed the session. Sue brought a list of questions, which we added to others already on hand.)

Good evening.

(*"Good evening, Seth."*)

And good evening to my traveling friends, here. We are going to begin our next chapter, to be called: "Reincarnational Relationships."

Now: Throughout your reincarnational existences you expand your consciousness, your ideas, your perceptions, your values. You break away from self-adopted restrictions, and you grow spiritually as you learn to step aside from limiting conceptions and dogmas.

Your rate of learning depends entirely upon you, however. Limited, dogmatic, or rigid concepts of good and evil can hold you back. Too narrow ideas of the nature of existence can follow you through several lives if you do not choose to be spiritually and psychically flexible.

These rigid ideas can indeed act as leashes, so that you are forced to circle like a tied puppy dog about a very small radius. In such cases, through perhaps a group of existences, you will find yourself battling against ideas of good and evil, running about in a circle of confusion, doubt, and anxiety.

Your friends and acquaintances will be concerned with the same problems, for you will draw to yourself those with the same concerns. I am telling you again, therefore, that many of your ideas of good and evil are highly distortive, and shadow all understanding you have of the nature of reality.

If you form a guilt in your mind, then it is a reality for you, and you must work it out. But many of you form guilts for which there is no adequate cause, and you saddle yourselves with these guilts without reason. In your dimension of activity there appear to be a wild assortment of evils. Let me tell you that he who hates an evil merely creates another one.

(9:45.) Now: From within your point of reference it is often difficult for you to perceive that all events work toward creativity, or to trust in the spontaneous creativity of your own natures. Within your system, to kill is obviously a moral crime, but to kill another in punishment only compounds the original error. Someone very well known who established a church — if you will, a civilization — once said, "Turn the other cheek if you are attacked." The original meaning of that remark, however, should be understood. You should turn the other cheek because you realize that basically the attacker only attacks himself.

Then you are free, and the reaction is a good one. If you turn the other cheek without this understanding, however, and feel resentful, or if you turn the other cheek out of a feeling of pseudomoral superiority, then the reaction is far from adequate.

Now all of this can be applied to your relationships in your reincarnational existences, and of course it also is highly pertinent to your current daily experience. If you hate another person, that hate may bind you to him through as many lives as you allow the hate to consume you. You draw to yourself in this existence and in all others those qualities upon which you concentrate your attention. If you vividly concern yourself with the injustices you feel have been done you, then you attract more such experience, and if this goes on, then it will be mirrored in your next existence. It is true that in between lives there is "time" for understanding and contemplation.

Those who do not take advantage of such opportunities in this life often do not do so when it is over. Consciousness will expand. It will create. It will turn itself inside out to do so. There is nothing outside of yourself that will force you to understand these issues or face them.

It is useless then to say, "When this life is over I will look back upon my experience and mend my ways." This is like a young man saying, "When I grow old and retire, I will use all those abilities that I am not now developing." You are setting the stage for your "next" life now. The thoughts you think today will in one way or another become the fabric of your next existence. There are no magic words that will make you wise, that will fill you with understanding and compassion, that will expand your consciousness.

(9:58.) Your thoughts and everyday experience contain the answers. Any successes in this life, any abilities, have been worked out through past experience. They are yours by right. You worked to develop them. If you look about you at your relatives, friends, acquaintances, and business associates, you will also see what kind of a person you are, for you are drawn to them as they are drawn to you, through very basic inner similarities.

If you examine your thoughts for five minutes at various times during the day for several times a month, you will indeed receive a correct impression of the kind of life you have so far arranged for yourself in the next existence. If you are not pleased with what you discover, then you had better begin changing the nature of your thoughts and feelings.

As you will see later in this book, you can do so. There is no rule saying that in each life you must meet again those whom you have known before; and yet through the nature of attraction, that is often the case.

You may take your break.

("Thank you." I was kidding.)

(Humorously): I do not keep you busy all the time, because you are such a good friend.

("Thanks a lot."

(10:04. Jane's pace had been good, with few pauses. During break the four

· 172 ·

of us talked about our activities of last Saturday night: After dancing we wound up the evening with hot sausage and pepper sandwiches at Toby's Bar and Grill. Resume at 11:15.)

Now: I can't compete with a sausage sandwich — but then, you do not have a sausage sandwich now. We will continue dictation.

You may be born into your present family for many reasons. You may find after death a much stronger relationship emotionally with a personality from a past life. If you are married, for example, and have no true rapport with your mate, you may instead find a past wife or husband waiting for you.

Oftentimes members of various groups — military groups, church groups, hunting groups, will in another life form family relationships in which they will then work out old problems in new ways. Families must be considered as gestalts of psychic activity; they have a subjective identity, of which no particular member of the group may be aware.

Families have subconscious purposes, though the individual members of the family may pursue these goals without conscious awareness. Such groups are set up ahead of time, so to speak, in between physical existences. Oftentimes four or five individuals will set themselves a given challenge, and assign to the various members different parts to play. Then in a physical existence the roles will be worked out.

The inner self is always aware of the hidden mechanisms of these family gestalts. Those who have been closely bound through emotional ties often prefer to remain in closely tied or loosely tied physical relationships that continue through many lifetimes. New relationships are always encouraged however, for you can have ingrown reincarnational "families." Many of these form physical organizations that are actually manifestations of inner groupings.

I spoke earlier of rigid concepts of right and wrong. There is only one way to avoid this problem. Only true compassion and love will lead to an understanding of the nature of good, and only these qualities will serve to annihilate the erroneous and distortive concepts of evil.

(10:28.) The simple fact is that as long as you believe in the concept of evil, it is a reality in your system, and you will always find it manifested. Your belief in it will, therefore, seem highly justified. If you carry this concept through succeeding generations, through reincarnations, then you add to its reality.

Let me try to throw some light upon what I am trying to tell you. First of all, love always involves freedom. If a man says he loves you and yet denies you your freedom, then you often hate him. Yet because of his words you do not feel justified in the emotion. This sort of emotional tangle itself can lead to continued entanglements through various lives.

If you hate evil, then beware of your conception of the word. Hate is restrictive. It narrows down your perception. It is indeed a dark glass that shadows all of your experience. You will find more and more to hate, and bring the hated elements into your own experience.

Now: If, for example, you hate a parent, then it becomes quite easy to hate any parents, for in their faces you see and project the original offender. In subsequent lives you may also be drawn into a family and find yourself with the same emotions, for the emotions are the problem, and not those elements that seem to bring them about.

If you hate illness you may bring upon yourself a succeeding life of illness, because the hate has drawn it to you. If instead you feel. . . .

(*10:35. Jane, as Seth, broke off. Our cat, Willy, waking up from a snooze, leaped up into her lap. I picked him up, but his claws on Jane's leg brought her out of trance. I put Willy in the closet. Jane sat quietly, then resumed dictation.*)

Now: If you expand your sense of love, of health, and existence, then you are drawn in this life and in others toward those qualities; again, because they are those upon which you concentrate. A generation that hates war (*Jane looked at Carl*) will not bring peace. A generation that loves peace will bring peace.

To die with hatred for any cause or people, or for any reason, is a great disadvantage. You have all kinds of opportunities now to recreate your personal experience in more beneficial ways, and to change your world.

In the next life you will be working with those attitudes that are now yours. If you insist upon harboring hatreds within you now, you are very likely to continue doing so. On the other hand, those sparks of truth, intuition, love, joy, creativity, and accomplishment gained now, will work for you then as they do now.

They are, you see, the only true realities. They are the only real foundations of existence. It is foolish, as Ruburt once said, to hate a storm or shake your fists at it and call it names. You laugh if you think of children or natives in such activities. It is useless to personify a storm and treat it as a demon, focusing upon its destructive elements, or those elements that to you appear destructive.

Change of form is not destructive. The explosive energy of a storm is highly creative. Consciousness is not annihilated. A storm is part of creativity. You view it from your own perspective, and yet one individual will feel within the storm the unending cycle of creativity, and another will personify it as the work of the devil.

Through all your lives you will interpret the reality that you see in your own way, and that way will have its effect upon you, and in turn upon others. The man who literally hates, immediately sets himself up in this fashion: He prejudges the nature of reality according to his own limited understanding.

Now I am emphasizing the issue of hate in this chapter on reincarnation because its results can be so disastrous. A man who hates always believes himself justified. He never hates anything that he believes to be good. He thinks he is being just, therefore, in his hatred, but the hatred itself forms a very strong claim that will follow him throughout his lives, until he learns that only the hatred itself is the destroyer.

Now you may take your break. Begin your chatter and I will listen.
("Okay.")

Are you following me in this material?
("Sure. Why do you ask?")

(Humorously, leaning forward): You are my first reader.

(10:51. Break came, to the laughter of Sue and Carl. Jane's pace had been fast most of the time. Resume at 11:08 in the same manner.)

Now: Far be it from me to interrupt your edifying conversation. Remember what you concentrate upon, and we will leave it at that. Now we will resume dictation.

I would like to make it clear that there is nothing to be gained, either, by hating hatred. You fall into the same trap.

What is needed is a basic trust in the nature of vitality, and faith that all elements of experience are used for a greater good, whether or not you can perceive the way in which "evil" is transmuted into creativity. What you love will also be a part of your experience in this life and others.

The most important idea to be remembered is that no one thrusts the experience of any given lifetime upon you. It is formed faithfully according to your own emotions and beliefs. *(As Seth, Jane delivered this material vigorously, her pace rapid.)* The great power and energy of love and creativity is apparent in the mere fact of your existence. This is the truth so often forgotten — that [the combination of] consciousness and existence continues and absorbs those elements that seem to you so destructive.

(Pause at 11:13.) Hate is powerful if you believe in it, and yet though you hate life, you will continue to exist. You have made appointments, each of you, that you have forgotten. They were signed, so to speak, before you were born in this existence. In many cases the friends that you make were close to you long before you met them in this present life.

This does not mean that every one in your present acquaintance-ship has been known to you, and it certainly does not imply a boring record played over and over again, for each encounter is a new one in its own way. Remembering what I said about families, realize also that towns and villages may also be composed of the past inhabitants of other such towns and villages, transposed with new experiences and backgrounds, as the group tries different experiments.

Now sometimes, there are also such variations in that the inhabitants of a particular town now may be the reborn inhabitants of those who lived, say, in 1632 in a small Irish village. They may be transposed to a town in Idaho.

Some who wanted to travel from the Old World to the New, may be reborn in the new one. You must remember also that abilities from past lives are at your disposal for your present use. You reap your own rewards. Information concerning these is often given to you in the sleep state, and there is a kind of gestalt type of dream, a root dream, by which those who have known each other in past lives now communicate.

In such dreams, general mass-information is given, that the individuals then use as they desire. Overall plans for development are made, as the group members, say, of a town decide upon its destiny. Some individuals always choose to be born as a part of some group — reborn, in other words, with past contemporaries, while others, disdaining such endeavors, return in much more isolated positions.

(11:25.) This is a matter of psychological feeling. Some individuals

are more at ease, more assured, and more capable working with others in this case. You could consider an analogy in which John Doe follows his kindergarten class all the way through high school. In a reincarnational situation, he would always choose to return with associates. Others, however, would rather skip from school to school, appearing alone, relatively speaking, with greater freedom, more challenge, but without the comforting framework of security chosen by the others.

In each case the individual is the judge, not only of each succeeding life, its time, environment, and historical date, but also of its overall character and methods of accomplishment. There are as many different ways to reincarnate, therefore, as there are inner selves, and each inner self will choose its own characteristic methods.

I will end our session now that the chapter is begun. I have the feeling that we will have some extra sessions in any case. I wish my friends over here a hearty good evening; and when you both travel next *(Seth has been helping Carl and Sue with astral travel),* I hope you bring your memories along with you — and *(to me)* you too.

("Okay. Good evening, Seth, and thank you."

(11:34. Jane's trance had been deep, her eyes very wide and dark. "Seth is still around," she told us.

(A spirited conversation sprang up now between the four of us. Sue brought up the question of overpopulation. How can this be, she wondered: If a certain number of entities were responsible for the creation of our physical world, where do the extra human beings come from? I told her that, according to Seth, each personality making up an entity could manifest itself physically as often as it chose to. Seth then interrupted us at 11:40.)

Now: Give me a moment here. *(Pause.)* First of all, as a species, in the context of normal usage, you have considered yourselves as apart from the rest of nature and consciousness.

Your own survival as a species was your main concern. You considered other species only in the light of their use to you. You did not have any true conception of the great sacredness of all consciousness, nor of your relationship within it. You were losing your grasp of that great truth.

In the present circumstances you are carrying that idea forward — of species survival regardless of the consequences, the idea of changing the environment to suit your own purposes; and this has led you to a disregard of spiritual truths.

In physical reality, therefore, you are seeing the results. Now those personalities who are returning are doing so for various reasons. Some of them are drawn to physical life again because of these attitudes. They are those who in the past, in your terms, strove for physical existence without consideration for the rights of other species. They are driven to return because of their own desires.

The species must learn the value of the individual man. The species is also learning its dependence upon other species, and beginning to comprehend its part in the whole framework in physical reality.

Now: Some individuals are being reborn at this time simply to help you understand. They are forcing the issue, and forcing the crisis, for you still have time to change your ways. You are working on two main problems, but both involve the sacredness of the individual, and the individual's relationship with others and with all physically oriented consciousness.

The problem of war will sooner or later teach you that when you kill another man, basically you will end up killing yourself. The overpopulation problem will teach you that if you do not have a loving concern for the environment in which you dwell, it will no longer sustain you — you will not be worthy of it. You will not be destroying the planet, you see. You will not be destroying the birds or the flowers, or the grain or the animals. You will not be worthy of them, and they will be destroying you.

You have set up the problem for yourselves within the framework of your reference. You will not understand your part within the framework of nature until you actually see yourselves in danger of tearing it apart. You will not destroy consciousness. You will not annihilate the consciousness of even one leaf, but in your context, if the problem were not solved, these would fade from your experience.

The crisis is a kind of therapy, however. It is a teaching method that you have set up for yourselves because you need it. And you need it now, before your species embarks upon journeys to other physical realities. You must learn your lessons now in your own backyard before you travel to other worlds. So you have brought this upon yourself for that purpose and you will learn. *(End session at 11:55 P.M.)*

Now, good evening.

("Good evening, Seth.")

We will resume dictation.

In each life you are meant to check the exterior environment in order to learn your inner condition. The outer is a reflection of the inner.

You are meant to understand the nature of your inner self, and to manifest it outward. As this is done, the exterior circumstances should change for the better as the inner self becomes more aware of its own nature and capabilities. Theoretically, then, in each life you would become stronger, healthier, wealthier, and wiser, but it does not work that way, for many reasons. As mentioned earlier, many personalities adopt different kinds of experiences, focusing upon development in certain specific areas, and ignoring others perhaps for a series of lives.

No consciousness has the same experiences or interprets them the same, and so each individual utilizes reincarnational opportunities in his own way. Sex changes, for example, are necessary. Some individuals alternate their sex in each (succeeding) life. Others have a series of female lives and then a series of male lives, or vice versa, but the entire reincarnational framework must involve both sexual experiences.

Abilities cannot be developed following a one-sex line. There must be experiences in motherhood and fatherhood. When you get to the point that you realize you are forming your day-to-day existence and the life that you know, then you can begin to alter your own mental and psychic patterns, and therefore change your daily environment.

(9:25.) This realization, however, should go hand in hand with a deep intuitional knowledge of the capabilities of the inner self. These two factors together can release you from any difficulties that have arisen in past lives. The entire structure of your existence will begin to change with these realizations, and an acceleration of spiritual and psychic growth will develop.

There is an inner logic to your current relationships, attitudes, and experiences. If in one life, for example, you hated women, you may very well be a woman in the next life. Only in this way, you see, would you be able to relate to the experience of womanhood, and then as a woman face those attitudes that you yourself had against women in the past.

If you had no sympathy for the sick, you may then be born with a serious disease, again now self-chosen, and find yourself encountering those attitudes that once were your own. Such an existence would usually also include other issues, however. No existence is chosen for one reason only, but would also serve many other psychological experiences.

A chronically ill existence, for example, might also be a measure of discipline, enabling you to use deeper abilities that you ignored in a life of good health. The perfectly happy life for example, on the surface, may appear splendid, but it may also be basically shallow and do little to develop the personality.

The truly happy existence, however, is a deeply satisfying one that would include spontaneous wisdom and spiritual joy. I am not saying, in other words, that suffering necessarily leads to spiritual fulfillment, nor that all illness is accepted or chosen for such a purpose, for this is not the case.

(9:35.) Illness is often the result of ignorance and lazy mental habits. Such a discipline may be adopted however by certain personalities who must take strong measures with themselves because of other characteristics. There is an overall pattern to relationships within lives, and yet this does not mean that you travel through various existences with the same limited and familiar number of friends and acquaintances, merely altered like actors with a change of face or costume.

Groups of individuals come together in various lives for certain purposes, separate, and may or may not come together again in a different time or place. Again, however, there is no rigid rule. Some families are literally reincarnations of their ancestors, but this is not the general case by any means. Deep relationships will continue in one way or another. Others will simply disappear.

The point I want to make is that the opportunity for development and knowledge is as present at this moment, in this life, as it will ever be. If you ignore day-by-day opportunities for development now, no one can force you to accept and utilize greater abilities after death, or between lives. The teachers are there in after-death experience, but there are also teachers here in your existence now.

Some families come together in a particular life not because of great attraction or love in a past existence, but for the opposite reason. Families may be composed, then, of individuals who disliked each other in the past and come together in a close relationship where they are to work together toward a common goal, learn to understand each other better, and work out problems in a different kind of context.

Jointly, each generation has its own purpose. It is this — to perfect inner knowledge, and to materialize it as faithfully as possible outward into the world. The changing physical scene throughout the centuries, as you know them, represents the inner images that have flickered through the minds of the individuals who lived within the world through the various ages.

Now you may take your break.

(*9:48. Jane's delivery had been fast but even so, she said, her trance hadn't been as deep as it usually is. She had been bothered by the sounds of people walking back and forth in the hallway outside our apartment. Ordinarily she wouldn't have noticed anything like this. Resume at 10:05.*)

Now: It is not necessary that you learn about your own past lives, though it may be helpful if you understand that you chose the circumstances of your birth this time.

If you examine your own life now carefully, the challenges that you have set for yourself will become apparent. This is not easy to do, but it is within the grasp of each individual. If you release yourself from hatred, then you automatically release yourself from any such relationships in the future — or any experiences that are based upon hatred.

Knowing your reincarnational background, but not knowing the true nature of your present self, is useless. You cannot justify or rationalize present circumstances by saying, "This is because of something I did in a past life," for within yourself now is the ability to change negative influences. You may have brought negative influences into your life for a given reason, but the reason always has to do with understanding, and understanding removes those influences.

You cannot say, "The poor are poor simply because they chose poverty, and therefore there is no need for me to help them." This attitude can easily draw poverty to you in the next experience.

(*10:13. Once again Jane's trance was broken when our cat, Willy, jumped up into her lap. Once more I put him in the closet while Jane gave me an "oh, well" look. Actually Willy doesn't interrupt us very often; but now I made a mental note that after this we'd go back to our old routine, and put him in another room before session time. Willy used to react strongly to these sessions when they began in 1963. Resume at 10:15.)*

Each individual is not at the same level of achievement even at the end of the reincarnational cycle. Some possess certain qualities that do not find a counterpart within human experience. Physical existence itself has a different effect upon various individuals. Some find it an excellent medium of expression and development. They are suited to it. They have the knack for expressing themselves in physical ways and objectifying inner feelings faithfully. Others find this difficult, and yet these same individuals may do much better in other levels of reality.

There are "hardy souls" who thrive in physical reality, and who may have difficulties acclimating to other nonphysical areas of activity. In all of these areas, however, deep spiritual or emotional contexts are never negated. Very close friends from past lives, who are in a position to do so, often communicate with you when you are in the dream state, and the relationships are continued though you do not realize it consciously.

On an unconscious basis, you are aware of the birth into physical life of someone you have known in the past. The strangers that you meet in your dreams are often, of course, people now alive — contemporaries — that you have also known in past lives.

There are also passing relationships, contacts made and then dropped. A mate from any given life, for example, may or may not represent someone with whom you have a deep abiding tie, and again you may marry someone because of highly ambiguous feelings from a past life, and choose a married relationship that is not based upon love, though love may emerge.

Twins, incidentally, almost always involve very deep, abiding psychic relationships of a strong, sometimes obsessive nature. I am speaking now of identical twins.

I suggest your break.

(10:29. This evidently wasn't our night. Again, Jane said upon coming out of trance, she had been aware of the footsteps of people passing back and forth

· 182 ·

in the hall outside our living room door. I had been hoping her trance was deeper this time. Resume at 10:37.)

Reincarnational goals also vary greatly. I want to stress that reincarnation is a tool used by personalities. They each use it in their own way. Some enjoy female existences, or have greater fondness for male lives. While both must be encountered, there is a great range of choice and activity. Some personalities will have difficulties along certain lines, and develop with relative ease in other ways.

Predetermination is never involved, for the challenge and circumstances are chosen. Some problems may be put off, for example, for several existences. Some personalities want to solve their strongest problems and get them over with, perhaps in a series of rather trying existences and exaggerated circumstances.

Others of a more placid nature will take their problems one at a time. Rest periods may also be taken, and they are highly therapeutic. For example, an excellent, satisfying life with a minimum of problems may be chosen either as a prelude to a life of concentrated challenge or as a self-adopted reward for a previous difficult life. Those that thoroughly enjoy the physical medium, without being obsessed by it, however, do very well indeed. The "laws" of reincarnation are adapted by the individual personalities to suit themselves.

I suggest that we end our session unless you have questions.

("No.")

My heartiest regards.

("Good night, Seth."

(10:47 P.M. At last, Jane's trance had improved. "I was just beginning to feel that I was getting into a deeper state," she said. "At least I wasn't aware of anything — but now it's all over. . . .")

CHAPTER 13

Reincarnation, Dreams, and the Hidden Male and Female Within the Self

SESSION 555, OCTOBER 21, 1970, 9:30 P.M. WEDNESDAY

(*S*ince September 30 Seth has held two ESP class sessions; held a session for our friend John Barclay, who is moving to Nevada; held two sessions concerning the work Jane and I are embarking upon because of this material; and spoken through Jane upon television once more — this time during our return visit to a Washington, D.C. station.*

(Early this month Jane and I bought an anthology containing a long section by Carl Jung, the Swiss psychoanalyst who died in 1961. Jane hadn't finished reading this part of the book when Seth suggested, in the 554th session for October 19, that she lay the book aside: "Let Jung go for now." He did not elaborate. This wasn't Jane's first contact with the writings of Jung by any means.

(It's interesting to note, however, the way in which Seth "takes off" from material like Jung's, developing it to include his own ideas and interpretations, as he does in this chapter.

(It had been raining all day. Jane had been to the chiropractor today and was very relaxed — so relaxed that I asked her if she felt like having a session. She wanted to, she said. Her eyes were half open, her voice very quiet, almost conversational, as the session began.)

Good evening.

("Good evening, Seth.")

Now: We will begin dictation.

(I thought I would get Seth's reaction to Jane's physical state. "How do you feel?")

I feel fine. One point to our friend. It is better if he does not go to the chiropractor when it is raining.

("Why is that?")

Partially because of the muscular reaction mentioned by the chiropractor, and partially because the body's healing mechanisms operate more effectively in clear weather. He will snap back more quickly after a treatment. There is one good benefit however: He rested the full amount specified *(one hour)* this time because he felt it necessary.

("Would you rather pass up the session tonight?")

We are fine for a session. It will be a short one considering, but a good one. I would like to elaborate, however, on these statements.

Such a *(chiropractic)* treatment causes, of course, a manipulation of the atomic structure that composes the vertebrae. The electrical reactions are different according to the weather and atmospheric conditions. In rainy weather, there is an added electrical resistance within the atomic structures themselves — a sort of delayed reaction, hardly perceptible in physical terms — a delayed period before the vertebrae come to rest again, so to speak, in the desired position.

While they take the desired position, there is still continued activity. In clear weather there is much less of a delayed reaction, and the activated, stirred-up atoms come more quickly to rest.

Now: Our next chapter will be called: "Reincarnation, Dreams, and the Hidden Male and Female Within the Self."

(By now Jane's pace had quickened a good deal.)

As I mentioned earlier, each person lives both male and female lives. As a rule, conscious memory of these is not retained. To prevent an overidentification of the individual with his present sex, within the male there resides an inner personification of femaleness. This personification of femaleness in the male is the true meaning of what Jung called the "anima."

The anima in the male is, therefore, the psychic memory and identification of all the previous female existences in which the inner self has been involved. It contains within it the knowledge of the present male's past female histories, and the intuitive understanding of all the female qualities with which the personality is innately endowed.

The anima, therefore, is an important safeguard, preventing the male from over-identifying with whatever cultural male characteristics have been imposed upon him through present background, environment, and education. The anima serves not only as a personal but as a mass-civilizing influence, mellowing strongly aggressive tendencies and serving also as a bridge both in communicating with women in a family relationship, and in communication also as it is applied through the arts and verbalization.

The male will often dream of himself, therefore, as a female. The particular way in which he does so, can tell him much about his own reincarnational background in which he operated as a female. Maleness and femaleness are obviously not opposites, but merging tendencies. The priestess, the mother, the young witch, the wife, and the old wise woman — these general types are archetypes, simply because they are "root elements" representing, symbolically, the various kinds of so-called female qualities and the various kinds of female lives that have been lived by males.

They have also been lived by females, of course. However, the women do not need to be reminded of their femaleness, but again, so that they do not overidentify with their present sex, there is what Jung called the "animus," or the hidden male within the woman.

Again, however, this represents the male lives with which the self has been involved — the young boy, the priest, the aggressive "jungle man," and the wise old man. These are types, representing generally and symbolically past male lives lived by present women. Women, therefore, can learn much about their reincarnational past as men, through studying those dreams in which these types appear, or in which they themselves appear as men.

Through the anima and the animus, so-called, present personalities are able to draw upon the knowledge and intuitions and background that was derived from past existences as the opposite sex. On some occasions, for example, the woman may go overboard and exaggerate female characteristics, in which case the animus or male within comes to her aid, bringing through dream experiences an onrush of knowledge that will result in compensating malelike reactions.

The same applies to a male when he over-identifies with what he believes to be male characteristics, for whatever reason. The anima or woman within will rouse him to make compensating actions, causing an upsurge of intuitive abilities, bringing a creative element to offset aggressiveness.

Ideally, left alone, these operations would result in a balance individually and *en masse*, where aggressiveness was always used creatively, as indeed it can and should be.

You may take your break.

(10:02. "Very good," I said to Jane as she came out of trance. "Yes," she said, "I could tell it was great, 'cause he's got a lot more to say." Yet she looked so limp and heavy-eyed, so bleary and yet relaxed, that I wondered if she could stay awake to continue. Resume in the same manner at 10:21.)

Now: The animus and the anima are, of course, highly charged psychically, but the origin of this psychic charge and the inner fascination are the result of a quite legitimate inner identification with these personified other-sex characteristics.

(Pace slower.) They not only have a reality in the psyche, however, but they are imbedded in genetically codified data by the inner self — a genetic memory of past psychic events — transposed into the genetic memory of the very cells that compose the body.

Each inner self, adopting a new body, imposes upon it and upon its entire genetic makeup, memory of the past physical forms in which it has been involved. Now the present characteristics usually overshadow the past ones. They are dominant, but the other characteristics are latent and present, built into the pattern. The physical pattern of the present body, therefore, is a genetic memory of the self's past physical forms, and of their strengths and weaknesses. *(10:29. Jane rubbed her eyes; she was speaking slowly, with many pauses.)*

I will try to put this as simply as possible. There are presently invisible layers within the body, the topmost layer that you see representing, of course, the present physical form. But enmeshed within this there are what amount to invisible layers, "shadow," latent layers that represent previous physical images that have belonged to the personality.

They are kept in abeyance, so to speak. They are connected electromagnetically to the atomic structure of the present body. To your way of thinking, they would be unfocused. They are a part of your psychic heritage, however. Often you can call up a past strength of a previous body, to help compensate for a present weakness. The body does not only carry memory biologically of its own past condition in this life therefore, but indelibly with it, even physically, are the memories of the other bodies that the personality has formed in previous reincarnations.

The anima and the animus are closely connected with these interior body images. These body images are highly charged psychically, and also appear in the dream state. They operate as compensations and reminders to prevent you from over-identifying yourself with your present physical body.

They are, of course, both male and female. When you are ill, in the dream state you often have experiences in which you seem to be someone else with an entirely healthy body. Often such a dream is therapeutic. An "older" reincarnational body has come to your aid, from which you draw strength through the memory of its health.

(10:44.) We will end the session, continuing our material next time, unless you have questions.

("No.")

My heartiest regards to you both then, and a fond good evening.

("Good evening, Seth. Thank you very much.")

(10:45. Once out of trance, Jane said she now felt as good or better than she had before the session began. She was surprised at the sudden ending. She had felt "really passive" during the session, and I had listened to her pace grow slower and slower as the session progressed.)

SESSION 556, OCTOBER 26, 1970, 9:08 P.M. MONDAY

Good evening.

("Good evening, Seth.")

Now: We will resume dictation.

Reincarnational experiences are a part of the framework of the self, a facet of the multidimensional reality of the living psyche. These experiences will, therefore, be reflected not only in the dream state, but in other layers of activity.

The fabric of the present self is interwoven with these reincarnational "pasts," and from them the present self draws unconsciously from its own bank of personality characteristics, activities, and insights. Often past-life memories come to the surface but are not recognized as such, since they appear in fantasy form, or are projected into art creations.

Many writers of historical pieces, for example, are writing out of direct experience with those times. Such instances represent an excellent working rapport between the present self and the unconscious, which brings these memories to the surface in such a way that current life is enriched. More often than not, true awareness of the situation often becomes almost conscious, and just beneath awareness the individual knows the source of his authentic material.

In dreams this reincarnational material is likewise cast into a dramatic mold very frequently. Beneath all this, the anima and the animus work together, again not opposites but blending characteristics. Together, of course, they represent the fount of creativity, psychically as well as physically.

The anima represents the necessary initial "inwardness," the brooding, caring, intuitive, inside-turning characteristics, the inward focusing from which creativity comes.

The word "passive" is a poor one to describe the characteristics of the anima, in that it suggests a lack of motion, and this is hardly the case. It is true that the anima allows itself to be acted upon, but the motive behind this is the desire and the necessity to tune into other forces that are supremely powerful. The desire to be swept along, therefore, is as strong with the anima as the opposite desire for rest. The characteristics of the animus provide the aggressive thrust that returns the personality back outward into physical activities, triumphantly holding the products of creativity that the anima characteristics have secured.

The whole self is obviously the sum of these characteristics, and more. After the final incarnation, the physical, sexual type of creativity is simply no longer needed. You do not need to reproduce physically, in other words. In simple terms the whole self contains male and female characteristics, finely tuned together, blended so that true identity can then arise — for it cannot, when one group of characteristics must be emphasized over the other group, as it must be during your present physical existence.

(9:30.) There are many reasons why the separation has been adopted within your dimension. The reasons have to do with the particular way in which mankind has chosen to evolve and use his abilities; and I will have more to say regarding this point, but it does not belong in this chapter.

The projection of the man's anima, or hidden female self, upon

[his] relations is quite natural, and allows him not only to understand them better but to relate with the other female existences of his own. The same is true of the woman's projection of the animus upon male relatives and friends. The reality of the anima and the animus is far deeper then than Jung supposed. Symbolically speaking, the two together represent the whole self with its diverse abilities, desires, and characteristics.

Together they act as a built-in, unconscious stabilizing factor, operating behind the faces of your civilization not only individually but culturally.

Personality as you know it, cannot be understood unless the true meaning of the anima and the animus is taken into consideration. The reincarnational pattern is generally speaking an open one, in that within it there is room for diversity. Each whole self has its own individual characteristics. It can live its lives as it sees fit within the guidelines. There may be a series of male or female existences, unbroken. Such a choice has some drawbacks.

There are, however, no rules dictating the sexual development in varying incarnations, except that experience with both sexes must be taken on, and the various characteristics developed. This does not mean that an equal number of male and female lives must be lived. Some, for example, find it far easier to develop as one sex or the other, and will need more opportunities for experience as the sex with which they experience difficulty.

The animus and the anima become even more important in these instances when a series of one-sex lives are chosen. The original pattern for the animus and anima comes from the whole self before reincarnations. The animus and the anima are born into the individual with the first physical life, and serve as an inner pattern, reminding the personality of its basic unity. Here is another reason for the strong psychic charge behind these symbols and the godlike quality that they can transmit and project.

(9:48.) The male yearns toward the anima because it represents to the deep unconscious those other characteristics of the whole self that, on the one hand, lie latent, and that, on the other hand, struggle for release. The tension between the two leads him to temper aggressiveness with creativity, or to use aggressiveness creatively.

Now there are deep correlations between these symbols and the struggle in which mankind is involved. Your consciousness as you know it, your particular present kind of consciousness, is a statement of awareness brought about by a particular kind of tension, a specific kind of focus arising from the true unconscious of the whole self.

(Jane, speaking as Seth, hadn't taken a break since the session began at 9:08. It was now 9:54.)

I know you are tired.

("I'm okay.")

The true unconscious is not unconscious. Instead, it is so profoundly and unutteringly conscious that it bubbles over. The life that you know is simply one of the many areas in which it is conscious. In each facet of its consciousness, literally tremendous power and balance must be maintained to hold aloft this particular consciousness-experience from all others.

(9:58.) Your reality exists in a particular area of activity in which aggressive qualities, thrusting-outward characteristics, are supremely necessary to prevent a falling back into the infinite possibilities from which you have only lately emerged. Yet from this unconscious bed of possibilities you derive your strength, your creativity, and the fragile yet powerful kind of individual consciousness that is your own.

The two-sex division was adopted, separating and balancing these most necessary but seemingly opposing tendencies. Only beginning consciousness needs these kind of controls. The anima and the animus, therefore, are embedded deeply with their necessary complementary but apparently opposed tendencies, and they are highly important in maintaining the very nature of your human consciousness.

Rest a moment.

(10:03. Jane, still in trance, sat quietly for a short time. I rested my writing hand. Resume at 10:04.)

There is also a natural tension, then, between sexes that is based on far deeper causes than physical ones. The tension results from the nature of your consciousness that arises from the anima, but depends for its continuation upon the "aggressiveness" of the animus. I have to some extent explained the fascination that one has for the other, as resulting from the inner knowledge of the whole self, that strives to attain true identity as it struggles to combine and fulfill the seemingly opposite tendencies that are a part of it.

At the end of the reincarnational cycle, the whole self is far more developed than it was before. It has realized and experienced itself in a dimension of reality unknown to it earlier, and in doing so, has of course increased its being. It is not a matter, then, of a whole self splitting in half, and then simply returning to itself.

(Long pause at 10:12.) Now there are many matters concerning the nature of conception that should be discussed here. Again, however, there is leeway and many variations. Usually between lives you choose ahead of time your children, and they choose you as parents.

(10:15.) If you are to be born as a male, then the mother serves as a stimulus to activate the symbol of the anima in you, so that the pattern of your own female lives becomes a portion of your next existence. Your mother, if you have known her in the past, will find at your birth an upsurge of dreams involving other existences in which the two of you were together.

These may not even be recorded consciously, but in many cases they are, and are then forgotten. Her own past male lives will help her relate to you as her son. In some cases new mothers may feel highly aggressive and nervous. These feelings are sometimes due to the fact that the male son causes an activation of the animus in her, with a resulting charge of aggressive feelings.

You may take your break. I wanted to get all of that through while we were doing so well.

("I think it's very interesting."

(10:22. "Wow — am I out . . . I can't get my eyes open," Jane said, trying to do just that. After several futile attempts she slumped back in her rocker. I thought she was close to a sleep state. I called her several times, then suggested she get up and exercise when she finally began to look around. She put her glasses back on, got up, and began to walk about.

(Jane's pace had been quite rapid except where noted. She had but a vague general idea of the material. I told her I thought it was excellent, all of it, with the last few pages even better.

(It turned out that break marked the end of material for Seth's book tonight. Seth then gave four pages of material for me. Here too Jane's pace was good. The session produced much more data than usual. It ended at 11:11 P.M. — with a good day's work done.)

SESSION 557, OCTOBER 28, 1970,
9:19 P.M. WEDNESDAY

(I had two questions which I explained to Jane, without necessarily expect-ing Seth to go into them tonight.

(1. In the 556th session, Seth said that many writers of historical pieces are writing out of direct past-life experience. My question concerned a hypothetical experiment in which, say, a hundred such writers would be hypnotized without being told what the purpose of the experiment was; once under, they would be queried about past-life memories. I wondered what percentage of them would recall any, and if such a test might furnish good evidence for reincarnation.

(2. What procedures are available to the nonphysical personality when it decides to incarnate physically for the first time? What is the initial life like? Is it apt to be savage, or more "cultivated" to some degree? Or is any sort of pre-determined pattern involved at all?

(Since I've been curious about these questions for some time, I thought the readers of Seth's book might be also. As things develop, however, Seth doesn't pay any attention to the first question now, and takes off from the second one in a most interesting way.

(Just before the session tonight I wondered aloud what the present Chapter Thirteen would have been like if Jane hadn't begun to read, early this month, the anthology containing the long section by Carl Jung, the Swiss psychoanalyst. As I mentioned, Seth suggested Jane lay the book aside on October 19, before she had time to finish it. See the notes at the beginning of the 555th session for Octo-ber 21. Neither of us has looked at the book since.

(An infusion from Jung cropped up in this chapter, of course — although handled in Seth's own way. But then such events in our own lives have influ-enced every other chapter in the book, too. The particular form of a chapter could be affected to some degree by just when the sessions for it were held, as well as by its intrinsic subject matter. Even interruptions, then, would play their part. . . .)

Good evening.

("Good evening, Seth.")

(Pleased and amused): Now I am glad that you approve of my book.

("I think it's great.")

There is much more in store.

("Very good.")

Now this is a living endeavor, and therefore we take advantage of

· 193 ·

those happenings in your own lives, and it was I myself who prompted Ruburt to pick up the book *(containing Jung)* in the first place.

("I hadn't thought of that." Nor, I was sure, had Jane.)

Then, I wanted him to put it aside for another time, after he had read so far. *(Pause.)* We will resume dictation.

(At this point, however, Seth requested that I lay my notebook aside for a bit, saying he regretted that I was kept so busy writing during sessions. We had a brief chat, a very pleasant exchange. Jane's eyes were wide and dark, her delivery lively; it was easy to sense the immediacy of Seth's presence. The interlude lasted less than a minute. Resume dictation at 9:20.)

The atoms that compose the fetus have their own kind of consciousness. The volatile awareness-consciousnesses that exist independently of matter, form matter according to their ability and degree. The fetus, therefore, has its own consciousness, the simple component consciousness made up of the atoms that compose it. This exists before any reincarnating personality enters it. The consciousness of matter is present in any matter — a fetus, a rock, a blade of grass, a nail.

The reincarnating personality enters the new fetus according to its own inclinations, desires, and characteristics, with some built-in safeguards. However there is no rule, then, saying that the reincarnating personality must take over the new form prepared for it either at the point of conception, in the very earliest months of the fetus's growth, or even at the point of birth.

The process is gradual, individual and determined by experience in other lives. It is particularly dependent upon emotional characteristics — not necessarily of the last incarnated self, but the emotional tensions present as a result of a group of past existences.

(Pause at 9:32.) Various methods of entry are adopted. If there is a strong relationship between the parents and the child-to-be, then the personality may enter at the point of conception if he is extremely anxious to rejoin them. Even here, however, large portions of self-awareness continue to operate in the between-life dimension.

In the beginning, the womb state under these conditions is a dreamlike one, with the personality still focused mainly in the between-life existence. Gradually the situation reverses, until it becomes more difficult to retain clear concentration in the between-life situation.

In these circumstances, when the personality attaches itself at conception, there is almost without exception strong past-life connections between parents and child, or there is an unceasing and almost obsessional desire to return to the earthly situation — either for a specific purpose, or because the reincarnating personality is presently obsessed with earthly existence. This is not necessarily detrimental. The personality can simply realize that it takes to physical experience well, is presently earth-oriented, and finds earthly atmosphere a rich dimension for the growth of its own abilities.

Some personalities are drawn to enter at conception as a result of seemingly less worthy motives — greed, for example, or an obsessional desire that is partially composed of unresolved problems. Other personalities who never completely take to earthly existence may hold off full entry for some time, and even then always remain at a certain distance from the body. At the other end of the scale, before death the same applies, where some individuals remove their focus from physical life, leaving the body consciousness alone. Others stay with the body until the last moment. In the early days of infancy, there is not a steady focus of the personality in the body in any case.

Take your break and we will continue.

(9:47 to 10:00.)

Now: In all cases the decisions have been made ahead of time, as I told you. The reincarnating personality is aware, therefore, when the conception for which it has been waiting takes place. And while it may or may not choose to enter at that point, it is drawn irresistibly to that time and point in space and flesh.

On occasion, long before conception takes place, the personality who will end up as the future child will visit that environment of both parents-to-be, drawn again. This is quite natural.

Between lives an individual may see flashes of the future existence, not necessarily of particular events, but experience the essence of the new relationship and in expectation remind himself of the challenge he has set. In these terms, the ghosts of the future are as real in your homes as the ghosts of the past.

You do not have completely empty shells of matter about to be filled, in that the new personality hovers in and about, particularly after conception and with greater frequency and intensity thereafter. The shock of birth has several consequences, however, that usually draw the personality full blast, so to speak, into physical reality. Before this, the conditions are fairly uniform. The body consciousness is nurtured almost automatically, reacting strongly but under highly controlled conditions.

At birth, all of this is suddenly over, and [new] stimuli [are] introduced with a rapidity that the body consciousness has never to that point experienced.

(10:10.) It greatly needs a stabilizing factor. Previously the body consciousness has been enriched and supported by deep biological and telepathic identification with the mother. The communication of the living cells is far more profound than you imagine. The identification is almost complete before birth as far as body consciousness alone is concerned.

Until the new personality enters, the fetus regards itself as a part of the organism of the mother. This support is suddenly denied at birth. If the new personality has not entered earlier to any full extent, it usually does so at birth, in order to stabilize the new organism. It comforts the new organism, in other words. The new personality, therefore, will experience birth to varying degrees according to when it has entered this dimension.

When it enters at the point of birth, it is fairly independent, not yet identified with the form it has entered, and acting in a supportive role. If the personality entered at conception or sometime before birth, then it has to some extent identified with the body consciousness, with the fetus. It has already begun to direct perception — though perception has begun whether or not it is so directed — and it will experience the shock of birth in immediate, direct terms.

(10:19.) There will be no distance between the personality and the experience of birth, then. The newly entered personality, as a consciousness, flickers, in that there is a while before stabilization takes place. When the child, particularly the young child, is sleeping, for example, the personality often simply vacates the body. Gradually the identification with the between-life situation dwindles until nearly full focus resides in the physical body.

There are obviously those who identify with the body far more completely than others. Generally speaking, there is an optimum point of focus in physical reality, a period of intensification that has nothing to do with duration. It can last for a week or thirty years, and from then onward it begins to dwindle, and imperceptibly begins to shift to other layers of reality.

Now. A crisis, particularly in very early or very late life, may so shatter the personality's identification with the body that he vacates it temporarily. He may do one of many things. He may leave so completely that the body goes into coma, if the body consciousness has also suffered shock. If the shock is psychological and the body consciousness is still operating more or less normally, then he may revert to an earlier reincarnational personality.

In such a case, this is simply a regression that often passes. Here we become concerned again with the animus and the anima. If a personality believes that it is doing a poor job in a male life, it may activate the anima's qualities, taking on the characteristics of a past female existence in which it handled itself well. Reversing the picture, the same can happen to a woman.

(10:30.) On the other hand, if the personality finds that it has so over-identified with its present sex that its individuality is deeply threatened, then it may also bring to the fore the opposite picture, going so far as to identify again with a past personality of the opposite sex.

The hold of the personality over the body is tenuous in the early years, and grows stronger. The personality, for its own reasons, may decide upon choosing a body that is not aesthetically pleasing. He may never relate to it, and while the existence will serve what purposes he had in mind, there will always be a basic sensed distance between the body and the personality within it.

Those mentioned earlier who enter at the point of conception are usually highly anxious for physical existence. They will, therefore, be more fully developed and show their individual characteristics very early. They seize upon the new body and already mold it. The control over matter is vigorous, and they usually stay within the body, dying either in accidents where death is immediate or in sleep or with a disease that strikes quickly. They are manipulators of matter as a rule.

(10:40.) They are emotional. They work out their problems in immediate, sometimes impatient, tangible ways. They work well with earth materials, and translate their ideas with great force into physical terms. They make cities, monuments. They are architects. They are concerned with forming matter and molding it to their desire.

As a rule, now, those who do not enter your plane of existence until the point of birth are less able manipulators in those particular terms. They are the mean, if such a term can be used, the mean or average.

Now there are some who resist the new existence, even though they chose it, as long as possible. To some extent they must be present at birth, but they can still escape any full identification with the born infant. They hover within and about the form, but half reluctantly. There are many reasons for such behavior. Some personalities simply prefer in-between-life existence and are much more concerned with the theoretical solving of problems than the practical application necessarily involved. Others have discovered that physical existence does not meet their needs as well as they thought it would, and they will progress much better in other fields of reality and existence.

(10:48.) Because of their own characteristics, however, some prefer to set up a certain distance between themselves and their physical existences. They are much more concerned with symbols. They look upon earthly life as highly experimental. They approach it almost with a jaundiced eye, so to speak. They are not interested so much in manipulating matter as they are curious as to the ways in which ideas appear within matter.

Again generally speaking, they are always more at home with ideas, philosophies, and nontangible realities. They are thinkers always a bit apart, their body types showing a lack of muscular development. Poets and artists, while somewhat of this nature, as a rule are more deeply appreciative of the physical values of earthly existence, although they have many of the same characteristics.

The attitude toward the body will always vary, therefore. Various types of bodies may be chosen, but there will still be overall preferences on the part of the whole self, and characteristics that will lead the whole self, so that generally the various lives lived will still have their own individual flavor.

It is almost impossible to speak of when the personality enters the physical body without discussing the ways in which it leaves it, for all this is highly dependent upon personal characteristics and attitudes toward physical reality. Decisions as to future lives may be made not only in between-life conditions but also in dream states in any given life.

You may have already decided for example, now, upon the circumstances for your next incarnation. Although in your terms your new parents may be infants now, or in your scale of time not even born, the arrangements may still be made.

Now you may take your break.

("That was very good."

(11:00 P.M. Jane's trance had been deep. She had a time getting her eyes to stay open. "I like it when he does it like that — when I'm just out," she said. "But when I come back I don't know what I'm doing. . . . I was really out."

(This break marked the end of book dictation for the evening. Seth finished the session by giving several pages of personal material for Jane and me.)

CHAPTER 14

STORIES OF THE BEGINNING, AND THE
MULTIDIMENSIONAL GOD

SESSION 559, NOVEMBER 9, 1970,
9:18 P.M. MONDAY

(E*xcerpts from the 558th session for November 5th are included in the Appendix.*)

Good evening.

(*"Good evening Seth."*)

Now for dictation. We will begin the next chapter. It will be called: "Stories of the Beginning, and the Multidimensional God." (*Leaning forward, smiling but intent*): How do you like <u>that</u>?

(*"It's very good."*)

As the present life of any individual rises from hidden dimensions beyond those easily accessible in physical terms, and as it draws its energy and power to act from unconscious sources, so does the present physical universe as you know it rise from other dimensions. So does it have its source, and derive its energy from deeper realities.

History, as you know it, represents but one single light upon which you focus. You interpret the events that you see therein, and you project upon its glimmer your interpretation of events that may occur. So entranced is your concentration, that when you wonder about the nature of reality you automatically confine your question to this one small flickering moment that you call physical reality. When you ponder upon the aspects of God, you unthinkingly speak of the creator of that one light. That light <u>is</u> unique, and if you truly understood what it was, you would indeed understand the nature of true reality.

History, as you think of it, represents but one thin line of probabilities, in which you are presently immersed. It does not represent the entire lifetime of your species or the catalogue of physical activities, or begin to tell the story of physical creatures, their civilizations, wars, joys, technologies, or triumphs. Reality is far more diverse, far richer and unutterable than you can presently suppose or comprehend. Evolution, as you think of it and as it is categorized by your scientists, represents but one probable line of evolution, the one in which, again, you are presently immersed.

(9:35.) There are, therefore, many other equally valid, equally real evolutionary developments that have occurred and are occurring and will occur, all within other probable systems of physical reality. The diverse, endless possibilities of development possible could never appear within one slender framework of reality.

With splendid innocence and exuberant pride, you imagine that the evolutionary system as you know it is the only one, that physically there can be no more. Now within the physical reality that you know, there are hints and clues as to the nature of other physical realities. There are, latent, within your own physical forms other senses, unused, that could have come to the front but in your probability did not. Now I have been speaking of earthly developments, realities therefore clustered about earthly aspects as you know them.

No evolutionary line is a dead one. Therefore if in your system it disappears, it emerges within another. All probable materializations of life and consciousness have their day, and create those conditions within which they can flourish; and their day, in your terms, is eternal.

I am speaking now, in this chapter, mainly about your own planet and solar system, but the same applies to all aspects of your physical universe. You are aware, then, of only one specific, delicately balanced but unique portion of physical existence. You are not only creatures of corporeal being, forming images of flesh and blood, embedded in a particular kind of space and time; you are also creatures rising out of a particularized dimension of probabilities, born from dimensions of actuality richly suited to your own development, enrichment and growth.

(9:53.) If you have any intuitive understanding as yet concerning the nature of the entity or whole self, you will see that it has placed you in

a position in which certain abilities, insights, and experience can be realized, and in which your unique kind of consciousness can be nurtured. Your slightest experience has far more repercussions within this multidimensional environment than the physical brain can conceive. For if you are intensely preoccupied with what may seem to be one infinitesimally minute aspect of reality, and while you seem to be completely embedded within it, only the most "surface" elements of the self are so entranced. I do not like the term "surface" in this regard, though I have used it to suggest the multitudinous portions of the self that are otherwise engaged — some of them as entranced in their reality as you are in yours.

The entity, the true multidimensional self, is aware of all of its experiences, and this knowledge is to some extent available to these other portions of the self, including of course the physical self as you know it. These various portions of the self in fact will eventually (in your terms) become fully aware. Period. This awareness will automatically alter what now seems to be their nature, and add to the multiplicitude of existence.

You may take a break.

(*10:03. Jane's pace had been quite slow for large portions of the delivery. I did some yawning during break. Resume at 10:15.*)

Now. We will have a brief session —

(*"I'm all right."*)

— now that I have begun on our next chapter. I have some comments, however. Give us a moment.

(*Seth continued with some personal material for Jane and one of the students in her ESP class.*)

Do you have other questions?

(*"No, I guess not."*)

We have indeed begun some excellent material. A hearty good evening.

(*"The same to you, Seth."*)

And my fondest regards to you both.

(*"Thank you. Good night." 10:34 P.M.*)

(Jane has been resting from sessions lately, except for a couple given for her ESP class.)

Now, good evening.

("Good evening, Seth.")

We will resume dictation.

There are many probable systems of reality, therefore, in which physical data predominates, but such physical probabilities represent but one small portion. Each of you also exist in nonphysical systems, and I have explained earlier that your slightest thought or emotion is manifested in many other ways than in your own field of existence.

Only a portion of your entire identity is "presently" familiar to you, as you know. Therefore, when you consider the question of a supreme being, you imagine a male personality with those abilities that you yourselves possess, with great emphasis upon qualities you admire. This imagined god has therefore changed throughout your centuries, mirroring man's shifting ideas of himself.

God was seen as cruel and powerful when man believed that these were desirable characteristics, needed particularly in his battle for physical survival. He projected these upon his idea of a god because he envied them and feared them. You have cast your idea of god, therefore, in your own image.

In a reality that is inconceivably multidimensional, the old concepts of God are relatively meaningless. Even the term, a supreme being, is in itself distortive, for you naturally project the qualities of human nature upon it. If I told you that God was an idea, you would not understand what I meant, for you do not understand the dimensions in which an idea has its reality, or the energy that it can originate and propel. You do not believe in ideas in the same way that you believe in physical objects, so if I tell you that God is an idea, you will misinterpret this to mean that God is less than real — nebulous, without reality, without purpose, and without motive action.

Now your own physical image is the materialization of your idea of yourself within the properties of matter. Without the idea of yourself, your physical image would not be; yet often it is all you are aware of.

The initial power and energy of that idea of yourself keeps your image alive. Ideas, then, are far more important than you realize. If you will try to accept the idea that your own existence is multidimensional, that you dwell within the medium of infinite probabilities, then you may catch a slight glimpse of the reality that is behind the word "god," and you may understand why it is almost impossible to capture a true understanding of that concept in words.

God, therefore, is first of all a creator, not of one physical universe but of an infinite variety of probable existences, far more vast than those aspects of the physical universe with which your scientists are familiar. He did not simply then send a son to live and die on one small planet. He is a part of all probabilities.

There have been parables told, and stories of beginnings. All of these have been attempts to transmit knowledge in as simple terms as possible. Often answers were given to questions that literally have no meaning outside of your own system of reality.

For example: There was no beginning, and there will be no end, yet parables have been given telling you of beginnings and endings simply because with your distorted ideas of time, beginnings and endings seem to be inseparable, valid events. As you learn to turn the focus of your attention away from physical reality and therefore experience some slight evidence of other realities, your consciousness will cling to old ideas that make true explanations impossible for you to understand. Multidimensional awareness is available to you in your dreams, however, in some trance states, and often even beneath ordinary consciousness as you go about your day.

This awareness gives personal experience with the multidimensional richness that exists not apart from but intermingled with, within, through, and all about your physical world of sense. To say that physical life is not real is to deny that reality pervades all appearance, and is a part of all appearance. In the same manner, God does not exist apart from or separate from physical reality, but exists within it and as a part of it, as he exists within and as a part of all other systems of existence.

(9:46.) Your Christ figure represents, symbolically, your idea of God and his relationships. There were three separate individuals whose history blended, and they became known collectively as Christ — hence many discrepancies in your records. These were all males because at

that time of your development, you would not have accepted a female counterpart.

These individuals were a part of one entity. You could not but imagine God as a father. It would never have occurred to you to imagine a god in any other than human terms. Earth components. These three figures worked out a drama, highly symbolic, propelled by concentrated energy of great force.

(Long pause at 9:52.) The events as they are recorded, however, did not occur in history. The crucifixion of Christ was a psychic, but not a physical event. Ideas of almost unimaginable magnitude were played out.

(Pause at 9:55.) Judas, for example, was not a man in your terms. He was — like all the other disciples — a blessed, created "fragment personality," formed by the Christ personality. He represented the self-betrayer. He dramatized a portion of each individual's personality that focuses upon physical reality in a grasping manner, and denies the inner self out of greed.

Each of the twelve represented qualities of personality that belong to one individual, and Christ as you know him represented the inner self. The twelve, therefore, plus Christ as you know him (the one figure composed of the three) represented an individual earthly personality — the inner self — and twelve main characteristics connected with the egotistical self. As Christ was surrounded by the disciples, so the inner self is surrounded by these physically oriented characteristics, each drawn outward toward daily reality on the one hand, and yet orbiting the inner self.

(10:03.) The disciples, therefore, were given physical reality by the inner self, as all of your earthly characteristics come out of your inner nature. This was a living parable, made flesh among you — a cosmic play worked out for your behalf, couched in terms that you could understand.

The lessons were made plain, as all the ideas behind them were personified. If you will forgive the term, this was like a local morality play, put on in your corner of the universe. This does not mean it was less real than you previously supposed. In fact, the implications of what is said here should clearly hint at the more powerful aspects of godhood.

(10:07.) When I go slow, you can rest between the lines.

("Yes." Note that Seth hasn't taken a break yet. Jane's pace has been very slow at times.)

The three Christ personalities were born upon your planet, and indeed became flesh among you. None of these was crucified. The twelve disciples were materializations from the energies of these three personalities — their combined energies. They were then fully endowed with individuality, however, but their main task was to clearly manifest within themselves certain abilities inherent within all men.

(10:12.) The same kinds of dramas in different ways have been given, and while the drama is always different, it is always the same. This does not mean that a Christ has appeared within each system of reality. It means that the idea of God has manifested within each system in a way that is comprehensible to the inhabitants.

This drama continues to exist. It does not belong, for example, to your past. Only you have placed it there. This does not mean that it always reoccurs. The drama, then, was far from meaningless, and the spirit of Christ, in your terms, is legitimate. It is the probable God-drama that you choose to perceive. There were others that were perceived, but not by you, and there are other such dramas existing now.

You may take your break.

(10:16. Jane's trance had been deep. Her eyes were heavy at break, slow to open. "I knew he was keeping me out until I got a good lot of that material through," she said. An hour and six minutes; this had been one of her longest trances. I told her I thought the material was excellent.

(As we talked, Jane recalled an image she'd had during the delivery. She couldn't explain it very well, even with gestures. "Something like Christ being a central pole, with twelve balls revolving around him but radiating outward at the same time," she said. "Christ created the twelve. . . ."

(So far, Seth has named two out of the three personalities making up the Christ entity — Himself, obviously, and John the Baptist. Resume at 10:37.)*

Now: Whether or not the Crucifixion occurred physically, it was a psychic event, and exists as do all the other events connected with the drama.

Many were physical but some were not. The psychic event affected your world quite as much as the physical one, as is obvious. The whole drama occurred as a result of mankind's need. It was created as a result of that need, grew out of it, but it did not originate within your system of reality.

*See Chapter Eighteen of *The Seth Material.*

(Pause at 10:41.) Other religions were based upon different dramas, in which ideas were acted out in a way that was comprehensible to various cultures. Unfortunately, the differences between the dramas often led to misunderstandings, and these were used as excuses for wars. These dramas are also privately worked out in the dream state. The God-personified figures first were introduced to man in the dream state, and the way then prepared.

In visions and inspirations, men knew that the Christ drama would be enacted and hence recognized it for what it was when it occurred physically. Its power and strength then returned to the dream universe. It had increased its vigor and intensity through the physical materialization. In private dreams, men then related to the main figures in the drama, and in the dream state they recognized its true import.

Now: God is more than the sum of all the probable systems of reality he has created, and yet he is within each one of these, without exception. He is therefore within each man and woman. He is also within each spider, shadow, and frog, and this is what man does not like to admit.

God can only be experienced, and you experience him whether or not you realize it, through your own existence. He is not male or female, however, and I use the terms only for convenience's sake. In the most inescapable truth, he is not human in your terms at all, nor in your terms is he a personality. Your ideas of personality are too limited to contain the multitudinous facets of his multidimensional existence.

(10:55.) On the other hand, he is human, in that he is a portion of each individual; and within the vastness of his experience he holds an "idea-shape" of himself as human, to which you can relate. He literally was made flesh to dwell among you, for he forms your flesh in that he is responsible for the energy that gives vitality and validity to your private multidimensional self, which in turn forms your image in accordance with your own ideas.

This private multidimensional self, or the soul, has then an eternal validity. It is upheld, supported, maintained by the energy, the inconceivable vitality, of All That Is.

(11:00.) It cannot be destroyed then, this inner self of yours, nor can it be diminished. It shares in those abilities that are inherent within All That Is. It must, therefore, create as it is created, for this is the great

giving that is behind all dimensions of existence, the spilling-over from the fountain of All That Is.

Now we will end our session.

("Okay. It's been very good.")

That body of material comes as one pattern, and we shall add others to it. I am finished with dictation. I will end the session unless you have any questions. . . .

(I did have a couple of questions pertaining to Jane and her dreams. Seth answered these, then ended the session at 11:09 P.M.)

SESSION 561, NOVEMBER 25, 1970,
9:55 P.M. WEDNESDAY

(Just as the session was about to begin at 9:15, Jane said she thought we'd be interrupted somehow, or have visitors. Not fifteen seconds later there was a knock at the door. It was Carl Jones. He teaches a high school course called "Inner and Outer Space," in a small city in Connecticut; the class uses Jane's book, The Seth Material, *as text. Carl was on his way to a destination near Niagara Falls, New York, for the Thanksgiving holidays.)*

Now: Good evening.

("Good evening, Seth.")

And good evening to our friend here, and I will take due note that you *(Carl)* are smiling this evening. Now: We are going to resume dictation on our book, so *(humorously to Carl)* you can see an author at work — an authentic ghost writer if you prefer.

I will in due time identify the figure of the third Christ personality. Now, however, I am concerned with the multidimensional aspects of All That Is. Such a reality can only be experienced. There are no facts that can be given that can portray with any faithfulness the attributes of All That Is.

This reality and those attributes will appear within various systems of actuality in keeping with the camouflage data of any given system. The inner experience with the multidimensional God can come in two main areas. One is through the realization that this prime moving force is within everything that you can perceive with your senses. The other method is to realize that this primary motive force has a reality independent of its connection with the world of appearances.

All personal contact with the multidimensional God, all legitimate moments of mystic consciousness, will always have a unifying effect. They will not, therefore, isolate the individual involved, but instead will enlarge his perceptions until he will experience the reality and uniqueness of as many other aspects of reality of which he is capable.

(10:05.) He will feel, therefore, less isolated and less set apart. He will not regard himself as being above others because of the experience. On the contrary he will be swept along in a gestalt of comprehension in which he realizes his own oneness with All That Is.

As there are portions of reality that you do not consciously perceive, and other systems of probability of which you are not consciously aware, so also are there aspects of primary godhood that you cannot at this moment comprehend. There are, therefore, probable gods, each one reflecting in its way the multidimensional aspects of a prime identity so great and dazzling that no one reality form or particular kind of existence could contain it.

(10:10.) I have tried to give you some idea of the far-reaching creative effects of your own thoughts. With that in mind, then, it is impossible to imagine the multidimensional creativities that can be attributed to All That Is. The term 'All That Is' can be used as a designation to include all of those probable gods in all of their manifestations.

Now it is easier perhaps for some of you to understand the simple stories and parables of beginnings of which I have spoken. But the time has come for mankind to take several steps further, to expand the nature of his own consciousness by trying to comprehend a more profound version of reality. You have outgrown the time of children's tales. When your own thoughts have a form and reality, when they have validity even in other systems of reality of which you are unaware, then it is not difficult to understand why other systems of probabilities are also affected by your own thoughts and emotions — nor why the actions of the probable gods are not affected by what happens in other dimensions of existence.

Now you may take your break.

(10:15. Jane's pace had been good. After an average-length break an unrecorded interval of material followed, with Seth mainly answering questions for Carl. A few points were mentioned, however, that I later wished I had written down. [This is usually the case when I don't take notes.] One such point had to do with Seth's statement that whenever a person thinks strongly about another

person, a portion of the "thinker" goes out to the "thought-subject," etc.

*(Another break followed. During it Carl left, to continue his holiday jour-
ney westward. . . . I had grown concerned lately that Jane was overdoing week-
end psychic work, including sessions for visitors. We talked about this now —
without expecting Seth to discuss it — and agreed that she'd have to slack off
on such extracurricular adventures, no matter how interesting the "provocation."*

(Resume at 11:10.)

Now: I have something to say. Your suggestion about weekends is
a good one, and Ruburt is prepared to follow it. When you are having
regular sessions, an occasional visitor will not annoy you, but such visits should be known in advance.

Ruburt is subconsciously aware of them in most cases, but seldom
brings this to consciousness, so it is simply a feeling of disquietude on
his part. He feels he will be interrupted, but is not consciously aware
of this, you see.

Now I suggest that our regular sessions for a while be held in one
of your back rooms, *(where my studio is),* for two reasons. You will know
the phone will not interrupt you, with both doors closed. Simply ignore
it. Let it be known that anyone who wants to attend private sessions must
then arrange so in advance. Otherwise you would not hear them at the
door.

The back room idea, however, will serve to reinforce the private
nature of the sessions in your own minds. All work dealing with other
people generally will be done in whatever room class sessions are held.

The idea of the back room will also serve as a psychological set for
withdrawal from ordinary physical concerns and relationships with others. I am not saying that you should not allow certain specific individuals at times to attend private sessions. I am now stressing, however, that
the two regular sessions should be held, and I am saying this now knowing that Ruburt is able and willing to follow my suggestions.

In the summertime the rooms in the back may or may not be beneficial. There were natural changes occurring in our work, and overall
Ruburt has done well in handling them. The unevenness in the timing
of our sessions was a result of the fact that often three regular sessions
were being expected from him, rather than two.

Often spontaneously we had class sessions, and as you noticed he
would miss our next session. He thought that two sessions were quite

enough. Our regular sessions will always be the primary source of the material, and the stress will always be laid upon them. Nevertheless, the class sessions serve an important purpose. They are a subsidiary or off-shoot, but they are not meant to supersede our own work.

At no time for now, and until I say so, should over three sessions a week be held. Now it may seem to you that it is merely a matter of my not being available if I think Ruburt should not have an extra session. *(I don't think this at all.)* Remember, however, what I told you much earlier. Sometimes I am very directly concerned in a session, and sometimes you get a session that has been programmed. This is putting it very simply, but you know what I mean.

So, using the psychological bridge at such times, Ruburt can have a session. I have made what I think clear and specific. Now: Work he does with impressions is an entirely different thing. He is not pulling in the same kind of energy. It is not a matter of a session taking something out of Ruburt. It is a matter of tuning into the kind of energy that he does in our sessions, and simply because of present circumstances and development, three times a week is sufficient.

Our two sessions should always be maintained, with the class sessions added as long as they do not drain Ruburt's resources. The phone should not be answered, however. Strangers who write can be invited to the Tuesday classes. On certain occasions, using your own discretions, you may have guests at our sessions, but these will be very occasional, and will not be a problem if you follow the procedure I have outlined.

Do you have questions?

("No.")

We will end the session, or take a break then as you prefer.

("We might as well end it then."

(11:30. This wasn't the end of the session after all. Seth returned after a short break, and we had a discussion about class sessions and other things that lasted until 11:50 P.M.

(Seth did make a prediction: Jane will write an excellent book about the class sessions, and this will lead many to read the regular Seth material. Seth added that the material itself, in session format, will be published in its entirety one day. This is a personal goal of mine.)

CHAPTER 15

REINCARNATIONAL CIVILIZATIONS,
PROBABILITIES, AND MORE
ON THE MULTIDIMENSIONAL GOD

SESSION 562, DECEMBER 7, 1970,
9:05 P.M. MONDAY

(*F ollowing Seth's suggestion of November 25, we held the session in my studio, at the back of our apartment. It's more private there but it isn't as warm, especially when doors are closed.*)

Good evening.

(*"Good evening, Seth."*)

Now: We will resume dictation, and we will begin with the next chapter. It will be called: "Reincarnational Civilizations, Probabilities, and More on the Multidimensional God."

In a manner of speaking, it can be said that you have reincarnational civilizations as well as reincarnating individuals. Each entity who is born in flesh works toward the development of those abilities that can be best nurtured and fulfilled within the physical environment. He has a responsibility to and for the civilization in which he has each existence, for he helps form it through his own thoughts, emotions, and actions.

He learns from failure as well as success. You think of physical history as beginning with the caveman and continuing up to the present, but there have been other great scientific civilizations; some spoken of in legend, some completely unknown — all in your terms now vanished.

It seems to you that you have, perhaps, but one chance as a species to solve your problems, or be destroyed by your own aggression, by your own lack of understanding and spirituality. As you are given many lives in which to develop and fulfill your abilities, so has the species in those terms been allotted more than the single line of historical development with which you are presently acquainted. The reincarnational structure is but one facet in the whole picture of probabilities. In it you have literally as much time as you need, to develop those potentials that you must develop, before leaving the reincarnational existences. Groups of people in various cycles of reincarnational activity have met crisis after crisis, have come to your point of physical development and either gone beyond it, or destroyed their particular civilization.

In this case they were given another chance, having the unconscious knowledge not only of their failure, but the reasons behind it. They then began with a psychological head start as they formed new primitive groupings. Others, solving the problems, left your physical planet for other points in the physical universe. When they reached that level of development, however, they were spiritually and psychically mature, and were able to utilize energies of which you now have no practical knowledge.

(Pause at 9:22.) Earth to them now is the legendary home. They formed new races and species that could no longer physically accommodate themselves to your atmospheric conditions. However, they also continued on the reincarnational level as long as they inhabited physical reality. Some of these have mutated and have long left the reincarnational cycle, however.

Those who have left it have evolved into the mental entities that they always were, you see. They have discarded material form. This group of entities still takes a great interest in earth. They lend it support and energy. In a way, they could be thought of now as earth gods.

(9:28.) On your planet they were involved in three particular civilizations long before the time of Atlantis; when, in fact, your planet itself was in a somewhat different position.

("Do you mean a different 'orbit'?")

For now, leave the word "position." Particularly in relationship to three of the other planets that you know. The poles were reversed — as they were, incidentally, for three long periods of your planet's history. These civilizations were highly technological; the second one being, in fact, far superior to your own along those lines.

Sound was utilized far more effectively, not only for healing and in wars, but also to power vehicles of locomotion, and to bring about the movement of physical matter. Sound was a conveyor of weight and mass.

(9:34. When Jane spoke the word "wars," above, her tone of voice and her facial expression had a "wouldn't you know it" connotation.)

The strength of this second civilization lay mainly in the areas now known as Africa and Australia, although at that time not only was the climate entirely different, but the land areas. There was a different attraction of land mass having to do with the altered position of the poles. Relatively speaking, however, the civilization was concentrated in area; it did not attempt to expand. It was highly ingrown and dwelled upon the planet simultaneously with a large, unorganized, dispersed, primitive culture.

Not only did it make no attempt to "civilize" the rest of the world, but it did everything in its power — which was considerable for a long period of time — to impede any such progress.

The members of this civilization were largely a fringe group from the earlier successful civilization, most of whom had decided to continue existence in other areas of your physical universe. These, however, were particularly enamored of earthly life, and also thought that they could improve upon the last experiment in which they had been involved, though they were free to move on to other layers of existence.

(9:42.) They were not interested in beginning from scratch again as an infant civilization, but in other areas. Therefore much of their knowledge was instinctive with them, and this particular group then went through what you would call the various technological stages very rapidly.

They were particularly concerned in the beginning with developing a human being who would have built-in safeguards against violence. With them, the desire for peace was almost what you would call an instinct. There were changes in the physical mechanism. When the mind signaled strong aggression, the body would not react. Now psychologically you can see vestiges of this in certain individuals, who will faint, or even attack their own physical system, before allowing themselves to do what they think of as violence to another.

This civilization, therefore, left the natives that surrounded them in peace. They did send out members of their own group, however, to live with the natives and intermarry, hoping peacefully to thus alter the physiology of the species.

The energy, often in your time given over to violence, went instead into other pursuits, but began to turn against them. They were not learning to deal with violence or aggression. They were attempting to short-circuit it physically, and <u>this</u> they found had complications.

You may take your break.

(9:52 to 10:05.)

Now: Energy must be allowed to flow freely through the physical system, controlled and directed mentally, or psychically if you prefer.

The physical alteration was a strain on the entire system. The creative function and basis that has been distorted into the idea of aggression — the urge to act — was not understood. In a manner of speaking, breathing itself is a violence. The built-in inhibition resulted in a tied-up system of mutual controls in which the necessary thrusting-out of action became literally impossible.

An overly conscientious, restrictive mental and physical state evolved, in which the organism's natural physical need for survival was in every way hampered. Mentally, the civilization progressed. Its technology was extremely activated, and propelled onward as it strove to develop, for example, artificial foods so that it would not need to kill for survival in any way.

(10:13.) At the same time it tried to leave the environment intact. It missed your stage of automobiles completely, and steam-driven vehicles, and concentrated rather early on sound. The sound could not be heard by physical ears.

The civilization was called Lumania, *(spelled out)*, and the name itself went down in legend and was used again at a later time.

The Lumanians were a very thin, weakly people, physically speaking, but psychically either brilliant or completely ungifted. In some, you see, the built-in controls caused so many blockages of energy in all directions that even their naturally high telepathic abilities suffered.

They formed energy fields around their own civilization. They were, therefore, isolated from contact with other groups. They did not allow technology to destroy them, however. More and more of them realized that the experiment was not a success. Some, after physical death, left to join those from the previous successful civilization, who had migrated to other planetary systems within the physical structure.

Large groups, however, simply left their cities, destroyed the force fields that had enclosed them, and joined the many groups of relatively uncivilized peoples, mating with them and bearing children. These Lumanians died quickly, for they could not bear violence nor react to it violently. They felt however, that their mutant children might have a resulting disinclination toward violence, but without the prohibiting nerve-control reactions with which they were endowed.

(One minute pause at 10:24.) Physically the civilization simply died out. Some few of the mutant children formed a small later group who traveled the area as itinerants in the following century, with large bands of animals. They cared for each other mutually, and many of the old legends concerning half-man and half-beast have come down through the ages simply from the memory of these old associations.

These people, as remnants, really, of the first great civilization, always carried within themselves strong subconscious memories of their origin. I am speaking of the Lumanians now. This accounted for their quick rise, technologically speaking. But because their purpose was so single-minded — the avoidance of violence — rather, say, than the constructive peaceful development of creative potential, their experience was highly one-sided. They were driven by such a fear of violence that they dared not allow the physical system freedom even to express it.

(10:33.) The vitality of the civilization was therefore weak — not because violence did not exist, but because freedom of energy and expression was automatically blocked along specific lines, and from out-side physically. They well understood the evils of violence in earthly terms, but they would have denied the individual's right to learn this his own way, and thus prevented the individual from using his own methods, creatively, to turn the violence into constructive areas. Free will in this respect was discarded.

As a child is physically protected from some diseases for a while after he emerges from his mother's womb, so for a brief period is the child cushioned against some psychic disasters for a short period after birth, and carries within him, still for his comfort, memories of past existences and places. So the Lumanians for some generations were supported by deep subconscious memories of the civilization that had gone before. Finally, however, these began to weaken. They had protected themselves against violence but not against fear.

They were, therefore, subject to all of the ordinary human fears which were then exaggerated, since physically they could not respond even to nature with violence. If attacked, they had to flee. The fight-or-flight principle did not apply. They had but one recourse.

(10:41.) Their god symbol was a male one — a strong, physically powerful male figure who would therefore protect them since they could not protect themselves. He evolved through the ages as their beliefs did, and into him they projected those qualities that they could not themselves express.

He was much later to appear as the old Jehovah, the God of Wrath who protected the Chosen People. The fear of natural forces was, therefore, initially extremely strong in them for the reasons given, and brought about a feeling of separation between man and those natural forces that nurtured him. They could not trust the earth, since they were not allowed to protect themselves against violent forces within it.

Their vast technology and their great civilization was largely underground. They were, in those terms, the original cavemen, and they came out from their cities through caves also. Caves were not just places of protection in which unskilled natives squatted. They were often doorways to and from the cities of the Lumanians. Long after the cities were deserted, the following natives, uncivilized, found these caves and the openings.

In the period that you now think of as the Stone Age, the men you think of as your ancestors, the cavemen, often found shelter not in rough naturally formed caves, but in mechanically created channels that reached behind them, and in the deserted cities in which once the Lumanians dwelled. Some of the tools fashioned by the cavemen were distorted versions of those they had found.

Now you may take your break — and keep warm.

(10:44. Jane's pace had been rather leisurely throughout. The studio had cooled off considerably by now — hence Seth's remark. Three pages of deleted material followed break, with the session ending at 11:25 P.M.)

SESSION 563, DECEMBER 9, 1970,
9:15 P.M. WEDNESDAY

(Again, the session was held in the studio. We sat for it as usual at about 9:00, but Jane didn't "feel Seth around" right away. Not that she was particularly tired, or bothered in any other way. . . .)

Now: Good evening.

("Good evening, Seth.")

We will resume dictation.

While the civilization of the Lumanians was highly concentrated, in that they made no attempt to conquer others or to spread out to any great extent in area, they did set out, over the centuries, outposts from which they could emerge and keep track of the other native peoples.

These outposts were constructed underground. From the original cities and large settlements there were, of course, underground connections, a system of tunnels, highly intricate and beautifully engineered. Since these were an aesthetic people, the walls were lined with paintings and drawings, and sculpture was also displayed along these inner byways.

There were various escalated systems, some conveying people on foot, some conveying goods. It was not practical to construct such tunnels to the many outposts, however, which were fairly small communities and relatively self-supporting; some were a good distance away from the main areas of commerce and activity.

(9:21.) These outposts were situated in many scattered areas, but there were a fairly large number of them in what is now Spain and the Pyrenees. There were several reasons for this, one having to do with the existence of rather giant-sized men in the mountain areas. Because of the timid nature of these [Lumanian] people, they did not enjoy outpost existence, and only the bravest and most confident of them were given such an assignment, which was temporary to begin with.

(A note, added later: Seth gives no dates for the Lumanian civilization. It's interesting to note however that in late July, 1971, about eight months after this session, newspapers carried the story — with photographs — of the unearthing of a "massive" subhuman skull in a cave in the French Pyrenees Mountains, very close to the Spanish border.

(The skull is at least two hundred thousand years old, and represents a race not identified before. It is now tentatively thought that several primitive races existed in Europe at that time. The period predates Neanderthal Man, and marks the start of the next-to-last Ice Age. This region in southern France is noted for its many caverns, easily eroded out of the limestone bedrock by flowing water. Jane has no paleontological background.)

The caves, again, served as doorways opening outward, and often what seemed to be the back of a cave was instead constructed of a material opaque from the outside but transparent from the inside. The natives of the area, using such caves for natural shelter, could therefore be observed without danger. These people reacted to sounds that are not audible to your ears. Their peculiar fear of violence intensified all of their mechanisms to an amazing degree. They were forever alert and on guard.

(9:29.) This is difficult to explain, but they could mentally pitch a thought along certain frequencies — a highly distinguished art — and then translate the thought at a given destination in any of a number of ways, into form or color, for example, or even into a certain type of image. Their language was extremely discriminating in ways that you could not understand, simply because gradations in pitch, frequency, and spacing were so precise and complicated.

Communication, in fact, was one of their strongest points, and it was developed to such a high degree simply because they feared violence so deeply and were constantly on the alert. They banded together in large family groups, again in need for protection. Contact between children and parents was at a very high level, and children were acutely uncomfortable if out of the sight of their parents for any amount of time.

(9:34.) For these reasons, those individuals who ran the outposts felt themselves to be in a very uncomfortable situation. They were limited in numbers and largely cut off from the main areas of their own civilization. They developed, therefore, an even greater telepathic activity, and a rapport with the earth above their head, so that the slightest tremor or footstep and the most minute movements above that were not usual, were instantly noted.

There were frequent peepholes, so to speak, through to the surface, from which they could make observations, and cameras situated there that kept the most precise pictures not only of the earth, but of the stars.

Of course, they had complete records of underground gas areas and intimate knowledge of the inner crusts, keeping careful watch upon and anticipating earth tremors and faults. They were as triumphant about their descent into the earth as any race ever was who left the earth.

(9:40.) This was, as I told you, the second, and perhaps most interesting of the three civilizations. The first followed generally your own line of development and faced many of the problems that you now do. They were largely situated in what you call Asia Minor, but they were also expansive and traveled outward to other areas. These are the people I mentioned earlier, who finally went on to other planets within other galaxies, and from whom the people of the Lumanian civilization came.

Now I suggest your break.

(9:43. Jane said her trance hadn't been very good. She had been smoking and the air in the studio wasn't fresh, so we opened the doors leading to the rest of the apartment. We usually keep windows closed because Seth's voice has the peculiar ability to carry well. Besides, it was a cold night. Resume at 9:55.)

Now: Before we discuss the third civilization, there are a few more points I would like to make about the second one.

This has to do with communication as it was applied to their drawings and paintings, and to the highly discriminating channels that their creative communications could take. In many ways their art was highly superior to your own, and not as isolated. The various art forms, for example, were connected in a fashion that is nearly unknown to you, and because you are so unfamiliar with the concept, it will be rather difficult to explain.

(10:00.) Consider, for example, something very simple — say a drawing of an animal. You would perceive it simply as a visual object, but these people were great synthesizers. A line was not simply a visual line, but according to an almost infinite variety of distinctions and divisions, it would also represent certain sounds that would be automatically translated.

An observer could automatically translate the sounds before he bothered with the visual image, if he wanted to. In what would appear to be a drawing of an animal, then, the entire history or background of the animal might also be given. Curves, angles, lines all represented, beside their obvious objective function in a drawing, a highly complicated series of variations in pitch, tone and value; or if you prefer, invisible words.

(10:07.) Distances between lines were translated as sound pauses, and sometimes also as distances in time. Color was used in terms of language in communication, in drawings and paintings; representing somewhat as your own color does, emotional gradations. The color however,

its value of intensity, served to further refine and define — for example, either by reinforcing the message already given by the objective value of the lines, angles, and curves, and by the invisible word messages already explained; or by modifying these in any given number of ways. Do you follow me here?

("Yes." Pause at 10:12.)

The size of such drawings also spoke its own message. In one way this was a highly stylized art, and yet it allowed for both great preciseness of expression in terms of detail, and great freedom in terms of scope. It was obviously highly compressed. This technique was later discovered by the third civilization, and some of the remnants of drawings done in imitation of it still exist. But the keys to interpretation have been completely lost, so all you could see would be a drawing devoid of the multisensual elements that gave it such great variety. It exists, but you could not bring it alive.

I should perhaps mention here that some of the caves, particularly in certain areas of Spain and the Pyrenees, and some earlier ones in Africa, were artificial constructions. Now these people moved mass with sound, and, as I told you earlier, actually conveyed matter through a high mastery of sound. This is how their tunnels were originally formed, and it was also the method used to form some of the caves in areas where originally there were few. Often drawings on the cave walls were highly stylized information, almost like signs in your terms in front of public buildings, portraying the type of animals and beings in a given area.

These drawings later were used as models by your early cavemen in the historical times to which you usually refer.

Do you want a break?

("Yes, I guess so.")

(10:20. I had started to cough during Jane's delivery because of the smoke from her cigarettes. She said she'd been aware of this, but that even so her trance had been better this time. We aired out the studio regardless of the outside temperature. Resume at 10:33.)

Now: Their communicative abilities, and therefore creative abilities, were more vital, alive, and responsive than yours are. When you hear a word you may be aware of a corresponding image in your mind. With these people, however, sounds automatically and instantly built up an amazingly vivid image that was not three-dimensional by any means, being internalized, but was far more vivid than your usual mental images indeed.

Certain sounds, again, were utilized to indicate amazing distinctions in terms of size, shape, direction, and duration both in space and time. Sounds automatically produced brilliant images, in other words. For this reason there was an easy distinction between what was called inner sight and outer sight, and it was quite natural for them to close their eyes when seated in conversation in order to communicate more clearly, enjoying the ever-changing and immediate inner images that accompanied any verbal interchange.

(10:41.) They learned quickly, and education was an exciting process, because this multisensuous facility automatically impressed information upon them not simply through one sense channel at a time but utilizing many simultaneously. For all this, however, and the immediacy of their perceptions, there was an inherent weakness. The inability to face up to violence and learn to conquer it meant, of course, that they also severely hampered a certain thrusting-out characteristic. Energy was blocked in these areas so that they actually lacked a forceful quality or sense of power.

I do not necessarily mean physical power however, but so much of their energy was used to avoid any meeting with violence that they were not able to channel ordinary aggressive feelings, for example, into other areas.

Now I am going to end the session, or you may take a break, if you prefer. I suggest however that you end it.

(I nodded in assent.) My heartiest regards and a fond good evening.

("Same to you, Seth, and thank you very much. Good night."

(10:48 P.M. Jane's trance had been quite variable this time, and I had continued to cough. She said that Seth finally ended the session because her trance actually fluctuated as I coughed. The material was of a type, Jane added, that was difficult to get while she contended with such distractions.)

SESSION 565, FEBRUARY 1, 1971,
9:05 P.M. MONDAY

(During the past few weeks Jane has had but a few sessions for her ESP class and a couple of personal ones for us. That's been it, even though I had hoped at various times that work could be done on Seth's book. Many things caused

us to lay it aside: other work, the holidays, the plain need for a change of pace,
travel, and the approaching death of my father. . . .

(Jane said she was nervous, now, about resuming dictation after the lay-
off. Her feelings were similar to those she'd had before starting the book. She hasn't
read it beyond the first part of Chapter Four, although I gave her a short excerpt
from Chapter Six to read to her ESP class. I had no doubt that when Seth resumed
dictation, it would be impossible to detect any sign of a break in continuity.

(Incidentally, we had gone back to holding sessions in the living room.)

Good evening.

("Good evening, Seth.")

Now: We will return to our book tonight and Wednesday, and the
following Monday and Wednesday, until it is finished.

Dictation now.

I have been speaking about the Lumanians in some detail because
they are a part of your psychic heritage. The other two civilizations were
in many ways more successful, and yet the strong intent behind the
Lumanians' experiment was extremely volatile. While they were not able
to solve the problem of violence as they understood it in your reality,
their passionate desire to do so still rings throughout your own psychic
environment.

Because of the true nature of "time" the Lumanians still exist as they
were in your terms. There are often bleed-throughs in the psychic atmosphere. These do not occur by chance, but when some kind of rapport
causes effects to leap between systems that otherwise appear quite separated. And so there have been such bleed-throughs between your own
civilization and the Lumanians'.

(9:13.) Various old religions picked up the idea of the Lumanians'
fierce god figure for example, in whom they managed to project their concepts of force, power, and violence, this god who had meant to protect
them when nonviolence would not allow them to protect themselves.

There is a bleed-through now in the making, so to speak, in which
the Lumanians' multidimensional concepts of art and communication
will be glimpsed by your own people, but in a rudimentary form.

Because of the nature of probabilities there is also, of course, a system of reality in which the Lumanians succeeded in their experiment
with nonviolence, and in which a completely different type of human
being emerged.

(9:19.) All of this may seem very strange to you, simply because your concepts of existence are so specific and limiting. Ideas of probable realities and probable men and gods may strike some of you as quite absurd, and yet as you read this book, you are but one of the probable you's. Other probable you's would not consider you real, of course, and some might indignantly question your existence. Nevertheless, the probable system of reality is not just a philosophical question. If you are interested in the nature of your own reality, then it becomes a highly personal and pertinent matter.

As the various qualities of the Lumanians are still present in your psychic atmosphere, as their cities still coexist in land areas now called your own, so other probable identities coexist with the identities you now call your own. In the following chapter we will discuss you and your probable selves.

(A note: According to Seth, the Lumanians were the second of a group of three highly technological civilizations that existed on our planet long before the time of Atlantis. In the 563rd session Seth mentioned that he would soon discuss the third of these cultures. This material was never received. It could have been, but because of the long break between the last two sessions on Seth's book, we simply did not remember to ask for it. . . .)

CHAPTER 16

PROBABLE SYSTEMS, MEN, AND GODS

(9:24.) And now we begin the next chapter: "Probable Systems, Men, and Gods."

In your daily life at any given moment of your time, you have a multitudinous choice of actions, some trivial and some of utmost importance. You may, for example, sneeze or not sneeze, cough or not cough, walk to the window or the door, scratch your elbow, save a child from drowning, learn a lesson, commit suicide, harm another, or turn your cheek.

It seems to you that reality is composed of those actions that you choose to take. Those that you choose to deny are ignored. The road not taken then seems to be a non-act, yet every thought is actualized and every possibility explored. Physical reality is constructed from what seems to be a series of physical acts. Since this is the usual criterion of reality for you, then nonphysical acts usually escape your notice, discretion, and judgment.

(9:30.) Let us take an example. You are reading this book when the telephone rings. A friend wants you to meet him at five o'clock. You stand considering. In your mind you see yourself (A) saying no and staying home, (B) saying no and going somewhere else instead, or (C) saying yes and keeping the engagement. Now all of these possible actions have a reality at that point. They are all capable of being actualized in physical terms. Before you make your decision, each of these probable

actions are equally valid. You choose one of these, and by your decision you make one event out of the three physical. This event is duly accepted as a portion of those serial happenings that compose your normal existence.

The other probable actions, however, are as valid as they ever were, though you have not chosen to actualize them physically. They are carried out as effectively as the one you chose to accept. If there was a strong emotional charge behind one of the rejected probable actions, it may even have greater validity as an act than the one you chose.

All actions are initially mental acts. This is the nature of reality. That sentence cannot be emphasized too thoroughly. All mental acts therefore are valid. They exist and cannot be negated.

Because you do not accept them all as physical events, you do not perceive their strength or durability. Your lack of perception cannot destroy their validity, however. If you wanted to be a doctor and are now in a different profession, then in some other probable reality you are a doctor. If you have abilities that you are not using here, they are being used elsewhere.

Now, again, these ideas may seem impossibly rich for your mental blood because of your propensity toward serial thought and three-dimensional attitudes.

(Humorously): You may take a three-dimensional break.

("Thank you." 9:43 to 9:55.)

Now these facts do not deny the validity of the soul, but instead add to it immeasurably.

The soul can be described for that matter, as a multidimensional, infinite act, each minute probability being brought somewhere into actuality and existence; an infinite creative act that creates for itself infinite dimensions in which fulfillment is possible.

The tapestry of your own existence is simply such that the three-dimensional intellect cannot behold it. These probable selves, however, are a portion of your identity or soul, and if you are out of contact with them it is only because you focus upon physical events and accept them as the criteria for reality.

(10:01.) From any given point of your existence, however, you can glimpse other probable realities, and sense the reverberations of probable actions beneath those physical decisions that you make. Some

people have done this spontaneously, often in the dream state. Here the rigid assumptions of normal waking consciousness often fade, and you can find yourself performing those physically rejected activities, never realizing that you have peered into a probable existence of your own.

If there are individual probable selves, then of course there are probable earths, all taking roads that you have not adopted. Beginning with an act of imagination in the waking state, you can sometimes follow for a short way into the "road not taken."

Go back to our man at the telephone, mentioned earlier. Let us say that he tells his friend he will not go. At the same time, if he imagines that he took another alternative and agreed on the engagement, then he might experience a sudden rift of dimensions. If he is lucky and the circumstances are good, he might suddenly feel the full validity of his acceptance as strongly as if he had chosen it physically. Before he realizes what is happening, he might actually feel himself leave his home and embark upon those probable actions that physically he has chosen not to perform.

(10:12.) For the moment, however, the full experience will rush upon him. Imagination will have opened the door and given him the freedom to perceive, but hallucination will not be involved. This is a simple exercise that can be tried in almost any circumstance, although solitude is important.

Such an experiment will not carry you too far, however, and the probable self who has chosen the action that you denied, is in important respects quite different from the self that you know. Each mental act opens up a new dimension of actuality. In a manner of speaking, your slightest thought gives birth to worlds.

This is not a dry metaphysical statement. It should arouse within you the strongest feelings of creativity and speculation. It is impossible for any being to be sterile, for any idea to die, or any ability to go unfulfilled.

(10:19.) Each probable system of reality of course then creates other such systems, and any one act, realized, brings forth an infinite number of "unrealized" acts that will also find their actualization. Now all systems of reality are open. The divisions between them are arbitrarily decided upon as a matter of convenience, but all exist simultaneously, and each one supports and adds to the other. So what you do is also

reflected to some degree in the experience of your probable selves, and vice versa.

To the extent that you are open and receptive, you can benefit greatly by the various experiences of your probable selves, and can gain from their knowledge and abilities. Quite spontaneously, again, you often do this in the dream state, and often what seems to you to be an inspiration is a thought experienced but not actualized on the part of another self. You tune in and actualize it instead, you see.

Ideas that you have entertained and not used may be picked up in this same manner by other probable you's. Each of these probable selves consider themselves the real you, of course, and to any one of them you would be the probable self; but through the inner senses all of you are aware of your part in this gestalt.

You may take your break.

(10:26 to 10:41.)

Now: The soul is not a finished product.

In fact it is not a product in those terms at all, but a process of becoming. All That Is is not a product, finished or otherwise, either. There are probable gods as there are probable men; but these probable gods are all a part of what you may call the soul of, or the identity of, All That Is; even as your probable selves are all a portion of your soul or entity.

The dimensions of actuality possible to All That Is of course far exceed those presently available to you. In a manner of speaking, you have created many probable gods through your own thoughts and desires. They become quite independent psychic entities, validities in other levels of existence. The one All That Is is aware not only of its own nature and of the nature of all consciousness, but is also aware of its infinite probable selves. We go here toward subjects in which words become meaningless.

The nature of All That Is can only be sensed directly through the inner senses, or, in a weaker communication, through inspiration or intuition. The miraculous complexity of such reality cannot be translated verbally.

Now give us a moment. End of dictation.

(Pause at 10:49. Jane's pace had been slower since break. Seth now proceeded to give some material for her regarding her writing.

("Thank you.")

And we will have book dictation Wednesday, with any personal material at the end.

("All right. Good night, Seth." End at 11:02 P.M.)

SESSION 566, FEBRUARY 15, 1971,
9:19 P.M. MONDAY

(For the last two weeks we have been busy with affairs related to the recent death of my father.)

Good evening.

("Good evening, Seth.")

Now: For a change we are going to have some dictation, though I may make a few remarks at the end of our session to you both.

Dictation then: Probabilities are an ever-present portion of your invisible psychological environment. You exist in the middle of the probable system of reality. It is not something apart from you. To some extent it is like a sea in which you have your present being. You are in it, and it is in you. Occasionally at surface levels of consciousness, you might wonder what might have happened had you made other decisions than those you have; chosen different mates, for example, or taken up residence in other portions of the country. You might wonder what would have happened had you mailed an important letter that you subsequently decided not to mail; and in such small wonderings only, have you ever questioned the nature of probabilities. But there are deep connections between yourself and all those individuals with whom you have had relationships, and with whom you were involved in deep decisions.

(9:28.) These are not nebulous. They are profound psychological interconnections that bind you each to each, particularly in a telepathic framework, though this may be beneath normal consciousness. The unrealized physical connections that might have occurred, but did not, are worked out in other layers of reality.

The invisible environment within your mind is not as lonely as you might think, and your seeming inner isolation is caused by the ego's persistent guard. It sees no reason, for example, why you should be informed of information that it does not consider pertinent to day-by-day daily activity.

(9:31.) I do not like the phrase, "to advance", yet in your terms "to advance" as a consciousness is to become more and more aware of these other materializations of your own identity. The probable selves are to gain awareness of the other probable selves, and realize that all are various manifestations of the true identity.

They are not "lost", buried or negated in some superself, without free will, self-determination, or individuality. Instead the identity is what they are, with full freedom to express all probable actions and developments, both in this reality and in others that you do not know.

As you sit reading this book in your present moment of time, you are positioned in the center of a cosmic web of probabilities that is affected by your slightest mental or emotional act.

(Pause at 9:36.) Your thoughts and emotions, therefore, go forth from you not only in all physical directions but in directions that are quite invisible to you, appearing in dimensions that you would not presently understand. Now you are also the receiver of other such signals coming from other probabilities that are connected with your own, but you choose which of those probable actions you want to make real or physical in your system, as others also have the freedom of choice in their systems.

You originate ideas then and receive them, but you are not forced to actualize unrealized probable acts that come to you from other probable selves. Now there is a natural attraction between yourself and other probable selves, electromagnetic connections having to do with simultaneous propulsions of energy. By this I mean energy that appears simultaneously both to you and probable selves in other realities; psychic connections having to do with a uniting, sympathetic, emotional reaction and a connection that shows up very strongly in the dream state.

In that state, with the functions of the ego somewhat stilled, there is some considerable communication between various portions of the entire identity. In dreams you may have glimpses of probable roads that you might have taken. You may think that these are fantasy, but instead you may be perceiving a legitimate picture of events that did occur within another system of probabilities.

Now you may take your break.

(9:45. Jane was surprised at the "little" amount of material delivered. She said she thought she'd "really been flying," with some great new material. Resume at 10:00.)

Now: One event can be actualized by more than one probable self, however, and you will resemble some probable selves more than others. Because you are involved in an intricate psychological gestalt such as this, and because the connections mentioned earlier do exist, you can avail yourself to some extent of abilities and knowledge possessed by these other probable portions of your personality.

The connections make for quite constant "bleed-throughs." Once you are aware of the probable system, however, you will also learn to become alert to what I will here call "benign intrusive impulses." Such impulses would seem to be disconnected from your own current interests or activities; intrusive in that they come quickly into consciousness, with a sense of strangeness as if they are not your own. These can often offer clues of various kinds. You may know absolutely nothing about music, for example, and one afternoon while in the middle of some mundane activity be struck by a sudden impulse to buy a violin.

(Pause at 10:06.) Such an impulse could be an indication that another probable portion of your identity is gifted with that instrument. I am not telling you to run off and buy one, but you could however act on the impulse as far as is reasonably possible — renting a violin, simply acquainting yourself with violin concerti, etc.

You would learn the instrument far quicker, you see, if the impulse was originating with a probable self. It goes without saying then that probable selves exist in your "future" as well as your past. It is very poor policy to dwell negatively on unpleasant aspects of the past that you know, because some portions of the probable self may still be involved in that past. The concentration can allow greater bleed-through and adverse identification, because that part will be one background that you have in common with any probable selves who sprang from that particular source.

(10:12.) To dwell upon the possibility of illness or disaster is equally poor policy, for you set up negative webs of probabilities that need not occur. You can theoretically alter your own past as you have known it, for time is no more something divorced from you than probabilities are.

The past existed in multitudinous ways. You only experienced one probable past. By changing this past in your mind, now, in your present, you can change not only its nature but its effect, and not only upon yourself but upon others.

Pretend a particular event happened that greatly disturbed you. In your mind imagine it not simply wiped out, but replaced by another event of more beneficial nature. Now this must be done with great vividness and emotional validity, and many times. It is not a self-deception. The event that you choose will automatically be a probable event, which did in fact happen, though it is not the event you chose to perceive in your given probable past.

(10:24.) Telepathically, if the process is done correctly, your idea will also affect any people who were connected with the original event, though they can choose to reject as well as accept your version.

This is not a book on techniques, so I will not go into this particular method deeply, but merely mention it here. Remember, however, that in a most legitimate way many events that are not physically perceived or experienced are as valid as those that are, and are as real within your own invisible psychological environment.

There are in your terms, then, unlimited probable future events for which you are now setting groundworks. The nature of the thoughts and feelings you originate and those that you habitually or characteristically receive set a pattern, so you will choose from those probable futures those events that will physically become your experience. *(Pause.)*

Because there are bleed-throughs and interconnections, it is possible for you to tune into a "future event," say of an unfortunate nature, an event for which you are headed if you continue on your present course. A dream about it, for instance, may so frighten you that you avoid the event and do not experience it. If so, such a dream is a message from a probable self who <u>did</u> experience the event.

(10:30.) So can a child then in a dream receive such communications from a probable future self, of such a nature that its life is completely changed. The entire identity is being now. All divisions are merely illusions, so one probable self can hold out a helping hand to another, and through these inner communications the various probable selves in your terms <u>begin</u> to understand the nature of their identity.

Now this leads to other adventures in which whole civilizations may be involved, for as individuals have their probable destinies, so do civilizations, nations, and inhabited planetary systems. Your historical earth as you know it has developed in many different ways, and there is a deeply unconscious connection that unites all such manifestations.

In their own way, even atoms and molecules retain a knowledge of the forms through which they have passed, and so the individuals that compose any given civilization contain deep within themselves the inner knowledge of experiments and trials, successes and failures, in which the races have also been involved at other levels of reality. You may take your break.

(10:39 to 10:55.)

In some probable realities, Christianity as you know it did not flourish. In some, males did not dominate. In others the makeup of physical matter simply followed different lines. Now all of these probabilities are in the air about you, so to speak, and I describe them as faithfully as I can, but I must relate them with concepts with which you are somewhat familiar. To some extent, then, the "truth" must be sifted through your own conceptual patterns in order for you to comprehend it at all.

Suffice it to say, you are surrounded by other influences and events. Certain of these you perceive in your three-dimensional reality. You accept them as real without realizing that they are only portions of other events. Where your vision fails, you think reality ceases, so again you must train yourselves to look between events, between objects, within yourself when you do not seem to be doing anything. Watch out for events that appear to make no sense, for they are often clues to larger invisible events.

End of dictation.

(Seth then briefly answered a couple of personal questions.)

So, if you have no more questions or comments . . . *(I shook my head.)* I intend to finish this chapter on Wednesday. My heartiest good wishes and a fond good evening, and when we get settled we will start on you.

("Okay. Thank you very much, Seth. Good night." 11:06 P.M.)

SESSION 567, FEBRUARY 17, 1971,
9:14 P.M. WEDNESDAY

Good evening.

("Good evening, Seth.")

Now: We will resume dictation.

The nature of matter itself is not understood. You perceive it at a certain "stage." Using your terms now and speaking as simply as possible, there are other forms of matter beyond those you see. These forms are quite real and vivid, quite "physical," to those who react to that particular sphere of activity.

In terms of probabilities, therefore, you choose certain acts, unconsciously transform these into physical events or objects, and then perceive them. But those unchosen events also go out from you and are projected into these other forms. Now the behavior of atoms and molecules is involved here, for again these are only present within your universe during certain stages. Their activity is perceived only during the range of particular vibratory rhythms. When your scientists examine them for example, they do not examine the nature, say, of an atom. They only explore the characteristics of an atom as it acts or shows itself within your system. Its greater reality completely escapes them.

(9:24.) You understand that there are spectrums of light. So are there spectrums of matter. Your system of physical reality is not dense in comparison with some others. The dimensions that you give to physical matter barely begin to hint at the varieties of dimensions possible.

Some systems are far heavier or lighter than your own, though this may not involve weight in the terms with which you are familiar. Probable actions emerge, then, into matter-systems quite as valid as your own, and quite as consistent. You are used to thinking in single-line thoughts, so you think of events that you know as complete things or actions, not realizing that what you perceive is but a fraction of their entire multidimensional existence.

(9:30.) In greater terms, it is impossible to separate one physical event from the probable events, for these are all dimensions of one action. It is basically impossible to separate the "you" that you know from the probable you's of which you are unaware, for the same reasons. There are always inner pathways, however, leading between probable events; since all of them are manifestations of an act in its becoming, then the dimensions between these are illusions.

The physical brain alone cannot pick up these connections with any great success. The mind, which is the inner counterpart of the brain, can at times perceive the far greater dimensions of any given event through a burst of sudden intuition or comprehension that cannot be adequately described on a verbal level.

(Pause at 9:35.) As I have said frequently, time as you think of it does

not exist, yet in your terms, time's true nature could be understood if the basic nature of the atom was ever made known to you. In one way, an atom could be compared to a microsecond.

It seems as if an atom "exists" steadily for a certain amount of time. Instead it phases in and out, so to speak. It fluctuates in a highly predictable pattern and rhythm. It can be perceived within your system only at certain points in this fluctuation, so it seems to scientists that the atom is steadily present. They are not aware of any gaps of absence as far as the atom is concerned.

(9:41.) In those periods of nonphysical projection, the off periods of fluctuation, the atoms "appear" in another system of reality. In that system they are perceived in what are "on" points of fluctuation, and in that system also then the atoms (seem to) appear steadily. There are many such points of fluctuation, but your system of course is not aware of them, nor of the ultimate actions, universes, and systems that exist within them.

Now the same sort of behavior occurs on a deep, basic, secret, and unexplored psychological level. The physically oriented consciousness, responding to one phase of the atom's activity, comes alive and awake to its particular existence, but in between are other fluctuations in which consciousness is focused upon entirely different systems of reality; each of these coming awake and responding, and each one having no sense of absence, and memory only of those particular fluctuations to which they respond.

Now you may take your break.

(9:47 to 10:06.)

Now: Resume dictation. These fluctuations are actually simultaneous. It would seem to you as if there would be gaps between the fluctuations, and the description I have used is the best one for our purposes; but the probable systems all exist simultaneously, and basically, following this discussion, the atom is in all these other systems at one time.

Now we have been speaking in terms of fantastically swift pulses or fluctuations, so smooth and "brief" that you do not notice them. But there are also "slower," "more vast," "longer" fluctuations from your end of the scale.

(10:14.) These affect entirely different systems of existence than any

closely connected with your own The experience of such kinds of consciousness is highly alien to you. One such fluctuation might take several thousand of your years, for example. These several thousand years would be experienced, say, as a second of your time, with the events occurring within it perceived simply as a "present period."

Now the consciousness of such beings would also contain the consciousness of large numbers of probable selves and systems, experienced quite vividly and clearly as multiple presents. These multiple presents can be altered at any of an actual number of infinite points; infinity not existing in terms of one indefinite line, but in terms of numberless probabilities and possible combinations growing out of each act of consciousness.

(10:25.) Such beings, with their multiple presents, may or may not be aware of your particular system. Their multiple present may or may not include it. You may be a part of their multiple present without even being aware of it. In much more limited terms your probable realities are multiple presents. *(Long pause.)* The image, for an analogy, of an e-y-e *(spelled out)* within an eye within an eye, endlessly repeated, may be useful here. End of that chapter.

(Pause at 10:29. Jane's delivery had been smooth and easy, seemingly effortless. I told her the material was excellent. I found statements like, "In one way, an atom could be compared to a microsecond," particularly evocative.

(After a very short break Jane gave several pages of material for us. The session ended at about 11:25 P.M.)

CHAPTER 17

PROBABILITIES, THE NATURE OF GOOD AND EVIL, AND RELIGIOUS SYMBOLISM

SESSION 568, FEBRUARY 22, 1971, 9:19 P.M. MONDAY

(*Jane felt very relaxed and sleepy by session time, yet she didn't want to miss a session. She began speaking at a slower pace than usual.*)

Good evening.

(*"Good evening, Seth."*)

Now: Dictation.

The chapter heading: "Probabilities, the Nature of Good and Evil, and Religious Symbolism."

Christian dogma speaks of the ascension of Christ, implying of course a vertical ascent into the heavens, and the development of the soul is often discussed in terms of direction. To progress is supposedly to ascend, while the horror of religious punishment, hell, is seen at the bottom of all things.

Development is therefore considered in a one-line direction only, in Christian terms. Seldom, for example, is it thought of in horizontal terms. The idea of evolution in its popular meaning promulgated this theory, as through gradual progression in a one-line direction, man emerged from the ape. (*Humorously*): Christ could just as well have disappeared sideways.

(*Pause at 9:26.*) The inner reality of the message was told in terms that man at the time could understand, in line with his root assumptions. Development unfolds in all directions. The soul is not ascending a series of stairs, each one representing a new and higher point of development.

Instead, the soul stands at the center of itself, exploring, extending its capacities in all directions at once, involved in issues of creativity, each one highly legitimate. The probable system of reality opens up the nature of the soul to you. It should change current religion's ideas considerably. For this reason, the nature of good and evil is a highly important point.

(9:30.) On the one hand, quite simply and in a way that you cannot presently understand, evil does not exist. However, you are obviously confronted with what seem to be quite evil effects. Now it has been said often that there is a god, so there must be a devil — or if there is good, there must be evil. This is like saying that because an apple has a top, it must have a bottom — but without any understanding of the fact that both are a portion of the apple. *(Pause; one of many.)*

We go back to our fundamentals: You create reality through your feelings, thoughts, and mental actions. Some of these are physically materialized, others are actualized in probable systems. You are presented with an endless series of choices, it seems, at any point, some more or less favorable than others.

You must understand that each mental act is a reality for which you are responsible. That is what you are in this particular system of reality for. As long as you believe in a devil, for example, you will create one that is real enough for you, and for the others who continue to create him.

(9:35.) Because of the energy he is given by others, he will have a certain consciousness of his own, but such a mock devil has no power or reality to those who do not believe in his existence, and who do not give him energy through their belief. He is, in other words, a superlative hallucination As mentioned earlier, those who believe in a hell and assign themselves to it through their belief can indeed experience one, but certainly in nothing like eternal terms. No soul is forever ignorant.

Now those who have such beliefs actually lack a necessary deep trust in the nature of consciousness, of the soul, and of All That Is. They concentrate upon not what they think of as the power of good, but fearfully upon what they think of as the power of evil.

(9:40.) The hallucination is created, therefore, out of fear and of

restriction. The devil idea is merely the mass projection of certain fears — mass in that it is produced by many people, but also limited in that there have always been those who rejected this principle.

Some very old religions understood the hallucinatory nature of the devil concept, but even in Egyptian times, the simpler and more distorted ideas became prevalent, particularly with the masses of people. In some ways, men in those times could not understand the concept of a god without the concept of a devil.

Storms, for example, are highly creative natural events, though they can also cause destruction. Early man could see only the destruction. Some intuitively understood that any effects are creative, despite their appearances, but few could convince their fellow men.

(Pause at 9:47.) The light-and-darkness contrast presents us with the same kind of picture. The good was seen as light, for men felt safer in the day. The evil was therefore assigned to nightfall. Within the mass of distortions, however, hidden beneath the dogma there was always a hint of the basic creativity of every effect.

There are, then, no devils waiting to carry anyone off, unless you create them yourself, in which case the power resides in you and not in the mock devils. The Crucifixion and attendant drama made sense within your reality at the time. It arose into the world of physical actuality out of the inner reality from which your deepest intuitions and insights also spring.

(9:52.) The race brought forth the events, then, that would best convey in physical terms this deeper nonphysical knowledge of the indestructibility of the soul. This particular drama would not have made sense to other systems with different root assumptions than your own.

You may take your break.

(9:54. Jane's trance had been good. Her delivery had picked up considerably. And of course I've often seen her respond to this infusion of energy and liveliness, seemingly from a source beyond Jane as I know her. If anything, her transformation is more pronounced when she's not at her best before a session begins. . . . Resume at 10:07.)

Now: The symbolism of ascent or descent, or of light and dark, would be meaningless to other realities with different perceptive mechanisms. While your religions are built around an enduring kernel of truth, the symbolism used was craftily selected <u>by</u> the inner self in line with its knowledge of those root assumptions you hold as valid in the physical universe. Other information, in dreams for example, will also be given to you with the same symbolism, generally speaking. The symbolism itself, however, was simply used by the inner self. It does not inherently belong to inner reality.

(10:13.) Many probable systems have perceptive mechanisms far different from your own. In fact, some are based upon gestalts of awareness completely alien to you. Quite without realizing it, your ego is a result of group consciousness, for example; the one consciousness that most directly faces the exterior world, is dependent upon the minute consciousness that resides within each living cell of your body; and as a rule you are only aware of one ego — at least at a time.

In some systems the "individual" is quite aware of having more egos than one, in your terms. The entire psychological organization is in a way richer than your own. A Christ who was not aware of this would not appear in such a system, you see. There are kinds of perception with which you are not familiar, worlds in which your idea of light does not exist, where almost infinite gradations of thermal qualities are absorbed in terms of sensation, not of light.

(10:21.) In any of these worlds, the Christ drama could never appear as it appeared within your own. Now the same thing applies to each of your great religions, though as I have said in the past, the Buddhists come closer, generally speaking, to a description of the nature of reality. They have not understood the eternal validity of the soul, however, in terms of its exquisite invulnerability, nor been able to hold a feeling for its unique character. But Buddha, like Christ, interpreted what he almost knew in terms of your own reality. Not only of your own physical reality, but your own probable physical reality.

(10:28.) The methods, the secret methods behind all of the religions, were meant to lead man into a realm of understanding that existed apart from the symbols and the stories, into inner realizations that would take him both within and without the physical world that he knew. There are many manuscripts still not discovered, from old monasteries particularly in Spain, that tell of underground groups within religious orders who kept these secrets alive when other monks were copying old Latin manuscripts.

There were tribes who never learned to write in Africa and Australia who also knew these secrets, and men called "Speakers" who memorized them and spread them upward, even throughout northern portions of Europe, before the time of Christ.

("Could you give a copy of one of those Speaker manuscripts in dictation?")

It is possible, and would take much time and excellent circumstances.

("Well, naturally I'd like to see it sometime.")

Offhand, the work involved could take five years, for there were several versions, and a group of leaders, each going in different directions, who taught their people. The world was far more ripe for Christianity than people suppose, because of these groups. The ideas were "buried" already throughout Europe.

(Pause at 10:36. "Buried" is the word Seth wanted here; I questioned him to make sure.

(A note: Seth has mentioned the Speakers just once before. This happened quite unexpectedly in the 558th Session for November 5, 1970. The apropos portion of that session, which was held for friends in an effort to resolve certain problems, is given in the Appendix, with notes. Jane and I find the idea of the Speakers most interesting. We'd like to learn more about this, and may make it a future project.)

Many important concepts were lost, however. The emphasis was on practical methods of living — quite simply — rules that could be understood, but the reasons for them were forgotten.

The Druids obtained some of their concepts from Speakers. So did the Egyptians. The Speakers predated the emergence of any religions that you know, and the religions of the Speakers arose spontaneously in many scattered areas, then grew like wildfire from the heart of Africa and Australia. There was one separate group in an area where the Aztecs dwelled at a later date, though the land mass was somewhat different then, and some of the lower cave dwellings at times were under water.

(10:41.) Various bands of the Speakers continued through the centuries. Because they were trained so well, the messages retained their authenticity. They believed, however, that it was wrong to set words into written form, and so did not record them. They also used natural earth symbols, but clearly understood the reasons for this. The Speakers, singly, existed in your Stone Age period, and were leaders. Their abilities helped the cavemen survive. There was little physical communication, however,

in those days between the various Speakers, and some were unaware of the existence of the others.

Their message was as "pure" and undistorted as possible. It was for this reason however, through the centuries, that many who heard it translated it into parables and tales. Now, strong portions of Jewish scriptures carry traces of the message of these early Speakers, but even here, distortions have hidden the messages.

Take your break.

(10:44. Jane said that after my questions she felt herself "go back and back and back," as she talked about the Speakers.

(It is of interest here to note that a current Biblical reference work, in dealing with the very early history of Israel, has much to say about the "oral traditions" which preceded — and thus helped shape — the written word by many centuries. During this long oral period many distortions, omissions, etc., took place for a variety of reasons. Recent work has shown that the early gathering and writing of traditions dates from about the twelfth century B.C. This in turn led to the biblical books. Resume at 11:02.)

Since consciousness forms matter, and not the other way around, then thought exists before the brain and after it. A child can think coherently before he learns vocabulary — but he cannot impress the physical universe in its terms. So this inner knowledge has always been available, but is to become physically manifest — literally made flesh. The Speakers were the first to impress this inner knowledge upon the physical system, to make it physically known. Sometimes only one or two Speakers were alive in several centuries. Sometimes there were many. They looked around them and knew that the world sprang from their interior reality. They told others. They knew *(pause)* that the seemingly solid natural objects about them were composed of many minute consciousnesses.

They realized that from their own creativity they formed idea into matter, and that the stuff of matter was itself conscious and alive. They were intimately familiar with the natural rapport existing between themselves and their environment, therefore, and knew that they could alter their environment through their own acts.

Now I will end here for the night, and continue with the Speakers at our next session.

("Was Ruburt, or Jane, ever a Speaker?")

Ruburt was.

(*"Were you?"*)

I was indeed. There were two others that you know of. The one mentioned in class material *(in the 558th session)*, and the other yourself. *(This was a distinct surprise to me.)* Now the Speakers themselves in the reincarnational process can also use or not use their abilities in any given life, or be aware of them. I bid you a fond good evening.

(*"The same to you, Seth. Thank you very much."*)

(Pause.) You must remember, as a postscript, that there have been millions of Speakers.

(*"Yes." 11:13 P.M. Jane said she remembered Seth saying that both of us had been Speakers. She'd had a quick, almost disbelieving reaction: "Now, that's just too pat." Then she had felt Seth return with the mention of the millions as an answer, blunting any particular uniqueness in the fact that both of us had been Speakers and were now producing the Seth material.*

(After the session I wondered if the Seth material itself could be a distorted version of the Speakers' messages. Jane said it might be possible. Actually, she felt, the Speakers' material was "probably more poetical.")

SESSION 569, FEBRUARY 24, 1971,
9:25 P.M. WEDNESDAY

Now —

(*"Good evening, Seth."*)

Dictation: Generally speaking *(smile)*, once a Speaker always a Speaker, in your terms. In some incarnations, the abilities might be used so powerfully that all other aspects of the personality remained in the background. At other times the capacities might be timidly used. The Speakers possess an extraordinary vividness of feeling and thought projection.

They can impress others with greater import through their communications. They can move from inner to outer reality with easy ability. They know instinctively how to use symbolism. They are highly creative on an unconscious level, constantly forming psychic frameworks beneath normal consciousness that can be used both by themselves and others in dream and trance states. They often appear to others in the dream condition, and they help dreamers in the manipulation of inner reality. They form images with which the dreamers can relate, images that can be used as bridges and then as gateways into kinds of consciousness more separated from your own.

(9:30.) The symbolism of the gods, the idea of the gods on Olympus, for example, the crossing-over point at the River Styx — that kind of phenomenon was originated by the Speakers. The symbolisms and frameworks of religion, therefore, had to exist not only in the physical world but also in the unconscious one. Outside of your own framework, houses as such or dwellings as such are not needed, and yet in trance encounters or dream encounters with other realities, such structures are frequently seen. They are transformations of data into terms that will be meaningful to you.

After death, for example, an individual may continue to create these — masses of individuals may — until they realize that the frameworks are no longer necessary. The Speakers were not confined in their activities, therefore, to waking consciousness. In all periods of your time they went about their duties both in the waking and sleep state. Much of the most pertinent information, in fact, was memorized by trainees during the dream condition, and passed on in the same manner. These unwritten manuscripts therefore were also illustrated, so to speak, by dream journeys or field trips into other kinds of reality. Such training still goes on. The particular psychic or story framework may vary. For example, conventional images of the Christian God and the saints may be utilized by the Speakers, with all of this highly vivid. The dreamer may find himself then in a magnificent harem, or instead in a brilliantly illuminated field or sky. Some Speakers confine their abilities to the dream state; and, waking, are largely unconscious of their own abilities or experience.

(Pause at 9:40.) Now it is meaningless to call such dreams or dream places hallucinations, for they are representations of definite "objective" realities that you cannot perceive as yet in their own guise. The Egyptian religion was largely based upon the work of the Speakers, and great care was given to their training. The outward manifestations given to the masses of the people became so distorted, however, that the original unity of the religion finally decayed.

However, efforts were being made then to map inner reality in ways that have not been attempted since. It is true that in the dream state and in some other levels of existence close to your own, there is strong individual play in the creation of images, and a magnificent use of symbolism, but all of this takes place, again, in an "objective" definite environment, an environment whose characteristics make such phenomena possible — a field of activity, then, with its own rules. Now the Speakers are familiar with those rules, and often serve as guides. They have at times worked within organizations as in Egypt, where they worked through the temples and became involved with the power structures. As a rule, however, they are far more solitary.

Because of the true simultaneous nature of time, they are, of course, speaking to all of your ages at once through their various manifestations. On occasion they also serve as mediators, introducing to each other two incarnations of one personality, for example.

You may take your break.

(9:51 to 10:04.)

Now: The rules within physical reality say that objects appear to be stationary and permanent. The rules of other realities are often far different, however. The nature of mental activities will follow different lines, and "continuity" in terms of time will not exist. Perceptual organization will exist by the use of different psychological groupings. *(Pause.)*

From the outside, such systems would seem meaningless to you even if you were able to perceive them. You would not be able to observe the pivot points about which actions occurred. The very definite rules of that system then would be quite obscure to you.

Now the Speakers are familiar with the rules within many systems. Still, however, most of these systems in larger terms are somewhat connected with your own kind of reality. There are an infinite number of inner universes. Only the very highest, most developed gestalt consciousness can be aware of anything like their totality. In this larger context, then, the Speakers must be called local. There is something like a chart mapping many of the nearby systems of reality, and I hope some day in your terms to make this available. In order to do so, Ruburt must be trained somewhat more intensely. There are points of coincidence where under certain conditions entry may be made from one of these systems to the other. They need not exist separately in space as you know it, of course.

(10:19.) These are called coordination points, where one camouflage merges into the other. Some of these are geographical in your system, but in all cases, a tuning-in of consciousness is a necessary

preliminary. Such entries can only be made in an out-of-body condition. Each individual in his dreams has access to the information possessed by the Speakers. There are adjacent states of consciousness that occur within the sleep pattern, that cannot be picked up by your EEG's — adjacent "corridors" through which your consciousness travels.

(An EEG, or electroencephalograph machine, traces brain wave patterns on graph paper.)

The higher centers of intuition are activated while physically oriented portions of consciousness remain with the body. The "absent" portion of the self cannot be traced through brain patterns, though the point of its departure and the point of its return may show a particular pattern. The "time out" itself, however, will not be detected in any way, the tracings showing only whatever characteristic pattern was being given immediately before departure.

Now this happens in every night's sleep. Two areas of activity are involved, one very passive and one acutely active. In one state this portion of consciousness is passive, receiving information. In the next stage it is active as it takes part through action — the concepts given it are then vividly perceived through participation and examples. This is the most protected area of sleep. The rejuvenating characteristics enter in here, and it is during this period that the Speakers act as teachers and guides.

(Pause.) This information is, then, often interpreted on return by other layers of the self such as the body consciousness and subconscious, where it is formed into dreams that will have meaning to these areas of the self and where general teaching, for example, may be translated into practical advice involving a particular matter.

You may take your break.

(10:34 to 10:45.)

Now: There are several very definite stages of sleep, and they all perform various services for the personality. They are also signals for different layers of consciousness, realization, and activity. They are accompanied by some physical variations, and there are some variations having to do with age.

In our next chapter I will speak of these in some detail. For now it is sufficient to realize that specific steps, definite alterations, occur as consciousness is shifted from the exterior to the interior reality, and that these changes are not random; that consciousness leaves through a very predictable route to its many destinations. Through the ages the Speakers have taught dreamers how to manipulate in these other environments. They have taught them how to bring back information that could be used for the good of the present personality. According to the intent, present purpose, and development, an individual may be aware of these travels to varying degrees. Some have excellent recall, for example, but often misinterpret their experience because of conscious ideas.

It is very possible for one dreamer who is a Speaker, to go to the aid of another individual who is having some difficulties in an inner reality within the dream state. The idea of guardian angels of course is highly connected here. A good Speaker is as effective within one reality as he is within the other, creating psychic frameworks within physical reality as well as within interior environments. Many artists, poets, and musicians are Speakers, translating one world in terms of another, forming psychic structures that exist in both with great vitality — structures that may be perceived from more than one reality at once.

(Pause at 10:57.) End of dictation. Now you may end the session or ask questions if you prefer.

("Have you got anything you want to say?")

Not specifically.

("Well, we might as well end it then.")

My heartiest regards to you both, and a fond good evening.

("Same to you, Seth. Thank you very much.")

Ruburt should fix foods that he knows he likes. Yes, and fuss with his table a bit. Think of food and its preparation in creative terms, tell him. Food comes last. He eats because he must. Have him think more in terms of the creative preparation of pleasant foods he likes, an emphasis on an old forgotten pattern. He enjoys cooking when he thinks in that fashion.

Let him coax himself with pleasant foods. He will not feel he is force-feeding himself then. He likes gravy and potatoes, but does not bother because of you. He will enjoy the cream. There are patterns to work on here, then.

A minor hobby. Under different circumstances cooking could be a hobby of his, so bank on that. The emphasis being physical as with the exercises. And now good evening.

("Good evening, Seth." 11:03 P.M.)

(As in the last session, Jane began speaking in an unhurried but quite businesslike manner.)

Now: Good evening.

("Good evening, Seth.")

Dictation: There are also various states of consciousness in waking life, upon which you do not focus, and of which you are usually quite unaware. Each state knows its own conditions and is familiar with a different kind of reality.

"You" presently have a once-centered consciousness, in that "you" close off from your experience these other stages of consciousness in which other portions of your entire identity are intimately involved. These other stages of consciousness create their own realities as you create your own. The realities are, therefore, byproducts of consciousness itself. If you could become aware of these, they might appear to be other places to you, rather than realms or fields of different kinds of activities. If you probe into these realms you will be forced to perceive them with the root assumptions of your own system, translating feelings of warmth and comfort, for example, into images of warm shelters or buildings, or feelings of fear into images of demons.

On occasion even in waking life a personality may spontaneously shift gears, so to speak, and suddenly find itself for a second or perhaps a few moments within another such realm. Disorientation usually occurs. There are those who do this quite deliberately with training, but often they do not realize that they are interpreting the experiences they have with the values of their "home" consciousness.

(Pause at 9:23.) All of this is not as esoteric as it might seem. Almost every individual has had bizarre experiences with consciousness, and knows intuitively that their greater experience is not limited to physical reality. Most dreams are like animated postcards brought back from a journey that you have returned from and largely forgotten. Your consciousness is already oriented again to physical reality; the dream, an attempt to translate the deeper experience into recognizable forms. The images within the dream are also highly coded, and are signals for underlying events that are basically not decipherable.

The Speakers help you in the formation of dreams which are indeed multidimensional artistic productions of a kind — dreams existing in more than one reality, with effects that dissect various stages of consciousness that are real, in your terms, to both the living and the dead and in which both the living and the dead may participate. It is for this reason that inspirations and revelations are so often a part of the dream condition.

Divorced from physical focus, you are in a better position to hear the Speakers, to translate their instructions, to practice with the creation of images, and to be guided in the methods of maintaining the health of the physical body. In the most protected areas of sleep, the apparent barriers between many layers of reality vanish. You are aware, for example, of some probable realities. You choose which probable acts you want to actualize in your system. You follow other probable acts through in the dream state. You do this individually, but you also do it *en masse* on national and global levels.

You may take your break.

(9:34. Break was a little early. Jane was surprised, since she thought much more time had passed. I told her the material was most interesting. Resume in the same deliberate manner at 9:40.)

Consciousness at different levels or stages perceives different kinds of events. In order to perceive some of these you have only to learn to change the focus of your attention from one level to another. There are minute chemical and electromagnetic alterations that accompany these stages of consciousness, and certain physical changes within the body itself in hormone production and pineal activity.

You usually glide from wakefulness through to sleep without ever noticing the various conditions of consciousness through which you pass, yet there are several. First, of course, with various degrees of spontaneity, there is the inward turn of consciousness away from physical data, from worries and concerns of the day. Then there is an undifferentiated level between wakefulness and sleep where you act as a receiver — passive but open, in which telepathic and clairvoyant messages come to you quite easily.

Your consciousness can seem to float. There are varying physical sensations, sometimes of growing large, sometimes of falling. Both sensations are characteristic of moments in which you almost catch yourself, almost become aware of this undifferentiated area, and then translate some of its experiences into physical terms. The sensation of largeness, for example, is a physical interpretation of the psychic expansion. The feeling of falling is an interpretation of a sudden return of consciousness to the body.

(Pause at 9:50.) This period can last for only a few moments, for half an hour, or can be returned to. It is a cushioning, supportive, and expansive stage of consciousness. Suggestions given during this time are highly effective. Following this period there is an active state, that can occur, of pseudodreaming, where the mind busies itself with physical concerns that have managed to cling through the first two stages.

If these are too vigorous, the individual may awaken. This is a vivid, intense, but usually brief stage. Another undifferentiated layer follows, this time marked quite definitely by voices, conversations, or images, as consciousness tunes in more firmly to other communications. Several of these may compete for the individual's attention. At this point the body is fairly quiet. The individual will follow one or another of these inner stimuli to a deeper level of consciousness, and form into light dreams the communications he is receiving.

Somewhere during this time he will go into a deeply protected area of sleep, where he is at the threshold to other layers of reality and probabilities. At this point his experiences will be out of all context to time as you know it. He may experience years though only minutes have passed. He will then return toward physical reality in an area marked as REM sleep by your scientists, where physically oriented dream productions will be created, putting the knowledge he has gained into use.

(10:00.) The cycle would then be repeated. Almost the same kinds of fluctuations and stages occur even when you are waking, however, though you are even less aware of them because then the egotistical self acts quite purposefully to blanket out these other areas of experience.

The precise stages are present beneath waking awareness, however, and with the same chemical, electromagnetic, and hormonal fluctuations. You simply are not aware of what your consciousness is doing. You cannot yourselves keep track of it for five full moments of your time. The dimensions of it can only be sensed by those determined enough to take the time and effort required to journey through their own subjective realities. Yet intuitively each individual knows that a part of his experience escapes from him all the time. When you suddenly cannot remember a name that you should know, you have in essence the same kind of feeling of which you are always subconsciously aware.

The purpose of the Speakers is to help you correlate and understand this multidimensional existence, and to bring as much as possible of it to your conscious attention. Only by learning to feel, or sense, or intuitively perceive the depths of your own experience can you glimpse the nature of All That Is. By becoming more aware of your consciousness as it operates in physical life, you can learn to watch it as it manipulates through these other less familiar areas. Probable realities are only probable to you because you are not aware of them.

Now you may take your break.

(10:11. Jane's trance had been good. Her delivery tonight, without voice effects, with only short pauses and a minimum of gestures, was the kind that seemingly could continue indefinitely. At break I asked if Seth would title the first eight chapters of his book, as he began doing from Chapter Nine on. Resume in the same manner at 10:26.)

Now: These stages of consciousness are all a part of your own reality. A knowledge of them can be most useful. You can learn to "shift gears," stand aside from your own experience, and examine it with much better perspective. You can prepare questions or problems, suggesting that they be solved for you in the sleep state. You can suggest that you will speak with distant friends, or convey important messages that you cannot convey verbally, perhaps. You can bring about reconciliations, for example, at another layer of reality though you cannot do so in this one.

You can direct the healing of your body, telling yourself that this will be accomplished by you at one of the other levels of sleep consciousness, and you may ask for the aid of a Speaker to give you any necessary psychological guidance that is needed to maintain health. If you have particular conscious goals and if you are reasonably certain that they are beneficial ones, then you can suggest dreams in which they occur, for the dreams themselves will hasten their physical reality.

Now unconsciously you do many of these things. You often go back in time, so to speak, and "relive" a particular event so that it has a different ending, or say things that you wish you had said. A knowledge of one state of consciousness can help you in other states. In a light trance the meaning of dream symbols will be given if you ask for them. The symbols may then be used as methods of suggestion that will be tailored for you personally. If you discover, say, that a fountain in a dream represents refreshment, then when you are tired or depressed, think of a fountain. In another layer of reality, of course, you will be creating one.

(10:35.) In the most protected areas of sleep you are dealing with experience that is pure feeling or knowing, and disconnected from both words or images. As mentioned, these experiences are translated into dreams later, necessitating a return to areas of consciousness more familiar with physical data. Here a great creative synthesis and a great creative diversification takes place, in which any given dream image has meaning to various layers of the self — on one level representing a truth you have lived and on other levels representing this truth as it is more specifically applied to various areas of experience or problems. There will be a metamorphosis, therefore, of one symbol turning into many, and the conscious mind may only perceive a chaos of various dream images, because the inner organization and unity is partially hidden in the other areas of consciousness through which the reasoning mind cannot follow.

The unconscious and subconscious areas, however, are aware of much more of this information than the ego, for it receives only the minute residue of dream material as a rule. The Speakers therefore may appear within dreams as historical characters, as prophets, as trusted old friends, or in whatever guise will impress the particular personality.

(Pause.) In the original experience, however, the true nature of the Speaker is apparent. The production of dreams is as "sophisticated" an endeavor as is the production of the objective life of a given individual. It is simply living on different terms.

Now that is the end of dictation, and just about the end of our chapter, though not quite.

(Pause.) Do not worry about the [first eight] chapter headings — we will get to them. We will end the session or answer any questions if you prefer.

("I guess not, Seth.")

Then my heartiest good wishes to you both — and tell our friend
Ruburt to try the suggestions given in the material this evening.

(*"I'd thought of that."*)

Three nights in a row. And now a fond good evening.

(*"Good evening, Seth. Thank you very much."*)

I'm glad you enjoy my book.

(*"I do." End at 10:45 P.M.*)

SESSION 571, MARCH 3, 1971,
9:17 P.M. WEDNESDAY

(*Seth-Jane's delivery soon had me writing along at a very brisk pace in order to keep up.*)

Good evening.

(*"Good evening, Seth."*)

Now: We will resume dictation.

(*"All right."*)

These various stages of consciousness and fluctuations of psychic
activity can also be examined through direct experience from the waking
state. In the following chapter we will let you become more aware
of these ever-active portions of your own reality. End of chapter.

(*Seth had told us last time that he was near the end of the chapter, but we
hadn't realized of course that he was to finish it with a sentence or two in the
next session. Nor did we know why he chose this method. It was as though the
break between sessions didn't exist for him.*)

(*I meant to quiz him about this tonight, but regretfully never did so. Since
Jane doesn't look at the book, she is unable to remind me of such points unless
I happen to discuss them with her, and I forgot to do that, too.*)

CHAPTER 18

VARIOUS STAGES OF CONSCIOUSNESS, SYMBOLISM, AND MULTIPLE FOCUS

The next chapter will be called: "Various Stages of Consciousness, Symbolism, and Multiple Focus."

Within your own personality all facets of your consciousness converge, whether or not you are aware of it.

(Long pause; the pace was still slow at this point.) Consciousness can be turned in many directions, obviously, both inward and outward. You are aware of fluctuations in your normal consciousness, and closer attention would make some of this quite clear. You expand or narrow the scope of your attention constantly. You may focus upon one object almost to the exclusion of everything else at times, so that you literally are not conscious of the room in which you sit.

You may be "conscious" and reacting to a remembered event so strongly that you are relatively unaware of present events. You take all of these fluctuations for granted. They do not disturb you. If you are lost in a book and unaware momentarily of your immediate environment, you are not afraid that it will be gone when you want to turn your attention back to it. Nor in a daydream do you usually worry about returning safely to the present moment.

To some extent, all of these are small examples of the mobility of your consciousness, and the ease with which it can be used. In a strange manner, symbols can be regarded as samples of the way you perceive at various levels of consciousness. Their changing guises can be used as signposts. Fire, for example, is a symbol made physical, so a real fire tells you obviously that you are perceiving reality with your physically attuned consciousness.

(9:33.) A mental picture of a fire automatically tells you that another kind of consciousness is involved. A fire mentally seen that has warmth but does not burn destructively obviously means something else. All symbols are an attempt to express feelings, feelings that can never be expressed adequately through language. Symbols represent the infinite variations of feelings, and in various stages of consciousness these will appear in different terms, but they will always accompany you.

There are several exceptions, however, in which pure knowing or pure feeling is involved without the necessity for symbols. These stages of consciousness are infrequent and seldom translated into normal conscious terms.

Let us take a particular feeling and follow it through as it might be expressed at various levels of consciousness. *(Pause.)* Begin with a feeling of joy. In normal consciousness, the immediate environment will be perceived in a far different manner than it would be, say, if an individual were in a state of depression. The feeling of joy changes the objects themselves, in that the perceiver sees them in a far brighter light. He creates the objects far more vividly and with greater clarity. In feedback fashion, the environment then seems to reinforce his joy.

(9:41.) What he sees, however, is still physical, the objects of the material world. Pretend now that he begins to daydream and falls into a reverie. Into his inner mind come pictures or symbols of material objects, people or events, from perhaps the past as well as present and future imaginings, the joy now being expressed with greater freedom mentally, but with symbols.

The joy stretches out, so to speak, into the future, sheds also its light into the past, and may cover greater areas of expansion than could be shown in physical terms at that moment. Now imagine that our individual from his reverie falls either into a trance state or into a deep sleep. *(Long pause.)* He may see images that are highly symbolic to him of joy or exuberance. Logically there may be little connection between them, but intuitively the connections are clear. He now enters into his mental experiences far more deeply than in the reverie state, and may have a series of dream episodes in which he is able to express his joy and share it with others.

He is still dealing with physically oriented symbols, however. Now since we are using this discussion as a case in point we will continue to follow it even further. He may form images of dream cities or people that are of a very joyful nature, translate the emotion itself into whatever symbols are pertinent to him. An exuberance may be translated into images of playing animals, flying people, or animals or landscapes of great beauty. Again, the logical connections will be lacking, but the entire episode will be connected by this emotion.

(9:51.) The physical body all the while is greatly benefitted, because the beneficial feelings automatically renew and replenish its recuperative abilities. The feelings of joy now may lead to images of Christ, Buddha, or the prophets. These symbols are the changing scenes characteristic of consciousness at various stages. The experiences are to be considered as creations; creative acts all native to consciousness at various stages.

Beyond this are states in which the symbols themselves begin to fade away, become indistinct, distant. Here you begin to draw into regions of consciousness in which symbols become less and less necessary, and it is a largely unpopulated area indeed. Representations blink off and on, and finally disappear. Consciousness is less and less physically oriented. In this stage of consciousness the soul finds itself alone with its own feelings, stripped of symbolism and representations, and begins to perceive the gigantic reality of its own knowing.

It feels direct experience. If we use joy as our example, all mental symbols and images of it would finally disappear. They had emerged from it, and would fall away from it, not being the original experience, but by-products. The soul would then begin to explore the reality of this joy in terms that can hardly be explained, and in so doing would learn methods of perception, expression, and actualization that would have been utterly incomprehensible to it before.

(10:01. Jane's pace had been consistently good. I told her I thought the session was excellent.

(At break each of us mentioned a question. I wanted to be sure that the material given on the Speakers, so far, adequately dealt with the methods by which they were able to contact others in both the waking and dream states. I wanted

to know more about the Speakers' training, by whom it was conducted, and their intuitions and dream experiences.

(Jane's question arose out of material in the 560th session in Chapter Fourteen: She wanted to know the name of the third personality making up the three-part Christ entity that Seth has postulated. [In Chapter Eighteen of Jane's own book, The Seth Material, *Seth gave as members of this entity Christ, of course, and John the Baptist.] I told Jane now that I thought Seth intended to go into this whole matter much more thoroughly later in this book.*

(Resume at a faster pace at 10:19.)

Now: Physical objects are the most obvious of your symbols, and precisely for that reason you do not realize that they are symbols at all.

At different levels, consciousness works with different kinds of symbols. Symbols are a method of expressing inner reality. Working in one direction the soul, using its consciousness, expresses inner reality through as many symbols as possible, through living, changing symbolism. Each symbol itself then is to its own extent conscious, individual, and aware.

In so doing, the soul continually creates new varieties of inner reality to be explored. Working in the opposite direction, so to speak, the soul divests itself of all symbols, all representations, and using its consciousness in a different way learns to probe its own direct experience. Without symbols to come between it and experience, it perfects itself in a kind of value fulfillment that you presently cannot understand except symbolically.

Now these efforts go on whether you wake or sleep. Once you are aware of these activities, however, it is possible to catch yourself in various stages of consciousness, and even at times to follow your own progress, particularly through dream states. Your body is your most intimate symbol at this point, and again your most obvious.

(10:23.) You will use the idea of a body in most stages of consciousness. When you leave your physical body in any kind of out-of-body experience, you actually leave it in another that is only slightly less physical. This in turn is "later" discarded for one still less physical, but the idea of the form is so important a symbol that you carry it through all of your religious literature, and stories of hereafter.

At one point it will vanish with the other symbols. Now there was a time, speaking in your terms, before the making of symbols; a time

· 257 ·

so divorced from your idea of reality that only in the most protected areas of sleep does any memory of it ever return. It seems to you that without symbols there would be nonbeing, but this is a natural enough deduction since you are so symbol-oriented.

(Jane's delivery had been fast ever since break, and continued so.)

Those stages of consciousness that occur after death still all deal with symbols, though there is much greater freedom in their use, and greater understanding of their meaning. But in higher stages of consciousness, the symbols are no longer necessary, and creativity takes place completely without their use.

Obviously you cannot become aware of that stage of consciousness now, but you can keep track of the way symbols appear to you in both waking life and the dream state, and learn to connect them with the feelings they represent. You will learn that certain symbols will appear personally to you at various stages of consciousness, and these can serve as points of recognition in your own explorations. When Ruburt is about to leave his body from the dream state for example, he will often find himself in a strange house or apartment that offers opportunities for exploration.

The houses or apartments will always be different, and yet the symbol is always a signpost that he has reached a particular point of consciousness, and is ready to enter another state of consciousness. Each of you will have certain symbols that serve the same kind of purpose, highly individual to you. Unless you make an effort at self-exploration, however, these symbolic guideposts will make no conscious sense.

(10:36.) Some such symbols stay with you for life. Some in periods of great change may also alter their character, bringing forth a certain feeling of disorientation as these unconsciously familiar symbols undergo transformation. The same sort of thing applies to your physical living. A dog may be a symbol to you of natural joy, for example, or of freedom. After seeing an accident in which a dog is killed, then dogs may mean something entirely different to you.

This of course is obvious, but the same sort of symbol changing may occur within dreams. The dog's accident may be a dream experience, for that matter, that then changes your conscious symbolic feeling toward dogs in the waking state. One person may symbolize fear as a demon, as an unfriendly animal, or even as some perfectly simple ordinarily harmless object; but if you know what your own symbols mean, then you can use the knowledge not only to interpret your dreams but also as signposts to the state of consciousness in which they usually occur.

These symbols will change, therefore, in various stages of consciousness. Again, the logical sequence is not present, but the intuitive creation will change the symbols much in the way that an artist might change his colors.

You may take your break.

(10:44. Resume at the same fast pace at 10:58.)

All symbols stand for inner realities, therefore, and when you juggle symbols, you are juggling inner realities. Any exterior move that you make is made within the interior environment, within all the interior environments with which you are involved.

Symbols are highly charged psychic particles and that includes physical objects that have strong characteristics of attraction and expansion, that stand for inner realizations and realities that have not been perceived through direct knowing. (By direct knowing here, I mean instant cognition and comprehension, without symbolization.)

Even the symbols, then, at various stages of consciousness will appear differently, some seeking to have stability and permanence as your physical objects, following the principles or root assumptions of corporeal reality, and some changing much more quickly, as in the dream state, these being more immediate and sensitive indicators of feeling. Various states of consciousness seem to have their own environments in which these symbols appear, again, as objects appear in a physical environment.

Seemingly nonstable mental objects appear in the dream environment at certain levels. The symbols follow rules then in both cases. As mentioned earlier, again, the dream universe is as "objective" as the corporeal one. The objects and symbols within it are as faithful representations of dream life as physical objects are of waking life.

The nature of the symbol, therefore, can serve as an indication not only as to your environment but your state of consciousness within it. In normal dreaming within the context of an ordinary dream drama, the objects seem permanent enough to you. You take them for granted. You are still physically oriented. You project upon dream images the symbolism of your waking hours.

(11:10.) In other states of dream consciousness, however, houses may suddenly disappear. A modern building may suddenly replace a shack. A child may turn into a tulip. Now the symbols are obviously behaving in a different manner. In this environment, permanency is not a root assumption. Logical sequence does not apply.

Symbols that behave in this way can be clues to you that you are now at another stage of consciousness, and within an entirely different interior environment. Expression of feelings and of experiences are not limited to the rigid framework of objects stuck into consecutive moments. Feelings are automatically transformed and expressed in a new, mobile, immediate manner. In a way the tune of consciousness is quicker.

Actualization does not need to wait for hours or days. Experience is free from a time context. In this realm of consciousness an entire book may be written, or one's life plans thoroughly scrutinized. Your present time is one of many dimensions that help form this particular stage of consciousness. Therefore your past, present and future exist within it, but only as portions of that interior environment. You have to learn your way about, for the states of consciousness and their environment stretch out in their own way as your world stretches out, say, in space. It is not difficult, however, to be aware of yourself in this stage through giving yourself proper suggestions before sleep. *(Pause.)* End of dictation. We have a good start. . . .

("I think it's very good. Most evocative.")

Unless you have questions I will end the session.

("How about my question concerning the Speakers?")

I believe that has been covered.

("And the third Christ information?")

That will be covered. *(Half humorously):* And if there are ever any points that you want to discuss with me, feel free to do so. *(Louder and more emphatically):* My heartiest good wishes, and I'm sorry you were not at our sensitivity (ESP) class last night.

("So am I, Seth, but you know I was busy. Thank you and good night."

(11:24 P.M. The pace had again been fast. My writing hand felt it.)

(The session was late in starting because we went to the tax office after supper this evening. Jane enjoyed getting out of the house, though, and the interactions with others. She started the session at a good pace.)

Good evening.

("Good evening, Seth.")

Now: We will resume dictation, and later I will have a few words for you.

To some extent this transmutation of symbol can be observed in various stages of waking consciousness also. When you are at rest, awake but with eyes closed, images and pictures will often appear to your inner eye. Some will be physical-like materializations, images of trees or houses or people. Others will be simply shapes that change swiftly and seem to flow one into the other. As a rule, even the images that are recognizable will quickly be replaced by others in a kaleidoscope of constantly changing forms.

There may seem to you to be no logic to these inner pictures, and certainly no connection between them and what you were thinking a moment before, or even an hour before. To some extent they seem disconnected from you and not of your doing. Often, however, they represent the characteristics shown by consciousness when it is somewhat turned away from physical stimuli. The form of symbols is changed as the states of consciousness change.

(Pause at 9:48.) The images that you see in this circumstance represent the thoughts and feelings experienced just before you closed your eyes, or those that were paramount in your mind somewhat previously. The minute your eyes are closed, the thoughts and feelings express themselves through this symbolism. Because the images may seem to have no direct connection logically to these thoughts and feelings, you do not recognize them either as your own, nor are you able to tie them up with what they represent.

I am putting this rather simply here. *(Pause.)* Imaginatively you have greater freedom to express feelings than you do practically. An earlier particular fear felt during the day involving, say, a loss of a job may then be translated when you close your eyes into a series of seemingly unrelated symbols, all however connected to that one fear.

You may see in a quick series of pictures a deep hole in the ground. It may be replaced by a street urchin, obviously poor and from another century. A casket may appear, or a black wallet fly through the air. You may see a severe, dark, wintry scene. The picture of a character from an old book long forgotten may appear and disappear. In between may be a grouping of opposing symbols, representing your hope — a spring flower, a table loaded with food, a new suit of clothes, any sign of abundance that would have meaning to you. Nowhere would the thought of the potential loss of a job enter in. It would seem to you that you had forgotten it.

(9:57.) Through the use of symbols, however, your feelings would be given full play, each image rising and falling in flow with feelings so far underneath consciousness — pools of emotion — that you were not aware of them. They would automatically bring about these images however. Now with reflection you could connect these with their origin, but usually they would pass you by.

If you let yourself lie still longer with eyes closed, the symbolism would continue to change character, losing perhaps some of its visual characteristics and growing more intense in other directions. You might think you smell a particular odor, for example, that is distasteful to you (following through with the situation as given). You might, instead, translate the fear into a frightening physical sensation, and suddenly feel that you are falling, or that something unpleasant touched you.

Any of these changing characteristics of symbols should alert you to the altered state of your consciousness. If you let yourself drift off into sleep here, you would most probably manufacture two or three dreams that symbolized the fear, dreams in which you consider and try out possible solutions within the dream context. The job situation might never appear as such within any of the dreams, of course.

Still, to the unconscious the problem has been set and given. In the following deep protected areas of sleep, the higher centers of the inner self are allowed to function and come to the aid of the three-dimensionally oriented portion of the personality. This more liberated self sees the situation much more clearly, suggests a given line of action (but does not order it), and informs the dreaming self. The dreaming self then manufactures a group of dreams in which the solution is stated within a symbolic dream situation.

(10:11.) The final and more specific interpretation is done in areas of dreaming closer to the waking self, when the symbols grow more and more specific. There is a much more narrow aspect to symbolism, therefore: The closer you get to waking consciousness, the more limited and narrow the symbol. The handier it is in a given physical circumstance, the less valuable it is as a waking lifetime characteristic symbol.

To some extent the more precise a symbol is, the less meaning it can contain. In the most important dream work, done in the deep protected sleep periods, the symbols are powerful enough and yet condensed enough so that they can be broken down, used in a series of seemingly unrelated dreams as connectives, retain their original strength and still appear in different guises, becoming in each succeeding dream layer more and more specific.

Now even as you go about your day, your consciousness fluctuates, and you can catch yourself "symbolizing" in these different ways if you get in the habit of observing but not interpreting the state of your mind. Each physical event that has happened to you is filed away within your psyche as a definite group of symbols. These do not represent the experience, they contain the experience. These represent your personal symbol bank as far as your present life is concerned.

(Pause at 10:20.) There is a great unity between your daytime symbols and your dreaming ones. In a miraculous shorthand, many symbols carry the burden of far more than one experience, of course, and one symbol will therefore evoke not only one given experience, but similar ones. Personal association, therefore, is highly involved with your personal bank of symbols, and it operates in the dream states precisely as in waking life — but with greater freedom, and drawing from the future, in your terms, as well as from the past.

Therefore, you have greater use of symbolism in the dream state, for you are aware of past and future symbols. These vary in intensity; often they cluster together. Such multidimensional symbols will appear then in many ways, not simply visually. They will affect not only your own physical reality, but all realities in which you are involved. In a manner of speaking the symbols that you know are but the tail end of greater symbols.

You may take your break.

(10:28. Jane's trance had been deep. She was extremely relaxed. She happened to mention that while in trance she often didn't know whether her eyes were open or closed. I told her that almost always she looked directly at whoever Seth might be addressing, and that she used a range of physical movements and voice effects that could vary considerably. Resume at 10:43.)

Now: Resume dictation. When I referred to your personal bank of symbols, I meant to specify that this bank was yours from the day of your birth and before. It contained the symbols of your past existences in your terms (and in your terms, you add to it in this life). This bank of symbols must be activated, however. For example, you have visual images when you are born, internal visual images, symbols that are activated the moment you open your eyes for the first time. These serve you as learning mechanisms. You keep trying to utilize your eyes properly until exterior images conform with the inner patterns. This is extremely important, and not understood by your scientists.

The eye-opening activates the inner mechanism. If there is something wrong physically with the eyes, if they are blind for example, then that particular mechanism is not activated at that time. The personality may have chosen to be born blind for his own reasons. If those reasons change, or if inner psychic developments occur, *(pause)* then the physical eyes will be healed and the inner mechanism activated. There are endless varieties of behavior along these lines. The inner banks of symbols, however, operate as a drawing account, latent unless you take advantage of them. You think before you learn language, as I mentioned earlier in this book, but you already have at your psychic fingertips past experiences from other lifetimes to guide you.

(Pause at 10:49.) Those who are born into the same nationality, say twice consecutively, learn to speak much quicker the second time around. Some infants will think in the language of a past life before the new language is learned. All of this has to do with the use of symbols.

Sound is itself a symbol. You understand that from a given point of silence, sound begins and grows louder. What you do not understand is that from that given point of silence, which is your point of non-perception, sounds also begin that grow deeper and deeper into silence, yet still have meaning and as much variety as the sounds that you know, and these are also symbols. The thought unspoken has a "sound" that you do not hear, but that is very audible at another level of reality and perception.

(11:00.) Trees as they stand <u>are</u> a sound that, again, you do not perceive. In your dreams and particularly beyond those dreams that you recall, are areas of consciousness in which these sounds are automatically perceived and translated into visual images. They operate as a sort of shorthand. Given certain sounds, you could recreate your universe as you know it unconsciously, and any one multidimensional symbol can contain all the reality that you know. End of dictation. *(Pause.)* Now a few remarks.

(There followed a page or so of personal data. End at 11:06 P.M.)

SESSION 573, MARCH 10, 1971,
9:37 P.M. WEDNESDAY

(The session was witnessed by Patty Middleton, who drove down to Elmira from Ottawa, Canada, yesterday to attend Jane's ESP class. We met Patty in Philadelphia, Pennsylvania in September, 1970, while we were on tour for Jane's own book, The Seth Material.

(Today Patty filled Jane in on her studies in operant conditioning; how, with a simple Yogalike technique, monitored by an electroencephalograph, she learned to "turn on" her alpha brainwaves. This resulted in her achieving a certain state of relaxed awareness, where perceptions and feelings were held in ideal balance.

(The alpha technique is thought to have many medical potentials, although it isn't really known how the state is produced. Each practitioner has his or her own explanation and "feeling" for it. Seth comments briefly on alpha at the beginning of the session.

(Patty enthusiastically told us that Seth's material on the various stages of consciousness, in the 569th and 570th sessions in Chapter Seventeen, closely agreed with her recent studies. In addition, her comments and information fit in so well with this present chapter that I began to wonder if something more than coincidence had led her to visit us now. We hadn't been corresponding with her.

(A note: Patty read the late chapters of Seth's book but Jane did not. The two of them discussed the material, though.)

Now.

("Good evening, Seth.")

(To Patty, amused): I did not think that you did a very good job

imitating my voice. Now surely I do not sound as badly as all that. . . .
I have a few remarks.

Now: The alpha state is a threshold, a preliminary state between
the physically oriented portions of the personality and the inner self.
Ruburt often propels himself through this state to deeper states, and
to a large extent is unfamiliar with it.

Characteristically, when he leaves his body he does the same thing,
hardly pausing at the threshold of alpha but taking off from there.

I want to do some dictation, though I may have some comments
later, so give us a moment here.

(Pause at 9:42.) Now: Physically, smell, sight, and sound are combined together to give you your main sense data and compose your physical senses. At other levels, however, these are separated. Odors therefore
have a visual reality, and, as you know, visual data can also be perceived
in terms of other sense perceptions.

The symbols can come together or fly apart, can be perceived separately or as a unity. As each event has its own symbol for you, so you
have your characteristic way of combining these. These symbols can be
translated and perceived in many terms; as a series of notes for example, as a combination of senses, as a series of images. At various stages
of consciousness you will perceive the symbols in different terms. The
multidimensional symbol in its entirety, then, has a reality in other states
of consciousness, but also at other levels of reality entirely.

(9:45.) You operate as if your thoughts were secret, though you
should know by now that they are not. Not only are your thoughts apparent through telepathic communications, for example, but without your
conscious awareness they also form what you may call pseudo-images
"beneath" the range of physical matter as you normally perceive it in
some cases, or "above" this same range.

It is, therefore, as if your thoughts appear within other realities as
objects — alive and vital in themselves, growing into other systems as flowers or trees grow up seemingly from nothing within physical reality.
These can then be used as the raw material, so to speak, in certain other
systems. They are the given "natural data," the raw material of creativity in the realities that you help seed but do not perceive.

In this manner of speaking, your thoughts then follow laws. Their
behavior follows laws, and their activities, that you do not understand,
though you call your thoughts your own. They are then manipulated,

independently of you, by other kinds of consciousness as ever-changing natural phenomena. The native consciousness within such systems is not aware of the origin of this phenomena, nor of your own reality. They take the evidence that appears to their senses as reality, as most of you do. It would not occur to them that this phenomenon originated outside of their own system.

If I were to make the same statement for example to any of my readers, I would be accused of saying that physical reality was composed of the discards of the universe.

I am not saying that, nor implying it in the case just mentioned. In your system you have a direct hand in the formation of physical reality. Your natural given data is the result of individual, mass, and collective thoughts, feelings, and emotions, materialized. Your system in this respect is more creative than the systems just mentioned. On the other hand, within these other systems there is a strong innovative group consciousness developing, in which identity is retained but greater inner play allowed between individuals, a large creative interchange of symbol-pools, a drawing upon mental and psychic symbols with greater facility. Because of this, these individuals recognize more clearly the connection between creative images and given sense data. They purposely alter and change their given sense data, and experiment with it.

(Pause at 10:00.) All of this involves a working with symbols in a most intimate manner. At certain levels of your personality you are aware of all the different ways in which symbols are used, not only in your system but in others. As mentioned earlier, no system of reality is closed. Your thoughts and images and feelings therefore alter the given sense data in some other systems.

The innovative patterns developed in those systems, however, can be to some extent perceived within your own. There are constant bleed-throughs. In your various stages of consciousness you pass through areas that can be correlated with many of these systems. Some stages through which you pass are native stages to other kinds of consciousness, and while passing through these you will find yourself using symbols in the way that is characteristic of that level.

Now you may take a break and rest your fingers. *(To Patty):* — and if you think a pretty thought, you may make a flower grow up there *(in the living room)* somewhere.

(10:03. Jane's trance had been good, her pace fast, her voice quiet. During break, while the three of us tried alpha states, Jane abruptly found herself projecting.

(A magnificent Seckel pear tree, well over two stories tall, used to grow on the property west of our apartment house. We often admired it from our living room windows. Last year the owner of the house next door, a professional man, had the tree cut down to make room for a parking lot. Jane said she seemed to use the alpha state as the base for a projection into the past and into this tree: she found herself, briefly, amid a cluster of its leaves, peering out. . . .

(Resume at 10:24.)

Now: Symbols should be fluid, ever-changing in their form. Some can be used as casements to house original experiences, as methods of deception therefore rather than illumination. When this happens fear is always involved.

Fear taken into the various stages of consciousness acts as a distorting lens, hiding the natural dimensions of all symbols, acting as a barrier and as an impediment to free flow. Symbols of an explosive nature serve as releasing agents, setting loose that which has been encased. Without physical storms you would all go insane.

The aggressive nature of symbols is little understood, nor the relationship between aggression and creativity. These are far from opposing characteristics, and without an aggressive thrust, symbols would lack their high mobility. They would exist in a permanent kind of environment.

It is both the creative and aggressive aspects of consciousness that allow it to use symbols, to move through various levels of experience, and the aggressive nature of thought that so propels it, despite your knowledge, into realities that you do not understand.

Aggressiveness and passivity are both behind symbols of birth, for both are needed. They are both beneath symbols of death, though this is not understood. Inertia results when aggressiveness and creativity are not in the proper proportions, when consciousness leans too severely in one direction or another, when the flow of symbols is either too quick or too slow for the particular psychological environment in which you dwell.

(10:32.) Pauses then occur. To put it as simply as possible, there is an almost inconceivable moment in which a no-reality occurs, in which

a symbol is caught between motion and no motion, a time of uncertainty. This is of course translated in many ways, and reflected. In such periods, certain symbols can be lost to all intents and purposes, dropping out of an individual's experience, leaving gaps of inertia.

These gaps exist quite literally in many systems. You encounter them on many levels. You may find yourself experiencing a state of consciousness, for example, in which nothing seems to happen, and no psychological landscape or recognizable symbols occur. These exist not only psychologically or psychically, but as blank areas in terms of space. The spaces may be filled finally with new symbols. If you are perceptive enough, you can sometimes catch yourselves encountering such states of reality in which nothing appears and no signs of any consciousness outside of your own is apparent.

Such blank spots can be seeded with new symbols, and are often used as channels through which new creative ideas and inventions are inserted. These gaps are recognized by others, therefore, and viewed as dark spaces. They also represent areas of no resistance for those mind-travelers who are probing inner realities. They represent uncluttered areas, but also open channels, inactive in themselves but passively waiting. Now some symbols also wait in such a passive manner to be activated.

They represent future experience, in your terms, that presently lies latent. These blank spots of inertia, therefore, are creative to some extent, in that these other symbols may swim into view within them.

Now you may take your break and we will return.

(*10:43. Jane's pace had been fast again for the most part. My writing hand was beginning to flag. Resume in the same manner at 11:12.*)

Now: We will end dictation; and give us a moment. (*Pause.*)

The alpha level is undifferentiated. The energy there is available to be used as you want to. It is the fountainhead or pool in which reservoirs of energy are held in reserve, pulled between the more interior self and the outer self. Into this area come signs and portents from deeper levels of the personality.

Because it is so situated, it is also of particular use in manipulating the physical organism. As you are learning, spontaneity is extremely important here. Your intent before you enter the alpha state largely predetermines the kind of experience you will have, automatically focusing your attention in those specified areas.

It is also beneficial to dip into those areas with no purpose in mind, for here whatever necessary information that you require without your conscious knowledge can be made available. When you learn to explore this region you can use it as a launching pad for other activities. In so doing you leave your physical body in good hands.

When your consciousness leaves your body, the alpha state maintains its good condition for you. It does this of course in any case. The answer to past lives lies in a deeper level, however. You can fish for it from the alpha state if you prefer.

(Patty: "Just randomly? Like throwing a line into the water? Or is it possible to use some direction?")

You can use direction to some extent, but you must seek the direction from the alpha state, requesting it from the deeper layers. Or you may enter those areas yourself, with more training. This is more direct.

(Patty: "Will I discover myself just by trying these various states?")

(Smile): You know that you will, or you would not have asked me the question.

(Patty: "That's a nice answer.")

(Over two more pages of material for Patty followed. After that, with my right hand practically numb, I put my notebook aside and joined Patty and Seth in an impromptu discussion. Seth's energy and vitality seemed to be inexhaustible — his pace even speeded up. The session ended at 11:37 P.M. All of us were weary.)

CHAPTER 19

ALTERNATE PRESENTS AND MULTIPLE FOCUS

SESSION 574, MARCH 17, 1971,
9:26 P.M. WEDNESDAY

(*No session was held Monday, since Jane needed to rest. She was very sleepy and relaxed before the session this evening also, but she wanted to hold it. Once she began speaking for Seth, however, her manner turned fairly active; her voice became very clear and precise, and slightly loud.*)

Good evening.

(*"Good evening, Seth."*)

Now: We will resume dictation, and begin our next chapter to be called: "Alternate Presents and Multiple Focus."

Let us begin with the normal waking consciousness that you know. But one step away from this is another level of consciousness into which you all slip without knowing. We will call it "A-1." It is adjacent to your normal consciousness, separated from it very slightly; and yet in it very definite effects can appear that are not present in your usual state.

At this level many abilities may be used, and the present moment can be experienced in many different fashions, using as a basis the physical data with which you are already familiar. In your normal state you see the body. In A-1 your consciousness can enter the body of another, and heal it. You can in the same manner perceive the state of your own physical image. You can, according to your abilities, manipulate matter from the inside consciously, with lucidity and alertness.

A-1 may be used as a side platform, so to speak, from which you can view physical events from a clearer standpoint. Using it you are released momentarily from bodily pressures, and with that freedom, you can move to relieve them. Problems that seem beyond solution can often, though not always, be solved. Suggestions given are much more effective. It is easier to form images, and they have a greater mobility. A-1 is a sidestep away, therefore, and yet an important one.

(Pause at 9:33. Jane has already discovered that she has very good abilities using A-1 as a "side platform." This is a natural method for her. As she puts it: "Just off to the right of my cheek there's this little figure, this tiny little me that I can send places and do things with." When requested to, she has been able to enter the bodies of others with this miniature self, to check on various maladies, their causes, etc. Trying my own version of this technique, I have been able to enter Jane's knee for instance.

(Jane's interest in these possibilities began to grow after I described the 570th session in Chapter Seventeen to her — it will be remembered that Seth suggested I do this — and my progress was accelerated through Patty Middleton's visit a week later, with her information about alpha states.)

Now it can be used as the first of a series of steps, leading to "deeper" states of consciousness. It can also be used as the first of a series of adjacent steps. Each of the deeper layers of consciousness can also be used as first steps leading to other adjacent levels. A-1 is simple to enter. When you listen to music that you like, when you are indulging in an enjoyable quiet pursuit, you can sense the different feeling. It may be accompanied by your own characteristic physical clues. You may tap your fingers in a certain way. There may be a particular gesture. You may stare or look dreamily to the left or right.

Any such physical clues can help you differentiate between this state of consciousness and the usual predominating one. You have only to recognize it, learn to hold it, and then proceed to experiment in its use. As a rule, it is still physically oriented, in that the abilities are usually directed toward the inner perception and manipulation of matter or physical environment. You can therefore perceive the present moment from a variety of unique standpoints not usually available.

You can perceive the moment's reality as it exists for your intestine, or your hand; and experience, with practice, the present inner peace and commotion that exist simultaneously within your physical body. This brings a great appreciation and wonder, a sense of unity with the living corporeal material of which you are physically composed. With practice you can become as intuitively aware of your internal physical environment, as [of] your external physical environment.

(Pause at 9:43.) With greater practice, the contents of your own mind will become as readily available. You will see your thoughts as clearly as your inner organs. In this case you may perceive them symbolically through symbols you will recognize, seeing jumbled thoughts for example as weeds, which you can then simply discard.

You can request that the thought content of your mind be translated into an intense image, symbolically representing individual thoughts and the overall mental landscape, then take out what you do not like and replace it with more positive images. This does not mean that this inner landscape must always be completely sunny, but it does mean that it should be well balanced.

A dark and largely brooding inner landscape should alert you, so that you begin immediately to change it. None of these accomplishments are beyond my readers, though anyone may find any one given feat more difficult than another. You must also realize that I am speaking in practical terms. You can correct a physical condition for example, in the manner just given. If so, however, by examining the inner landscape of thoughts, you would find the source here that initially brought about the physical ailment. *(Pause.)*

Feelings can be examined in the same way. They will appear differently, with much greater mobility. Thoughts, for example, may appear as stationary structures, as flowers or trees, houses or landscapes. Feelings will appear more often in the changing mobility of water, wind, weather, skies and changing color. Any physical ailment, then, can be perceived in this state by looking inward into the body and discovering it; then by changing what you see you may find yourself entering your body or another's as a very small miniature, or as a point of light, or simply without any substance, yet aware of the inner body environment.

(9:54.) You change what needs to be changed in whatever way occurs to you, then — by directing the body's energy in that direction, by entering the flesh and bringing certain portions together that need this adjustment, by manipulating areas of the spine. Then from this adjacent platform of A-1 consciousness, you perceive the mental thought

patterns of yourself or the other person in whatever way you find characteristic of you.

You may perceive the thought patterns as quickly flashing sentences or words that are usually seen within your mind or within the other mind, or as black letters that form words. Or you may hear the words and thoughts being expressed, or you may see the earlier mentioned "landscape" in which the thoughts symbolically form into a picture.

This will show you how the thoughts brought about the physical malady, and which ones were involved. The same thing should then be done with the feeling pattern. This may be perceived as bursts of dark or light colors in motion, or simply one particular emotion of great force may be felt. If it is very strong, one emotion may be felt in many such guises. In the case of both thoughts and emotions, with great confidence you pluck out those that are connected with the malady. In such a manner you have made adjustments on three levels.

A-1 may be used also as a great framework for creativity, concentration, study, refreshment, rest and meditation. You may evolve your own image of this state to help you, imagining it as a room or a pleasant landscape or platform. Spontaneously, you will find your own symbol for this state.

You may take your break.

(10:02. Jane's trance had been deep, and my writing hand could attest to her fast delivery. In spite of being sleepy just before the session, she said, she had "felt Seth as clear as a bell." She had indeed spoken with an extra clarity. She'd also been aware of what Seth was saying, which usually isn't the case.

(This material was another instance of how Seth developed an idea in an original way. At first I wondered whether his A-1 state would merely repeat the alpha data given to us by Patty Middleton, but it soon developed that he was using alpha only as a takeoff point. Already he was well beyond it.

(Resume in the same fast manner at 10:21.)

Now: This state may be used also as a step to the next state of consciousness, leading to a deeper trance condition; still relating however to the reality system that you understand.

Or it may be used as a step leading to an adjacent level of consciousness; two steps away, therefore, on the same level from normal reality. In this case it will lead you not into a deeper examination and perception of the present moment, but instead into an awareness and recognition of what I will call alternate present moments.

You will be taking steps aside from the present that you know. This leads to explorations mentioned earlier in this book, into probabilities. This state can be extremely advantageous when you are trying to solve problems having to do with future arrangements, decisions that will affect the future, and any matters, in fact, in which important decisions for the future must be made. In this state you are able to try out various alternative decisions and some probable results, not imaginatively but in quite practical terms. *(Pause.)*

These probabilities are realities, regardless of which decision you make. Say, for example, that you have three choices and it is imperative that you select one. Using this state, you take the first choice. The alternative present is the moment in which you make that choice. Having made it the present is changed, and quite clearly you perceive exactly the way it is changed and what actions and events will flow from the change into the future that belongs to that particular alternate present.

(10:30.) You do the same with each of the other choices, all from the framework of that state of consciousness. The methods in each case are the same. You make the decision. You then become aware in whatever way you choose of the physical effects within your body. You enter the body as you did in the way I gave earlier for healing. With great sensitivity you are able to see what physical effect the decision will have — whether the state of the body remains the same, whether there is a great sense of health within it, or the incipient beginning of great difficulties.

In like manner you explore the mental and feeling aspects, then you turn your attention "outward," toward the environment that results from this alternate present. Mentally, events will appear to you. You may experience these strongly, or merely view them. They may become so vivid that you momentarily forget yourself, but if you maintain your contact with this level of consciousness, this will happen seldom. As a rule you are very aware of what you are doing.

According to the situation, you can do the same thing to find out the effect of this decision on others specifically. You then return to normal consciousness, going through the A-1 state that you used as a preliminary. After a period of rest, return and make the second decision, and again the third, following through in the same manner. Then in your normal state of consciousness, of course, you make the decision that you want from the information and experience that you have received.

(10:36.) The names make little difference. For simplicity's sake call this level of consciousness A-1-a.

There is an A-1-b, you see, still adjacent to this one, and still starting off from an alternate present that can be used for many other purposes.

(Pause.) It is not as easy for the ordinary individual to enter, and it deals with group presents, with mass probabilities, racial matters, the movement of civilization. It is one that would be most beneficial to politicians and statesmen, and it also can be used to probe into probable pasts as well. Here it would be of benefit in learning of old ruins for example, and vanished civilizations, but only if the specific probable past were probed in which these existed.

The next adjacent level now would be A-1-c, which is an extension of the one just given, in which there is greater freedom of action, mobility and experience. Here to some extent there is some participation in the events perceived. There is no need to go deeply into any of these beyond this point, because ordinarily you will not be involved with them, and they lead into realities that have little reference to your own. They are states of consciousness too divorced, and under usual circumstances, this is as far as your present consciousness is able to go in that particular direction.

The first state, A-1-a, is the most practical and the easiest for you, but often you must still have a good feeling for the A-1 level before you are willing to take that next adjacent step. It allows for great expansion, however, within its limitations. Using it, you can discover for example what would have happened if "I did this or the other." Remember, these are all adjacent levels, going out horizontally.

(10:47.) Directly beneath A-1, now, you will have A-2, which is a slightly deeper state, using the analogy of up and down direction. It is less physically oriented than A-1. You still have excellent lucidity and awareness. This state can be used to explore the past in your terms of reference, within the probable system that you know.

Reincarnational pasts are known to you here, and if some personal malady cannot be solved from A-1, you may have to go to A-2 discovering that it originated from another existence. This state is distinguished by a slower breathing pattern and, unless other directions are given, by a somewhat lowered temperature and longer alpha waves; a slower frequency.

There is still relation to environment, however, and awareness of it. This may be purposely blocked off for greater efficiency, but it is not necessary. In many cases the eyes may be open, for example, though it may be easier to close them. Here sensitivity is quickened. Without necessarily following the methods given in A-1, the mental, physical and feeling aspects of past personalities will appear.

(10:55.) They may be perceived in various ways according to the characteristics of the individual who is in this state. This can be used to discover the origin of an idea in the past, or to find anything that has been lost there, as long as it is within your probability system.

Directly beneath this is A-3. You have an extension, again, here dealing with mass issues — movements of land, the history of your planet as you know it, the knowledge of the races that inhabited it, the history of the animals, the layers of gas and coal, and of the various ages that swept across the planet and changed it.

You may take your break.

(10:59 P.M. Jane's trance had again been very good. She had experienced many images, but couldn't put them into words now. My writing hand was lame; because of this we didn't resume the session, much as I wanted to.

(Seth, Jane said, already had other "directions" in mind, involving the right and left; although he hadn't moved into these areas yet to any great degree via analogies, he had it all planned. She could "see" these directions. They had to do with probabilities.

(Jane told me that had the session continued, Seth was going to say that Patty Middleton's visit last week had been incipient from the time we met her in Philadelphia, in September, 1970. Seth knew there was a high probability that she would be here when he was working on the section of his book concerning stages of consciousness. This confirms my own speculations about the timing of her visit; see the notes prefacing the 573rd session in Chapter Eighteen.

(This isn't to say that Patty's journey here was preordained. Free will always operates. She simply "picked up" that this was a good time to see us, and chose to make the trip. Seth then used her information about alpha as an impetus for his own material on A-1, A-1-a, A-2, etc.)

(Compared to her intense approach in recent sessions, long portions of Jane's delivery tonight were quiet and easy.)

Good evening.

("Good evening, Seth.")

Now: We will resume dictation.

A-4 brings you to a level that is beneath matter formations, a level in which ideas and concepts can be perceived, although their representations do not appear in the present physical reality that you know.

From this layer many of the deepest inspirations come. These ideas and concepts, having their own electromagnetic identity, nevertheless appear as "the symbolic landscape" at this level of consciousness. This is difficult to explain. The thoughts do not appear as pseudoimages for example, or assume any pseudomaterialization, yet they are felt vividly, perceived and picked up by portions of the brain — those seemingly unused portions for which science has found no answer.

These ideas and concepts obviously came from consciousness. However, they represent incipient latent developments that may or may not occur in physical reality. They may or may not be perceived by any given individual. The characteristic interest and abilities of the personality involved will have much to do with his recognition of the realities within this layer of consciousness.

(Pause at 9:16. Jane, as Seth, took a lengthy pause as a fire engine passed the house, its siren screaming.)

The material available, however, represents building blocks for many probable systems. It is an open area into which many other dimensions have access. It often becomes available in sleep states. Complete innovations, world-shattering inventions — these all lie waiting, so to speak, in this huge reservoir. Strong personal "conversions" are often effected from this level. *(Pause.)*

Now any individual can pass through these levels and remain relatively untouched and unaware, can travel through them unperceiving. The overall intentions and characteristics of the personality will determine the quality of perception and understanding. The material mentioned is available in each of the levels of consciousness given, but it must be sought out, either through conscious desire or strong unconscious desire. If it is not, then the gifts available and the potentials simply remain unused and unclaimed.

(9:25.) The states of consciousness merge also one into the other, and it is obvious that I am using the terms of depth to make the discussion easier. Starting with the ego or waking consciousness as the outer self focused toward exterior reality, these states are broad, more like plains to be explored. Each one, therefore, opens in great adjacent areas also, and there are many "paths" to be taken according to your interest and desire.

As your ordinary waking state perceives an entire universe of physical data, so each of these other states of consciousness perceive realities as complicated, varied, and vivid. It is for this reason that it is so difficult to explain the experiences possible within any given one. *(Long pause.)*

A-5 opens up a dimension in which the vital consciousness of any personality can at least theoretically be contacted. This involves communicating not only with past personalities in your terms, but future ones. It is a level of consciousness very seldom reached. It is not, for example, the layer used by most mediums. It is a meeting ground in which personalities from any time or place or probable system can communicate with each other in clear terms understood by all.

Since past, present, and future do not exist, this is a level of crystal clear communication of consciousness. Those involved have an excellent knowledge of their own backgrounds and histories, of course, but in this state possess also a much larger perspective, in which private and historical backgrounds are seen as a portion of a greater perceivable whole.

(9:35.) At this level, messages literally flash through the centuries from one great man or woman to another. The future speaks to the past. The great artists have always been able to communicate at this level and while living literally operated at this level of consciousness a good deal of the time. Only the most exterior portions of their personalities bowed to the dictates of historical period.

For those who reach this state and utilize it, communication is clearest. It must be understood that this communication works in both ways. Leonardo da Vinci knew of Picasso, for example. There are great men and women who go unknown. Their contemporaries ignore them.

Their achievements may be misunderstood or physically lost, but at this level of consciousness they share in these communications, and at another level of existence their achievements are recognized.

I do not mean to imply, however, that only the great share in this communication of consciousness. *(Pause.)* A great simplicity is necessary, and out of this, many of the most lowly in men's terms also share in these communications. There is an unending conversation going on throughout the universe, and a most meaningful one. *(Long pause.)* Those from both your past and your future have a hand in your present world, and at this level the problems that have been met and will be encountered are being discussed. This is the heart of communication. It is most usually encountered either in a protected deep level of sleep or in a sudden spontaneous trance state. Great energy is generated.

Now you may take your break.

(9:47. Jane was aware that her pace had been quite slow most of the time. Resume at a faster rate at 10:05.)

Now: The information received in any of these states of consciousness must be interpreted for the normal waking consciousness, if any physical memory is to be maintained.

In many cases memory remains unconscious as far as waking self is concerned, but the experiences themselves can completely change the structure of an individual life. Disastrous courses can be averted through such inner communications and illuminations, whether or not the ego is aware of them.

The experiences at these various levels may be interpreted symbolically. They may appear in the form of fantasy, fiction, or art work, without the conscious self realizing their origin. Now at any of these various stages of consciousness, other phenomena may also be perceived — thought-forms for example, energy manifestations, projections from the personal subconscious, and projections from the collective unconscious. Any or all of these may take symbolic form, and may appear beneficial or threatening according to the attitude of the personality involved. They should be regarded as quite natural phenomena, often neutral in intent.

Often they are incipient forms given activity by the personality who encounters them. The nature of their activity, therefore, will be projected outward from the personality onto the relatively passive materialization. The person encountering these has only to turn his attention away to "deactivate" the phenomenon. This does not mean that the phenomenon is not real. Its nature is simply of a different kind and degree.

It has some energy of its own, but needs additional energy from a perceiver for any interrelationship to take place. If such a materialization appears threatening, then simply wish it peace and withdraw your attention from it. It draws its main activating energy from your focusing, and according to the intensity and nature of your focus. You must not take the root assumptions of physical existence with you as you journey through these levels of consciousness. Divest yourself of as many of them as possible, for they can cause you to misinterpret your experiences. *(Pause.)*

There are other layers of awareness beneath this one, but here there is a much greater tendency for one to merge into the other. In the next level, for example, communication is possible with various kinds of consciousness that have never been physically manifested, in your terms — personalities who do not have a physical reality in either your present or future, yet who are connected with your system of reality both as guardians and custodians.

Almost all experiences from this level will be symbolically represented, for otherwise they would have no meaning to you. The experiences will all have to do in one way or another with nonphysical life, noncorporeal consciousness and forms, and the independence of consciousness from matter. These experiences will always be supportive. Out-of-body experiences will often be involved here, in which the projectionist finds himself in an unearthly environment or one of great beauty and grandeur.

The "stuff" of the environment will have its origin in the mind of the projectionist, being symbolic of his idea, for example, of life after death. A Speaker or Speakers will appear in whatever guise will be most acceptable to the projectionist, whether it be the guise of a god, an angel or a disciple. This is the most characteristic kind of experience from this level. *(Pause.)*

According to the abilities and understanding of the projectionist, however, more thorough messages can be given, and it may be quite obvious that the Speakers are indeed only symbols of greater identities. Some will be able to understand the communications more clearly. The true nature of the nonphysical Speakers may then be made known.

Deeper projections into that environment may then be possible. In this state also great vistas of historic pasts and futures may be seen. All of these levels of consciousness are filled with the tapestry of various communications that can be followed through according to the purpose of the personality involved.

(10:33.) Molecular structures send out their own messages, and unless you are tuned in to perceive them, they may be interpreted as static or meaningless noise. Any one of these levels of consciousness can be covered in a twinkling, and no notice taken of it; or, at least theoretically, you could spend a lifetime exploring any given level.

You may have several quite valid experiences in level four for example, without any awareness of the first three. The stages are there for those who know what they are and how to use them. Many quite spontaneously find their own way. The other adjacent levels on the horizontal line, now, involve you in various alternate realities, each one a greater distance from your own. Many of these involve systems in which life and death as you know it does not occur, where time is felt as weight; systems in which the root assumptions are so different from your own that you would only accept any experiences as fantasy.

For this reason, you are much less apt to travel in those directions. In some there are built-in impediments. Even projection from your universe into a universe of antimatter is most difficult, for example. The electromagnetic makeup even of your thoughts would be adversely affected, and yet theoretically this is possible from one of these adjacent levels of consciousness.

I suggest your break.

(10:42. Jane's trance had been excellent, her delivery faster yet. Resume at 10:55.)

Often you visit such areas of consciousness in the dream state where you fall into them spontaneously, remembering in the morning a fantastic dream. Consciousness must use all of its parts and activities, even as the body must. When you are sleeping, therefore, your consciousness turns itself in many of these directions, often perceiving, willy-nilly, bits and pieces of reality that are available to it at its different stages. This also happens beneath your normal physical focus to some extent, even as you go about your waking activities. The alternate presents of which I spoke are not simply alternate methods of perceiving one objective present. There are many alternate presents, with you focused only in one of them.

When you let your attention waver, however, you may often fall into a state in which you momentarily perceive glimpses of another alternate present. The whole self, the soul, knows of its reality in all such systems, and you, as a part of it, are working toward the same state of self-awareness and development.

When you are proficient you will not be swept willy-nilly into other stages of consciousness as you sleep, but will be able to understand and direct these activities. Consciousness is an attribute of the soul, a tool that can be turned in many directions. You are not your consciousness. It is something that belongs to you and to the soul. You are learning to use it. To the extent that you understand and utilize the various aspects of consciousness, you will learn to understand your own reality, and the conscious self will truly become conscious.

You will be able to perceive physical reality because you want to, knowing it to be one of many realities. You will not be forced to perceive it alone, out of ignorance.

(11:02.) End of dictation. Now, you may ask me any questions that you have, or end the session as you prefer.

("I hope you'll cover for your book the question Jane and I were discussing at the supper table this evening, about what you actually see when you're speaking to a group of people — focusing upon each of us as individuals in this time and place.")

I will see that it is covered for you. My perceptions were dealt with in the earlier chapters of the book, but not in just that way. . . .

(In the ESP class session of February 9, 1971, Seth gave an excellent account of the particular aspect of his perceptions that I was referring to now. Ever since then I've wanted to ask him to say more about this in his own book. Here's an extract from the class session, which was recorded as usual:

("Now [humorously]*: no one asked me what it was like when I go into a trance. To go into a trance is simply to focus intensely in a highly specific area of reality. Therefore, I throw or project a part of what I am here because I am able to utilize greater areas of my personality than those with which you are now*

acquainted in yourselves. I can do this in a conscious manner, and yet still, as I have mentioned, when I am here I find a difficulty in looking at you and relating to the selves that you think you are within your given moment of time; for I see the composites. So it takes some training on my part to pinpoint you in the time and space with which you are acquainted.

("You are aware of the selves that sit in this room on a particular evening of a snowstorm, with certain members of the class present, certain members absent, and with some new people here. I am familiar with the inner portions of your selves that you also know, however, but that the egotistical self has hidden from you, and so I must think constantly to myself: 'Oh, yes, our Lady of Venice [Seth's affectionate term for a class member] *thinks that she sits in this specific room at this specific hour, and is wearing a blue outfit.'*

("But I am aware of a Lady of Venice, you see, in several different manifestations in various existences, all occurring at once. I must remember that she is not aware of these, and when I speak to her I must use a designation that will make sense to her at this particular time.

("To some extent, I serve as a communicator from one level of your selves to other levels of your selves, for I remind you of what you are. You have been much given to thoughts of death this evening. Now, I have been a very lively corpse many times; but then, so have you all. The inner portions of your selves know this well. You have walked away from more graves than you can remember — and will indeed, many of you, walk away from more. Why, then, do you worry about justifying your own existence in this hour?")

(Seth's delivery now speeded up considerably, and we exchanged views on the subject just quoted in a lively manner. I made no effort to record the conversation.)

I am sure you will like my book when you read it.

("I like it now." After another short exchange):

Now I will bid you a fond good evening. . . .

("Good night, Seth, and thank you very much." 11:05 P.M.)

SESSION 576, MARCH 29, 1971,
9:17 P.M. MONDAY

(Through March 26 to 28, Jane had a notice running under Personals *in the* Elmira Star Gazette, *stating her intention to form a class in creative writing. This is something she's wanted to do for a long time. Today she has been receiving calls as a result, and took one this evening just as we sat for the session at 9.*

(Seth had some comments, although we hadn't asked for them.)

Now: Good evening.

("Good evening, Seth.")

As far as helping other people is concerned, [Ruburt] can help far better in his psychic class, or in another additional one. I am not telling him not to have his creative writing class. He can do as he likes. He will be using the same ideas, but different methods, in any case. The people who have called about creative writing are only using that as an excuse. They feel a need of development in many areas.

(Oddly enough, the notice about the writing class has spurred calls about the ESP class. Jane was concerned about the influx of people for the latter, since she has run out of room in the apartment. She told me the problems made her "nervous but happy" as she considered them.)

Now: Give us a moment. *(Pause.)* Your suggestions as to the séances and Ruburt's as to other experiments — these ideas are both good ones.

His regular classes cannot get larger. There are physical limitations. There are other less tangible limitations, however, having to do with the interactions of the people involved. There are also other possibilities here that you have not thought of.

(Long pause at 9:27.) Now: Give us a moment and we will resume dictation. You may ask questions on that material later.

The various levels of consciousness discussed here may appear to be very divorced from ordinary waking ones. The divisions are quite arbitrary. These various stages all represent different attributes and directions inherent within your own soul; clues and hints of them, shadows and reflections appear even in the consciousness that you know. Even normal waking consciousness, then, is not innocent of all other traces of existence, or devoid of other kinds of awareness. It is only because you usually use your waking consciousness in limited ways that you do not encounter these clues with any regularity.

They are always present. Following them can give you some idea of those other directions, and those other levels of which we have spoken. Often, for example, seemingly unrelated symbols or images may rise into your mind. Usually you ignore them. If instead you acknowledge them and turn your attention to them, you can follow them to several other layers, at least, for example, A-1 and A-2, with ease.

(9:35.) The symbols or images may change as you do so, so that you

perceive little similarity between, say, the initial image and the next one. The connection may be highly intuitional, however, associative, and creative. Often a few moments' reflection afterward will allow you to see why the one image merged into the other. A single image may suddenly open up into an entire mental landscape, but you will know none of this if you do not acknowledge the first clues that are just beneath present awareness, and almost transparent if you are only willing to look.

Alternate focus is merely a state in which you turn your consciousness in other than its habitual direction, in order to perceive quite legitimate realities that exist simultaneously with your own. You must alter your perception to perceive any reality that is not geared practically toward material form. This is something like looking out of the corner of your eye or mind, rather than straight ahead. *(Pause.)*

Using alternate focus, with practice it is possible to perceive the different physical formations that have filled any given area of space, or that will fill it in your terms. In some dream states you may visit a particular location and then perceive the location as it was, say, three centuries ago and five years hence, and never understand what the dream meant. It seems to you that space can be filled only by a given item at a time, that one must be removed to make room for another.

Instead you only perceive in this fashion. In alternate focus you can dispense with the root assumptions that usually guard, direct, and limit your perception. You are able to step aside from the moment as you know it, and return to it and find it there. Consciousness only pretends to bow to the idea of time. At other levels it enjoys playing with such concepts and perceiving great unity from events that occur outside of a time context — mixing, for example, events from various centuries, finding harmony and points of contact by examining both historical and private environments, plucking them out of the time framework.

Again, you even do this in your sleep. If you do not do it in the waking state, it is because you have held your consciousness in too tight a rein. Now you may take your break.

(9:48. The pace had been fast. Resume at 10:05.)

Now: As mentioned somewhat earlier in this book, while your normal waking consciousness seems continual to you, and you are aware usually of no blank spots, nevertheless it has great fluctuations. To a large extent it has memory only of itself and its own perceptions. In normal consciousness, then, it seems as if there are no real other kinds of consciousness, no other areas or levels. When it encounters "blank spots" and "returns," it blots out awareness that the moment of non-function occurred.

It forgets the stumble. It cannot be aware of alternate kinds of consciousness while being itself, unless methods are taken that allow it to recover from this amnesia.

(*10:13. We had forgotten to put our cat, Willy, in another room before the session. Now he jumped into Jane's lap, so I had to lay my notebook aside. He purred as I carried him back to the studio. Jane sat waiting patiently in trance.*)

It plays hopscotch in and out of reality. It is gone sometimes and you are not aware of it. On such occasions your attention is focused elsewhere, in what you might call mini-dreams or hallucinations, or associative and intuitive processes of thought that go quite beyond normal focus.

In these lapses you are perceiving other kinds of reality — with other than normal waking consciousness. When you return, you lose the thread. Normal waking consciousness pretends there was never any break. This happens with some regularity, and to varying degrees, from fifteen to fifty times an hour, according to your activities.

At various times many people do catch themselves, the experience being so vivid that it leaps the gap, so to speak, with perception so intense that even normal waking consciousness is made aware of it. These intervals are quite necessary to physical consciousness. They are woven through the fabric of your awareness so cleverly and so intimately that they color your psychic and feeling atmosphere. (*Pause.*)

Normal waking consciousness weaves in and out of this infinite supportive webwork. Your inner experience is so intricate that verbally it is almost impossible to describe. Normal waking consciousness, while having memory of itself, obviously does not retain all memory all of the time. It is said that memory of past events drops back into the subconscious. It is still intensely alive, and by alive I mean living and active, although you do not focus upon it.

Inner portions of your personality also have memory of all of your dreams. These exist simultaneously, and suspended, so to speak, like lights over a dark city, illuminating various portions of the psyche. These memory systems are all interconnected. Now in the same way you have your memory of past lives, all quite complete and all operating in the entire memory system.

(Pause at 10:23.) In periods of conscious "blank spots" or certain fluctuations, these memory systems are often perceived. As a rule the conscious mind with its own memory system will not accept them. When a personality realizes that such other realities exist and that other experiences with consciousness are possible, then he activates certain potentials within himself. These alter electromagnetic connections both within the mind, the brain, and even the perceptive mechanisms. They bring together reservoirs of energy and set up pathways of activity, allowing the conscious mind to increase its degree of sensitivity to such data. The conscious mind is set free of itself. To a large measure it undergoes a metamorphosis, taking on greater functions. It is able to perceive, little by little, some of the content before closed to it. It need no longer perceive the momentary "blank spots" fearfully, as evidence of nonexistence.

The fluctuations mentioned earlier are often quite minute, yet highly significant. The conscious mind knows well of its own fluctuating state. When once it is led to face this, it finds not chaos, or worse, nonexistence, but the source of its own abilities and strength. The personality then begins to use its own potential.

Now you may take your break.

(10:35. Even though her trance had been deep, Jane had been aware of her slower delivery. She said this was because Seth wanted her to use just the right words. She had had many images, also, which she couldn't verbalize now. She could only say things like "systems of lights for memories," etc. I told her I thought the material was very rich and evocative. Resume at 10:47.)

Now: Periods of reverie and creative moments of consciousness both represent excellent entryways into these other areas. In the usual creative state of consciousness, the regular waking consciousness is suddenly supported by energy from these other areas. Waking consciousness alone does not give you the creative state. Indeed, normal waking consciousness can be as afraid of creative states as it is of blank states, for it can feel that the I is being thrust aside, can feel the upthrust of energy that it may not understand.

It is precisely in the low points of fluctuation that such experiences originate, for normal consciousness is momentarily at a weak state and in a period of rest. The whole physical organism undergoes such normal fluctuations, again, that are usually quite unnoticed. These periods also fluctuate, following rhythms that have to do with the characteristic personality. In some the waves of motion are comparatively long and slow, the valleys within being sloped; with others, the reverse is true.

With some, the lapses are more noticeable, outside of the norm. If the situation is not understood, then the personality may find it difficult to relate to physical events. If he is able to perceive the other areas of consciousness, he may find himself in still more difficulty — not realizing that both systems of reality are valid.

(10:55.) The fluctuations also follow seasonal changes. Events from any given layer of consciousness are reflected in all other areas, each being actualized according to the characteristics of the given layer. As one dream is like a stone thrown into the pool of dream consciousness, so any act appears in this pool also in its own guise. Alternate focus allows you to perceive the many manifestations of any given act, the true multidimensional reality of a given thought. It enriches the normal consciousness.

You are active in these other layers whether or not you are aware of it. You learn not only in physical life and in the dream state, but in these interior existences of which you have no memory. Creative abilities of a specific nature, or healing abilities, are often trained in this fashion, only then emerging into physical actuality.

Your future thoughts and acts are as real in these dimensions as if they had already occurred, and as much a part of your development. You are formed not only by your past but by your future, and by alternate existences. These great interactions are only a part of the framework of your soul. You can, therefore, change present reality as you understand it from any of these other layers of consciousness.

End of dictation, and very nearly the end of the chapter.

(Pause at 11:04. Seth then gave some personal material for Jane, dealing with her writing class and other matters. End at 11:12 P.M.)

SESSION 577, MARCH 31, 1971, 9:13 P.M. WEDNESDAY

(This afternoon Jane held her first creative writing class.)

Now, good evening.

("Good evening, Seth.")

We will begin dictation.

Any one of these various layers of consciousness can be used as the normal acting consciousness, reality being viewed from that specific standpoint.

Physical reality is therefore glimpsed by other kinds of personalities in other systems, from their own unique viewpoint. Peering at it from this angle, so to speak, you would not recognize it as your own home system. From some of these viewpoints, your physical matter has little or no permanency, while to others your own thoughts have a shape and form, perceived by observers but not by yourselves.

In traveling through the states of consciousness, these other personalities would try to attain some focus and perceive your environment, trying to make sense of data with which they are largely unacquainted. Since many of them are unaware of your idea of time, they would find it difficult to understand that you perceive events with intervals between, and would not perceive the inner organization that you thrust upon your normal environment. Yours is obviously a probable system to other fields also touched by the field of probabilities.

(9:20.) As these systems are adjacent to yours, so is yours adjacent; alternate focus allows personalities from other realities to perceive your own, then, as it can theoretically at least allow you a glimpse into their existence.

End of chapter.

And now I have an assignment for you, and the opportunity to participate in my book. You may take the rest of the session to make up an <u>excellent</u> — underlined twice *(humorously)*, list of questions that will appear in the next, question-and-answer chapter.

If you have questions already given by others, by all means include these. But they should be questions from you rather than questions posed by me. They will be more pertinent to the reader.

Then present these to me at our next session, or one at a time, or two, as you prefer, and I will answer them. You may organize the questions under headings, but you need not do so. If several happen to fall under one large subject heading, this would simply be a convenient way of handling it.

("Can Ruburt ask questions too?")

You may both make up the list. You need not have the whole list by the next session. One answer may take some time.

(*"That's what I was wondering about."*)

I suggest, then, that you both get to work.

(*The telephone began to ring while I was writing. Jane was still in trance but didn't appear to be bothered. Feeling some irritation, I let it ring until it stopped.*)

I will be around to inspire you.

(*9:30 P.M. This had been the shortest session in several years. I was still surprised at the quick ending; I didn't even say good night to Seth. Already I was wondering whether we should ask questions we thought others were interested in, or just those we spontaneously came up with ourselves.*)

(*Jane checked the outline Seth had given us for his book in the 510th session for January 19, 1970. Sure enough, he had listed a question-and-answer chapter. I had forgotten this. For some reason I felt uneasy now; perhaps I thought it might not be a good idea to interrupt the flow of the book in such a manner.*)

(*Jane hasn't read any of Seth's book since the 521st session, in Chapter Four; in spite of temptations, she has always felt it better to be free of concern about it. We didn't think her not looking at it would interfere with her having questions. She has of course had contacts with the book, aside from her own imperfect memory. I gave her a couple of short passages to read to her ESP class. She discussed the book to some extent with Patty Middleton recently; and I've talked about it at times, although without referring back to the typed page.*)

(*Within an hour after the session ended, we had fifteen questions listed. We'll write a longer list for the session on Monday, April 5.*)

CHAPTER 20

QUESTIONS AND ANSWERS

SESSION 578, APRIL 5, 1971,
9:30 P.M. MONDAY

(A *s instructed by Seth in the last session, I had compiled a list of questions for this chapter. It wasn't complete but, surprisingly, it already ran to five typed pages and some fifty-two items. I contributed a lot of them, but also consulted with Jane. The list included some of the many interesting questions Sue Watkins had asked; we had saved these, along with those raised by ourselves and others in connection with various older sessions. All of the questions, we thought, had a timeless quality.*

(Earlier today I told Jane that I was afraid the questions weren't very representative of Seth's book, and that to assemble a truly relevant list of them would require an intimate study of each chapter. This we hadn't done, of course — partly because of time limitations; partly because Jane hadn't wanted to be that involved consciously. We were left hoping that intuitively the list would be an appropriate one.

(We sat for the session at 9:00, as we almost always do, but Seth didn't appear with his usual promptness. As the time passed, Jane said she thought she was somewhat uptight because of the questions; she had read them after supper. The session was held in my studio for more privacy. Finally, Jane took off her glasses.)

Now: Good evening.

("Good evening, Seth.")

(Humorously): Begin with your famous list of questions.

("Well, first I'll read you this paragraph heading the list: Some of these

questions may refer to subjects you plan to cover in later chapters. If so, let us know and we'll just pass them by for consideration in this chapter.")

I will indeed.

("Okay. Here's question number one: You said you'd tell us about the third Christ. Also, do we need to know more about the other two personalities belonging to the Christ entity: Christ Himself, and John the Baptist?")

Let the religious questions go for now.

("Does that include data on the Speakers?" I planned to ask several questions about the Speakers.)

No — just the questions about the world religions, and those pertaining to the third Christ and allied subjects.

("All right, question number two: Was the statement given by Jane, while speaking for you, correct, that there have been millions of Speakers? Or was this distorted?" See the 568th session, in Chapter Seventeen.)

It was not distorted. The Speakers are gifted according to their own characters, some having far more abilities than others, but all playing roles in the communication of inner data. In your terms, therefore, some Speakers would be much more accomplished than others. For example, there have been a far smaller number of truly prominent Speakers than the number given.

There have been less than thirty great Speakers. Give us time here.

(Pause at 9:35. Jane's pace was quite slow.) The Christ entity was one. The Buddha was another. These Speakers are as active when they are nonphysical as when they are physical. The Christ entity had many reincarnations before the emergence of the Christ "personality" as known; as did the Buddha.

The greatest Speakers do not only translate and communicate inner data, but also go much further into these inner realms of reality than others connected with your physical system. They add, then, to the basic inner data. The greatest Speakers have not needed the intensive training necessary for most. Their unique combination of characteristics has made this unnecessary. *(Pause. One of many.)*

At another level, Emerson was a Speaker.

A man named Marbundu. . . . *(My phonetic interpretation.)*

("Do you want to spell that?")

M-A-U-B-U-N-D-U, in Africa, 14 B.C. The Speakers, more than most, are highly active through all aspects of existence, whether physical or nonphysical, waking or sleeping, between lives or at other levels of reality. As certain physical data are carried along in the gene structure, so this inner information is codified within whatever psychological structures the Speakers may inhabit; but far more readily available than it is to other personalities. It needs, often, trigger points to release it, however. These can take place in either the waking or dream state, and they serve to open up the reservoirs of knowledge and make past training available.

I know that one of your questions has to do with a first Speaker.

(*"Yes. Number four: Is it possible to name, or describe, a first Speaker?"*)

Now: In greater terms, there was no first Speaker. Imagine that you wanted to be ten places at once, and that you actually sent one portion of yourself to each of these ten places. Imagine that you could scatter yourself in those ten directions, and that each of the ten portions were conscious, alert, and aware.

You — being the ten of you — would be aware of existence in each of the ten places. It would be impossible to ask which of the ten arrived first, except to say that all began with the original who decided to visit the ten locations. So it is with the Speakers, who in the same way do not originate in the locations or in the times in which they may appear.

Do you have more Speaker questions?

(*"Well, that brings me to number three, which you've already been getting into: What is the original source of the Speaker data? Where did it come from, and when?"*)

The original source of the Speaker data is the inner knowledge of the nature of reality that is within each individual. The Speakers are to keep the information alive in physical terms, to see that men do not bury it within and dam it up, to bring it — the information — to the attention of the conscious self.

They speak the inner secrets, in other words. In some civilizations, as mentioned earlier in this book, they played a much stronger part, practically speaking. At times they were consistently, consciously and egotistically aware of this information. It was then that it was memorized. They realized it was always available at an unconscious level.

They imprinted it, however, upon the physical brain through the use of memory. There was always great interaction however between inner and outer existence for them, as there is today. Valid information gained in the dream state was memorized in the morning. One Speaker heard another's <u>lesson</u> in the dream state. On the other hand, pertinent physical data was also communicated one to another in the dream state, and both states were utilized to a high degree. *(Pause.)*

Do you have any more Speaker questions?

("Number five: Were any of the disciples Speakers?")

I will save that one for the religious chapter. It can be handled more simply.

("Number six: Can Speakers work with us while they are between physical lives?")

I believe that has been answered.

("Yes." See the data at 9:35. I was so busy writing I didn't realize the question had already been considered.)

They can, and do indeed. Both of you are being trained by other Speakers who are themselves between lives, this occurring in your dream states. The Speakers themselves obviously attain varying degrees of efficiency.

(And of course, the above data gives rise to more questions: such as who is training us? Have we known them in past lives, etc.? Not knowing what to do, I asked no questions. . . .)

The large amount of their work is done from a nonphysical state, earthly existences being somewhat like very important field trips.

("Number seven: Are you going to talk about Seth II in this book?")

I am indeed. We will leave that one for now.

(Here there was an exchange between Seth and me, in which I didn't have to take notes. Seth said this chapter was intended as a change of pace from the long excerpts included in the book. It was also designed to make the reader think of his own questions. "Then I suppose you'll want to handle question number eight later, too: Are you a medium for Seth II?")

Also later.

("Number eleven: In Chapter Seventeen you said it would require more training on Jane's part before she could deliver a Speaker manuscript, and that even then the work involved could take five years. What kind of training?")

I was speaking specifically of what you would term an ancient Speaker's manuscript, and I thought that was what you were referring to.

("Yes.")

Ruburt would not be familiar with a good many of the words and phrases used, even if translation from the original languages was made. There is a difference even in some basic concepts. To maintain any purity of translation, training in different kinds of inner perception would be necessary. Some of these languages dealt with pictures rather than words. In some the symbols had multidimensional meanings. To deliver such information through Ruburt would be an immense task, but it is possible. Oftentimes words were hidden within pictures, and pictures within words. We speak of manuscripts, yet most of these were not written down.

Some were, but at much later dates, and portions exist underground and in caves — in Australia, parts of Africa, and in one area of the Pyrenees.

Now I suggest your break.

(10:12. Jane's pace had speeded up considerably, as though she had lost some sort of nervousness. She said that now she felt much better about the question-and-answer format. So did I. The studio had cooled off considerably. Jane said she hadn't been cold in trance, but was now.

(I told her that question number nine was next on the list. It had to do with Seth's perceptions while speaking through her, and had been inspired by the ESP class session for February 9, 1971; excerpts from this are included in the 575th session in Chapter Nineteen. In the meantime I thought of another Speaker query, which I wrote down. Resume at 10:40.)

Now which of the two questions do you want me to answer first?

("We'll call this eleven-a: Wouldn't you say then that these sessions are Speaker training for Jane and me, raised to a conscious level?")

They are indeed. The inner information must be consciously recognized. In your terms, by the time an individual is in his last physical life *(pause)*, all portions of the personality are then familiar with it at the time of death. The personality is not swept willy-nilly back to another earthly existence, as might be the case otherwise.

The conscious physically oriented portions of the self become acquainted with the inner information. To some extent the reality of thought is consciously perceived as the innovator behind physical matter. Such an individual then can understand the nature of hallucinations at the point of death, and with full conscious awareness enter into the next plane of existence. The information made conscious is then passed on to others where it can be physically recognized and applied.

Now, as to the next question.

("Number nine: You told us you were going to elaborate upon what you perceive when you are speaking through Jane to a roomful of people. In that ESP class session, you mentioned going into a trance yourself, and the effort required by you to pinpoint us in our time and space.")

I perceive people in a room in a far different manner than they perceive themselves; their various past and future reincarnated personalities, but not their probable selves, are perceivable to me.

I "see" the reincarnated aspects, the various manifestations taken in that regard. In your terms it would be as if you saw a series of quickly moving pictures, all representing various poses of one personality. I must remember, in all communications with those in the room, to limit my remarks and focus to the specific reincarnated "present self."

I see this composite image myself. It is not registered by Ruburt's eyes *(pause)*, which do not have the multidimensional depth perception necessary. I see the composite image clearly, whether or not I am looking through Ruburt's eyes. I use his eyes because they narrow down the focus for me, to the one "present" self of which the individual is aware.

Communicating with your system in such a manner demands great diligence and greater discrimination, according to the "distance" of the communicator from the physical system. I am not based within the physical system, for example. The discrimination comes to bear upon the precision needed to enter your reality at the precise time, the precise point in time and space, upon which you are concentrated.

Present and future experience of those in the room are available to me, and as real as their present experience. Therefore I must remember what they think has already happened, or not yet occurred, for to me it is one. These patterns of activity, however, are also constantly changing. I say for example that I am aware of their past and future actions and thoughts; and yet what I am aware of, actually, are ever-shifting and changing patterns, both in the future and in the past.

(11:00.) Some of the events that I see connected very clearly with these persons in the future may not, in your physical system, occur. They exist as probabilities, as potentials, actualized in thoughts but not turned into definite physical form. I told you that no events were

predetermined. I would have to tune into a future date, in your terms, and probe it with all of its ramifications in order to ascertain which of the probable actions I saw in your earlier would be actualized in your later.

To a large extent the methods of communication may vary. A personality based within physical reality, between lives for example, would find entry in many ways easier. The information he would be able to give, however, would also be limited because of his experience. I do have a memory of physical existence however, and this automatically helps me in translating your mental data into physical form. I do perceive objects, for example. Using Ruburt's mechanism is of great help here also. At times I see the room and the people as he, or rather his perceptive mechanisms, do.

In this case I translate or read that data and use it as you might a computer's. Will that answer your question?

("Excellent.")

I am ready for the next.

("Number ten: Are you going to tell us about some of the ways you contacted Jane before these sessions began?")

I mentioned some of that in an earlier chapter. Much of her training, as Jane, took place in the dream state. There were frequent out-of-body projections in which she attended classes, taught initially by various Speakers. The information gained was often brought to conscious layers through the poetry. *(Long pause at 11:15.)*

There was concentrated training that allowed her to focus inward; an exterior environment that forced her to look inward for answers, and a strong religious structure in which initial growth could take place. That is enough.

(A long pause while I scanned the next three questions: twelve, thirteen, and fourteen.)

If this is the reincarnational material, let that go for now.

(It was. I skipped down to number nineteen, a question I almost hadn't bothered to write down. "Do you have any interest in perceiving our daily lives when you're not speaking through Jane? Is this possible?")

I do not make it a practice to observe. We are connected, however, in our psychological gestalt, and so I am aware of any intense feelings on your part, or strong reactions of any kind. This does not mean that

I am necessarily aware of all events within your lives, or that I always break down the feelings I receive from you into specifics.

(Pause at 11:25.) I am generally aware, therefore, of your condition. If anything upsets Ruburt, he automatically sends me messages about it. I am aware, within the limitations mentioned, of future events in your lives. *(Pause.)* I am much more concerned with your overall spiritual vitality than I am with what you had for breakfast.

I think that will do for that one.

("Okay. That was very interesting. I don't know whether to ask for a break or end the session.")

I will handle the questions on evolution and fragments probably together, and suggest they wait for the next session. You may end the session or take a break as you prefer.

("I guess we'd better end it then, sorry to say.")

They were good questions, as I knew they would be.

("I was kind of concerned about them.")

I hope you are relieved now.

("Very pleased, yes.")

My heartiest regards, and a fond good evening.

("Thank you very much, Seth, and good night." 11:30 P.M.)

SESSION 580, APRIL 12, 1971, 9:13 P.M. MONDAY

(Wednesday's session, the 579th, was held for a husband and wife who have an acute problem involving one of their children. The family lives in another state and we have never met. We learned later that Seth's material was very helpful.

(Before the session tonight I discussed two questions with Jane that I hoped Seth would consider. We also wanted some personal material. The session was held in my studio once again.

("Good evening, Seth.")

Now: Do you want to begin with questions or with personal material?

("How about a question first?")

You give it to me then.

("Number twenty: If everything exists now, or at once, how can it be added to through constant creation and expansion? Or to put it another way: If we are constantly creating, how can All That Is exist as complete now?")

All That Is is not done and finished.

(Long pause. Jane's pace was alternately fast and slow.)

Everything within your three-dimensional system occurs simultaneously. Each action creates other possibilities of itself, or other actions from the infinite energy of the universe, which itself is never still. The answer is that the whole is more than the sum of its parts. *(Pause.)*

All That Is simultaneously and unendingly creates itself. Only within your particular frame of reference does there seem to be a contradiction between action that is simultaneous and yet unending. This has to do mainly with the necessary distortions arising from your time concept and the idea of duration; for duration to you presupposes existence continued within a time framework — predisposing to beginnings and endings.

Experience existing outside of that reference is not dependent upon duration in your terms. There is no "perfect ending," no completed perfection beyond which further experience is impossible or meaningless. *(Long pause.)* All That Is is a source of infinite and unending simultaneous action. Everything happens at once, and yet there is no beginning and end to it in your terms, so it is not completed in your terms at any given point.

(9:25.) Your idea of development and growth, again, implies a one-line march toward perfection, so it would be difficult for you to imagine the kind of order that pervades. Ultimately a completed or finished God, or All That Is, would end up smothering his creation. For perfection presupposes that point beyond which development is impossible, and creativity at an end.

There would be an order in which only predestination could rule, each part fitting in with a particular order without freedom to change the pattern given it. There is order, but within this order there is freedom — the freedom of creativity, that characteristic of All That Is, that guarantees its infinite becoming.

Now in that infinite becoming, there are states that you would call perfected, but had creativity rested within them, all of experience would be destined to grind to a halt. Yet this great complexity is not unwieldy; it is as simple, in fact, as a seed.

(9:32.) All That Is is inexhaustible. Infinity rests within simultaneous action, in a way that you cannot presently understand.

Give us a moment. *(Long pause.)* All That Is is alive within the least of itself, aware within for example the molecule. It endows all of its parts — or its creations — with its own abilities that then act as inspiration, impetus, guiding lines and principles, by which these parts then seek to further create themselves, their own worlds and systems. This is freely given.

(Long pause at 9:37.) These powers and abilities will be used by these creations in various ways. In your own case mankind is forming his reality through the use of these gifts. He is learning to use them efficiently and well. He uses them to exist. They form the basis of his reality. Within that framework, individually and as a whole, mankind may seem to make errors, to bring ill health, death or desolation upon himself, but he is still using those abilities to create a world.

Through observing his creations he learns how to use these abilities better. He checks on his inner progress by seeing the physical materialization of his work. The work, the reality, is still a creative achievement, although it may portray a tragedy or unspeakable terror in your terms at any given time.

("Well, you're leading into the next question then. Number twenty-one: How do you account for the pain and suffering in the world?" Many people have asked us this question.)

(9:43.) I am indeed. A great painting of a battle scene, for example, may show the ability of the artist as he projects in all its appalling drama the inhuman and yet all-too-human conditions of war. The artist is using his abilities. In the same way, man is using his abilities, and they are apparent when he creates a real war.

The artist who paints such a scene may do so for several reasons: because he hopes through portraying such inhumanity to awaken people to its consequences, to make them quail and change their ways; because he is himself in such a state of disease and turmoil that he directs his abilities in that particular manner; or because he is fascinated with the problem of destruction and creativity, and of using creativity to portray destruction.

In your wars you are using creativity to create destruction, but you cannot help being creative.

(9:48.) Illness and suffering are not thrust upon you by God, or by

All That Is, or by an outside agency. They are by-products of the learning process, created by you, in themselves quite neutral. On the other hand, your existence itself, the reality and nature of your planet, the whole existence in which you have these experiences, are also created by you, using the abilities of which I have spoken.

Illness and suffering are the results of the misdirection of creative energy. They are a part of the creative force, however. They do not come from a different source than, say, health and vitality. Suffering is not good for the soul, unless it teaches you how to stop suffering. That is its purpose.

Within your particular plane of activity, and speaking practically, no one fully or completely can use all the energy available to them, or completely materialize the inner sensed identity that is multidimensional. This inner identity is the blueprint however against which you judge, ultimately, your physical actions. You strive to express as best you can the entire potential that is within you.

(9:58.) Within that framework, it is possible to have sane and healthy minds within healthy bodies, to have a sane planet. The release and use of creative energy expended simply to maintain your planet and your existence, is impossible to conceive of. The great amount of energy available to you gives you great leeway in its use.

I have mentioned before that everyone within your system is learning to handle this creative energy; and since you are still in the process of doing so, you will often misdirect it. The resulting snarl in activities automatically brings you back to inner questions.

Now you may take your break.

(10:02. This was the end of the material on Seth's book. The balance of the session was taken up with personal material. End at 11:06 P.M.)

SESSION 581, APRIL 14, 1971,
9:16 P.M. WEDNESDAY

(On Thursday night, April 8, Jane and I were visited by three women from Rochester, New York. They were very interested in talking about Jane's book, The Seth Material. They also gave me several questions for Seth to answer in his own book, if he chose to do so. Jane and I went over them briefly before the session.)

Good evening.

("Good evening, Seth.")

Now: Suppose we begin with the first question that you were discussing.

(By M.H. Her query was based on a theory that, as it happened, I'd heard of also: A group of scientists has postulated the existence of a class of subatomic particles called "tachyons," or "meta-particles," that always travel faster than the speed of light.

(According to the theory of relativity, no particle can be accelerated to the speed of light because its mass would become infinitely large as it approached light's velocity; but this barrier is bypassed by stating that the particles in question have an imaginary proper mass — not rest mass — that is never less than the speed of light. M.H. asked, then: "Are these faster-than-light particles the same as, or like, the electromagnetic energy or EE units Seth discusses in the Appendix of The Seth Material*?")*

I told you some time ago that there were many gradations of matter, or form, that you did not perceive. In your terms many of these particles making up such constructions do move faster than the speed of your light.

Your light, again, represents only a portion of an even larger spectrum than that of which you know; and when your scientists study its properties, they can only investigate light as it intrudes into the three-dimensional system. The same of course applies to a study of the structure of matter or form.

There are indeed universes composed of such faster-than-light particles. Some of these in your terms share the same space as your own universe. You simply would not perceive such particles as mass. When these particles are slowed down sufficiently, you do experience them as matter.

Some of these particles drastically alter their velocity, appearing sometimes at your slower rate, usually in cyclic fashion. The inner vortex of some such particles has a much greater velocity than the orbiting portions. EE units are formed spontaneously from the electromagnetic reality of feelings emitted from each consciousness, as, for example, breath automatically goes out from the physical body.

(9:27.) EE units are, then, emanations from consciousness. The intensity of the thought or emotion determines the characteristics of the units themselves. As certain ranges are reached, they are propelled

into physical actualization. Whether or not this occurs in your terms, they will exist as small matter particles — as, say, latent matter or pseudo-matter.

Some of these will fall into the faster-than-light groupings, and have a perceivable vitality within that framework. These faster-than-light particles of course exist in their own kind of form then. There are many ranges and great varieties of such units, all existing beyond your perceivable reach. To lump them together in such a way, however, is misleading, for within all of this there is great order.

(9:33.) You are not <u>utterly</u> unaware of the existence of some of these units, though you do not experience them as mass. You interpret some of them as events, dream events, so-called hallucinations; and sometimes certain ranges of these units are interpreted by you as movement-through-time.

All of them cast certain "atmospheric conditions" or reflections that color physical events as you know them. Some of your own feelings are propelled into a reality within such systems, adopting within that framework their own mass and form. In the creation and maintenance of your normal reality, you focus your daily waking consciousness so that it becomes effective within the ranges necessary. Ideas and feelings that you want made physical carry within them the mechanisms that will put them in the proper range, well within the electromagnetic field necessary for physical development.

(Pause at 9:40.) Your consciousness, however, is equipped to create realities in other fields as well. Now in certain dreams and out-of-body experiences, your own consciousness moves faster than the speed of light, and under such conditions you are able to perceive some of these other forms of "mass or matter."

The EE units are quite simply incipient forms of reality: seeds automatically given birth, suited for different environments, some appearing within the physical framework, and some not conforming at all to its prerequisites. Now some systems of reality are "bounded" with centers of faster-than-light particles. These begin to slow down at a rhythmic rate toward the peripheries, in your terms over great distances, until actually the outside slower particles to some extent imprison the center masses even though they move much more quickly, but within a confined area.

(9:45.) The behaviors of such units, as you can now see, form the particular camouflage within any given system, while the peripheral activities effectively set up inner identities and outer boundaries. These are all variations, generally speaking and very simply put, on matter as you think of it. The same applies to negative or antimatter however, which you do not perceive in any case. But the gradations of activity within such systems are as diverse.

Basically, however, no system is closed. Energy flows freely from one to another, or rather permeates each. It is only the camouflage structure that gives the impression of closed systems, and the law of inertia does not apply. It appears to be a reality only within your own framework and because of your limited focus.

Now the duration and relative stability of such "matter" within other systems varies considerably, with intensity determining the strength of all such manifestations. The invisible EE units form your physical matter and represent the essential and basic units from which any physical particle appears.

(9:52.) It will not be physically perceived. You see only its results. Since consciousness can travel faster than the speed of light, then when it is not imprisoned by the slower particles of the body it can become aware of some of these other realities. Without training, however, it will not know how to interpret what it sees. The physical brain is the mechanism by which thought or emotion is automatically formed into EE units of the proper range and intensity to be used by the physical organism.

Now you may take your break.

(9:56. Jane's delivery had alternated between slower and faster states, but her trance had been deep. When I told her the material was a great answer to the question, she said, "I just know I was way away. . . ."

(A note, pertaining to faster-than-light effects. On the Sunday following this session, a leading New York City newspaper reported that astronomers have observed two components of a quasar flying apart at, apparently, ten times the speed of light. This is an astonishing discovery, one that is impossible according to the laws of physics.

(Quasars — quasi-stellar radio sources — are extraordinarily powerful sources of light and radio waves. Most scientists believe they exist on the edge of our observable universe. If this is so, they are so far away that their energy has taken billions of years to reach us. Resume at 10:20.)

These EE units, then, are the psychic building blocks of matter. Now: You may go on to another question.

(*"Number twenty-three: Are you in contact with, or speaking through, any other humans as you are with Jane?"*)

No. As mentioned earlier in this book, I do contact some in other levels of reality, however.

(*Seth paused, so I asked him a second question from M.H.: "Is experiencing inner vibrational touch akin to reading an aura?"**)

No. Inner vibrational touch is a much more personal experience, more like "becoming a part of" that which you perceive, rather than for example a reading of an aura. (*Pause.*)

(*"Ready for the next question?"*)

I am waiting.

(*"Number twenty-four: Does Jane ever prevent your coming through when you want to?"*)

On several occasions I have communicated my willingness in particular circumstances. I knew more about those circumstances than Ruburt. Some of these occasions occurred fairly early in our sessions, when Ruburt was worried about spontaneous trances, so after making my presence known to him, I acquiesced to his decision at the time. On a few occasions certain conditions have been poor. Usually Ruburt reacted to these adversely at his end — that is, the interference was such that it would bother his situation rather than mine.

(*Many sessions ago, Seth told us he had a dog fragment personality still here on Earth. He wouldn't tell us where it was, though. "Number twenty-five: Do you have any physical fragments of any kind still here on earth?"*)

I do not now. My dog is gone.

(*"Number twenty-six: Are animals fragments of human beings?"*)

(*Smile.*) It is a good question, and you had better give me a moment to explain it clearly.

(*10:30.*) In one manner of speaking, you are fragments of your

---

*Inner vibrational touch is one of our Inner Senses. Seth lists these in Chapter Nineteen of *The Seth Material*. To paraphrase: Using this sense, an observer standing on a typical street would feel the experience of *being* anything he chose within his field of notice: people, trees, insects, blades of grass. He would retain his own consciousness, and would perceive sensations somewhat in the way we now feel heat and cold. This sense is like empathy, but much more vital.

entities. Yet you consider yourselves quite independent, and not thrust-off second-handed selves; so dogs and other animals are not simply the manifestation of stray psychic energy on the part of human beings.

Animals have varying degrees of self-consciousness, as indeed people do. The consciousness that is within them is as valid and eternal as your own, however. There is nothing to prevent a personality from investing a portion of his own energy into an animal form. This is not transmigration of souls. It does not mean that a man can be reincarnated in an animal. It does mean that personalities can send a portion of their energy into various kinds of form.

(10:35.) Perhaps reincarnations are over for a given individual, for example, yet within him is still some sense of yearning for the natural earth with which he has so often been involved. So he may project a fragment of his consciousness in such a way into an animal form. When this is done, the earth is then experienced in the way natural for the form. A man is not an animal, then, nor does he invade, say, the body of one.

He simply adds some of his energy to that present in the animal, mixing this vitality with the animal's own. This does not mean that all animals are fragments in this manner, however. Animals, as any pet owner knows, have their own personalities and characteristics, and individual ways of perceiving the reality available to them. Some gobble experience. Their consciousness can be immeasurably quickened by contact with friendly humans, and emotional involvement with life is strongly developed.

The mechanics of consciousness remain the same. They do not change for animals or men. Therefore there are no limitations set upon the development of any individual consciousness, or growth of any identity. Consciousness both in the body and without finds its own range, its own level. A dog, then, is not limited to being a dog in other existences.

A certain level, again, of consciousness is necessary, a certain kind of knowledge, a certain understanding of energy organization before an identity can manipulate a complicated physical organism.

(10:45.) As you know, consciousness has a great tendency to maintain individuality, and yet to join in gestalts at the same time. An animal consciousness after death may form such a gestalt with other such

consciousnesses, in which abilities are pooled and the combined cooperation makes possible, for example, a change of species.

In these and other cases, however, the innate individuality is not lost but remains indelibly imprinted. Consciousness must by its nature change, and so identities must also change — not one blotting out the other, but building upon it while each succeeding step is main-tained and not discarded, you see.

In such interrelationships, the steps or identities are each immeasurably enriched by the added perception of the others. As mentioned earlier, thoughts, containing their own electromagnetic reality, have form whether or not you perceive it. With each thought, then, you send out from yourself shapes and images that can be quite legitimate realities to those within the system of reality into which they are propelled.

In the same way, personalities from other systems can send energy to yours. Since such events do not originate within your system, you do not understand their import.

Now you may take your break.

(10:54. Jane's trance had again been good, her delivery variable. This was the end of the material on Seth's book for the evening. The rest of the session was taken up with matters involving ourselves and others. End at 11:20 P.M.)

SESSION 582, APRIL 19, 1971,
9:20 P.M. MONDAY

(Before the session we read over a letter Jane had received on March 16, 1971, from Mrs. R. Her son had disappeared on June 28, 1970. Jane had written her on April 4, promising some information soon.)

Good evening.

("Good evening, Seth.")

Now. Begin with your program. What do you have for me first?

("How about answering the letter from Mrs. R. first?" As Seth, Jane reached out for the letter.)

Hand it to me. Now. Give us a moment.

(Eyes closed, Jane leaned back in her rocker with the folded letter in her right hand.)

The boy has been in several locations, with one stop, a brief one, in a hospital. He seemed to have some difficulty with a lung, or his lungs. I believe he visited Detroit. *(Pause.)* Also the state of Florida, near a small town beginning with a P, but a long enough name.

California was in his mind strongly, also. Thirty-six. *(Pause.)* He had one job, in what seems to be a factory location, in a rather dark environment, with rows of what I assume to be machinery and large windows, treated so that the sunlight did not shine through brightly.

Either this or the place was half below ground level. The name "George" connected with him. A friend perhaps. Also he sent a telegram I believe, either to someone, or he will send one to his mother.

There is a connection with two young women. *(Long pause.)* The mother will hear from him, however. That is all I have for now.

(The above data was delivered at a crisp pace. We have no way of knowing how long Seth's reply to a query like Mrs. R's will be. Whatever the length — one, five, or ten pages — we send a copy of it to the writer as soon as I get the session typed up. We ask for a reply, to see if it's possible to check the material. In this case, we didn't hear from Mrs. R.)

We will try to give an explanation of your question concerning the nature of evolution.

(Number twenty-seven: Is evolution, as it is commonly thought of, a fact or something greatly distorted?

(Apropos of this question, in ESP class eight days later Seth had this to say about Charles Darwin and his theory of evolution:

("He spent his last years proving it, and yet it has no real validity. It has a validity within very limited perspectives only; for consciousness does, indeed, evolve form. Form does not evolve consciousness. All consciousness does, indeed, exist at once, and therefore it did not evolve in those terms. It is according to when you come into the picture, and what you choose to observe, and what part of the play you decide to observe. It is more the other way around, in that evolved consciousness forms itself into many different patterns and rains down on reality. Consciousness did not come from atoms and molecules scattered by chance through the universe, or scattered by chance through many universes. Consciousness did not arrive because inert matter suddenly soared into activity and song. The consciousness existed first, and evolved the form into which it then began to manifest itself.

("Now, if you had all been really paying attention to what I have been saying for some time about the simultaneous nature of time and existence, then you would have known that the theory of evolution is as beautiful a tale as the

theory of biblical creation. Both are quite handy, and both are methods of telling stories, and both might seem to agree within their own systems, and yet, in larger respects they cannot be realities. . . . No — no form of matter, however potent, will be self-evolved into consciousness, no matter what other bits of matter are added to it. Without the consciousness, the matter would not be there in the universe, floating around, waiting for another component to give it reality, consciousness, existence, or song."

(A class member: "Every bit of matter already has consciousness?"

("Indeed, and the consciousness came first. You are quite correct. I thank you for bringing up the matter. [Smile.] There are many ways of bringing up matter.")

(9:30.) At the risk of really repeating myself, let me state that time as you know it does not exist basically and that all creations are simultaneous. *(Amused.)* That should answer your question.

("I've already thought of that," I said. As I told Jane at our first break, the knowledge that time is actually simultaneous is sometimes confounding when one asks certain types of questions; this knowledge half answers the question, yet we want the rest of the question considered.)

We will elaborate.

("All right.")

All of the ages of Earth, in your terms both past and present, exist, as do future ages. Now. You may make that a capital now. Some life forms are being developed in what you think of as present time. They will not appear physically until you reach your future time. Do you follow me?

("Yes.")

They exist now, however, as certainly as do, say, the dinosaurs. You only choose to focus your attention upon a highly specific field of space-time coordinates, accepting these as present reality, and closing yourselves off from all others. Specifically, complicated physical forms are not the result of previous simpler ones. They all exist in larger terms at once.

On the other hand, more complicated organizations of consciousness are necessary to form, enter, and vitalize the more complicated physical structures. All structure is formed by consciousness. Defined in your terms, a fragment is a consciousness not as developed as your own. The living portions of nature are the result of your own creativity, projections and fragments of your own energy; energy that comes to you from All That Is and goes outward from you, forming its own image manifestations as you form yours.

(*Pause at 9:42.*) Since you do not perceive the future and do not understand that life goes out in all directions, then it seems only logical to suppose that present forms must be based upon past ones. You do close your eyes to evidence that does not support this theory. (*Heartily, smiling*): And of course I am not speaking of you personally, Joseph.

There is no single-line development, in other words. The fragment elements directed outward by you as a species also add of course to your physical reality, for without the fine balance maintained, and without this cooperation, your particular kind of environment would not be possible.

I have told you often that you do yourselves a grave injustice by limiting your conception of the self. Your sense of identity, freedom, power, and love would be immeasurably enhanced if you could understand that what you are does not end at the boundaries of your skin, but continues outward through the physical environment that seems to be impersonal, or not-self.

Biologically it should be easy to understand that you are physically a part of earth and everything within it. You are made of the same elements, you breathe the same air. You cannot hold the air that you take within you and then say, "This is myself, filled with this air. I will not let it go," or you would find out very quickly that you were not nearly so independent.

You are biologically connected, chemically connected with the earth that you know; but since it is also formed naturally and spontaneously from your own projected psychic energy, since you and the seasons even have a psychic interaction, then the self must be understood in a far greater context. Such a context would allow you to share in life experiences of many other forms, to follow patterns of energy and emotion of which you barely conceive, and to sense a world-consciousness in which you have your own independent part.

You may take your break.

(*9:54. I told Jane that she had delivered this excellent answer to my question at a considerably faster pace. Resume at 10:04.*)

Now: I finished with the last question, so continue.

("Number twenty-eight: Have I painted any portraits of Speakers?")

You have indeed. One was a painting purchased by Carl and Sue Watkins *(which, half jokingly, we had called Moses)*; one, the portrait of me *(pause)*; and one that you have not completed — that the Dean *(Seth's friendly title for Tom M., one of the members of ESP class)* asked about recently, of a woman. And your blue man. *(Pause.)* That is your answer.

(In Chapter Seventeen Seth told Jane and me that we'd both been Speakers. Since I haven't painted any self-portraits I wouldn't have been included in the list anyhow, but Seth did neglect to mention my painting of Jane. I didn't catch the omission, so I didn't ask about it. . . .

(When Seth tells me I've done a Speaker's portrait, I translate this to mean that I've tuned-in on but one personality out of the very many making up that Speaker's entity.

(After the sessions began I started a series of portraits of people I don't "know" consciously. At first I understood little about the possible sources for their inspiration; I simply put my urge to paint them to work. Ideas for the portraits "come" to me spontaneously when I am mentally occupied with something else. I am always surprised. Sometimes I see an outright vision, objectified quite clearly and in full color. The vision is either of the finished painting, or of the individual who is to be portrayed. On several occasions I have "known" the subject was dead. Few of the paintings are of Speakers, obviously, and in no case did I realize I was working with such a personality.

(I recently finished the blue man that Seth refers to. I painted a male in modern garb, but in reality, according to an amused Seth, the subject was a female clairvoyant who lived in Constantinople in the fourteenth century; unconscious distortions in my own perceptions led me to the male figure. Seth has given her the name Ianodiala. The oil is very successful, and is done in blue and green.

(Such sources of inspirational material were entirely unsuspected by me in earlier years. I believe now that they are among those usually present at unconscious levels; but in order to expand the potentials for the creative act as much as possible, I would like to see others learn to cultivate such visions and perceptions on a deliberate, conscious basis. It seems to me the benefits would be many. There is much to be learned here.

("Do you want to deal now with the question about the Dead Sea Scrolls and Yahoshua?" This was in reference to a letter Jane had received on April 12, having to do with Seth's third-Christ data in The Seth Material.*)*

We will save that for our religious chapter. In it we will answer your other related questions.

("Number fifty-two: In the 429th session for August 14, 1968, you said: 'Also, minutes and hours have their own consciousness.' You didn't elaborate.")

(Smile.) And now you want me to elaborate.

("Well, I don't know. I'm wondering if perhaps the question is too complicated for a quick answer.")

Give us a moment. *(Pause.)* What you perceive of time is a portion of other events intruding into your own system, often interpreted as movement in space, or as something that separates events — if not in space, then in a way impossible to define without using the concept of time.

What separates events is not time, but your perception. You perceive events "one at a time." Time as it appears to you is, instead, a psychic organization of experience. The seeming beginning and end of an event; the seeming birth and death, are simply other dimensions of experience as, for example, height, width, weight. Instead it seems to you that you grow toward an end, when an end is a part of a particular experience, or if you prefer, person-event.

(10:26.) We are speaking then of multidimensional reality. The whole self or entity or soul can never be completely materialized in three-dimensional form. A part of it can be projected into that dimension however, extending so many years in time, taking up so much space, and so forth.

The entity sees the whole event, the whole person-event, with the time element, or age in your terms, as simply another characteristic or dimension. The person-event is not cut off, however. Its greater reality simply cannot appear within three dimensions. It is instead composed of atoms and molecules that you do not perceive, both above and below the physical range of intensities — and all of these in their own way possess consciousness.

In greater terms, seconds and moments do not exist, either, but the reality that is behind time or that you perceive as time, the "outside time" events, are composed of units that also have their own kind of consciousness. They form what appears as time to you, as atoms and molecules form what appears as space to you. *(Pause.)*

Now these are units moving faster than the speed of light, excellent energy sources intruding into and impinging upon matter without ever materializing. They will be interpreted differently in other systems. That is the end. *(Smiling.)*

(10:35. Of book dictation, that is. This was actually a break. Seth finished the session with several pages of material dealing with other matters. End at 11:10 P.M.)

SESSION 583, APRIL 21, 1971,
9:30 P.M. WEDNESDAY

(Last night, Tuesday, I went to bed while Jane was holding ESP class in the living room. It was about 11:30. As I lay dozing I gave myself suggestions that I would recall my dreams in the morning and write them down. Oddly enough, I didn't mention "astral projection."

(I slept rather uneasily, waking up several times while class was still in progress. Finally, I was hazily aware of hearing the cars of class members as they pulled out of the parking lot next to the house. Then I slept. Jane said later that she came to bed at 12:45 A.M.

(The next thing I knew, I was hovering in the air in our darkened bathroom. I was in a bodiless state without being at all upset.

(The bathroom is in the center of our apartment; the living room is on one side of it, the bedroom and my studio on the other. In order to keep our cat, Willy, off our bed at night, we put him in the living room and close the door on that side of the bathroom. Now I found myself hanging in front of that door, unable to penetrate it.

(I felt no panic, no fear. My astral eyes were functioning. A weak light came through a narrow open window to my right. The closed door was in deep shadow, but I knew I was before it. Although my body lay sleeping beside Jane in the bedroom "behind" me, I wasn't concerned about it. I didn't realize that I was projecting at first — I didn't have the presence of mind, say, to order myself to burst through the door into the living room. But that I was out of my body, and in this very pleasant weightless state, did slowly make itself known to me. I had no memory of actually leaving my body and moving into the bathroom.

(This was the first time that no element of fear was present in any of my rather infrequent projections. I believe my ordinary conscious ideas that doors can't be penetrated held me back, though. I fell asleep again briefly after encountering the impasse posed by the closed door. When I became aware again, evidently a

few moments later, I found myself floating just above my physical body as it lay in bed.

(It happened that I lay sleeping flat on my back with my arms down at my sides. My astral body was in the same approximate position, perhaps six inches above. My state was remarkably steady and pleasant: I felt awake, aware of what I was up to, and quite free and weightless. I heard myself snoring, without paying much attention to that fact — yet. I knew I wasn't dreaming. I even remembered reading at various times that when projecting one knows the difference between that state and a dreaming one. This I could now attest to at firsthand. I was very pleased.

(I had a different kind of vision this time. In some fashion I was aware of my legs especially, suspended above my physical ones. I took great pleasure in wiggling them about, shaking them up and down, enjoying the marvelous sense of freedom and lightness they possessed. I knew my physical legs couldn't move that freely, although they are in good shape. My astral legs felt quite rubbery, so loose and flexible were they — and somehow, from my prone position, I could see that they were light-colored and translucent from the knees down!

(Since my projection state seemed to be so reliable, I began to think it offered great opportunities. I felt no fear, again, only confidence. I thought that this would be a great time to do something. Now was the time for a fine adventure. I told myself I was willing to try anything — a visit to some other reality, a plunge through the door into the living room, a trip down the street in front of the house. . . .

(All this time Jane lay beside me. She said afterward that I was snoring loudly when she came to bed. My attention now began to change its focus; for the first time I really heard myself. I was amazed at the loudness of the sounds that came from my physical head, just beneath "me." I couldn't possibly duplicate them while awake.

(Without success, I made several quite conscious and deliberate attempts to "get going," and travel away from my body. My efforts didn't break the projection spell; I merely remained hovering where I was. Then I had an idea: I would use the sound of my snoring as an impetus to send myself soaring off into other dimensions, leaving my body far behind me on the bed.

(Deliberately I began to snore even louder, if possible. I wanted to build up a massive sound-impetus that I would use as a propellant, although I didn't know how this was supposed to work. The strange thing is, I enjoyed both the feeling of lying just above my physical body, and my ability to use the latter to *produce sound. This implies a dual consciousness here, since I was aware of both bodies.*

(Either I heard my snoring actually increase in volume, or I focused upon it even more acutely. My idea wasn't working, anyhow. I don't know whether I would have eventually succeeded in taking off, for Jane now said to me: "Honey, you're snoring. Turn over," as she usually does when she gets tired of listening to me. I heard her clearly. I stopped snoring at once, but didn't move. I don't remember rejoining my physical body. Finally I nudged her, and with an effort told her something of what had transpired. She thought I sounded as though I was still in a trance.

(I felt as though I might project again, so I kept trying while Jane lay quietly beside me. I had no success, although the very pleasant aura surrounding the whole episode lingered most definitely. The projection, small as it was, had seemed so easy and natural that I wondered why it wasn't a commonplace. I knew all the while that much more was possible than I was able to accomplish — that just beyond my abilities of the moment lay wonderful possibilities if I could just break that . . . barrier. I never did feel any alarm, and at no time did I see, or feel, the "astral silver cord." Finally I slept.

(The experience gave rise to a couple of questions which I added to the list for Chapter Twenty: 1. My own projection was so enjoyable, but more importantly contained so many potentials, that I wonder why Western man isn't more aware of these abilities. 2. Why doesn't he cultivate them and put them to use? I hoped Seth would comment tonight.)

Now: Good evening.

("Good evening, Seth.")

And congratulations.

("Thank you.")

This is to you: You tried the experiment when you did, having an ace in the hole, so to speak, in case you became frightened, knowing full well that Ruburt would be coming to bed. You were ready to try again, however, and picked a slow and easy method, pleasant surroundings, to make it easy for you also, so that you could become familiar with the sensation before you actually did anything too adventurous with it.

("Did I try this before Jane came to bed?")

No. You began your attempts before, but did not succeed until Ruburt came to bed. The time sense outside the body can be quite different than the body's. You knew that with one successful experience you would be much more free, and so you chose the best of circumstances.

You could have left the apartment indeed. The snoring was also, however, supposed to be a signal to Ruburt. You knew he would awaken you. This was the original motivation for it. If you did not like the experiment, you see, it would have been terminated. In the meantime, however, you were delighted, and decided upon the noise as a propellant, but Ruburt's usual reaction to the snoring took place.

You should find yourself remembering quite a few such experiences now.

(It is Sunday, April 25, as I type up this session from my notes. Ever since April 21 I have been waiting expectantly, and in vain, for another projection. On a different occasion I had a rather small out-of-body that trailed behind it, for almost two weeks, a series of incomplete projections or dream experiences containing distorted elements of such phenomena. Strangely, an analogy might be the aftershocks following a quake. . . .)

Now in answer to your questions: Western man has chosen to focus his energy outward and largely ignore inner realities. The social and cultural aspects, and even the religious ones, automatically inhibit such experiences from childhood on. There is no social benefit at all connected with projections in your society, and many taboos against it.

(9:40.) This is, of course, chosen by those involved in that civilization. There are also balances that exist before moderation and understanding are reached. Some personalities choose to be reincarnated in exteriorly oriented societies, in compensation for lives that were lived with great concentration inward, and very poor physical manipulation. Man learns, you see, that inner reality and outer reality both must be understood and used constructively.

Projections occur of course in the sleep state constantly, whether or not they are remembered. They are recalled when there is some reason to do so, some merit or obvious achievement involved, as in societies where it is considered highly advantageous to use dreams and projections.

If you are presently experiencing a life in which you have chosen high emphasis upon physical locomotion, for example, then through vague dream memories of flying you can be inspired toward, say, the invention of airplanes or rockets; but if you actually understand the fact that your own consciousness can indeed travel outside of the body, then the impetus toward physical developments in locomotion is not nearly so intense.

Now. What questions do you have?

("Number fifty-three: In the 429th session for August 14, 1968, you said that some personalities can be a part of more than one entity.")

I have mentioned this many times. There are no boundaries to the self, and no barriers put upon its development. A personality may "originally" be a part of a given entity, and on its own develop interests quite different. It can on its own take a lonely way, or it can instead attach itself or gravitate toward other entities with interests like its own. The original connection will not be severed, but new ones made and formed.

(Pause at 9:47. "Number forty-six. In Chapter Nineteen of The Seth Material *you gave a list of the inner senses. Are there more of these that you haven't told us about?")*

There are indeed. They have to do, however, with experiences that you will not normally encounter in your particular system, that lie latent. *(Pause.)*

Almost any cell has the capacity for growing into any given organ, or forming any part of the body. It has the capacity for developing sense organs that, practically speaking, will not be developed if the cell becomes an elbow or a knee, but the capacity is there. This applies not only to your own species but in many cases between species, and there are basic units in all living matter capable of forming animal or vegetable life, capable of developing the perceptive mechanisms inherent in any of these.

It is therefore theoretically possible for you to see the world through a frog's eye, or a bird's or an ant's. We are speaking here of physical senses. The inner self has also latent inner senses beside the ones that it normally uses while the consciousness is tuned into a particular camouflage system.

Some, however, are inexpressible in physical terms, and only analogies could be used to hint of their nature. In this book there is no need to discuss them. They belong in a book given more specifically to interior methods of perception.

("Number fifty-five: This question comes from the answer you gave to

number eleven, when I asked you about the training Jane would need in order to deliver one of the ancient Speaker manuscripts. You said some of those old languages involved pictures and symbols. With your help while she's in trance, could Jane make drawings of a few picture-words or symbols? I'm just curious to see if she could approximate one of the Speaker languages.")

This is possible.

("That would be very interesting." Seth paused, so I asked, "Can she try it now?")

This is not the time. *(Pause.)* There are many distorted inner connections between these. Some hieroglyphics and the symbols were used by the Mu civilization.

I suggest a break then while you check your questions.

("Okay."

(10:00. Jane and I went over some of the remaining questions, but since she seemed to be tiring I suggested we end this part of the session. The rest of it was given over to personal material. End at 10:58 P.M.)

SESSION 584, MAY 3, 1971,
9:35 P.M. MONDAY

(Except for ESP class, Jane rested from psychic work last week.)

Now: Good evening

("Good evening, Seth.")

I will answer questions that do not deal with reincarnation or religion.

(We had been talking about those subjects just before the session, although I hadn't planned to refer to them tonight. "Number fifty-eight: Are there any more Laws of the Inner Universe, other than those you gave in the 50th session for May 4, 1964?")

There are, but since I am not covering those in this book, I will give them to you at another time.

(I asked the question because I thought Seth's answer to number forty-six, in the last session, touched upon one of those propositions: "The Law of Infinite Changeability and Transmutation." In view of his reply now, though, I didn't pursue the matter further.

("Number forty-four: If you hadn't been able to speak through Jane, would you try to do so through another — or are you doing so anyhow?")

I have spoken through others. The arrangements "this time" were already made, you see. It is true that Ruburt need not have accepted the arrangement. If so the material would have been given, but in different fashion.

I would not have spoken in this way, for this work requires a certain specific rapport, and definite characteristics on the part of the personality involved. Material could have been given in a much more simple fashion through another, but I wanted it as undistorted and fully dimensional as possible. Had Ruburt not been available, the material would have been given to a Speaker, living in your terms, who was also involved in the creative field.

There is no one else presently alive in your system with whom I had any great rapport in the past, except yourselves. Such a Speaker would have received the information largely in the dream state, and written it in a series both of treatises and fictionalized narrative.

Had Ruburt not accepted, however, it is most probable that he would have chosen another life in which to fulfill the task, in which case I would have waited. The decision was always his, however, and had he not accepted at all, other arrangements would have been made.

(To me): Now you early foresaw your part in these sessions, and our work. One of the paintings you did many years ago clearly foreshadowed the development of your psychic endeavors. This was the one you sold, of the man that hung for some time in the position in which my portrait now hangs. That was a portrait of Joseph; in other words of your own inner identity as you intuitively perceived it at the time. You were not consciously aware of the connection, but you were consciously aware of the painting's strong impact.

(I know the painting, of course. I painted it in Florida in 1954, before Jane and I were married. I have photographs of it, and intend to repaint it some day. This means, of course, that I'll only be painting a new version of the old. It would be impossible to truly duplicate it. I have no regrets about selling the painting, though.)

It represented also the searching, creatively dissatisfied portion of you, looking for further understanding and knowledge. The peculiar relationship existing between you and Ruburt was also a prerequisite, and so your permission and acceptance was also needed.

Had you remained apart, the sessions would not have begun. You have been connected with the same entity, though you have sprung apart from it, but the inner relationship adds to the power available. You help steady the circuit, so to speak. You also generated initial energy and impetus to help Ruburt's own.

Such work does not only necessitate the choosing of one individual, but is also an endeavor in which many other elements are taken into consideration. It was known, for example, that Ruburt would need your support, as it was also known that the work itself would help your own creative abilities.

All of this was decided by you both, and by me before you began this particular lifetime. Even Ruburt's intellectual questioning and often deep reluctance was known in advance, and adapted to aid in the work involved.

The information was not to be given to "born believers," but to intelligent people, and to a "medium" who questioned it, not only for himself but for all those given to the same kind of questioning. As Ruburt grows to understand, therefore, and as he continues to develop, he triumphs not only for himself but for all those who follow his ventures. And yet we wanted a balance also, and so you stand as a man who intuitively recognized the value of inner information and the importance of the material, even though you were unacquainted with such ideas.

(10:00.) It goes without saying that on much deeper levels there is no reluctance on Ruburt's part, or the abilities would not have developed in this fashion. His criticism in the beginning served also as reassurance to the ego, in its first experiences, that it would not be shoved aside or damaged in any fashion.

The characteristics needed for "mediumship" are much like those needed by any strongly creative person. A strong supportive ego is a necessity, particularly in initial stages. In periods of severe personality disturbances that can occur simultaneously with great creativity, the ego becomes terrified of the strength of the creative ability, fearing that it can be crushed beneath.

In such cases the ego is too rigid, and does not expand with the nature of the personality's whole creative experience. Of course this could happen with mediumship, as with any other such activity. In this case, however, Ruburt's ego gradually began to let its rigidity go, in a gradual process that allowed the whole personality, itself included, to expand.

End of dictation for now, and a personal note. You can see where the above information ties in with Ruburt. The idea of letting the muscular armor go, as in your current reading, is good.

You can take your break, and then we will resume the session.

(10:09. Jane's trance had been deep, her delivery fast. She said she could see the 1954 painting very clearly while Seth talked about it, including its wide, old-fashioned gold frame. At first she had forgotten what the frame looked like, she told me, but now correctly described it. Naturally, the painting was sold before we had any conscious awareness of its import. This would be not only before the sessions began, but before we even suspected such possibilities. The balance of the session is deleted from the record. End at 10:28 P.M.)

CHAPTER 21

THE MEANING OF RELIGION

SESSION 585, MAY 12, 1971,
9:35 P.M. WEDNESDAY

(Before the session Jane and I went over the questions remaining on the list we had prepared for Chapter Twenty. "I hope Seth will just do those chapters on religion and reincarnation, and get them over with," she said. We've realized for some time that Jane is sensitive to those subjects, particularly religion; she had strict training in that field as a youngster. Coupled with that, however, she developed a very strong, literal, religious drive on her own. She is well aware that such an early environment leaves its marks, even though she had left her church by the time she was nineteen. . . .

(Somewhat to my surprise Seth started Chapter Twenty-one this evening, but I soon realized that he wasn't leaving our questions behind. The session was held in my studio again, and because of its rather small size Jane decided not to smoke. It had been raining all day, and still was.)

Good evening.

("Good evening, Seth.")

Now: The questions on religion and reincarnation will be answered in due time, as mentioned. I will deal with several of your other questions also along with the text. Therefore we will begin the next chapter, called: "The Meaning of Religion."

There are internal realizations always present within the whole self. There is comprehension of the meaning of all existence within each personality. The knowledge of multidimensional existence is not only in the background of your present conscious activity, but each man knows within himself that his conscious life is dependent upon a greater dimension of actuality. This greater dimension cannot be materialized in a three-dimensional system, yet the knowledge of this greater dimension floods outward from the innermost heart of being, and is projected outward, transforming all it touches.

This flooding-out imbues certain elements of the physical world with a brilliance and intensity far surpassing that usually known. Those touched by it are transformed, in your terms, into something more than they were. This inner knowledge attempts to find a place for itself within the physical landscape, to translate itself into physical terms. Each man, then, possesses this inner knowledge within himself, and to some extent or other he also looks for confirmation of it in the world.

(Pause at 9:45. The above paragraph is, incidentally, an excellent little description of the results flowing from Jane's own psychic initiation in September, 1963. Her transcendent experience led to her manuscript, The Physical Universe as Idea Construction, *which in turn led to these sessions. See her Introduction to this book.*

(A note: I was amused, now, to see Jane light a cigarette while she was in trance.)

The outer world is a reflection of the inner one, though far from perfect. The inner knowledge can be compared to a book about a homeland that a traveler takes with him into a strange country. Each man is born with the yearning to make these truths real for himself, though he sees a great difference between them and the environment in which he lives.

An internal drama is carried on by each individual, a psychic drama which is finally projected outward with great force upon the field of history. The birth of great religious events emerges from the interior religious drama. The drama itself is a psychological phenomenon in a way, for each physically oriented self feels thrust alone into a strange environment, without knowing its origins or destination or even the reason for its own existence.

This is the dilemma of the ego, particularly in its early states. It looks outward for answers because this is its nature: to manipulate within physical reality. It also senses, however, a deep and abiding connection that it does not understand, with other portions of the self that are not under its domain. It is also aware that this inner self possesses knowledge upon which its own existence is based.

As it grows, in your terms, it looks outward for confirmation of this inner knowledge. The inner self upholds the ego with its support. It forms its truths into physically oriented data with which the ego can deal. It then projects these outward into the area of physical reality. Seeing these truths thus materialized, the ego then finds it easier to accept them.

Thus you deal often with events in which men are touched by great illumination, isolated from the masses of humanity, and endowed with great powers — periods of history that appear almost unnaturally brilliant in contrast with others; prophets, geniuses, and kings shown in greater-than-human proportion.

(10:00.) Now these people are chosen by others to manifest outwardly the interior truths that all intuitively know. There are many levels of significance here. On the one hand, such individuals receive their unearthly abilities and power from their fellows, contain it, exhibit it in the physical world for all to see. They play the part of the blessed inner self that actually cannot operate within physical reality uncloaked by flesh. This energy, however, is a quite valid projection from the interior self. *(Long pause.)*

The personality so touched by it actually does then become, in certain terms, what he seems to be. He will emerge as an eternal hero in the external religious drama, as the inner self is the eternal hero of the interior religious drama.

(10:08.) This mystic projection is a continual activity. When the strength of one great religion begins to diminish and its physical effects grow less, then the internal drama begins once again to quicken. The highest of man's aspirations, therefore, will be projected upon physical history. The dramas themselves will differ. Remember, they are built up internally first.

They will be formed to impress world conditions at any given time, and therefore couched in symbols and events that will most impress the populace. This is craftily done, for the inner self knows exactly what will impress the ego, and what kinds of personalities will be best able to personify the message at any given time. When such a personality appears in history then, he is intuitively recognized, for the way has long been laid, and in many cases the prophecies announcing such an arrival have already been given.

The individuals so chosen do not just happen to appear among you. They are not chosen at random. They are individuals who have taken upon themselves the responsibility for this role. After their birth they are aware to varying degrees of their destiny, and certain trigger experiences may at times arouse their full memory.

They serve quite clearly as human representatives of All That Is. Now since each individual is a part of All That Is, to some extent each of you serve in that same role. In such a religious drama however *(long pause)*, the main personality is much more conscious of his inner knowledge, more aware of his abilities, far better able to use them, and exultantly familiar with his relationship to all of life.

Now you may take your break.

(10:25. Following break, Seth-Jane delivered five excellent pages of data about my painting and related subjects. The session ended at 11:03 P.M.

(Jane, knowing Seth had started his chapter on religion, was both relieved and very curious. I finally ended up giving her a copy of the material, in order to answer all of her questions. She liked it so much that she read it to ESP class, as she has done with a few previous segments from the book.)

SESSION 586, JULY 24, 1971,
9:01 P.M. SATURDAY

(This is the first regular session since May 12. There were many factors behind the long layoff: Jane's sheer need for rest; problems and questions of our own that we had wanted to deal with, but had put off for a long time; some work with others; a vacation; and the acquisition of several more rooms across the hall from our original apartment. Jane held ESP classes for some of this time, though, and gave a few sessions within that format.

(Jane preferred that Seth simply start in where he had left off on the chapter — a feat I was sure he was quite capable of. "But I don't care what he does," she laughed, "as long as we have a session." She was somewhat nervous because of the break in dictation, in spite of my reassurances. She was strongly interested in seeing that Seth finished his book, although she still has to read most of it.

(The session was held in our old bedroom, which, having been cleared out now, is an adjunct to my studio. The additional space we've acquired is most welcome.)

Now: Good evening.

("Good evening, Seth.")

(Smiling): And welcome back. . . . Now give me a moment, and we will begin by resuming our chapter on religion. *(Pause.)*

Ideas of good and evil, gods and devils, salvation and damnation, are merely symbols of deeper religious values; cosmic values if you will, that cannot be translated into physical terms.

These ideas become the driving themes of these religious dramas of which I have spoken. The actors may "return," time and time again, in different roles. In any given historic religious drama, therefore, the actors may have already appeared on the historic scene in your past, the prophet of today being the traitor of the past drama.

These psychic entities are real, however. It is quite true to say that their reality consists not only of the core of their own identity, but also is reinforced by those projected thoughts and feelings of the earthly audience for whom the drama is enacted.

(9:05.) Psychic or psychological identification is of great import here and is indeed at the heart of all such dramas. In one sense, you can say that man identifies with the gods he has himself created. Man does not understand the magnificent quality of his own inventiveness and creative power, however. Then, say that gods and men create each other, and you come even closer to the truth; but only if you are very careful in your definitions — for how, exactly, do gods and men differ?

The attributes of the gods are those inherent within man himself, magnified, brought into powerful activity. Men believe that the gods live forever. Men live forever, but having forgotten this, they remember only to endow their gods with this characteristic. Obviously, then, beyond these earthly historic religious dramas, the seemingly recurring tales of gods and men, there are spiritual realities.

(9:10.) Behind the actors in the dramas, there are more powerful entities who are quite beyond role-playing. The plays themselves, then, the religions that sweep across the ages — these are merely shadows, though helpful ones. Behind the frame of good and evil is a far deeper spiritual value. All religions, therefore, while trying to catch "truth" must to some large degree fear its ever eluding them.

The inner self alone, at rest, in meditation, can at times glimpse portions of these inner realities that cannot be physically expressed. These values, intuitions, or insights are given each to each according to his understanding, and so the stories told about them will often vary.

For example, the main character in a religious historical drama may or may not consciously be aware of the ways in which such information is given to him. And yet it may seem to him that he does know, for the nature of a dogma's origin will be explained in terms that this main character can understand. The historical Jesus knew who he was, but he also knew that he was one of three personalities composing one entity. To a large extent he shared in the memory of the other two.

The third personality, mentioned many times by me, has not in your terms yet appeared, although his existence has been prophesied as the "Second Coming" *(Matthew 24).* Now these prophecies were given in terms of the current culture at that time, and therefore, while the stage has been set, the distortions are deplorable, for this Christ will not come at the end of your world as the prophecies have been maintaining.

(9:20.) He will not come to reward the righteous and send evil-doers to eternal doom. He will, however, begin a new religious drama. A certain historical continuity will be maintained. As happened once before, however, he will not be generally known for who he is. There will be no glorious proclamation to which the whole world will bow. He will return to straighten out Christianity, which will be in a shambles at the time of his arrival, and to set up a new system of thought when the world is sorely in need of one.

(9:25.) By that time, all religions will be in severe crisis. He will undermine religious organizations — not unite them. His message will be that of the individual in relation to All That Is. He will clearly state methods by which each individual can attain a state of intimate contact with his own entity; the entity to some extent being man's mediator with All That Is.

By 2075, all of this will be already accomplished.

You may make a note here that Nostradamus saw the dissolution of the Roman Catholic Church as the end of the world. He could not imagine civilization without it, hence many of his later predictions should be read with this in mind.

The third personality of Christ will indeed be known as a great psychic, for it is he who will teach humanity to use those inner senses that alone make true spirituality possible. Slayers and victims will change roles as reincarnational memories rise to the surface of consciousness. Through the development of these abilities, the sacredness of all life will be intimately recognized and appreciated.

Now there will be several born before that time who in various ways will rearouse man's expectations. One such man has already been born in India, in a small province near Calcutta, but his ministry will seem to remain comparatively local for his lifetime.

Another will be born in Africa, a black man whose main work will be done in Indonesia. The expectations were set long ago in your terms, and will be fed by new prophets until the third personality of Christ does indeed emerge.

He will lead man behind the symbolism upon which religion has relied for so many centuries. He will emphasize individual spiritual experience, the expansiveness of soul, and teach man to recognize the multitudinous aspects of his own reality.

Now you may take your break.

("Thank you."

(9:37. Seth spoke humorously about break, since the pace had been mostly fast, with few pauses. Jane's trance had been good. I had to work harder than usual taking notes because I was out of practice; I also discovered I'd temporarily forgotten some of the symbols I use in my own version of Speedwriting.

(During the break Jane read over parts of Chapter Eighteen of The Seth Material, *then announced that she thought there was a contradiction, between that material — originally from the 491st session on July 2, 1969 — on the three Christs, and the information given by Seth this evening. Here are the paragraphs in question from pages 246–47 of the chapter on "The God Concept":*

("There were three men whose lives became confused in history and merged, and whose composite history became known as the life of Christ. . . . Each was highly gifted psychically, knew of his role, and accepted it willingly. The three men were a part of one entity, gaining physical existence in one time. They were not born on the same date, however. There are reasons why the entity did not return as one person. For one thing, the full consciousness of an entity would be too strong for one physical vehicle. For another, the entity wanted a more diversified environment than could otherwise be provided.

("The entity was born once as John the Baptist, and then he was born in two other forms. One of these contained the personality that most stories of Christ

· 329 ·

refer to. . . . I will tell you about the other personality at a later time. There was constant communication between these three portions of one entity, though they were born and buried at different dates. The race called up these personalities from its own psychic bank, from the pool of individualized consciousness that was available to it."

(I too had begun wondering. All along we'd been thinking the three personalities making up the Christ entity had already lived and died, but now here Seth was talking about the third personality returning in the next century. What was the explanation? We weren't upset; yet we did feel uneasy as the session resumed at 9:57.)

Now: Let us resume.

The third <u>historical</u> personage, already born in your terms, and a portion of the entire Christ personality, took upon himself the role of a zealot.

This person had superior energy and power and great organizing abilities, but it was the errors that he made unwittingly that perpetuated some dangerous distortions. The records of that historical period are scattered and contradictory.

The man, historically now, was Paul or Saul. It was given to him to set up a framework. But it was to be a framework of ideas, not of regulations; of men, not of groups. Here he fell down, and he will return as the third personality, just mentioned, in your future.

In that respect, however, there are not four personalities.

("I understand.")

Now Saul went to great lengths to set himself as a separate identity. His characteristics, for example, were seemingly quite different from those of the historical Christ. He was "converted" in an intense personal experience — a fact that was meant to impress upon him the personal and not organizational aspects. Yet some exploits of his in his earlier life have been attributed to Christ — not as a young man, but earlier.

(10:05.) All personalities have free will and work out their own challenges. The same applied to Saul. The organizational "distortions," however, were also necessary within the framework of history as events are understood. Saul's tendencies were known, therefore, at another level. They served a purpose. It is for this reason, however, that he will emerge once again, this time to destroy those distortions.

Now he did not create them on his own, and thrust them upon

historical reality. *(Jane paused, a hand to her eyes.)* He created them in so far as he found himself forced to admit certain facts: In that world at that time, earthly power was needed to hold Christian ideas apart from numberless other theories and religions, to maintain them in the middle of warring factions. It was his job to form a physical framework; and even then he was afraid that the framework would strangle the ideas, but he saw no other way.

("Why the two names, Paul and Saul?")

He was called both. *(Pause.)* When the third personality reemerges historically, however, he will not be called the old Paul, but will carry within him the characteristics of all the three personalities.

(Jane paused again. "Can I ask a very stupid question?")

You may.

(There followed a short exchange between Seth and me, which isn't recorded verbatim because it was too rapid. I was interested in learning whether, and when, the three personalities of the Christ entity had met as physical beings. It seemed that superior psychic interactions would have taken place among them, and I wanted to know more about this. Jane, as Seth, listened politely to my groping questions.)

It is easy to see that you have no knowledge of the Bible —

("True.")

— for this would be fairly apparent to those who have.

Paul tried to deny knowing who he was, until his experience with conversion. Allegorically, he represented a warring faction of the self that fights against his own knowledge and is oriented in a highly physical manner. It seemed he went from one extreme to another, being against Christ and then for him. But the inner vehemence was always present, the inner fire, and the recognition that he tried for so long to hide.

His was the portion that was to deal with physical reality and manipulation, and so these qualities were strong in him. To some extent they overruled him. When the historical Christ "died," Paul was to implement the spiritual ideas in physical terms, to carry on. In so doing, however, he grew the seeds of an organization that would smother the ideas. He lingered after Christ, [just] as John the Baptist came before. Together the three spanned some time period, you see.

John and the historical Christ each performed their roles and were satisfied that they had done so. Paul alone was left at the end unsatisfied, and so it is about his personality that the future Christ will form.

The entity of which these personalities are part, that entity which you may call the Christ entity, was aware of these issues. The earthly personalities were not aware of them, although in periods of trance and exaltation much was made known to them.

Paul also represented the militant nature of man, that had to be taken into consideration in line with man's development at the time. That militant quality in man will completely change its nature, and be dispensed with as you know it, when the next Christ personality emerges. It is therefore appropriate that Paul be present.

(10:27.) In the next century, the inner nature of man, with these developments, will free itself from many constraints that have bound it. A new era will indeed begin — not, now, a heaven on earth, but a far more sane and just world, in which man is far more aware of his relationship with his planet and of his freedom within time.

Now you may take a break in time.

(10:30. Jane's pace had been good again for the most part, but she came out of trance easily. She was relieved that Seth had named the third personality of the Christ entity. Although she said she hadn't been worrying about this data, I knew she had been more than usually concerned about getting it.

(Our discussion at break concerned several other points I thought readers might be interested in: One was the zealot designation Seth applied to Paul. At first I'd thought he was going to say there was a connection between Paul, or Saul, and the Zealots, one of the religious sects the Jewish people had been divided into in Judaea in the first century A.D. The Holy Land was occupied by the Romans then, and Paul was a Jew and a Roman citizen. I'd been reading about these sects recently in a book on the Dead Sea Scrolls, and had been somewhat puzzled by my interest in both the scrolls and the sects; but after hearing Seth tonight I assumed he wasn't going to say much about these subjects.

(Another question concerned a name and country for the appearance of the third Christ in the next century. Also, could or would Seth give any data on the religious figure already born in India, and the black man to be born in Africa?

(As we continued to talk during break, Jane then told me she knew the answers to the questions I had asked. The answers had "come" to her. She didn't get this information in exact words, she said, but felt it and had to translate it:

(1. Seth had intended the word zealot, as applied to Paul, to be descriptive of his temperament — not a reference to the Zealot sect. A note, added later: More was to come on Paul and the Zealots, though.

(2. The country — with a name and dates — which would see the appearance of the third Christ in the next century, would not be given to us now, but might be in later years. Seth, she said, had deliberately refrained from being more specific. This was to prevent any overreactions to every personage born in a particular country, who might seem to fit descriptions and dates given. This would be very unfair and misleading.

(3. For the same reason Seth wouldn't say more at this time concerning the Indian religious figure, and the to-be-born African who would work in Indonesia.)

(Resume at 10:50.)

Now: Let us continue.

Ruburt was correct in the answers he just gave you.

I would like to make certain points clear. The "new religion" following the Second Coming will not be Christian in your terms, although the third personality of Christ will initiate it.

This personality will refer to the historical Christ, will recognize his relationship with that personality; but within him the three personality groupings will form a new psychic entity, a different psychological gestalt. As this metamorphosis takes place, it will initiate a metamorphosis on a human level also *(emphatically)*, as man's inner abilities are accepted and developed.

The results will be a different kind of existence. Many of your problems now result from spiritual ignorance. No man will look down upon an individual from another race when he himself recognizes that his own existence includes such membership also.

(10:55.) No sex will be considered better than the other, or any role in society, when each individual is aware of his own or her own experience at many levels of society and in many roles. An open-ended consciousness will feel its connections with all other living beings. *(Pause.)* The continuity of consciousness will become apparent. As a result of all this the social and governmental structures will change, for they are based upon your current beliefs.

Human personality will reap benefits that now would seem unbelievable. An open-ended consciousness will imply far greater freedom.

From birth, children will be taught that basic identity is not dependent upon the body, and that time as you know it is an illusion. The child will be aware of many of its past existences, and will be able to identify with the old man or woman that in your terms it will become.

(11:02.) Many of the lessons "that come with age" will then be available to the young, but the old will not lose the spiritual elasticity of their youth. This itself is important. But for some time, future incarnations will still be hidden for practical reasons.

As these changes come about, new areas will be activated in the brain to physically take care of them. Physically then, brain mappings will be possible in which past-life memories are evoked. All of these alterations are spiritual changes in which the meaning of religion will escape organizational bounds, become a living part of individual existence, and where psychic frameworks rather than physical ones form the foundations for civilization. *(Pause, eyes closed, at 11:05.)*

Man's experience will be so extended that to you the species will seem to have changed into another. This does not mean there will not be problems. It does mean that man will have far greater resources at his command. It also presupposes a richer and far more diverse social framework. Men and women will find themselves relating to their brethren, not only as the people that they are, but as the people that they were.

Family relationships will show perhaps the greatest changes. There will be room for emotional interactions within the family that are now impossible. The conscious mind will be more aware of unconscious material.

I am including this information in this chapter on religion because it is important that you realize that spiritual ignorance is at the basis of so many of your problems, and that indeed your only limitations are spiritual ones.

(11:14.) The metamorphosis mentioned earlier on the part of the third personality, will have such strength and power that it will call out from mankind these same qualities from within itself. The qualities have always been present. They will finally break through the veils of physical perception, extending that perception in new ways.

Now, mankind lacks such a focus. The third personality will represent that focus. There will be, incidentally, no crucifixion in that drama. That personality will indeed be multidimensional, aware of all its incarnations. It will not be oriented in terms of one sex, one color, or one race.

(11:20.) For the first time, therefore, it will break through the earthly concepts of personality, liberating personality. It will have the ability to show these diverse effects as it chooses. There will be many who will be afraid to accept the nature of their own reality, or to be shown the dimensions of true identity.

For several reasons, as mentioned by Ruburt, I do not want to give any more detailed information as to the name that will be used, or the land of birth. Too many might be tempted to jump into that image prematurely.

Events are not predestined. The framework for this emergence has already been set, however, within your system of probabilities. The emergence of this third personality will directly affect the original historical drama of Christ as it is now known. There is and must be interactions between them.

You may take your break, or end the session as you prefer.

("We'll take the break."

(11:25. I asked for a break on the chance that more information might come through for the chapter. Jane said she couldn't remember any of the data given since last break. She'd had no sense of time passing while in trance.

(Both of us were getting tired. We were also hungry, so we thought of ending the session and watching an old mystery or horror movie on TV while we had something to eat. Then I remembered that Seth hadn't given headings for the first eight chapters of his book. He'd told us not to worry about this in Chapter Seventeen. Could he give the headings now, or would Jane have to go over that early material first? Impossible as it seemed, well over a year had passed since she had stopped reading the book, session by session, early in Chapter Four. Resume at 11:39.)

Now: I will bid you a fond good evening after a few remarks in answer to your question. Again, Ruburt picked this up from me this afternoon: When I deviated from the original outline as given *(in the 510th session for January 19, 1970),* I gave chapter headings. Otherwise those statements made in the outline apply. You can simply add them if you prefer. I inserted many chapters where none were mentioned, and so used the headings from then onward.

Now, do you have more questions?

(*"Yes, but I guess we'll ask them later."*)

(*Humorously, eyes wide and very dark*): You did not come to [ESP] class, so you could not have missed me very much.

(*"I missed you a great deal."*)

We will have a personal session also, and continue with our book. And I missed our private sessions.

(*"So did I."*)

You can still record and chat with me, without notes, some evening for your own freedom.

(*"That's why I'm having our recorder fixed."*)

My fondest regards then, and good evening.

(*"Thank you very much, Seth. It's been a pleasure."*)

It's always a pleasure.

(*I laughed at the humorous emphasis. "Good night." End at 11:45 P.M.*)

SESSION 587, JULY 28, 1971,
9:17 P.M. WEDNESDAY

Good evening.

(*"Good evening, Seth."*)

Now: We will resume dictation.

The exterior religious dramas are of course imperfect representations of the ever-unfolding interior spiritual realities. The various personages, the gods and prophets within religious history — these absorb the mass inner projections thrown out by those inhabiting a given time span.

Such religious dramas focus, direct, and, hopefully, clarify aspects of inner reality that need to be physically represented. (*Long pause, eyes closed.*) These do not only appear within your own system. Many are also projected into other systems of reality. Religion *per se*, however, is always the external facade of inner reality. The primary spiritual existence alone gives meaning to the physical one. In the most real terms, religion should include all of the pursuits of man in his search for the nature of meaning and truth. Spirituality cannot be some isolated, specialized activity or characteristic.

Exterior religious dramas are important and valuable only to the extent that they faithfully reflect the nature of inner, private spiritual existence. To the extent that a man feels that his religion expresses such inner experience, he will feel it valid. Most religions *per se*, however, set up as permissible certain groups of experiences while denying others. They limit themselves by applying the principles of the sacredness of life only to your own species, and often to highly limited groups within it.

(Pause at 9:30.) At no time will any given church be able to express the inner experience of all individuals. At no time will any church find itself in a position in which it can effectively curtail the inner experience of its members — it will only seem to do so. The forbidden experiences will simply be unconsciously expressed, gather strength and vitality, and rise up to form a counter projection which will then form another, newer exterior religious drama.

The dramas themselves do express certain inner realities, and they serve as surface reminders to those who do not trust direct experience with the inner self. They will take the symbols as reality. When they discover that this is not so, they feel betrayed. Christ spoke in terms of the father and son because in your terms, at that time, this was the method used — the story he told to explain the relationship between the inner self and the physically alive individual. No new religion really startles anyone, for the drama has already been played subjectively.

What I have said, of course, applies as much to Buddha as it does to Christ: Both accepted the inner projections and then tried to physically represent these. They were more, however, than the sum of those projections. This also should be understood. Mohammedanism fell far short. In this case the projections were of violence predominating. Love and kinship were secondary to what indeed amounted to baptism and communion through violence and blood.

In these continuous exterior religious dramas, the Hebrews played a strange role. Their idea of one god was not new to them. Many ancient religions held the belief of one god above all others. This god above all others was a far more lenient god, however, than the one the Hebrews followed. Many tribes believed, quite rightly, in the inner spirit that pervades each living thing. And they often referred to, say, the god in the tree, or the spirit in the flower. But they also accepted the reality of an overall spirit, of which these lesser spirits were but a part. All worked together harmoniously.

The Hebrews conceived of an overseer god, an angry and just and sometimes cruel god; and many sects denied, then, the idea that other living beings beside man possessed inner spirits. The earlier beliefs represented a far better representation of inner reality, in which man, observing nature, let nature speak and reveal its secrets.

(9:45.) The Hebrew god, however, represented a projection of a far different kind. Man was growing more and more aware of the ego, of a sense of power over nature, and many of the later miracles are presented in such a way that nature is forced to behave differently than in its usual mode. God becomes man's ally against nature.

The early Hebrew god became a symbol of man's unleashed ego. God behaved exactly as an enraged child would, had he those powers, sending thunder and lightning and fire against his enemies, destroying them. Man's emerging ego therefore brought forth emotional and psychological problems and challenges. The sense of separation from nature grew. Nature became a tool to use against others.

Sometime before the emergence of the Hebrew god these tendencies were apparent. In many ancient, now-forgotten tribal religions, recourse was also made to the gods to turn nature against the enemy. Before this time, however, man felt a part of nature, not separated from it. It was regarded as an extension of his being, as he felt an extension of its reality. One cannot use oneself as a weapon against oneself in those terms. *(Pause.)*

In those times men spoke and confided to the spirits of birds, trees, and spiders, knowing that in the interior reality beneath, the nature of these communications was known and understood. In those times, death was not feared as it is in your terms, now, for the cycle of consciousness was understood.

Man desired in one way to step out of himself, out of the framework in which he had his psychological existence, to try new challenges, to step out of a mode of consciousness into another. He wanted to study the process of his own consciousness. In one way this meant a giant separation from the inner spontaneity that had given him both peace and security. On the other hand, it offered a new creativity, in his terms.

I suggest your break, before I get into that.

(10:01. Jane's pace had speeded up considerably after a slow start. I told her the material was excellent. Tonight's session was being held in our living room,

since the house was empty except for us. The air conditioner had been on since before the session, yet Jane felt warm at break. In trance, she said, she hadn't been bothered by any sort of physical discomfort.

(During break I went over a few questions about the relationships between the three members of the Christ entity — John the Baptist, Jesus Christ, and Paul. After listening for a bit, Jane asked me not to pursue this subject now; she suggested I ask these questions at the end of the chapter, if Seth hadn't volunteered the answers before then. Resume at 10:13.)

Now: At this point, the god inside became the god outside.

Man tried to form a new realm, attain a different kind of focus and awareness. His consciousness turned a corner outside of itself. To do this he concentrated less and less upon inner reality, and therefore began the process of inner reality only as it was projected outward into the physical world.

Before, the environment was effortlessly created and perceived by man and all other living things, knowing the nature of their inner unity. In order to begin this new venture, it was necessary to pretend that this inner unity did not exist. Otherwise the new kind of consciousness would always run back to its home for security and comfort. So it seemed that all bridges must be cut, while of course it was only a game because the inner reality always remained. The new kind of consciousness simply had to look away from it to maintain initially an independent focus.

I am speaking here in more or less historic terms for you. You must realize that the process has nothing to do with time as you know it, however. This particular kind of adventure in consciousness *(smile)* has occurred before, and in your terms will again.

(Here Seth was making a little joke, for Jane has been doing some writing lately which she has tentatively entitled "Adventures in Consciousness.")

Perception of the exterior universe then changed, however, and it seemed to be alien and apart from the individual who perceived it.

(10:24.) God, therefore, became an idea projected outward, independent of the individual, divorced from nature. He became the reflection of man's emerging ego, with all of its brilliance, savagery, power, and intent for mastery. The adventure was a highly creative one despite the obvious disadvantages, and represented an "evolution" of consciousness that enriched man's subjective experience, and indeed added to the dimensions of reality itself.

To be effectively organized, however, inner and outer experience had to appear as separate, disconnected events. Historically the characteristics of God changed as man's ego changed. These characteristics of the ego, however, were supported by strong inner changes.

(Jane, as Seth, gestured emphatically and often as she spoke. Her pace had been fast since her break.)

The original propulsion of inner characteristics outward into the formation of the ego could be compared with the birth of innumerable stars — an event of immeasurable consequences that originated on a subjective level and within inner reality.

The ego, having its birth from within, therefore, must always boast of its independence while maintaining the nagging certainty of its inner origin.

(Pause at 10:30. Still in trance, Jane took time to sip at a beer and light a cigarette. Then):

We'll have a good chapter.

("Great.")

The ego feared for its position, frightened that it would dissolve back into the inner self from which it came. Yet in its emergence it provided the inner self with a new kind of feedback, a different view not only of itself; but through this, the inner self was able to glimpse possibilities of development of which it had not previously been aware. In your terms, by the time of Christ, the ego was sure enough of its position so that the projected picture of God could begin to change.

The inner self is in a state of constant growth. The inner portion of each man, therefore, projected this knowledge outward. The need, the psychological and spiritual need of the species, demanded both interior and exterior alterations of great import. Qualities of mercy and understanding that had been buried could now surface. Not only privately but *en masse* they surged up, adding a new impetus and giving a natural "new" direction — beginning to call all portions of the self, as it knew itself, together.

(10:38.) So the concept of God began to change as the ego recognized its reliance upon inner reality, but the drama had to be worked out within the current framework. Mohammedanism was basically so violent precisely because Christianity was basically so gentle. Not that

Christianity was not mixed with violence, or that Mohammedanism was devoid of love. But as the psyche went through its developments and battled with itself, denying some feelings and characteristics and stressing others, so the historic religious exterior dramas represented and followed these inner aspirations, struggles, and searches.

(Slower now): All of this material now given must be considered along with the fact that beneath these developments there are the eternal aspects and creative characteristics of a force that is both undeniable and intimate. All That Is, in other words, represents the reality from which all of us spring. *(Pause, one of several.)* All That Is, by its nature, transcends all dimensions of activity, consciousness, or reality, while being a part of each.

(10:45.) Behind all faces there is one face, yet this does not mean that each man's face is not his own. The further religious drama of which I have spoken, in your terms still to come, represents another stage in both the internal and external dramas in which the emergent ego becomes aware of much of its heritage. While maintaining its own status, it will be able to have much greater commerce with other portions of the self, and also to offer to the inner self opportunities of awareness that the inner self on its own could not procure.

The journeys of the gods, therefore, represent the journeys of man's own consciousness projected outward. All That Is, however, is within each such adventure. Its consciousness, and its reality, is within each man, and within the gods he has created. That last is in small letters, and gods shall always be in small letters. All That Is is capitalized.

The gods attain, of course, a psychic reality. I am not saying therefore that they are not real, but I am to some extent defining the nature of their reality. It is to some extent true to say: "Be careful of the gods you choose, for you will reinforce each other."

Now: Take a break.

(10:55. The pace had been consistently fast, and my writing hand felt it. As Seth had promised, it was a good chapter. Jane said she could feel him pause briefly at times to make sure that she chose just the right word while delivering the material. She would still be in trance, she said, and even speaking, but Seth would wait. Yet she didn't remember any of the material at break. Resume at 11:08, with the air conditioner still on.)

Now: Such an alliance sets up certain fields of attraction. A man who attaches himself to one of the gods is necessarily attaching himself largely to his own projections. Some, in your terms, are creative, and some destructive, though the latter are seldom recognized as such.

The open concept of All That Is, however, frees you to a great extent from your own projections, and allows a more valid contact with the spirit that is behind the reality that you know.

In this chapter I would also like to mention several other pertinent points.

Some ancient tales have come down through the centuries that tell of various gods and demons who guard the gates, so to speak, of other levels of reality and stages of consciousness. Astral levels are neatly laid out, numbered, and categorized.

There are tests to pass before entry. There are rituals to be acted out. Now, all of this is highly distorted. Any attempt to so rigorously and precisely express inner reality is bound to be abortive, highly misleading, and in your terms sometimes dangerous; for you do create your own reality and live it according to your inner beliefs. Therefore, be careful also of those beliefs that you accept.

Let me take this moment to state again that there are no devils or demons, except as you create them out of your belief. As mentioned earlier, good and evil effects are basically illusions. In your terms all acts, regardless of their seeming nature, are a part of a greater good. I am not saying that a good end justifies what you would consider an evil action. While you still accept the effects of good and evil, then you had better choose the good.

(11:25.) I am saying this as simply as possible. There are profound complications beneath my words, however. Opposites have validity only in your own system of reality. They are a part of your root assumptions, and so you must deal with them as such.

They represent, however, deep unities that you do not understand. Your conception of good and evil results in large part from the kind of consciousness you have presently adopted. You do not perceive wholes, but portions. The conscious mind focuses with a quick, limited, but intense light, perceiving from a given field of reality only certain "stimuli." It then puts these stimuli together, forming the liaison of similarity. Anything that it does not accept as a portion of reality, it does not perceive.

The effect of opposites results, then, from a lack of perception. Since you must operate within the world as you perceive it, then the opposites will appear to be conditions of existence. These elements have been isolated for a certain reason, however. You are being taught, and you are teaching yourselves to handle energy, to become conscious cocreators with All That Is, and one of the "stages of development" or learning processes includes dealing with opposites as realities.

In your terms, the ideas of good and evil help you recognize the sacredness of existence, the responsibility of consciousness. The ideas of opposites also are necessary guide lines for the developing ego. The inner self knows quite well the unity that exists.

Now: End of dictation, and very near the end of the chapter. And at the end of the chapter ask those questions that you have in mind.

("Okay." As the chapter progressed, though, Seth was automatically answering many of our questions about religion; originally we'd included these in our list for Chapter Twenty.)

I bid you a fond good evening; and *(with smiling emphasis)* we were in great form last evening.

("You certainly were. Thank you, Seth, and good night."

(11:57 P.M. Seth referred to Jane's ESP class. A long session had been recorded during the class, as happens quite often. And it can be added that Seth was in great form this evening, too.)

SESSION 588, AUGUST 2, 1971,
9:01 P.M. MONDAY

(Jane and I each noted questions before the session this evening.

(In the 586th session, earlier in this chapter, Seth stated that by the year 2075 the third Christ — Paul or Saul — would have enacted the Second Coming, exerting of course a profound effect upon religion and world history. Jane thought a period of less than a century was much too short a time to encompass so many dramatic changes. She wanted me to ask Seth if she had distorted this data while delivering it.

(When, for instance, would the personality be born, in order to have time to bring about such tremendous changes? We supposed there was a chance distortion had occurred.

(My questions concerned relationships between the three personalities of the Christ entity: John the Baptist, Jesus Christ, and Paul. What sort of psychic

interactions had taken place between them in any strong or exceptional way? Were their dreams and other psychic experiences — other than the recorded instances — outstanding on a regular basis as they lived out their lives day by day?

(All of the following historical dates are quite approximate, but they show the overlapping pattern of the physical lives of the three personalities making up the Christ entity.

(John the Baptist was born between 8 and 4 B.C., and died in A.D. 26 to 27. Jesus Christ was born between 8 and 5 B.C., and died in A.D. 29 to 30. Paul [Saul] of Tarsus was born between A.D. 5 and 15 and died in A.D. 67 to 68.

(Elizabeth, the mother of John the Baptist, was a cousin of Christ's mother, Mary. John baptized Christ at the beginning of his ministry in A.D. 26 to 27, when he was about thirty. John was already active in his own ministry, and often called himself a "forerunner of one who would be nobler and stronger." Shortly after he baptized Jesus, John was imprisoned by Herod Antipas in the fortress Machaerus, near the Dead Sea.

(It isn't known for sure that Christ and Paul ever met. Paul was converted several years after Christ's death; before that he had been a zealous persecutor of Christians. Nor does it appear that John and Paul met.

(According to history, all three members of the Christ entity met violent ends. Christ was crucified near Jerusalem at the order of Pontius Pilate; Herod had John beheaded; and Paul was beheaded near Rome during the reign of Nero.

(Readers of The Seth Material *had asked Seth to elaborate upon data of the three Christs given in Chapter Eighteen, "The God Concept," of that book. Some wanted to know if one of the three Christs could have been the Teacher of Righteousness; this personage was the leader of the Zealot sect in Judaea early in the first century A.D. There were four known Jewish sects flourishing there at the birth of Christianity.*

(Other questions concerned a variety of names for Christ himself. Jane and I had been saving these, and we went over them now before the session. Jane's pace as the session opened was quite a bit slower than usual.)

Good evening.

("Good evening, Seth.")

Now: Give us a moment, and we will resume.

In any given historical period, one religious drama may finally emerge as the exterior representation, but there will also be many minor dramas, "projections," that do not entirely take. These represent,

· 344 ·

of course, probable events. Any of them could supersede the actual exterior drama. In the time of Christ there were many such performances, as many personalities felt the force of inner reality and reacted to it.

There were probable Christs, in other words, living in your terms at that time. For several reasons that I will not go into here, these projections did not mirror inner events faithfully enough. There were, however, a score of men in the same general area, physically, who responded to the inner psychic climate and felt upon themselves the attraction and responsibility of the religious hero.

(Pause at 9:09.) Some of these men were too tinged, too caught in the torment and fervor of the period to rise sufficiently above it. The cultures used them. They could not use the various cultures as launching ground for the new ideas. Instead they became lost in the history of the times.

Some carried on following the same pattern taken by Christ, performed psychic feats and healings, had groups of followers, and yet were not capable of holding that powerful focus of psychic attention that was so necessary.

The Lord of Righteousness, so called, was such a person, but his over-zealous nature held him back.

(In the literature I've been reading on the subject, the Zealot leader was always called the Teacher of Righteousness. *The interpretation of scanty records, including the Dead Sea Scrolls, has given rise to debate, but it appears he was either Menahem ben Judah, who was killed in* A.D. *66 in Jerusalem, or a nephew, who survived and succeeded him.)*

His rigidity prevented the spontaneity necessary for any true great religious release. He fell, instead, into the trap of provincialism. Had he performed the role possible, he could have been of benefit to Paul. He was a probable personality of the Paul portion of the Christ entity.

(Long pause at 9:17. Jane's pace was still quite slow.)

These men innately understood their part in this drama, and also their position within All That Is. They were all highly clairvoyant and telepathic, given to visions and hearing of voices.

In their dreams they were in contact. Consciously Paul remembered many of these dreams, until he felt pursued by Christ. It was because of a series of recurring dreams that Paul persecuted the Christians. He felt that Christ was a kind of devil who pursued him in his sleep.

On an unconscious level, however, he knew the meaning of the dreams, and his "conversion," of course, was only a physical event following an inner experience.

John the Baptist, Christ, and Paul were all connected in the dream state, and John was well aware of Christ's existence before Christ was born.

Paul needed the strongest egotistical strength because of his particular duties. He was far less aware consciously of his role for this reason. The inner knowledge, of course, exploded in the physical conversion experience.

This material has been given in answer to your questions.

("It's very interesting."

(Jane took a long pause at 9:25. Still in trance, she lit a cigarette and sipped a drink.)

Now in answer to Ruburt's question: The birth will occur at the time given; by the time given *(the year 2075)*. The other changes will occur generally over the period of a century, but the results will show far before that time.

Because of the plastic nature of the future, in your terms, the date cannot be considered final. All probabilities point in its direction, however, for the inner impetus is already forming the events.

Unless you have other questions, that is the end of the chapter.

("As a matter of curiosity: can you say how the Teacher of Righteousness met his end?" This is one of the questions correspondents have asked.)

Give us a moment.

The name given was correct, though it is itself a translation. He died with a small group of men in a cave that he held as a point of refuge in the middle of a battle, killed by members of another sect. The murderers took with them certain manuscripts that they found there; but others they did not find, and these have not as yet come to light.

The final place of refuge was near Damascus. For some time the Lord of Righteousness tried to hide himself within the city. His identity was discovered, however, and he and a band of men took to caves that were between Damascus and another nearby town, much smaller, that had been used at one time as a fortress. They were heading there.

Now you may take your break, and then I will begin the next chapter.

(9:35. But instead of taking a break, Jane sat quietly, still in trance.)

One small note for those interested. The Zealots, the sect, were also divided into two main groups, one splitting finally from the other main one. Other documents will be found that will clear several important matters concerning the historical times. *(Pause.)* During one short period of his life, Paul joined a Zealot group. This is unknown. It has not been recorded.

(Jane sat in trance so long that I began to ask a question; but then she raised a hand to indicate that I wait.)

In fact, for a period he led a double life as a member of the Zealots. He turned against them vehemently, however, as he was later to turn against the Romans to join the Christians. Before his conversion, he knew he had a purpose and mission, and flung himself with all the passion of his being into whatever answers he thought he had found.

Now take your break.

(9:40. Jane's pace had been slow to begin, but had picked up as her delivery progressed. Her trance had been deep. She said she "really went out when Seth started in on the biblical data."

(I was finding Seth's information intensely interesting. It was unavoidable in many cases, but Jane said she much preferred not to know anything about the historical period Seth would be discussing. She hadn't read anything about the Dead Sea Scrolls, for instance, although I'd explained a little about them to her at various times. Nor is she familiar with the Bible.

(Of course, we hadn't known just how Seth was going to present his material in the chapter on religion on the third Christ and related data. Both of us were surprised to hear him declare a connection between Paul and the Zealots. Many questions automatically came to our minds; but we had to stop somewhere, so we reluctantly decided not to ask them.

(Jane's attitude about biblical history is in keeping with her feelings about some other facets of her abilities: she has often told me she felt much freer giving a reading for a person when she wasn't acquainted with him. The same was true when she was trying for the contents of sealed envelopes. She preferred not to know who had prepared them, or their origin, etc.)

CHAPTER 22

A Goodbye and an Introduction: Aspects of
Multidimensional Personality
as Viewed Through My Own Experience

(*Resume at 10:00. Jane's voice, as Seth, was a little different from usual. More controlled, perhaps, not quite as jovial or as much at ease.*)

Now: We will begin the next chapter, and we will call it: "A Goodbye and an Introduction: Aspects of Multidimensional Personality as Viewed Through My Own Experience."

(*"That's all in the chapter heading?"*)

Yes, a colon to separate the two divisions. And give us a moment. (*Pause.*)

In the historical time of Christ, I was a man called Millenius, in Rome. In that life my main occupation was that of a merchant, but I was a highly curious gentleman, and my travels gave me access to many different groups of people.

Physically I was round and stout, not at all patrician in my bearing, and given to untidiness in my dress. We had a type of snuff made from a certain kind of straw. I used it constantly, often spilling some upon my robe.

My house was in the busiest, northwestern part of the city, just beyond what you would call the heart of town. Among my wares I sold bells for donkeys. This may not sound like a very grand product, and yet families on the farms outside of Rome found these highly useful. Each had a special sound, and a family could tell by the sound of the bell their own donkey from innumerable similar ones.

(10:08.) Donkeys were also used in many businesses within Rome itself as carriers of burden, particularly in the lower occupations. The number of bells, their particular pitch, even the colors, all had meaning. In the tumult of the city the particular bells could be recognized, therefore, by the poor and by the slaves who waited to buy products — often wilted foods from the laden carts.

The bells were only a small portion of my business, which dealt largely with cloths and dyes, but they fascinated me. Because of my interest in them I did far more traveling about the countryside and the region than any prudent man should. The bells became my hobby. My curiosity drove me to journey in search of different kinds of bells, and led me into contact with many people I would not otherwise have encountered.

(10:11.) While I was not literate, I was shrewd and lively of mind. Special bells, I discovered, were used by various sects of Jews, both within Rome and without. While I was a Roman and a citizen, my citizenship meant little except for providing me with minimal safety as I went about my daily way, and in my business I encountered as many Jews as Romans. I was not too far above them socially. *(This was Seth's first bit of humor in the chapter.)*

The Romans had no clear idea of the number of Jews in Rome at that time. They went by guesswork. The bells on donkeys belonging to the Zealots had upon them the symbol of an eye *(Jane, as Seth, pointed to one of her eyes).* They came secretly into town, hiding as much from other Jews as from Romans. They were good bargainers and often did me out of more than I deserved to lose.

I learned about the Lord of Righteousness from a cousin of his named Sheraba —

("Can you spell that?" Seth did so, and it turned out that our versions agreed.

(It can be seen from the above paragraphs that Seth shifts his physical location from Rome to Judaea without saying just how or when he did so. I wanted to know more about the mechanics of the transfer but decided not to interrupt further just now.)

— who was, as clearly as I could figure out at the time, a "sacred" assassin. He was drunk the night I spoke to him in a stinking stall outside of Jerusalem. It was he who told me about the symbol of the eye. He also told me that the man, Christ, was kidnapped by the Essenes. I did not believe him. Nor at the time he told me did I know who Christ was.

(Pause at 10:28. Jane's pace had been slow. The four major Jewish sects known to flourish in the Holy Land at the beginning of the first century were the Sadducees, the Pharisees, the Zealots and the Essenes.)

At the time that Christ lived his existence was known to very few, comparatively speaking. To put it bluntly *(and humorously)* I knew that someone had the ball, but I was not certain of the person. In dream states, the situation finally became known to me and to many others.

The Christians, generally speaking, did not want Roman converts. I was later one of these, and because of my nationality was never trusted. My part in that drama was simply to acquaint myself with its physical foundation; to be a participant, however small, in that era. Much later in your terms I would end up as a minor pope in the third century, meeting again some of those I had known — and, if you will forgive a humorous note, once more familiar with the sound of bells.

(Seth first referred to his incarnation as a minor Pope in Jane's ESP class session for May 25, 1971. Some eighteen people were present. The session was recorded, so the quotes that follow are verbatim. Seth was in a high, if somewhat ribald, mood:

(". . . for I was a pope in A.D. 300. I was not a very good pope.

("I had two illegitimate children [class laughter], *a mistress that sneaked into my private study, a magician that I kept in case I did not do too well on my own, a housekeeper who was pregnant every year that I had her, and three daughters who joined a nunnery because I would not have them — and I am referred to in barely three paltry lines, for my reign did not last very long.*

("Now: I had a large family — that is, I came from a large family, and I was ambitious, as all intelligent young men of that time were. I did not go for the military, so there was nothing to do but go to the church.

("For a while I was not in Rome but held my religious call elsewhere. I wrote two Church laws. It should all go to show you that some good ends up from everything. I died of trouble with my stomach because I was such a glutton. My name was not Clement [in answer to a question from a class member] *although Clement is a lovely name.*

("I was originally called Protonius. Now give me a moment. The last name is not nearly so clear, and this is not my papal name, but my — if you will forgive the term — common name: Meglemanius, the third. From a small village.

("Unless I summon the self that I was at that time, the memories for details are not that clear. But as I now recall them, without directly checking on our friend

the Pope, who has, you must understand, gone his own way, I am coming as close as I can. We did not have as many guards at that time, but we had many stolen paintings and jewels of great merit. Now some of these jewels, as well as the money, went for expeditions that you do not realize were adopted at the time, having to do with commerce and ships sent to Africa; and this interest had to do with my later life when I was involved with the oregano [as a spice merchant in Denmark, in the 1600's]. My sniffing goes back for centuries.

("There were two brothers strongly united in control of Italy at the time. Perhaps I should say two males, one in the higher capacity and the other his chancellor, with whom I was involved as Pope; and I sent armies to the north also.

("We had not yet begun the strong insistence upon indulgences, so I did not have that extra cash that indulgences would bring in. I believed and did not believe, as you [to a class member] earlier believed and did not believe, and I did a good job of hiding from myself what I believed and what I did not believe. And the higher one gets in power, the harder it is to hide such things from one's self.

("I was very fond of my first mistress, whose name was Maria. And there were no such sane rules as those in which you now sit, and there were no governments as secure in which you could reside as those you now enjoy.

("I did believe implicitly in the God in which I was brought up, and in that belief. It was only later that I wondered how such a god would choose me for such a position — and then I began to wonder. I had four lives following that of the most adverse circumstances, to make sure that I understood the difference between luxury and poverty, pride and compassion. And there were days in other centuries that I walked the same streets that I had walked as Pope. I touched these streets lightly as Pope; but as a peasant I walked with a heavy foot and great weight, until I learned the lessons that I had to learn, as all of you will also learn your own lessons."

(At this writing we do not know which pope Seth referred to. When I came to type up this session I wondered if Seth-Jane's mention of the third century might be an error. [If so, I hadn't been quick enough to catch it; I could have asked about it at once.] Since Seth gave A.D. 300 in the class session for last May, I personally think it more likely that his papal incarnation followed this date, taking place in the fourth century. The fourth century encompasses the years A.D. 301 to 400, since our modern computation of time is based upon the assumed date of the birth of Christ. The Encyclopaedia Britannica lists eleven popes and two antipopes between A.D. 296 and 401. Some of the reigns were very brief, some of the dates of tenure uncertain or estimated.

(Of course we would like to learn more about the incarnation in question. As Seth has already indicated, there is a wealth of information here waiting to be acquired. This brings up a dilemma Jane has confronted often: what to investigate out of the many possibilities available at any given time; then, the choice made, how to find the time to carry out the study.)

It is not my purpose to go into my past existences in any great detail, but to use them to make certain points. First of all, I have been many times both man and woman, and I have immersed myself in various occupations, but always with the idea of learning so that I could teach. I had a firm background in physical existence, therefore, as a prerequisite for my present "work."

I did not play the part of any towering personality of historical note, but became experienced in the homey and intimate details of daily life, the normal struggle for achievement, the need for love. I learned the unutterable yearning of father for son, son for father, husband for wife, wife for husband, and fell headlong into the intimate webs of human relationships. Before your idea of history, I was a Lumanian, and was later born in Atlantis.

Using your historical reference, I returned at the time of the cavemen, operating as a Speaker. Now I have always been a Speaker, regardless of my physical occupation. I have been a spice merchant in Denmark, where I knew Ruburt and Joseph. In several lives I was black — once in what is now called Ethiopia, and once in Turkey.

My lives as monks followed my experience as a pope, and in one of these, I was a victim of the Spanish Inquisition. My experience in female lives varied from that of a plain Dutch spinster to a courtesan at the time of the biblical David, to several existences as a humble mother with children.

Now when I began contacting Ruburt and Joseph, I hid from them the fact of my numerous lives. *(Smile):* Ruburt, in particular, did not accept reincarnation, and the idea of such multiple life experiences would have been highly scandalous to him.

The times and names and dates are not nearly as important as the experiences, and they are too numerous to list here. However, I will see to it at some time that these are made fully available. Some have been given in Ruburt's class sessions, and some, though few, have appeared in *The Seth Material* itself.

In a book on reincarnation, I hope to have each of my previous personalities speak for themselves, for they should tell their own story. You should understand, therefore, that those personalities still exist and are independent. While what I am once seemed to be contained within those personalities, I was but the seed for them. In your terms, I can remember who I was; in greater terms, however, those personalities should speak for themselves.

Perhaps you will see an analogy here when you compare the situation with age regression under hypnosis. Those personalities are not locked up inside of what I am, however. They have progressed according to their own fashion. They are not negated. In my terms, they coexist with me, but at another layer of reality.

Now: Take your break.

(10:56. Jane said she'd really been out. As sometimes happens, memory and images connected with the material began to come back to her as we talked. She experienced a sense of expansion, an impression of great crowds. Then she remembered a stinking stall with dirty straw, and "three men wearing dirty brown robes, of pretty rough cloth."

(Jane sat half in trance, "seeing more stuff now than in the session itself." It was as though a light within her focused upon one small area. She saw grease or wax from a candle, falling upon one of the robes and staining it. In the stall there were long oval bundles of straw, stacked one upon another "to keep it dry, pretty high up to the roof. Each bundle is tied but not covered."

(Now she smelled something very rancid. "Seth has some kind of soap with his wares — some awful mixture with lye and rosewater," she said, unbelieving, her nose wrinkling. "This was in some kind of woven sack; a double one like you'd throw over a horse. . . . I can almost see it in front of me. I could draw the shape of it, though it's not any big deal.

("That's it — all that opened up after you started talking about it," she said finally. "I didn't have any bigger vision, and I didn't know how far to go along with it. When I saw the double sack, that's all I saw. . . ."

(Jane was obviously much more relaxed now than when she'd started this chapter. She was yawning deeply, again and again, her eyes watering. I suggested an end to the session, but she wanted to continue. Resume at 11:19.)

In several lives I was consciously aware of my "past existences." Once as a monk I found myself copying a manuscript that I myself had written in another life.

Often I was given to the love of weight, and possessed it. Twice I died of starvation. I always found my deaths highly educational — in your terms, afterwards. It was always a lesson between lives to trace the thoughts and events that "led to a given demise."

None of my deaths surprised me. I felt during the process the inevitability, the recognition, even a sense of familiarity: "Of course, this particular dying is mine and no other." And I accepted even the most bizarre circumstances then, feeling almost a sense of perfection. The life could not be finished properly without the death.

There is a great sense of humility, and yet a great sense of exaltation as the inner self senses its freedom when death occurs. All my deaths were the complement of my lives, in that it seemed to me that it could not be otherwise.

(*Long pause at 11:29.*) If I choose, in your terms I can relive any portion of those existences, but those personalities go their own way. Do you understand me?

(*"Yes."*)

On a subjective level I acted as a teacher and a Speaker in each of my lives. In a few highly intuitive existences I was aware of this fact. You do not understand as yet the high importance of the underside of consciousness. Beside your objective role in each life, your reincarnational challenges also involve your dream states, rhythms of creativity that flow and ebb beneath the daily world you know. So I became highly proficient in this way as a Speaker and a teacher in several lives that were externally uninteresting by contrast.

My influence, work, and concern in such cases was far more vast than my quiet objective pursuits. I give you this information hoping to help you understand the true nature of your own reality. My reincarnational existences do not define what I am, however, nor do yours define you.

Now, you may take a break or end the session as you prefer.

(*"We'll take the break." 11:35. When I feel that Jane might choose to continue a session, I ask for a break instead of ending the session. It had been a slow delivery, and Jane knew she hadn't been out long.*

(*"I don't know what to do now, about continuing," she said after we'd talked briefly. "I know what Seth's got planned, but I don't know how he's going to go about it.*

· 354 ·

("What's up? I don't understand — "

("He's going to let Seth Two come through."

(Seth Two is dealt with at length in Chapter Seventeen of Jane's book The Seth Material. *This personality speaks occasionally in ESP class, but relatively seldom in our private sessions. In the outline Seth gave for this book before dictation began, we were told that Seth Two would be explained. Some of our questions for Chapter Twenty had concerned Seth Two also. I'd forgotten both points for the moment — hence my surprise.*

(But now, at 11:40, Jane didn't know whether to end the session, as I'd suggested earlier, or continue. She finally decided to "just sit quietly for a minute." Then: "I don't know whether to shut it down or not — it could go on for another hour. . . ." I told her I was game if she was. Seth resumed at 11:45.)

Now: The soul knows itself, and is not confused by terms or definitions. Through showing you the nature of my own reality, I hope to teach you the nature of your own.

You are not bound to any category or corner of existence. Your reality cannot be measured any more than mine. I hope to illustrate the function of consciousness and personality through writing this book and enlarging your concepts.

Now I began by telling you that I was dictating this material through the auspices of a woman of whom I was quite fond. Let me now tell you that there are other realities involved. The following paragraphs will be written by another personality, who stands relatively in the same position to me as I stand to the woman through whom I am now speaking.

(Pause at 11:51. I now watched a transformation begin to take place in Jane, as our familiar Seth retreated and Seth Two began to come to the fore. At the same time I knew that subjectively Jane was experiencing the feeling of a "cone" or "pyramid" coming down over the top of her head. Jane has often told me that whereas she feels Seth come to her in a very warm and alive and friendly manner, she feels her consciousness going out of herself to meet Seth Two — "up the invisible pyramid like a draft up a flue." She doesn't know where she goes or how she gets back. Her body seems to be left behind.

(Jane sat very formally in her Kennedy rocker, her forearms upon the arms of the chair, her feet flat upon the rug. It was a muggy night; our living room windows were open, and now I became conscious of traffic noise. I heard someone moving about in the apartment upstairs.

(Jane's eyes were closed, but occasionally they opened slightly. She smiled

faintly as she spoke for Seth Two. The voice that began to issue from her was very high, very distant and formal, with little volume or emphasis. Each word was carefully and deliberately, almost delicately, spoken. It was as though Seth Two wasn't familiar with vocal chords or words, and so took pains to use those mechanisms in just the right way. The contrast between the two Seths couldn't have been more complete.)

We are the voices who speak without tongues of our own. We are sources of that energy from which you come. We are creators, yet we have also been created. We seeded your universe as you seed other realities.

We do not exist in your historical terms, nor have we known physical existence. Our joy created the exaltation from which your world comes. Our existence is such that communication must be made by others to you.

Verbal symbols have no meaning for us. Our experience is not translatable. We hope our intent is. In the vast infinite scope of consciousness, all is possible. There is meaning in each thought. We perceive your thoughts as lights. They form patterns. *(Each syllable was so carefully and separately pronounced.)*

Because of the difficulties of communication, it is nearly impossible for us to explain our reality. Know only that we exist. We send immeasurable vitality to you, and support all of those structures of consciousness with which you are familiar. You are never alone. *(Pause.)* We have always sent emissaries to you who understand your needs. Though you do not know us, we cherish you.

Seth is a point in my reference, in our reference. He is an ancient portion of us. *(Pause.)* We are separate but united. *(Long pause.)* Always the spirit forms the flesh.

(12:06 A.M. This was the end of the session. As usual when Seth Two speaks, the end was unannounced, and came without any of the warmth and emotional exchange that often involves Seth, Jane, and me.

(Jane's eyes were heavy. For some few minutes she had trouble keeping them open. She hadn't changed her position in her rocker for the duration of the delivery, and she'd experienced the usual cone effect. I'd had to ask for a word or two to be repeated when it had been obliterated by a burst of traffic noise.)

(We were ready for the session early this evening, for a change. I told Jane I hoped Seth would discuss a dream she'd had last night. It involved the two of us and was very optimistic; I was sure that in symbolic terms it dealt with our work. Seth did analyze the dream at the end of the session, so that material is deleted from the dictation on his book.

(With the approach of 9:00 Jane began to acquire a typical bearing. She became quiet as she sat waiting, and started glancing sideways from lowered eyes; she seemed to be alert for a certain subjective signal. Then she told me Seth was "around" and that the session would begin in a moment. When she took her glasses off and placed them upon the coffee table before her, she was in trance. Her pace was quite slow at the beginning.)

Now: We will continue. There are kinds of consciousness that cannot be deciphered in physical terms. The "personality" who originated the paragraphs you have just read is such a one.

As mentioned, there is the same kind of connection between that personality and myself as the one that exists between Ruburt and myself. But in your terms, Seth Two is far further divorced from my reality than I am from Ruburt's. You can imagine Seth Two as a future portion of me if you prefer, and yet far more is involved.

I am myself using simple terms here to try and make these ideas clearer. In a trance state, Ruburt can contact me. In a state in some ways similar to a trance, I can contact Seth Two. We are related in ways quite difficult to explain, united in webs of consciousness. My reality includes, then, not only reincarnational identities but also other gestalts of being that do not necessarily have any physical connections.

The same applies to each reader of this book. The soul is open-ended, therefore. It is not a closed spiritual or psychic system. I have tried to show you that the soul is not a separate, apart-from-you thing. It is no more divorced from you than — capital — God is.

There is no need to create a separate god who exists outside of your universe and separate from it, nor is there any need to think of a soul as some distant entity. God, or All That Is, is intimately a part of you. "His" energy forms your identity, and your soul is a part of you in the same manner.

(9:18.) My own reincarnational personalities, probable selves, and

even Seth Two exist within me now, as I exist within them. In your terms, Seth Two is more advanced. In your terms, he is more alien, since he cannot relate to your physical existence as well as I do because of my background in it.

Still, my experience enriches Seth Two, and his experiences enrich me to the extent that I am able to perceive and translate them for my own use. In the same way, Ruburt's personality is expanded through relationship with me, and I also gain through the experience, as even the best of teachers learns from each dimension of activity.

In larger terms, my soul includes my reincarnational personalities, Seth Two, and probable selves. I am as aware of my probable selves, incidentally, as I am of my reincarnational existences. Your concept of the soul is simply so limited. I am not really speaking in terms of group souls, though this interpretation can also be made.

Each "part" of the soul contains the whole — a concept I am sure will startle you. As you become more aware of your own subjective reality you will therefore, become familiar with greater portions of your own soul. When you think of the soul as a closed system you perceive it as such, and close off from yourself the knowledge of its greater creativity and characteristics.

(9:27.) Seth Two does represent what I will become, to some extent, and in your terms, yet when I become what he is he will be something different. In the same terms now, only, Ruburt may become what I am, but then I will be something far different.

Each of you are involved in the same kind of relationships, whether or not you are aware of them. Though it seems to you that reincarnational existences involve past and future events, they are existences parallel or adjacent to your own present life and consciousness. Other aspects of your greater identity exist, relatively speaking, about or around these.

(Jane was speaking intently as Seth, her eyes wide and very dark. She made a series of large circular motions in the air.)

The answers to the nature of reality, the intimate knowledge of All That Is that you all seek, is within your present experience. It will not be found outside of yourselves, but through an inner journey into yourself, through yourself and through the world that you know.

Give us a moment. *(A one-minute pause, eyes closed, at 9:32.)*

I was once a mother with twelve children. Ignorant in terms of education, far from beautiful, particularly in later years, with a wild temper and raucous voice. This was around Jerusalem in the sixth century. The children had many fathers. I did my best to provide for them.

My name was Marshaba. We lived wherever we could, squatting in doorways and, finally, all begging. Yet in that existence, physical life had a contrast, a sharpness greater than any I had known. A crust of bread was far more delicious to me than any piece of cake, however well-frosted, had ever been in lives before.

When my children laughed I was overwhelmed with delight, and despite our privations, each morning was a triumphant surprise that we had not died in our sleep, that we had not succumbed to starvation. I chose that life deliberately, as each of you choose each of yours, and I did so because my previous lives had left me too blasé. I was too cushioned. I no longer focused with clarity upon the truly spectacular physical delights and experiences that earth can provide.

Though I yelled at my children and screamed sometimes in rage against the elements, I was struck through with the magnificence of existence, and learned more about true spirituality than I ever did as a monk. This does not mean that poverty leads to truth, or that suffering is good for the soul. Many who shared those conditions with me learned little. It does mean that each of you choose those life conditions that you have for your own purpose, knowing ahead of time where your weaknesses and strengths lie. *(Pause.)*

In the gestalt of my personality, as in your terms I lived later richer lives, that woman was alive again in me — as, for example, the child is alive in the adult, and filled with gratitude comparing later circumstances to the earlier existences. She urged me to use my advantages better.

So in you, your various reincarnational existences in a large manner co-occur. Using the analogy of adulthood again, it is as if the child within you is a part of your own memory and experience, and yet in another way has left you, gone apart from you as if you are only one adult that the child "turned into." So the people that I have been have gone their own way, and yet are a part of me and I of them.

I am alive in Seth Two's memory, as a self from which he sprang. Yet the self I am now is not the self from which he sprang. Only your rigid ideas of time and consciousness make these statements seem strange to you; for in a larger context, again, I can remember Seth Two. All of these connections therefore are open. All psychological events affect all others.

You may take your break.

(*To me, louder*): If you do not understand something clearly, mention it — because if you do not, then the reader will not.

(*"Okay." 9:55. Jane had no images of the woman Seth had been discussing. She remembered how, in early sessions, Seth had talked about a minimum of three reincarnational existences for most entities — and how "scandalized" she'd been later when she began to realize that Seth had lived many lives. Now, she finds that the idea of simultaneity of "reincarnational" lives is quite acceptable; this fits her emotional and intellectual temperament. When the sessions began, Jane was especially bothered by what she called the trite and popular ideas about reincarnation, mixed up as they were with ideas of good and evil, punishment, etc.*

(*"I go along wholeheartedly with Seth's statement that reincarnation is as much a myth as a fact," she said now, referring to an ESP class session. In that session, for May 4, 1971, Seth said in part: "So what you understand of reincarnation, and of the time terms involved, is a very simplified tale indeed. . . . Reincarnation, in its own way, is also a parable. It seems very difficult for you to understand that you live in many realities — and many centuries — at one time. . . ." 10:22. Resume at a slow pace.*)

All of existence and consciousness is interwoven. Only when you think of the soul as something different, separate, and therefore closed, are you led to consider a separate god — a personality that seems to be apart from creation.

All That Is is a part of creation, but more than what creation is. There are pyramid gestalts of being impossible to describe, whose awareness includes knowledge and experience of what would seem to be to you a vast number of other realities. In the terms of which I am speaking for your benefit, their present might, for example, include the life and death of your planet in a moment of their "time." Seth Two's existence is at the outside fringes of one such galaxy of consciousness.

(*Pause at 10:30.*) When Seth Two speaks, Ruburt initially is aware of the following: His consciousness strains upward, following an inner psychic pathway, an energized funnel, until quite simply it can go no further. It seems to him then that his consciousness goes out of his body through an invisible pyramid whose open top stretches far up into space.

Here he seems to make contact with impersonal symbols whose message is somehow automatically translated into words. That point actually represents a warp in dimensions, a place between systems that has far more to do with energy and psychological reality than it has to do with space, for space is meaningless.

I am almost always present as a translator at such times. My knowledge of both realities is necessary for the communication.

(Long pause.) Seth Two is familiar with an entirely different set of symbols and meanings, so that, in this case, two translations are being given — one by me and one by Ruburt.

Hopefully, certain concepts will be delivered in this way that could not be delivered otherwise. These minglings of reality and experience, these messages from one system to another, occur in various ways continually, emerging in your world in one guise or another — as inspiration of many kinds. You are being helped, in other words.

You are also using your own abilities, however, for your own characteristics largely determine the amount of help you receive. The symbolism apparent to Ruburt when Seth Two speaks works well, but outward is also inward, and so consciousness travels as far inward as it seems to him to go outward.

Such contacts and knowledge are available to each individual. All That Is speaks to all of its parts, not with sounds, trumpets, and fanfare from without, but communicates its messages through the living soul-stuff of each consciousness.

Now: If you want something on the dream, I suggest we end dictation for this evening. You may take a break or I will begin the interpretation as you prefer.

(10:45. "You might as well begin.")

Give us a good moment. *(Pause.)*

(Seth then delivered two excellent pages explaining Jane's dream. The session ended at 11:05 P.M.)

SESSION 590, AUGUST 9, 1971,
10:05 P.M. MONDAY

(The session began late this evening because Jane and I first attended a twenty-fifth wedding anniversary surprise party for a member of ESP class. The affair was a great success.

(At the supper table this evening we had been speculating about the times Seth had given in connection with his life as a pope, both in the ESP class session for May 25, 1971, and the 588th session in this chapter. When I wondered if I was right in thinking it likely that Seth's papal incarnation took place in the fourth century, Jane said she "got" the year A.D. 325. This seemed like a confirmation. To our further surprise, Seth added to the data concerning that life in tonight's session.)

Good evening.

("Good evening, Seth.")

It was in the 300's.

("Thank you.")

A few extra notes for your own edification. Often during that time, and for some time afterward, the records are rather unreliable. They were doctored. Sometimes the name of one man would be given as a reign covering a span of years.

The original man may have been assassinated, another taking his place, carrying on as if there had been no change as far as the populace was concerned. Poison was the usual method, and even those who suspected the truth would not dare speak out.

The records would show one reign of one pope; but one, two, or even three different men may have filled the position. A change of policy is the clue in such cases; vacillation.

Now give us time. *(Pause at 10:11.)* There were also men called "Little Popes," those in training of an ambitious nature, and catered to. If they were seriously in the running, you see, the rewards would be great to their followers. These men, incidentally, were no worse, particularly, in their actions than the rest of the populace. Their positions simply gave them greater leeway.

The dates 325 and 375 come to mind in connection with my own life at that time. Again, the names and dates have little meaning to me now. In that life I learned to understand the interplay between men and their ambitions, the gulf that often exists between ideals and practical action.

You must also understand that politics was a legitimate hand of the church in those days, and a churchman was expected to be an excellent politician. I seem to have spent some time in a place that sounds like Caprina, also during that lifetime.

(Long pause at 10:20.) A cousin or brother was important to me. He ended up in severe difficulties, caught in some smuggling business to the Spanish.

There was at the time a secret group called "Followers of the Motherhood of God." They were considered heretics, and several times petitions were given to me against them. This concerned the position of "the Virgin" within the dogma of the church.

Now we are finished with those notes and you may take a break.

(10:25. "I knew he was doing that," Jane said, then added that she just went along with it. Her pace had been rather slow, but picked up when she resumed at 10:32.)

Now. We will resume dictation.

You are not fated to dissolve into All That Is. The aspects of your personality as you presently understand them will be retained. All That Is is the creator of individuality, not the means of its destruction.

My own "previous" personalities are not dissolved into me any more than your "past" personalities. All are living and vital. All go their own way. Your "future" personalities are as real as your past ones. After a while, this will no longer concern you. Out of the reincarnational framework, there is no death as you think of it.

My own frame of reference, however, is no longer focused on my reincarnational existences. I have turned my attention in other directions.

Since all lives are simultaneous, all happening at once, then any separation is a psychological one. I exist as I am while my reincarnational lives — in your terms — still exist. Yet now I am not concerned with them, but turn my concentration into other areas of activity.

(10:41.) Personality changes whether it is within a body or outside of it, so you will change after death as you change before it. In those terms, it is ridiculous to insist upon remaining as you are now, after death. It is the same as a child saying: "I am going to grow up, but I am never going to change the ideas that I have now." The multidimensional qualities of the psyche allow it to experience an endless realm of dimensions. Experience in one dimension in no way negates existence in another.

You have been trying to squeeze the soul into tight concepts of the nature of existence, making it follow your limited beliefs. The door to the soul is open, and it leads to all the dimensions of experience.

(10:50.) If you think, however, that the self as you know it is the end or summation of yourself, then you also imagine your soul to be a limited entity bounded by its present ventures in one life alone, to be judged accordingly after death on the performance of a few paltry years.

In many ways this is a cozy concept, though to some it can be quite frightening with its connotations of eternal damnation. It is far too tidy an idea, however, to hint at the rich embellishments that are at the heart of divine creativity. The soul stands both within and without the fabric of physical life as you know it. You are not separated from the animals and the rest of existence by virtue of possessing an eternal inner consciousness. Such a consciousness is present within all living beings, and in all forms.

You may take your break.

(10:55 P.M. This proved to be the end of the session.)

SESSION 591, AUGUST 11, 1971, 9:03 P.M. WEDNESDAY

(Again, this was a short session. Jane and I had grown very used to living with Seth's production of his book; we had come to look forward to each development. But now . . . "I almost don't want to hold the session," Jane said as we waited for 9:00. "It's a real funny feeling — almost nostalgic. I can feel — I know — that Seth's going to end his book soon now, probably tonight, and I don't want it to happen, I guess." She'd mentioned such feelings occasionally before, since Seth began work on the last two chapters.)

Good evening.

("Good evening, Seth.")

Now: We will resume dictation. *(Now Jane's pace was rather fast, her voice quiet.)*

I titled this chapter "A Goodbye and an Introduction." The goodbye is my own, since I am now finishing this book. The introduction applies to each reader, for I hope that you will now be able to meet yourself face to face with a greater understanding of who and what you are.

I would like, therefore, to introduce you to yourself.

You will not find yourself by running from teacher to teacher, from book to book. You will not meet yourself through following any particular specialized method of meditation. Only by looking quietly within the self that you know can your own reality be experienced, with those connections that exist between the present or immediate self and the inner identity that is multidimensional.

There must be a willingness, an acquiescence, a desire. If you do not take the time to examine your own subjective states, then you cannot complain if so many answers seem to elude you. You cannot throw the burden of proof upon another, or expect a man or teacher to prove to you the validity of your own existence. Such a procedure is bound to lead you into one subjective trap after another.

As you sit reading this book, the doorways within are open. You have only to experience the moment as you know it as fully as possible — as it exists physically within the room, or outside in the streets of the city in which you live. Imagine the experience present in one moment of time over the globe, then try to appreciate the subjective experience of your own that exists in the moment and yet escapes it — and this multiplied by each living individual.

This exercise alone will open your perceptions, increase your awareness and automatically expand your appreciation of your own nature.

The "you" who is capable of such expansion must be a far more creative and multidimensional personality than you earlier imagined. Many of the suggested small exercises given earlier in the book will also help you become acquainted with your own reality, will give you direct experience with the nature of your own soul or entity, and will put you in contact with those portions of your being from which your own vitality springs. You may or may not have your own encounters with past reincarnational selves or probable selves. You may or may not catch yourselves in the act of changing levels of consciousness.

Certainly most of my readers, however, will have success with some of the suggested exercises. They are not difficult, and they are within the capabilities of all.

Each reader, however, should in one way or another sense his own vitality in a way quite new to him, and find avenues of expansion opening within himself of which he was earlier unaware. The very nature of this book, the method of its creation and delivery, in themselves should clearly point out the fact that human personality has far more abilities than those usually ascribed to it. By now you should understand that all personalities are not physically materialized. As this book was conceived and written by a nonphysical personality, and then made physical, so do each of you have access to greater abilities and methods of communication than those usually accepted.

I hope that in one way or another this book of mine has served to give each of you an introduction to the inner multidimensional identity that is your own.

(Louder): And that, my dear friend, is the end of dictation, and the book is finished.

("Excellent, Seth.")

Now you may take a break. A well-deserved one.

(9:30. The end of the book seemed to come abruptly even though we were prepared for it. Once out of trance, Jane again expressed her peculiar regret that Seth's book was done, even though this was what we'd been working for. "What's he going to do now?" she asked. "I can't really believe it's over, you know."

("We'll just have to wait and see," I replied. We made various joking remarks about what would come next in the sessions, but I could see that Jane didn't really feel humorous. Actually, Seth's own book contained so many ideas for future sessions that our problem would be what to explore first — and we would have the unaccustomed opportunity to carry out these studies at our leisure.

(Finally Jane told me: "I'm just trying to relax. . . . He's got something for you, I think, about those biblical times; the Crucifixion . . . The thing is, I know what Seth's going to start telling you, but it's confusing. It doesn't sound right."

("Well it's nice to know you haven't run out of words," I said. The following material is included because it supplements Seth's data in Chapter Twenty-one. After Seth began that chapter Jane and I realized we could become quite interested in biblical history, but our time for learning had been brief. Resume at 9:50, at a slower pace.)

Now: For your edification:

Christ, the historical Christ, was not crucified. . . . You will have to give me time here. *(Pause.)*

He had no intention of dying in that manner; but others felt that to fulfill the prophecies in all ways, a crucifixion was a necessity.

Christ did not take part in it. *(Pause.)* There was a conspiracy in which Judas played a role, an attempt to make a martyr out of Christ. The man chosen was drugged — hence the necessity of helping him carry the cross *(see Luke 23)* — and he was told that he was the Christ.

He believed that he was. He was one of those deluded, but he also himself believed that he, not the historical Christ, was to fulfill the prophecies.

Mary came because she was full of sorrow for the man who believed he was her son. Out of compassion she was present. The group responsible wanted it to appear that one particular portion of the Jews had crucified Christ, and never dreamed that the whole Jewish people would be "blamed."

(Pause at 10:00.) This is difficult to explain, and even for me to unravel. . . . The tomb was empty because this same group carted the body away. Mary Magdalene did see Christ, however, immediately after *(see Matthew 28)*. *(Long pause.)* Christ was a great psychic. He caused the wounds to appear then upon his own body, and appeared both physically and in out-of-body states to his followers. He tried, however, to explain what had happened, and his position, but those who were not in on the conspiracy would not understand, and misread his statements.

Peter three times denied the Lord *(Matthew 26)*, saying he did not know him, because he recognized that that person was not Christ.

The plea, "Peter, why hast thou forsaken me?" came from the man who believed he was Christ — the drugged version. Judas pointed out that man. He knew of the conspiracy, and feared that the real Christ would be captured. Therefore he handed over to the authorities a man known to be a self-styled messiah — to save, not destroy, the life of the historical Christ.

(10:05. Jane's pace had speeded up considerably by now.)

Symbolically, however, the crucifixion idea itself embodied deep dilemmas and meanings of the human psyche, and so the Crucifixion *per se* became a far greater reality than the actual physical events that occurred at the time.

Only the deluded are in danger of, or capable of, such self-sacrifice, you see, or find it necessary. Only those still bound up in ideas of crime and punishment would be attracted to that kind of religious drama, and find within it deep echoes of their own subjective feelings.

Christ knew however, clairvoyantly, that these events in one way or another would occur, and the probable dramas that could result. The man involved could not be swerved from his subjective decision. He would be sacrificed to make the old Jewish prophecies come true, and he could not be dissuaded.

(10:10.) In the Last Supper when Christ said, "This is my body, and this is my blood," He meant to show that the spirit was within all matter, interconnected, and yet apart — that his own spirit was independent of his body, and also in his own way to hint that he should no longer be identified with his body. For he knew the dead body would not be his own.

This was all misunderstood. Christ then changed his mode of behavior, appearing quite often in out-of-body states to his followers. *(See John 20, 21; Matthew 28; Luke 24.)* Before, he had not done this to that degree. He tried to tell them however that he was not dead, and they chose to take him symbolically. *(A one-minute pause.)*

His physical presence was no longer necessary, and was even an embarrassment under the circumstances. He simply willed himself out of it.

Now you may take your break.

("Thank you. It's very interesting.")

(10:17. "Wow," Jane said after she came out of trance, "nobody'll like that. But I tried to relax and let it come out, because I had so many questions about those times myself. . . .")

(I questioned Jane, but she hadn't retained any images nor could she add to the material just given. The short delivery that follows answers some of the points we discussed at break. Resume at 10:28.)

Now: He knew that without the wounds, they would not believe he was himself, because they were so convinced that he died with those wounds. *(See John 20.)* They were to be a method of identification, to be dispensed with when he explained the true circumstances.

He ate to prove he was still alive, for example *(John 21, Luke 24, etc.)*, but they took this simply to mean that the spirit could partake of food. They wanted to believe that he had been crucified and arisen.

Now: I will end our session for the evening. I bid you a fond good evening.

("All right. Thank you.")

Tell Ruburt there will be other books. And I thank you for your help, cooperation, and patience.

("I've been glad to do it.")

We will have a private session next time.

("Okay. Good night and thank you." End at 10:30 P.M.

(In the last two chapters Seth has answered just about all of the questions remaining on the list we had prepared originally for Chapter Twenty.

(A note: Beneath a larger agreement, there are many differences in the details of the Gospels of Matthew, Mark, Luke, and John. For instance, in John 19 it is said that Christ carried his own cross; in Luke 23, Simon from Cyrene is named as carrying Christ's cross for him. Many complicated questions and reasons have been advanced in dealing with various aspects of the Gospels: their possible foundation in oral tradition and older common literary or documentary sources; whether any of them embodies an eyewitness account of the life of Christ [it has been very recently claimed that Mark's was written only a few years after Christ's death, for example], whether the Gospels should simply be regarded as expressing a single tradition, the fact and atmosphere of Christ, regardless of anything else, etc.

(With a good deal of anticipation and not a little nervousness — Jane now began to read Seth's book from page one. She was amazed.)

APPENDIX

S eth devoted three full sessions and portions of two others to this
Appendix. It includes additional information on several topics already mentioned in the book proper, such as coordination points, biblical times and records, objects as symbols, reincarnation, and expansion
of consciousness. Sessions 592 and 594 are particularly intriguing in that
events occurring during the sessions highlighted and illustrated the dictated material.

We also added portions of six other sessions. Five are class sessions;
one is included because it is relevant to the discussion on after-life organization in Chapter Nine. Another contains an excellent description
of true spirituality. In the remaining class excerpts, Seth answers questions that readers might also have in mind.

These sessions also show Seth as he relates to others in personal contact. To an engineer he gives an explanation of the pulsations of atoms,
discusses mental health with a nurse and aggression with a minister —
all class members. The sixth presentation is from a session held for a
student in which Seth mentioned the Speakers for the first time.

SESSION 592, AUGUST 23, 1971,
9:35 P.M. MONDAY

(Since I knew so little about the time of Christ, it's taken me a while to do
the extra reading necessary so that I could write appropriate session notes. Sue

Watkins, a member of Jane's ESP class and our personal friend, has been very helpful; she has loaned me books on the period so that I could be sure of historical references.

(Jane and I were tired from our recent activities and might have missed the session, except that she didn't want to interrupt the rhythm we'd built up. Sue sat in as a witness. All of us expected an easygoing session — one that might touch upon current events involving the three of us, from a very ill feline, say, to our impromptu Friday evening "reincarnational dramas." But we certainly didn't expect Seth to continue the material he'd begun in his book relating to biblical times.)

Good evening.

("Good evening, Seth.")

I should frighten you by saying, "Chapter One," but I will not. And good evening to our friend here *(Sue).* You will shortly be able to read my book in its entirety. *(To me):* I have a few notes for your edification.

("All right." Seth's pace was rather fast.)

Give us a moment. Now. The Essenes had deep roots in some of the mystery religions of the Greeks. Some of the Essenes set up schools that were not what they appeared to be. Subterfuge was used. There were various tests applied before an initiate could come close to the interior doctrines. *(Pause.)* There were other groups of Essenes, therefore, beside the one generally spoken of.

(The Essene group generally known would be the Jewish sect in the Holy Land during the time of Christ, early in the first century. Historically they are thought of as a peaceful group.)

The Essenes, as they are known, were a surviving group from a larger and more ancient brotherhood. Some existed in Asia Minor. Efforts were made to infiltrate into national or group cultures. Certain basic ideas united the Essenes, therefore, though often they went by different names. *(Pause.)* There were three basic groups: the one generally thought of, an offshoot in Africa, and the Asia Minor group mentioned earlier. Little contact existed between these groups, however, and gradually the inner doctrines themselves showed important variations.

The schools often pretended to be giving an education in other areas. The stranger would be kept in this outer group. Some attended such schools without ever knowing of the inner initiates, and the more important work being carried on beneath the camouflage.

Some of the members of the Zealots were originally Essenes. The Essenes predated them. John the Baptist was an Essene in all important ways; yet a man who steps forward in such a way automatically steps out of his group, and so did your friend, John.

(Here Seth humorously referred to my recent interest in John the Baptist. The Zealots were a much more aggressive, semipolitical Jewish sect that also existed in the Holy Land early in the first century — as I discovered from my recent reading.)

(9:46.) There was some jealousy, then, from certain members of the Essenes at John's progress. At one time John attempted to join various divergent groups together as one brotherhood, but he failed. The failure weighed heavily upon him. Fire is seldom gentle, and John the Baptist was as filled with fire as Paul.

He was a far more gentle man, and yet in his own way as fanatical as any of the other main characters of that day. He was much more against what he was against, than for what he was for. Christ, you see, was to deliver the message and John was to prepare the way for it.

John had an alliance with a female cousin, as a youth. He fled from the knowledge of this for the rest of his life, believing it sinful.

Now these were men filled out like sails with the energy of their roles, yet they had to have the personality characteristics of their time. They had to appear as men before men, before Christ could proclaim himself as anything beyond the natural man.

The entanglements were those that were necessary in the context of that religious drama. They were creative in that they bore within them the only seeds that could grow, in your terms, within that place and that time. *(More heartily):* Now, we do not have to be so formal. Book dictation is over.

("Is it?")

It is indeed.

("Okay.")

You may ask me a question or take a break as you prefer.

("We'll take the break then.")

(To Sue): I talk to this one in the dream state often. I do not want to take up all your waking time besides.

(9:56 to 10:00.)

Now: Records were often falsified; completely doctored, and false records were often planted. Religion was politics. It implied sway and power over the masses. It was the business of the rulers to know in which direction the religious winds blew. There were deliberate falsifications of fact, then and later. Some sects kept false records on purpose as blinds, so that if these were stolen, the robbers would think they had what they were after.

In some cases the falsified records have been found — the misrepresentations — while the true records behind them have not as yet been discovered.

(Pause.) You had better remember in what session that information was given you.

("I don't quite get what you mean.")

Before too long you may have reason to check upon what I have said, for records will appear that seem to contradict previous ones — as indeed they shall — and because of the reasons just given.

The Essenes kept sets of records to confuse the Zealots, and another set to confuse the Romans, and they very carefully guarded the inner set from which all the facts were made. They were not as violent as the other groups, but they were as shrewd.

(10:06.) There were various marks made, however, to distinguish the various sets of records, true and false. *(Jane paused as Seth, a hand to her eyes.)* Now, I do not know whether or not we can get this through clearly . . . Give Ruburt a piece of paper, and together we will see.

(The session was being held in our living room. Jane sat in her rocker, facing Sue and me on the couch. Our long coffee table separated us. There was a light to Jane's left, and one lit beside me. Sue handed Jane a piece of paper and a pen, while I continued to take notes.

(This was the first time Jane had written anything while in trance. Actually she was making some small diagrams or symbols, moving the pen quite deliberately, squinting down at the paper.

(Sue sat just opposite Jane, and I gestured for her to number the symbols when Jane lay the pen down and began to describe them for Seth. About a minute had passed. Tracings of the symbols are shown below, numbered in the sequence in which Seth-Jane produced them.

(Two attempts were made at both the first and last signs.)

Now, number one is an attempt to get at number two, which was simply a sign of a copy made, a distorted or doctored copy. The middle one,

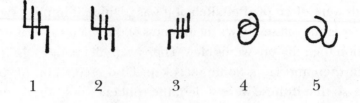

1   2   3   4   5

(three), was a mark made for a much less distorted copy, and the last mark, *(five),* was for an undoctored record.

These are poor versions. This looked more like a snake, a serpent.

(Speaking emphatically for Seth, Jane pointed at the last symbol as she held the paper up for Sue and me to see.

(Concerning symbols . . . In 1947 scholars began acquiring the seven now famous Dead Sea Scrolls. They had been found in a cave situated above the usually dry Qumran wadi, or riverbed, which leads to the Dead Sea a mile or so away. Excavations in the Judaean desert nearby soon revealed the ruins of a monastery which had been occupied by a divergent Jewish group, for varying periods, between 180 B.C. and A.D. 68. The Qumran settlement was but fifteen miles from Jerusalem and Bethlehem. It has been linked with the peaceful Essene sect by some authorities, while others just as strongly associate it with the more aggressive Zealots.

(Some weeks after this session Jane and I were interested to read that the St. Mark's Isaiah Scroll, from the Qumran find, contains marginal symbols that had still not been deciphered by the 1960's; this according to the last printing of the reference work we consulted. Some of the symbols, which were illustrated, bear more than a little resemblance to those Seth-Jane drew — especially the last one.)

It would be nearly impossible for anyone except one of the innermost circle to distinguish between some of the versions presented. These signs would not appear isolated, but in such a fashion that only those who knew how to look for them would find them. They were not blazed in gold on the title page. *(Humorously.)*

There were other clues also, certain other signs to be taken in conjunction with these, that appeared within the texts.

(10:17.) Now, in some of these records, the dating, for example, would be just off enough so that only one well-versed would recognize a discrepancy. Some would include an obvious error. Those in the know would immediately recognize that the record was a fake.

Some of the distorted records have been taken as fact, and it is a good joke to realize that the Vatican holds some of these. At the time, the church believed that these records could harm it. In the case of these particular errors, the records instead could have helped the churchmen, but they did not have the sense to know the truth from the false.

Now you may take your break. *(A gesture to Sue):* She is not used to my speaking so slowly.

(10:20. Sue is used to hearing Seth speak more rapidly in ESP class, where tape recorders are used. I don't record Seth usually but make direct verbatim notes, using my own kind of shorthand; this saves much time later when I type up the material. Still, Seth often speaks fast enough in our own sessions to keep me writing at top speed.

(No doubt Seth's amusement at the Vatican holding doctored records stems from his own brief tenure as Pope in one of his lives.

(Now Seth returned as Sue and I began to discuss the drawings Jane had done in trance.)

Since these are meaningless to Ruburt, it is difficult to get the symbolism across to him clearly. They should be drawn much more tightly, for example, not so loosely. In actuality the signs would appear as tightly concentrated symbols, and thicker in line.

(10:24. At break, Jane told us she couldn't draw versions of the symbols based upon those she'd done in trance. "I saw them quite clearly, mentally, when I was doing them," she said. "I don't see anything now, though." Looking at the last drawing, number five, Jane did say that the serpent's tail was supposed to be represented by the lower loop. Resume at 10:45)

Now: Give us a moment. *(Pause.)* In many cases records were faithfully reproduced, but with the names changed to protect the innocent.

Think of the language used presently by governments and diplomats. Think of the difference between what your government knows, and what is told to the people. Often when you hear a denial in such circumstances, you immediately leap to the correct conclusion — that in a month or so an affirmative answer will be given to the same question.

Words, therefore, are often used to cover up as well as to reveal. Great efforts are taken so that knowledge is kept, often, from a majority and for a few. In Biblical times this was all the more true. Literary devices themselves served as formalized methods of seeming to indulge certain information, while actually offering instead falsified data. No question in those days was answered directly *(emphatically)* — not by those who were at all literate.

To answer a question directly meant that you were simpleminded and lacked any appreciation of the questioner's greater intelligence, for he seldom asked a question he really wanted answered. It was highly ritualized behavior; understood, however, in those terms.

In other words, you do not understand how to translate the material properly from many of those records, even when the translations *per se* are correct.

You would call whole pages of the [Dead Sea] Scrolls tremendous put-ons, since whole pages, in literal terms, are not true. But these were expected exaggerations and embellishments that preceded the giving of information.

(10:55.) All professions, to one extent or another, had such fashions. The records meant life or death if they were discovered at the wrong time. Falsifications were often put in simply to lead any readers astray if the books fell in the wrong hands.

Again, those in the know had no worries. They would not be misled. To them the information was clear and the distortions obvious. Now the Scrolls are full of such protective distortions. The signs mentioned were but some of the clues used. They appeared in many guises, sometimes intertwined with signatures.

These people were much given to codes; even the arrangement of the letters upon the pages, as you think of pages, had their meanings. The weight or thickness of various strokes had meaning in terms of emphasis. There were even certain ways of handling a preceding word, so that the word would be a clue that the next word was false. Only those in the know would recognize this, of course, and the others would merrily digest the false information.

Descriptions of important individuals were changed to insure their safety, and backgrounds were often fictional for the same reason. These were life and death struggles. Some of the falsified records had poison on the manuscripts — deadly reading material indeed.

(In spite of the humor, Seth-Jane was very emphatic and serious in giving this material. The pace was fast. Pause at 11:00.)

Many of the men involved did lead double lives then, known in their villages by one name, and in their brotherhoods by another. In some cases, their more mundane identities were never divulged but to a few. Later, when the Christians were being persecuted, there were many safe-guards taken — particularly by those who believed they had a responsibility to live long enough to see the new creed find fertile ground.

Often Paul, or Saul, seemed to be where he was not, for example. Word would be sent that he would travel to such and such a location, and stories planted there of his arrival, while instead he journeyed to an entirely different place.

Now you may take a break or end the session as you prefer.

("We'll take the break, thank you."

(11:05. Jane's pace had been fast through the delivery. "Boy, he sure has energy," she said when she came out of trance. "I felt like I was going right through the wall. . . ." Resume in a bantering manner at 11:15.)

Now, I will not keep you from your beauty sleep.

(Thanks. I need it. . . . No, I don't. I'm beautiful enough.")

I suppose you are putting this into the session for the use of future historians.

("No, I'm not." Though, obviously, I kept writing out of habit.)

You should be getting some more reincarnational material on your own.

("I feel that it's available now.")

It is easily available. It will also open up greater activity in out-of-body experiences.

("That should be interesting.")

I will let you all go. *(To Sue):* I am glad you attended the session.

(Sue: "So am I.")

You should be ready for some more experiences in probabilities. *(Louder):* I must save my voice because we may have a class session tomorrow night. *(Humorously, to me):* You do want to be able to hear me over there, don't you?

("Sure. I usually do."

(Our apartment is divided by a long hall. When ESP class is held in the living room, I'm usually typing material in one of the rooms on the other side of the corridor. Sometimes I can hear Seth through the two closed doors.)

(To Sue): Again, I am glad you came, and a fond good night to you two.

(Sue: "Thank you."

("Good night, Seth. Thank you very much."

(11:20 P.M. Seth's reference to reincarnational material of my own concerned the "reincarnational dramas" that Jane, Sue, myself and a few others have undertaken on our own, usually at our Friday night gatherings. This is a relatively new activity for us. It's been both surprising and very rewarding, and is an outgrowth of experiments Seth initiated in ESP class.)

SESSION 593, AUGUST 30, 1971,
9:06 P.M. MONDAY

(The regularly scheduled session for Wednesday, August 25 was not held.

(This material came after the second break in this session. First we received several pages about a very interesting development in Jane's psychic faculties: her growing ability to perceive a beneficial "helper," as she has taken to calling it. . . . There is much to be learned here.

(Earlier in the week Jane received word that her editor wanted an Introduction from her for Seth's book, and an Appendix. She wondered if the 592nd session would be suitable, and I told her that I thought Seth had planned it that way. She was surprised, then agreed. We decided to leave it entirely up to Seth to produce whatever material he wanted for the Appendix.

(Jane's pace as she continued this session at 10:30 was quite fast, animated and emphatic.)

Now: For our Appendix.

The great religions of the world all had their births near the major coordination points. *(See Chapter Five.)*

In such localities, changes are apt to appear rapidly, for ideas and emotions are propelled into physical actuality with great vigor. Ideas sweep like fire among the people. The psychic atmosphere is fertile.

Creativity springs forth easily, and so such locations are not necessarily peaceful, although they would be the best ground in which peace could grow. Any ideas for good or bad become materialized with such strength, however, that the contradictory feelings of mankind are more apparent near coordination points.

There are effects, not as yet ascertained by your scientists, that appear in such areas: effects that were known however at the time of Atlantis, and also utilized by the Lumanians. In a strange manner, space puckers to an unobservable degree, as far as your instruments are concerned, near these coordination points.

Some of my readers may be familiar with "black" and "white holes" in space, that your scientists have recently discovered.

(Some theoretical physicists have postulated recently that when the nuclear fires of very massive stars are finally extinguished, their enormous gravity causes them to collapse so completely that they literally squeeze themselves out of existence. A "black hole" is thus left in space, and surrounding matter can disappear into this.

(It's been further suggested that this vanishing matter can show up elsewhere, either in our universe or others, through "white holes." There would be a flow of matter in our universe and also between universes, keeping things in balance.)

These points have somewhat the same qualities. The electromagnetic aspects of thoughts and emotions, the animations, are drawn through points that <u>can</u> compare to miniature black holes. Here their energy momentarily disappears from your system, is immeasurably <u>accelerated</u>, however, and returned through what you might call a miniature white hole — concentrated now, and highly directed back into your system of reality.

This is only an analogy, but for working purposes it is a fair enough one. There is, again, a wrinkling effect about these points, though not as yet observable to you, where space itself, it seems, yearns to disappear inside the first point. There are other distortions in physical laws. A few of these have been observed, but ignored as pertinent signs. *(With gestures, eyes wide open):* The activities of atoms and molecules quicken as they approach these points, but the distance <u>between</u> the atoms and molecules remains the same. That is important.

(Pause at 10:45.) These coordination points also serve to give your system additional sources of energy. The law of entropy does not apply, therefore. The coordination points are actually, then, sources of additional energy. They only open however when concentrations of energy build up within your system. I would like to make the idea clearer. A physical vehicle, a spaceship, for example, could never survive that kind of exit and reentry from your system.

(Long pause at 10:50. Jane's delivery had been very animated.

(A note: The second law of thermodynamics tells us that while the total energy in a closed system such as our universe remains constant, the amount of energy available for useful work is constantly decreasing. A mathematical factor that

measures the unavailable energy is called entropy. Seth has insisted from the very
beginning of our sessions that the law of entropy doesn't apply, and that there
are no closed systems.)

In Atlantis there were those who utilized this knowledge, accelerating certain thoughts through concentration, emphasizing certain feelings so as to send them through these coordination points. Great stability was therefore achieved as far as roads, buildings, and the like were concerned. Such projects were carried out with great consideration for their position between various coordination points.

This pocketing-of-space effect can be perceived in certain trance states.

("Can Ruburt do this?"

(I didn't think Seth heard me; there was a burst of traffic noise through our open living room window just as I asked the question. The answer came easily, though.)

This can be compared almost to a wadding-up of air.

Now sit quietly with your eyes closed and <u>try</u> to ascertain the directional proximity of main or subordinate coordination points. Here are some aids to help you.

With the intent in mind, you will find your inner vision inclining toward a particular direction of the room, and even your thoughts will seem to follow in the same direction. An imaginary line will help you properly identify the place, in any given location, closest to any given coordination point. Imagine a line drawn from the point of your inner vision, coming from the inner eye you seem to be using, outward. Let it be joined by an imaginary line from the top of your skull, following the same direction in which your thoughts seem to flow.

You have an imaginary line, then, in this case, from here, and here. There is an angle, and then both lines form together. They will point unerringly to the direction closest to a coordination point.

(To illustrate this as she spoke for Seth, Jane touched her eyes with one hand and the top of her head with the other. She extended her hands from these points until they met at arm's length, somewhat off to her right. I sat roughly south of Jane as she faced me, so this meant she indicated the western corner of our living room.)

The subordinate points permeate space. Ruburt will be able to tell you, for example, the nearest point in this room. Sometimes the angle will be longer, but the two lines will point in the right direction. Energy is, therefore, most effective in those areas.

(Long pause.) Now you may take a break or end the session as you prefer.

("We'll take a break."

(11:02. Jane was quiet after coming out of a deep trance. I wondered aloud where the nearest coordination point was. This brought forth a torrent of information from her — she'd forgotten it until my remark reminded her of what had happened.

(Jane said that while speaking for Seth, she knew the two lines she was indicating met in the west-by-south corner of our room. She walked over to the spot most positively. It was just inside the wall, between two of our bay windows and in back of an old-fashioned, exposed steam pipe. Unfortunately it was crowded between a heater and bookcase, and wasn't a spot we could put into easy use.

(Walking about the room, Jane said she felt her thoughts "lean" in just that direction. Now that she knew where the coordination point was, it seemed incredible to her that she hadn't always known its location. She couldn't possibly lean mentally in any other direction, she said. She turned her back to the spot, and gleefully announced that she felt the "lines" go out to it from the back of her head. Resume at 11:10.)

Now: Using this analogy of the white hole and the black hole: To make this clearer, the white hole is within the black hole. Do you follow me?

("Yes.")

Electromagnetic properties are drawn into the black hole, and accelerated beyond imagination. The acceleration and the activities within the black hole draw unbelievable proportions *(I checked this word with Seth)* of additional energy from other systems.

This greater acceleration changes the very nature of the units involved. In the meantime, the characteristics of the black hole itself are changed by this activity. A black hole is a white hole turned inside out, in other words. The electromagnetic "matter" may reemerge through the same "hole" or "point" which is now a white hole.

The reemergence, however, again alters its characteristics. It becomes "hungry" once more, and again, a black hole. The same sort of activity goes on in all systems. The holes, therefore, or coordination points, are actually great accelerators that reenergize energy itself.

We will end this material for this evening.

(An abrupt ending, then, after a long pause. But Seth returned):

Put a note after the material on coordination points, indicating the Appendix. This is not our book *(humorously)*, this is the Appendix to our book.

("Okay.")

My heartiest good wishes to you and a fond good evening.

("Thank you very much, Seth.")

And when you find time for the recorder, I will find time for you.

("All right. Good night, now."

(11:21 P.M. After the session, Jane tried Seth's method for finding coordination points once more. Again she found herself pointing to the west-by-south corner of the room. "I got a whole bunch of stuff that time," she said, meaning that she received some extra information after trance. "Those lines form triangular or flue shapes that contain energy. That's why psychics talk about pyramid forms — those lines keep the energy concentrated."

("Sure; that's why I get the triangle effect with Seth Two," she exclaimed. "Only when I'm in a Seth Two trance, the coordination point is in a different direction. It goes up from the top of my head, way out of the room and the house into a different reality."

(Jane then thought of having the members of her ESP class try Seth's method. She wanted to see if they would locate the same spot that she had.)

SESSION 594, SEPTEMBER 13, 1971,
9:40 P.M. MONDAY

(Only one session was held last week, and that was a long overdue, promised one for friends.

(Sue Watkins witnessed tonight's session. She intended to leave before session time, but Jane invited her to stay at 8:50. Sue's unexpected presence is a fine example of how spontaneous events can influence a session in a very creative way — as Sue's notes, quoted later, will show.

(As usual, Jane had no idea of what tonight's session would include. "Stuff for the Appendix, I hope," she said. She was in an excellent mood, even a hilarious one. This quality also turned up in the session, in Seth's funny, over-elaborate requests for me to use just the right punctuation and paragraphing.

(We were late getting started because of my own work in the studio. Talking and laughing, Jane and Sue waited for me to join them in the living

room with my notebook. Jane's delivery was quite brisk, with an occasional short pause.)

Now: I bid you good evening, and our friend *(Sue)*. I would have some interesting comments to make regarding the relationships between you, but we must be up and about with our Appendix, and so we will continue that. The other information will come in its own time.

Objects are the symbols.

You usually think of them simply as realities. You think of thoughts, images, and dreams sometimes as being symbolic of other things, but the truth is that physical objects are themselves symbols. They are the exterior symbols that stand for inner experience.

There are, therefore, mass physical symbols upon which you all agree, as well as private, personal symbols.

The whole nature and structure of physical life as you know it, is a symbolic statement made by groups of entities who choose to work with physical symbolism. So the body is a symbol for what you are, or what you think you are — and these may be two different things indeed.

(Seth actually made an elaborately humorous request for the dash in the last sentence: Jane, her eyes very dark, leaned far forward over our coffee table and spoke to me in a soft voice.)

Any physical ailment is symbolic of an inner reality or statement. Your entire life is a statement in physical terms, written upon time as you understand it.

New paragraph. *(Very quietly):* Once you understand the symbolic nature of physical reality, then you will no longer feel entrapped by it. You have formed the symbols, and therefore you can change them. You must learn, of course, what the various symbols mean in your own life, and how to translate their meaning.

To do so, you must first of all remind yourself frequently that the physical condition is symbolic — not a permanent condition. Then you must look within yourself for the inner actuality represented by the symbol. This same process can be followed regardless of the nature of the problem, or of your challenge.

(9:50.) Your intimate physical environment is, therefore, a symbolic statement of an inner situation. The inner situation is a fluid one, for you are always in a state of becoming. Left alone, you will automatically translate the freely moving, spontaneous inner events into physical reality, therefore altering your environment and changing the symbols.

If however you imagine that the environment or physical condition is the reality, then you can feel trapped by it, and spend your efforts fighting a paper dragon. The environment is always altered from the inside. There is instant feedback between the interior and exterior conditions, but the mobility, the necessity and the method of changing the physical environment will always come from within.

New paragraph. *(Again, a very quiet, smiling, and polite request. "I'm way ahead of you this time, Seth.")*

Many of the ideas given in this book can be used most advantageously to solve personal problems. If these concepts are understood, then the individual should realize the freedom he has to operate purposefully within the structure of physical life. Many of you are so used to looking outward — and accepting the physical world as the criterion for reality — that it has not occurred to you to look within. The entire framework of your existence, therefore, is constantly flowing from within outward, and being projected into those physical symbols that you mistake, then, for reality.

(To Sue, who sat beside me on the couch): I am pretty good on details too. New paragraph.

(Seth burst out with loud and emphatic humor this time because of the work Jane and I have done in recent weeks as we proofread this book, checking all my notes that are included, and so forth.)

The interior drama, therefore, is always the important one. The "story of your life" is written by you, by each reader of this book. You are the author. There is no reason, therefore, for you to view the drama and feel trapped by it. The power to change your own condition is your own. You have only to exercise it.

To some other types of consciousness, your physical reality is clearly understood in its symbolic form. Objects, as symbols, help construct the very framework of your existence. They, the objects, can then be manipulated quite freely.

You may take your break.

("Thank you."

(10:00. Jane's pace had been fairly good. Her eyes had been closed often, however, which is rather unusual.

(The first thing she wanted to know when she came out of trance was if the session contained new material. I had to tell her I didn't know; I'd been too busy

writing. Nor could I keep all of Seth's book in mind, even though I was working with the manuscript just now. But then, Jane said, neither could she — and she'd just finished reading the whole thing over.

(A note: Jane was halfway through the final draft of her Introduction to Seth's book when this session was held.

(Sue said the material had a great deal of meaning for her, and that she now realized that it hadn't been an "accident" that she'd dropped in this evening. She had much more to say here, especially concerning her impressions of Jane, Seth, and the great energy involved in these sessions. It developed that Sue had begun to experience and formulate some impressions both before and during the session.

(Sue's comments were so very good that I asked her to write them down. She wrote them during the rest of break, then added to them occasionally through the rest of the session. They are presented here in slightly abridged form:

("As I sat here before the session," Sue wrote, "I got an impression of Seth that I'd never had before. It was as though Jane, Rob, and I were traveling at a certain familiar speed while we were talking, although this has nothing to do with motion. When Seth came 'around' just before the session, it seemed that something within Jane began to crank up, to whirl or accelerate faster and faster until a certain incredibly other speed was reached — a part of Jane's consciousness that is called Seth.

("At that point the speed was right and things 'clicked' somehow. Jane took off her glasses, as she always does. I could almost hear this action; then the Seth personality began to communicate. The Seth Two experience would be an even greater acceleration of this speed, reached at the point of the pyramid effect Jane describes.

("Even while I told Jane about this during break, I could feel this acceleration begin again, as Jane's consciousness prepared to continue the communication. It was almost an inside-out process of going into trance, and as I watched Seth a few minutes later it seemed that Jane's consciousness was rushing past her open eyes, beyond my comprehension of what speed is. I now must wonder how the communication ever gets back down to words.

("I don't mean to say by this that I think Seth and Jane are the same personality; rather, my feeling is that this acceleration connects portions of the same consciousness that are normally so diverse as to be two separate personalities for all practical purposes. I can recognize the same feeling of acceleration when I'm writing well myself, or even talking enthusiastically; but the feeling of vast, incomprehensible speed behind Seth's eyes goes way beyond that. I could sense the notion *of speeds very clearly, both in Jane and Seth, and I felt partly carried along by them.*

("When Jane came out of trance it was, again, an almost audible experience for me — a feeling of slowing down from a high airy whine to our normal 'sound' or speed. There was a great sense of change. It was as though part of this acceleration was connected with a dimension where sound was more than a hearing *thing. It's a terrific, vital feeling. I could feel it starting up toward the end of each break."*

(Jane resumed at 10:25 at a slower pace.)

Now: Our friend Sue's observations came very close to an excellent description of Ruburt's subjective feelings, as he told you during break.

I refer readers to Ruburt's Introduction, in which he compares his own creative experiences as a writer to those he feels in our sessions. There are several points he did not understand, and so here I would like to clear them. *(With a pause):* New paragraph.

In our own sessions he is not aware, consciously, of the creative work that is being done, precisely because he has gone out of the range that the conscious mind can follow. He has projected a portion of himself into an entirely different kind of subjective reality, a different dimension of activity entirely.

Referring to his Introduction again, he remarks that he misses the excitement of the chase, encountered in his own creative work. Here, you see, the acceleration is so rapid and intense that he is not consciously able to follow it. The unconscious, so-called, has little to do with this phenomenon. It is, however, related strongly to qualities inherent within each consciousness. Such ability is rarely used to full advantage. Connections are made so rapidly that the physical brain is not aware of them.

(Pause, one of many, at 10:30.) Ruburt has indeed always possessed this ability to a strong degree. For various reasons, reincarnationally speaking, he allowed himself to remain ignorant of the ways in which the ability could be used for the early portion of his life. During sessions, however, all the characteristics of the inner being are accelerated; the knowing, intuitional, creative abilities, working at a rate far beyond what you would call the norm.

This is a dimension of existence native to consciousness, however, when it is not physically oriented. Ruburt can, and will, learn to explore this dimension even further. Only his lack of confidence in the past held him back.

The acceleration propels him into a state in which he can operate quite well, while going beyond all those normal psychological realities that he would personally call his own. *(Pause.)*

In such a state he literally uses incredible power, in terms of energy, now; and the volume of the voice in many cases is an attempt to help him use some of this, and discharge it, while he learns how to use it, and until he is taught other purposes to which it can be put. The volume, of course, can also be used as an excellent demonstration of the vitality with which he is in touch.

Now you can take a break. Finish your notes.

("Okay.")

And I will give Super-Jane a rest. *(Pause, pointing to Sue):* This one here is waiting for him to come back, so she can feel the difference.

(10:37. Sue was on the edge of the couch, watching Jane closely as she came out of a deep trance. Once again she talked about the change in Jane's "speeds." "A sound goes along with those speeds that I can't describe," Sue said. "It's like being in a dimension where music is the reality — where sound is more than just hearing things. Then when you leave it — " Sue whistled, imitating the Doppler effect of a train whistle receding into the distance.

(When Sue and Jane questioned me about this, I had to tell them that I didn't feel anything out of the ordinary, but then I seldom do during sessions. Concentrating on writing helps close out other effects also. I am always writing, it seems— just as I wrote through most of this break period.

(Again Sue watched Jane expectantly as we waited for Seth to return. "Wow, the acceleration's terrific," Sue exclaimed; and just before going back into trance, Jane told us she felt the chair vibrating beneath her. . . . Resume, with pauses, at 10:57.)

Now: Many of the experiences that Ruburt has during our sessions he cannot recall afterward. As physical objects are symbols, existing as realities within certain frequencies, so there are other realities, of course, at different frequencies; but here objects are not the main symbols.

Experience within such a dimension is extremely difficult to translate when Ruburt is back within the physical system. On my part, there are also adjustments that must be made. I step down several levels for example, so that contact can be made.

I then attempt what is indeed a creative endeavor, in which Ruburt participates — the act of translating such inner data into physical terms, bringing into your reality those clues that I can bring you of these other realities of which you are part.

(Pause at 11:00. In a quietly amused manner now, Seth was giving frequent instructions regarding punctuation, etc. Jane's eyes were closed often.)

Seen or viewed from my natural perspective, your objects do not exist. Your inner reality does, of course. Now Ruburt's system physically undergoes some changes, although these are largely native to his constitution. *(Humorously):* He saw to that before this life began.

He uses nervous connections in a way that is unusual, and to his purpose. His pulse rate is normal. The acceleration begins, however, on a physical level, with the use of hormones and chemicals, and then leaps from there. Both halves of the brain spark, and from those connections, speaking physically now, the acceleration is initiated, and its effects on the body are cut off.

Many cases of missing persons can be explained somewhat in the same manner: when the acceleration was strong enough, unexpected enough, to sweep the entire personality out of your system.

Now for our friend's sake, I am speeding up the acceleration to see if she can perceive it. This often takes place during the dream state — and when it seems to you that you have briefly entered an astonishing new dimension, the dream state itself involves such an acceleration.

(As I wrote, I took a quick look at Sue, beside me. She sat very quietly, watching Jane. Jane's eyes were open now, her pace faster, her voice somewhat louder.)

To some extent or another, each artistic creation, though to a lesser degree, involves the same principle. Now, I cannot keep the additional acceleration up, or the voice will go so quickly that our friend cannot keep to his notes —

(Jane's voice abruptly grew much louder with the last sentence — an effect Sue and I have witnessed often. This volume was far from her potential when speaking for Seth, however. On some occasions her voice has been so loud that my ears rang. I've heard Jane keep up very strong voice effects, with such ringing peaks, for an incredible several hours, and without any signs of strain afterward.)

Now, do not take notes. . . .

(His loud and rapid voice soon quieting, Seth explained to me that he would give a "fine demonstration of an acceleration" in a session in which we used our recorder. Sue could sit in on it, and hopefully I would experience the acceleration as clearly as she does. This interlude ended in a break at 11:10.

(When Jane came out of trance, Sue was again "drastically aware of the drop" in Jane's speed. She also had some visual effects that were hard to describe; in an effort to pin these down, she began adding to her own notes, and these are quoted at the end of the session.

("Sometimes in ESP class, I could take the whole class with me on a real acceleration adventure, if they could go," Jane said. She used the contrasting example of trees in a forest, comparing their passive state to the feeling of acceleration, of "being able to go right through the wall" that she sometimes gets. There was more here that I didn't get down.

(Resume at 11:20.)

Now: I am going to end the session shortly. It was, of course, no coincidence that our friend came here this evening. Besides giving you necessary information for the Appendix, some of the information given on objects and symbolism definitely applied to Sue.

(To me): I feel sorry for you —

("Why?")

Because you have been writing so steadily.

("I'm okay.")

There is one point I can add here, in connection with the religious drama of Christ and the disciples.

As Ruburt said after reading the body of the book, the interior drama is the "real" one. Christ became the Crucified, Judas became the betrayer, though Christ was not crucified and Judas did not betray him. The reality, therefore, was in the myth. The reality was the myth. In such cases the interior events will always predominate, regardless of the physical facts, which are only symbols for those events.

Now I bid you a fond good evening.

("Good evening, Seth. It's been a pleasure.")

(To Sue): And I will let my friend, Ruburt, slide back down.

(Sue: "All right. Good night."

(11:25 P.M. Once out of trance, Jane had little to say. "I'm just sitting here, watching you two busy bees," she grinned, as Sue and I worked on our separate notes.

("Before break at 11:10," Sue wrote, "when Seth told me that he was speeding up the acceleration to see if I could perceive it, I had the definite feeling of greater speed and a visual change in Jane's body. It seemed to become smaller, as though I were looking at it through the wrong end of binoculars. This was again connected with motion, as though the physical frequency was also changed, and Jane's body was rushing past me, even while staying in the same place.

("Then when Jane came out of trance at last break, I felt as though a force had been released in front of me, so that if I wasn't careful I could topple over. And the same thing now, after the session.")

SESSION 595, SEPTEMBER 20, 1971, 9:01 P.M. MONDAY

(The first part of the session was given over to a friend who needed help with a personal problem. She taped Seth's information, then left when break came at 9:45.

(I had two questions for our portion of the session, and we expected that Seth's answers would be included in the Appendix of his book. The first question: According to Seth, he, Jane and I lived in Denmark in the 1600's. I simply wanted clarification of the data on my lifespan, as given in the notes at the end of the 541st session, in Chapter Eleven.

(The second question: Did Seth intend to title Part One and Part Two of his book, as he had his chapters? Resume at 10:05.)

Now.

("Good evening, Seth.")

Now: I have to speak more slowly, you see.

The information on the Denmark life in Chapter Eleven is correct, except for a misinterpretation. That was one life divided into two separate periods — literally a life divided in terms of interests, concentration of abilities, and life styles.

Aside from the information given in that chapter, there have been distortions in some past material concerning that life. These were not caused by Ruburt's feeling about reincarnation. They were simply a result of correlating many details into the correct specific pattern.

Some of the names given, for example, applied to friends rather than to yourselves. The overall picture, the validity of the existence, carried through the distortions, however. I was a spice merchant. You were originally an artist, who turned rather dramatically into a landowner, and against your youthful ways.

Ruburt was a dabbler in art as a young man also, and you resented this, grown fat and prosperous. You wanted him to go into more acceptable work, and you were ashamed of your own early wanderings as an itinerant artist.

Here the division was set between the idea of owning property, as opposed to being an artist. In this life that has caused you considerable unease.

(10:13. This is very true. And for whatever reasons, in this life I have insisted upon being an artist in spite of all obstacles.

(In the 223rd session for January 16, 1966, Seth said that my name in the Denmark life was Larns Devonsdorf. My wife then was named Letti Cluse. My son — who is now Jane — was Graton. Seth, a prosperous merchant, traveler, and family friend, was named Brons Martzens.)

The general itinerary of my journeys as given in that session by Ruburt was correct. There were some distortions in other portions of that session, however.

(Long pause at 10:15.) The details that so concern you now are, of course, important, and yet in a larger way it is the deep emotional experience of your life that is "later" remembered. Basically the names and dates are meaningless to the inner self. Therefore in reincarnational data the emotional values will come through more vividly, and with much less distortion.

You place upon names and dates an importance you presently find of critical import. You insist upon them to add to the validity of past life narratives, yet these are precisely those things that are forgotten first, and that have least value psychologically.

(10:20.) Certain names will, therefore, spring into immediacy. You insist that the names be neatly placed, and yet often the inner self has great difficulty in this regard, for names simply do not matter. Persons and events of meaning, carrying strong emotional charges, will come through far clearer. Dates that are associated with emotional events will also be recalled. The past life is *(smile)* like a crossword puzzle that must be put together, but at its center is the emotional reality from which the puzzle springs.

(Seth smiled because of Jane's recently developed, rather strong interest in crossword puzzles. I enjoy them also. We've been speculating about the symbolic reasons behind our involvement.)

Many such reincarnational narratives are liberally sprinkled with names and dates simply to satisfy those who insist upon them, because the emotional and psychological validity may not be accepted otherwise. This applies to any kind of reincarnational material, however it may be obtained.

Now if the life in question is a recent one, in your terms, the details may be more readily recalled and far more precise. Even a life centuries ago may be perfect in detail however if it included, for example, battles or events of great import, where the dates themselves were impressed upon the personalities because of the occurrences at those times.

(10:29.) Any emotional experience that is highly charged will carry a barrage of details along with it, but usual dates and usual names have little meaning. They have little meaning in your own reality. Basically speaking, relationships are far more important, and these you do not forget.

These lives exist simultaneously across the board, however. This you should not forget. The useless paraphernalia is not important to the various personalities, however, "now" or "then." Do you follow me?

("Yes.")

The reincarnational structure is built along the same lines of existence that you know now. Some individuals are more intrigued by detail than others: A particular "previous personality" may be one who had a great love of detail, in which case you would discover the richness of it. The particular likes and dislikes of any given personality will also have much to do with the descriptions given of a particular reincarnational episode.

It will do no good to ask deep questions concerning the history of the times of some personality who was impoverished, ignorant, and limited. He simply would not know the answers. The picture of any given life, therefore, usually comes through the experience of the personality who lived it.

(Pause at 10:35.) Again, those details will emerge that were important to him. In my particular case, I am so unfocused on my own reincarnational selves, and they have gone so far on their own, that I have little feeling of immediacy. Since we *[Seth, Jane, and I]* have been so involved however, those relationships remain important, and in your

terms our present relationship was latent then. The Denmark life exists as much as this one does for you. "You" are simply focused within this picture of reality.

Now you may take your break.

(*"Thank you."*)

(*10:37 to 10:50.*)

Now: The reincarnational structure is a psychological one. It cannot be understood in any other terms. The distortions and interpretations that have built up about it are natural enough, considering what seems to be your practical experience with the nature of time.

The reality, the validity, the immediacy of those lives do exist simultaneously with your present life. The distance between one life and another exists psychologically, and not in terms of years or centuries. The psychological distance, however, can be far more vast. There are certain lives, as there are certain events in this life, that you may not want to face or deal with. There may be great temperamental differences in some cases, between your personality in one given life and another — so that your present self simply could not relate to the other's experience.

You will be more strongly drawn to those "past lives" that somehow reinforce your own at this time. You realize that your early memories are sparse. Most of you remember little of the years spent as an infant and child. You make use of the knowledge gained then, and while it is part of you, you are not aware of it consciously; and so you are not consciously aware of other reincarnational existences. (*In a whisper, humorously*): New paragraph.

Earlier in this book I mentioned alternate presents on several occasions, and reincarnational lives are indeed alternate presents. There is interaction between you and your reincarnational selves constantly. There is, as your friend Sue Watkins said, "constant action across the board."

(*11:01.*) Those selves are not dead, in other words. Your understanding of this must be limited because you automatically think in terms of one life experience at a time, and in linear patterns of development. In your terms, a reincarnational self can be aware of your environment, and interact sometimes through your own relationships.

Certain "present happenings" can, indeed, spark such interactions.

In quite other terms, however, the reincarnated personality, while interacting with or through you, can still be having other kinds of experience at other levels.

(Jane's delivery was quite animated and positive here, as though Seth wanted her gestures to underscore the material.)

Because time is open-ended, as you think of it, you can also affect what you would think of as past reincarnational selves, and at times react in and to their environment. You would usually do this in the dream state, but this is often accomplished just below the level of waking consciousness, and is blotted out by you as you go about your daily business.

(11:07.) Strong emotional associations can often trigger such responses. *(Pause.)* Reincarnation, as it is usually explained, in terms of one life before another, is a myth; but a myth enabling many to partially understand facts that they would otherwise dismiss — insisting as they do upon the concept of a continuity of time.

Now you may take a break or end the session.

("We'll take the break, Seth."

(11:10. Jane had been "way out" as she often puts it. She remembered only the first sentence or so of the material. All of her trances have been deep this evening. It takes her a bit longer to leave such a state; her eyes roll up occasionally, etc.

(At break I repeated my question about titles for Parts One and Two of Seth's book. Resume in the same manner at 11:24.)

Now: We do not need to name the two portions separately. I had thought of specifically having the first part deal with inner and outer immediate environments, and then to lead to the larger reality of the soul and its perception in the second part. This is what I did, but the material is so interwoven that I felt the given separation enough, and did not want to reinforce the idea of a division.

(Smiling:) Now I could go on for hours, but I suggest that you get your rest.

("It will be appreciated — the rest, that is."

(And although I was getting weary, it was apparent that Seth could easily shift into a state where his energy would seem inexhaustible.)

I bid you a most fond good evening.

("I thought the personal material you gave for our witness tonight [before first break] was excellent.")

It was indeed. It was tailor-made for her.

Now: When the Appendix is done and your work with this book is finished, I will give you as many sessions as you would like, within reason, for yourself. And use the recorder.

("Okay. Good night, Seth, and thank you."

(11:27 P.M. "That was funny," Jane said, after she rested for a few minutes. "I was really out that last time but it was for such a short time that I really felt the transitions from 'here' to 'there' and back. That word Sue used — 'acceleration' — is a good one. . . ." See the 594th session.)

SESSION 596, SEPTEMBER 27, 1971,
9:24 P.M. MONDAY

(Jane and I worked on proofreading Seth's book for an hour or so after supper, and then went for a walk. It was a warm and rainy fall evening, already dark and very pleasant. There was a scattering of wet fallen leaves about.

(By 8:30 we were back home. We sat in the living room with the lights off, so that we could see outside easily. Jane had finished the Introduction to Seth's book today. This in turn reminded her of her own manuscript, The Physical Universe As Idea Construction, *which she discusses in the Introduction. She had read it again today, and it still intrigues her. She said again that she'd like to do something with it on her own eventually.*

(9:00 passed almost unnoticed as we talked. I turned on a couple of lights when we finally got down to the business of holding a session. Jane wanted more material for the Appendix of Seth's book. She said that the living room seemed "different" this evening, significant; but it was a "nice difference," she added. She began speaking for Seth in a very quiet voice. Her pace was rather slow, her eyes closed often.)

Good evening.

("Good evening, Seth.")

Now: *The Physical Universe as Idea Construction,* mentioned by Ruburt in his Introduction, did indeed represent our first <u>formal</u> contact, although Ruburt was not aware of it at that time.

The experience came within a framework that he could accept — that of highly accelerated inspiration. His consciousness left his body only after he was in the throes of what seemed <u>to him</u> to be inspiration of almost unbearable intensity. Had his habits instead led him, say, to regular prayer, then <u>that</u> framework could also have been used. In all such cases several qualities are apparent: an ability to look inward, to concentrate deeply, to lose the sharp edges of the physically oriented self in contemplation, and an intense desire to learn. These must be coupled with the inner confidence that pertinent knowledge can be directly received. To those who believe that all answers are known, there is little need to search.

Such information, such inspired writing, usually appears within frameworks of the personality that have already been set and formed. The context in which such knowledge appears will often vary, therefore. In some cases, the framework itself is used for a final time, with the initial inspired knowledge — the knowledge itself — escaping from the framework and growing out of the context that allowed for its birth.

(Pause at 9:35, one of many. Jane's delivery was more vigorous by now, however.)

Above all, individuals who receive such information in states of expanded consciousness are already those who feel deeply within themselves connections not only with the earth itself, but with deeper realities. Consciously they may often be unaware of this basic quality within themselves. They do not accept answers given by others, but insist upon finding their own.

These searches may appear erratic. There is a fine impatience, a divine discontent that drives them on until the frontiers within their own personalities are finally opened. The knowledge gained must then be integrated by the physical personality, and yet by its nature, valid knowledge of this kind will shed out its light and make its own way.

The energy generated by some such experiences is enough to change a life in a matter of moments, and to affect the understanding and behavior of others. These are intrusions of knowledge from one dimension of activity to another. They are highly charged and volatile. Unknowingly, the individual who receives such information is himself a part of it. The entire feeling-tone of his present personality is changed — and directly — by the information he receives.

To the extent that he is true to his own vision, possibilities of expansion are available to him that he could hardly have achieved otherwise. Often the information given clashes with previously held ideas and beliefs, however. Otherwise, there would be no need for the sometimes explosive, intrusive qualities of such experiences, for there would be no barriers.

(Long pause at 9:45.) Such personalities often then must learn to correlate their intuitive knowledge, to reform intellectual frameworks strong enough to support it. Such personalities also are usually gifted with the ability to draw upon unusual amounts of energy. Often they must learn at a fairly young age not to dissipate the energy. They can seem, for example, to go off in many directions at once, before this lesson is brought home.

The late thirties and early forties are frequently involved simply because the need to know in such personalities often reaches a peak then. The required patterns of behavior are sufficiently set. The energy has been directed, and the individual has had enough time to realize that the accepted frameworks and answers make little sense to him.

At their strongest, such experiences can propel intuitive knowledge from the private domain to change civilization. The incredible charge is always in the initial experience. Contained within it is the condensed energy from which all other developments come.

The personality involved can react in many ways. Great adjustments are necessary, and often changes of behavior. The individual now realizes that he is indeed a living web of reality, and this becomes immediate conscious knowledge.

(This of course, is what happened to Jane. Pause at 9:58.)

Such knowledge requires not only more responsive and responsible behavior, but involves a sympathy with life that may earlier have been lacking. The sympathy brings with it a sensitivity that is strong, challenging and intense. Many individuals have experienced unusual, quite valid and intense expansions of consciousness, but found themselves unable to correlate the new knowledge with past beliefs, to make the changes necessary to handle the sensitivity. Indeed, they were not strong enough to contain the experience. In such cases, they tried to close it off, deny it, forget it.

(10:05.) Others never allowed it to escape from the framework or the context from which it had sprung. They were then unable to escape. They could not free themselves. If the information seemed to be coming initially from their God, for example, they continued to think in their particular way about God, even though the experience and the information given should have brought them far beyond such a point.

(Jane's voice was still relatively quiet as she spoke for Seth, but her delivery was faster and much more intense now, and she used many gestures.)

Ruburt, for example, would have made the same error had he not been led by his experience beyond the framework of inspiration that had given it birth. *(Pause.)* In his case, then, he was propelled into new concepts because he had the sense to reject old ones, and the courage to go ahead.

The going-ahead involved him *(long pause)* with my ideas of the god concept. Before our sessions, he was so disillusioned that he would not even consider any questions dealing with "religious matters."

(To me): Are you tired?

(We hadn't had a break yet, but I nodded no. It was raining harder now. Along with that sound, I had been hearing someone move back and forth in the apartment above us.)

Now such experiences or such doorways to knowledge are available to each individual, and to some extent each individual partakes in them. They appear in much less conspicuous form, often in intuitive decisions made with seeming suddenness, beneficial changes, intuitive hunches. Often midway in life an individual will suddenly seem to see things clearly in a physical manner, straightening out his affairs. A life that seems headed for disaster will suddenly become victorious, for example. These are all variations of the same experience, though in lesser form.

(Pause at 10:15.) In normal living and in day-by-day experience, all the knowledge you need is available. You must, however, believe that it is, put yourself in a position to receive it by looking inward and remaining open to your intuitions, and most important, by desiring to receive it.

I said a few paragraphs back that individuals such as Ruburt are themselves a portion of the knowledge they receive. This applies to each person, each reader. *(Long pause.)* There is a great fallacy operating. People believe that there is one great truth, that it will appear and they will know it. Now a flower is a truth. So is a lamp bulb. So is an idiot and a genius, a glass and an ant. There is little exterior similarity, however.

(10:24.) Truth is all of these seemingly distinct, separate, different realities. So Ruburt is a part of the truth he perceives, and each of you are part of the truths that you perceive.

"Truth," reflected through Ruburt, becomes in a way new truth, for it is perceived uniquely, (as it would be for each individual who perceived it). It is not less truth or more truth in those terms. It becomes new truth.

Now you may take your break.

(10:26. It took Jane a few minutes to come out of a very deep trance. Her voice had remained quiet for the most part, but had become very intent. She had no idea that she'd been speaking for just over an hour. "Wow, he sure had me out that time," she said. "I know why, too. The noise upstairs really began to bother me, so Seth put me under even deeper."

("I knew I was going to get something on Idea Construction *for the Appendix, though," she continued. "It's been a most enjoyable evening." She was very happy about the session. I thought she was sensitive to noise tonight because she didn't want to be interrupted while getting this particular material. The upstairs apartment was quiet now.*

(The effects of the deep trance lingered. Jane yawned again and again. She walked about the room, sipping a beer and smoking a cigarette. The warm rain continued. I asked Jane if she wanted to end the session, but she chose to continue in spite of her yawns.

(Resume in the same manner at 10:45.)

Now: Such "new truths" can still be very ancient indeed, but truth is not a thing that must always have the same appearance, shape, form, or dimension. Those who persist, therefore, in shielding their truths from questions threaten to destroy the validity of their knowledge.

Again, those who are so certain of their answers will lack that need to know that can lead them into still greater dimensions of understanding. Any valid expansion of consciousness is itself, of course, a part of the message. The personality finds itself encountering living truth, and knows that truth only exists in those terms.

I have used the term "expansion of consciousness" here rather than the more frequently used "cosmic consciousness" *(pause)*, because the latter implies an experience of proportions not available to mankind at this time. *(Pause.)* Intense expansions of consciousness by contrast to your normal state may appear to be cosmic in nature, but they barely hint at those possibilities of consciousness that are available to you now, much less begin to approach a true cosmic awareness.

(10:55.) The ideas presented in this book should allow many

readers to expand their perceptions and consciousness in ways they may not have believed possible. The book itself is written in such a way that all those ready to learn will benefit. There is meaning not only in the written words themselves, but connections existing between them that do not appear, and that will have meanings to various levels of the personality.

(Jane, in trance, tried to light a book match several times, but it was evidently too damp. She finally had to put her new cigarette aside.)

The integrity of any intuitive information depends upon the inner integrity of the person who receives it. Expansion of consciousness, therefore, requires honest self appraisal, an awareness of one's own beliefs and prejudices. *(Long pause at 11:01.)* It brings a gift and a responsibility. All who wish to look within themselves, to find their own answers, to encounter their own "appointment with the universe," should therefore become well acquainted with the intimate workings of their own personality.

That is it. *(As Seth, Jane leaned forward, her eyes open wider and quite dark.* *("Okay.")*

And it is for our Appendix. You may ask questions, take a break, or end the session as you prefer.

("We'll take the break, then." 11:02 to 11:09.)

Such self knowledge is in itself highly advantageous, and in one way is its own reward. It is impossible, however, to look inward with any clearness if you are unwilling to change your attitudes, beliefs, or behavior, or examine those characteristics that you consider uniquely your own.

You cannot examine reality without examining yourself, in other words. You cannot hold encounters with All That Is apart from yourself, and you cannot separate yourself from your experience. *(Pause.)* You cannot use "truth." It cannot be manipulated. Whoever thinks he is manipulating truth is manipulating himself. You are truth. Then discover yourself.

And now, I will say good evening. *(As Seth, Jane slapped her knee, grinning.*

("Okay, Seth. Thank you very much.")

We will still have our own sessions when circumstances allow.

("All right. Good. When this book is finished, I guess.")

My heartiest regards.

("The same to you. Thanks. Good night."

(11:16 P.M. "Gee, I really feel good," Jane said, when she finally came out of another deep trance, "but I think I can just about make it to bed." She was yawning again, and very relaxed. The soft pleasant rain continued.)

ESP CLASS SESSION:
TUESDAY, JUNE 23, 1970

(Some sixteen members of Jane's ESP class were present when this session was taped. In the session, here slightly abbreviated, Seth discusses organization in our present reality, among others. See the 537th session in Chapter Nine for material on after-death organization.)

Now: If you want organization then you shall have it — at any time. You structure your own existence, and you choose those realities that have exactly as much organization as you need at any given time.

In this reality, you very nicely emphasize all the similarities which bind you together; you make a pattern of them, and you very nicely ignore all the dissimilarities. Out of a vast field of perception, you choose to focus your attention upon certain specific areas and to ignore all others, and so there is perfect agreement among you as far as this small area is concerned. The vastness that you do not perceive does not bother you at all, and you do not ask questions about it. And yet it exists.

I have said this before: If you were able to focus your attention upon the dissimilarities, merely those that you can perceive but do not, then you would be amazed that mankind can form any idea of an organized reality. *(As Seth, Jane looked at the couch, where Mary and Art were sitting.)* I look now between the two of you. When the others look at our friends here on the fancy blue couch, they see a picture of true organization. There is an individual there *(pointing)*, and an individual there, with space between. The picture is equalized. It appears perfect and organized.

However, the space between our two friends is not vacant. You think of it as vacant because you do not perceive what is there. The picture appears to be very organized. As soon as you realize that the picture is not complete, however, then you must begin to ask new questions, and the old idea of the perfect organization is gone.

Now: As you know, you do not perceive the atoms and molecules that swim about the room, nor those that fill the space between our two friends, nor the forces — the field forces — that exist. The couch serves to unite them since they sit upon it. And what do they sit upon? Emptiness that you perceive as solidity.

Now without your particular physical senses you would not perceive the couch as solid. Consciousness that has different perceptive mechanisms than your own is unaware of our now famous blue couch. <u>You</u> make the organization. <u>Your</u> thoughts perceive an organization. You enforce the organization, and indeed create it.

(Question from a class member: "Do we all create the same organization and see the same couch?"

(To Mary and Art): You each generally agree, I am sure, that you sit upon a couch. You do not perceive the same couch. You only perceive your own idea constructions. You cannot see those of another. Telepathically, you transpose your ideas in line with what you know of the other person's thinking. You agree that the couch is here. Now it is true that within your physical system — for I know this will come next — you can measure your couch. I expect at any moment that someone will get a ruler and measure it, and then say to me that the couch is so long: How can I say it is not one couch?

However, within your physical system the instruments themselves are distorted, and of course they will agree with what they measure. There is no reason why they should not. Telepathically you all agree on the placement of objects, and their dimensions.

Now: You use atoms and molecules in a strange way. You transpose your ideas upon them. You perceive them in a certain fashion. I am not blaming you. I have done it too, in my time, and there is good reason for it. But the fact is that physical matter is not solid except when you believe that it is, and that organization is transposed from within upon the without. It is not transposed from the without upon you. You form the reality that you know, and even though the table holds up your arms and you may lean upon it and write, I still tell you that the table is not solid.

This makes little difference as long as you can write upon it. It makes little difference as long as you can sit upon your blue couch. But when you leave your physical system and when physical perception is no longer the rule, then you must learn new root assumptions.

Root assumptions are those laws upon which you agree in any system of reality. You agree, for example, upon what objects are physical — it makes little difference whether they are or not, as long as you agree upon this. Your consciousness belongs in a body. You would not be caught DEAD with your consciousness outside of your body. It is taboo! Now the fact is that your consciousness is not imprisoned within your body; but as long as you believe that it is, again, you will not be caught dead outside of it. And when you are caught dead outside of it, there will be some amazement, indeed.

There are other root assumptions that you take as a basis of reality. And in other levels of reality, there are other root assumptions. These are the seeming laws by which you govern your experiences. Our note takers are doing very well, considering that the paper is not solid and neither are their pens. It is amazing what you can do with nothing!

(Break, and discussion.)

You are truly multidimensional personalities, as I have said before. At some point in your development you will become more and more aware of the true nature of your identity. There is, for example, a part of you who is very aware of the pulsations you have just been discussing, and who is aware of the pulse-like nature of memory. When the pulse is in this physical reality, then you, as you know yourselves, have memory of this existence. When the pulse is in another dimension, there is memory of that existence. Now a portion of your entire identity has memory of both. The entire personality structure dwells in many dimensions, and simultaneously.

You are at the very beginning of any idea of psychology. You simply do not realize what you are now; and as I've said before, when you ask me questions about life after death, you automatically transpose — — if you will forgive me — this lack of knowledge into the next realm. Therefore, sometimes I am at a loss to answer your questions. You are learning to know yourselves. At the rate you are going, it will take you some time!

Now: When you properly understand how to use psychological time, then to some extent you can learn to alter the nature and focus of your consciousness. You can turn it in many directions. You can focus it in other ways, away from physical reality. This does not mean that you will be left high and dry here. It does mean that you will begin to explore the reality of yourselves, and of those other dimensions in which you have your existence.

There must be, however, a willingness to admit that there are other dimensions in which you exist. You must also have faith in your physical self — faith that it will be here when you get back, and I assure you that it will. There is <u>no other way</u> — and I repeat this — there is no other way of getting firsthand information about other realities except by the exploration and manipulation of your own consciousness.

Now when I speak to you I very seldom use such words as "love." I do not tell you that a God is waiting for you on the other side of a golden door. I do not reassure you by telling you that when you are dead, God will be waiting for you in all his majestic mercy, and that that will be the end of your responsibility. And so as I said last evening, in my latest chapter, I offer no hope for the lazy, for they will not find eternal rest.

However, through traveling within yourselves, you will discover the unity of your consciousness with other consciousnesses. You will discover the multidimensional love and energy that gives consciousness to all things. This will not lead you to want to rest upon the proverbial blessed bosom. It will instead inspire you to take a better hand in the job of creation; and that feeling of divine presence you will find indeed, and feel indeed, for you will sense it behind the dance of the molecules, and in yourselves and in your neighbors. What so many want is a God who walks down the street and says, "Happy Sunday, I am I, follow me." But God is hidden craftily in his creations, so that he is what they are and they are what he is; and in knowing them, you know him.

(Break, and discussion.)

Now: There are many words for psychological time. I do not mean my method of meditation alone. I do mean subjective activity on your part, and exploration. Do you follow me? I am glad!

Actually, you are with God now. It is you who do not realize this. You see, you have believed many tales, and symbolically they were very important. As was mentioned earlier, they have their place in your lives and your development, but there are times when you must leave them behind, and you may feel lonesome for a while without them.

(Question: "Then we need those beliefs as part of our development, even though we cast them off later?")

Yes, even though someone like myself will come along and take off the comfort blankets — for after a while they hamper your development, where earlier they helped you grow. The fact remains, however: You do not have to die to find God. All That Is, is now, and you are a part of All That Is now. As I have told you often, you are a spirit now. The avenues for development are open now. You can, now, set out to explore environments that are not physical if you want to, but I do not see any rush of students at that invisible door!

Now I am going to close our session, but I would like you all to read carefully a copy of what I have said. And now and then, when you have nothing else to do — nothing better to do — then try, try to sense that lapse in the pulsation of your consciousness. Try to leap that gap!

I bid you all good evening.

(11:25 P.M.)

ESP CLASS SESSION:
BEFORE JUNE 23, 1970

(This remnant, saved by one of Jane's students, is all that is left from one of the few class sessions that were either lost or not fully recorded. See Chapter Nine.)

True spirituality is a thing of joy and of the earth, and has nothing to do with fake adult dignity. It has nothing to do with long words and sorrowful faces. It has to do with the dance of consciousness that is within you, and with the sense of spiritual adventure that is within your hearts.

That is the meaning of spirituality; and as I have told you before, if I could I would do a merry dance about the room to show you that your vitality is not dependent upon a physical image. It is not dependent upon your youth, it is not dependent upon your body. It rings and sings through the universe, and through your entire personality. It is a sense of joy that makes all creativity probable.

So do not think you are being spiritual when you are being long-faced, and do not think you are being spiritual when you berate yourself for your sins. The seasons within your system come and go. The sun falls upon your face whether you think you are a sinner or a saint. The vitality of the universe is creativity and joy and love, and that is spirituality. And that is what I shall tell the readers of my book.

And now, take the break I promised you. . . .

*(This excerpt from the session contains Seth's first mention of the Speakers
and their functions in the reincarnational process, and supplements the Speaker
data in Chapter Seventeen.*

*(The session came about because Ron B. and his wife, Grace, members of
ESP class, requested help with a problem involving their family. After winding
up some very interesting material concerning that situation, Seth launched into
the Speaker data at about 11:15. All of us present were surprised. The term
"Speaker," as Seth uses it, was as unknown to Jane and me then as it was to Ron
and his family.)*

We have known several people who were monks in a previous
existence. Now. *(To Ron):* In a life in the east before the time of Christ,
1200 B.C., you were a member of a body of men who belonged to an esoteric heritage. You were wanderers and traveled also through Asia Minor.

You carried with you in your heads messages and laws that had been
given to one of your kind in a time that was already nearly forgotten.
These were codes of ethics. They originated from the time of Atlantis.
Before that, these codes were given by a race from another star. This
race had to do with the origin of Atlantis. The messages were put into
words and language and written down at the time of Atlantis, but after
that they were handed down by word of mouth.

Your people learned them from their elders, and they were called
Speakers. You were a Speaker. This is why you find it so easy to call others your brothers. Now: Three men in particular who are under you
(in the manufacturing plant where Ron holds a supervisor's position), were part
of that original band of men. Your wife, your daughter-in-law and your
son *(all present this evening)* were also members of that band. Your wife
and your daughter-in-law, however, were brothers. Now give us a
moment here. *(Pause.)*

You traveled through Asia Minor in a time of great turmoil, and
wherever you went you spoke — which means you gave utterance to the
ethics. It took you twelve years of training to memorize this code of
ethics.

Now later the Essenes were involved. I am not sure of the word.

*(The Essenes were one of the four known Jewish sects active in the Holy Land
at the time of Christ. They were a peaceful, contemplative group. They aren't*

mentioned in the Bible. If Seth means that the Essenes were promulgating the Speakers' codes of ethics in, say, the first century A.D., *then this of course is a time many centuries later than Ron's life in 1200* B.C.

(Ron's wife, Grace: "Seth, did we fulfill our purposes in that time?")

In that existence, yes. You must give me time. There was turmoil within the group, disagreement. There was disagreement over the meaning of the words that were recalled. The group became divided. One portion of the group traveled to the land we now call Palestine, and the other migrated, in the next century, appearing in southern Europe.

There was a major distortion having to do with B-A-E-L *(spelled)*. A group gathered together with Bael as their idea of God. You *(Ron)* were with the other group. There was a city in a jungle — M-E-S-S-I-N-I *(spelled)* as nearly as I can translate it. In Asia Minor, and fragments of a past civilization were then there. A new city was built which in its turn also disappeared. There were writings on rocks, however, as the old messages were once again put into written symbols. But your people were gone, and you are only now finding them again.

(11:27. Jane's trance had been very good. She had trouble opening her eyes, then in keeping them open. She had seen images while giving the material, she said, but couldn't describe them to us now.

(Ten sessions after this one, Seth told Jane and me that we had been Speakers also, although he said nothing about dates or countries, or whether Jane, Ron, or I might be renewing acquaintances made in other, perhaps very ancient times. It seems to me that in this life at least, Ron and I encountered each other in quite a strange way: almost of an age, we grew up in the same small town near Elmira many years ago; we knew of each other's family — and yet we didn't meet until 1970. . . .

(Possibly reflecting his early Speaker practices — which may be continuing on subjective levels — Ron is active in lay church work, and knows much about the Bible and related subjects. He elaborated upon some of Seth's data; later, I checked portions through various reference works. Jane, since she knows practically nothing about the historical periods in question, was very pleased that Seth's data was so evocative.

(Seth-Jane spelled the god's name Bael. Most sources spell it Baal, possibly pronounced as Bael. The Akkadian form, Bel, was used in ancient Mesopotamia. Baal — lord — was the name or title of a number of local deities of ancient Semitic peoples. Baal worship appeared in Syria and Israel many centuries before

the birth of Christ — as early as 1400 B.C., according to Syrian cuneiform texts. This date is very interesting, in light of the 1200 B.C. Seth mentions for Ron, and the conflict within his group over Baal. Baal was most often a god of fertility, its image of stone probably a phallic one. According to orthodox Israelite belief, Baal or nature worship was idolatrous, a denial of any moral values.

(While we were talking about the city of Messini, about which none of us knew anything, Seth returned briefly):

Now: Write down R-A-M-A *(spelled)*. It is another city. Give us a moment and then we will indeed say good evening. . . .

(Ramah is the name of several Palestinian towns, and means "height" in Hebrew. Biblical allusions associate the name with some of the "high places" of cultic practice. These sites, rejected as immoral and threatening to Israelite belief, contained objects of illegitimate worship — the sacred pillar of Baal being one such. I discovered all of this information through research after the session. None of it was known to us at the time. Resume at 11:48.)

In your terms, and in your terms only, the coming of Christ was the Second Coming. *(Pause.)* In those terms — and, again, this is important — in those terms only, he appeared at the time of Atlantis, but the records were destroyed and forgotten except in the memory of a few who survived.

Now, again in those terms, he is an entity who appears time and time again within your physical system, but he has been recognized on only two occasions. Once in Atlantis, and once in the Christ story as it has come down to you in all of its distortions. He appears and reappears therefore, sometimes making himself known and sometimes not. He was not one personality, as I have told you, but a highly developed entity, sometimes appearing as a fragment of himself.

In your terms he eternally weaves himself within the fabric of your time and space, born again and again into the world of flesh, being a part of it while also independent of it, even as you are all a part of it but independent of it.

Now: Since our little friend over here *(Ron's daughter-in-law, Sherry)* is worried lest I annoy the neighbors *(very loudly)*, I will smile what I hope is a gentle smile, and bid you a gentle good evening, with what blessings I have to give.

(End at 11:55 P.M. Jane's trance had again been deep, and it took her a while

to come out of it. "Wow," she said, "I feel that energy so strongly now, going through me, carrying me along. . . ."

(After the session Ron explained the Second Coming as given in the Bible in Matthew 24. He also told us about Jesus predicting his own death and resurrection several times in Matthew, Mark and Luke, and of the resulting uncertainty and misunderstanding of the disciples. Even after his crucifixion the risen Jesus wasn't recognized on various occasions.)

ESP CLASS SESSION:
TUESDAY, JANUARY 5, 1971

(This session followed a class discussion on reincarnation and probabilities. Seth's comments and the students' questions show the give-and-take characteristic of class sessions, and demonstrates their scope.)

Now: Ancient Rome exists, and so does Egypt and Atlantis. You not only form the future, as you think of it, but you also form the past. You have been told simple tales, and they are delightful ones; but if you were not ready to hear more you would not be in this room.

You and your reincarnated selves, or personalities, are not imprisoned in time. There is a constant interchange going on between what you think of as your present self, and your past and future selves. If this were not the case, then I would not be speaking here, for I am not Ruburt's past self. Each personality is free. Time has open ends in all directions or such a thing as probabilities would not exist. Therefore, actions that you make now can help a so-called past personality; and a so-called future personality may step in and help you along your weary way.

Also, your actions now can affect the future personality as well as the past one. You must try to stretch your imagination and feel these realities, because the intellect alone cannot comprehend them. Psychological time is your best method for perceiving these actualities.

You can feel what you cannot necessarily describe verbally, for you are more than the physical brain that you have now. I am no poet, but as in one of Ruburt's poems, think of the brain as a web you form about the inner self. This webwork helps you manipulate in a world of space and time, and is as nebulous, precarious and delicate as any spider's web — and in as precarious a balance. You form this and then perceive the world, but your viewpoint is very small and the garden you perceive very intimate. You have, however, far greater abilities of perception. I want you to understand the nature of your inner self, or soul, for it is a focal point of reality from which other realities spring. It is not imprisoned in tiny boxes of days or weeks or months, or even of centuries.

Now I will let you all take a break, and I will return in a moment.

(During break a student, Janice S., wanted to know if Seth was a part of Jane's personality.)

Now: Ruburt cannot answer you as easily as I can. We were originally a portion of the same entity. I evolved along my own ways and he evolved along his. Therefore we are both independent.

(Janice S.: "In other words, all parts of the entity are evolving? Are they developing as one?")

I evolved to form my own entity. Ruburt will also, but he is not at that stage yet, in your terms. In another frame of reference he is, of course. He also contains those portions of himself that are less developed, for they all exist as one. All the parts of himself are aware of this correspondence. In your terms only, I could be referred to — and I have told Ruburt this — as a sixth self of his in his future; but this is only to get the idea across, for he will not become what I am. That is impossible. I am myself.

There are certain answers that cannot be given verbally, but must be intuitively understood. Yet the fact that I exist and can communicate should show you, in simple terms, that other "higher aspects" of your personality can help you out on occasion.

(Janice S.: "Have you always taught on reincarnation?")

Teaching has been my main object, but I have not always been a teacher. I was a spice merchant at one time. A round and fat and heavy spice merchant.

(Janice S.: "But handsome.")

(Smiling): I do not know what to do with you. We learned what spices would do long before the present generation got hung-up on grass. We got high on the high seas, sniffing oregano. *(In the 1600's.)* We brought spices to Denmark; we had delightful trips indeed. We explored far down the coast of Africa. I was quite a gourmet.

Now: All of your so-called pasts exist within you now, and you can recapture your memories and discover what they are. You are not imprisoned in time unless you believe that you are, and there is nothing more important than belief. If you believe that you exist only within the context of this life, that you are born only to death and annihilation, then you will not use your freedoms in this existence. You deny their abilities when they show themselves, yet no one forces this bondage upon you but yourself. To understand your multidimensional self is to use it.

(Janice S. commented that Seth did not give many predictions.)

I am not cautious, I am simply realistic. When you understand the nature of reality, then you realize that predictions of future events are basically meaningless. You can predict some events and they can occur, but you create the future in every moment.

Time, in your terms, is plastic. Most predictions are made in a highly distorted fashion; they can lead the public astray. Not only that, but when the predictors fall flat on their faces it does not help "The Cause." Reality does not exist in that fashion. You can tune in to certain probabilities and predict "that they will occur," but free will always operates. No god in a giant ivory tower says, "This will happen February 15 at 8:05." And if no god predicts, then I do not see the point of doing so myself.

(Annie G.: "What about precognitive dreams?")

Some are entirely legitimate. Often, however, the suggestion involved in a dream brings about the event, so it seems when the dream becomes real that you have looked into a future that already existed. Instead you have formed the event, not realizing that it had its origins at the time you slept. The question cannot be answered simply for there are many ramifications, but from this instant of reality you form and change not only the future, but the past. In the operation of probabilities this has great significance, for this means that you change and affect all events, and that your books are a delightful fiction that tell you only your current ideas about the past.

(Sally W.: "How can I change my way of thinking to keep my family well, instead of making them sick?")

Back here, we have a question from the gallery. *(Smiling.)* You must realize that you do not form events alone. You are involved in a cooperative venture. Usually then you alone are not responsible for an event, because others participate in its creation — for their own reasons. The question cannot be answered simply in one evening, but each consciousness has its own defense system and its own vitality; you should trust your own.

You cooperate together to form the physical reality that you know, telepathically, through ways and means that are unknown to you. You weave webs of psychic reality that then coalesce into physical reality. You do not necessarily weave them alone, but together. Your thoughts intertwine with those of others. You are responsible for your own thoughts. You need to learn the power of thought and emotion, but this should fill you with the joy of creativity. Once you realize that your thoughts form reality, then you are no longer a slave to events. You simply have to learn the methods.

(Sally W.: "But I don't know how to learn them.")

You will learn them here. You will learn them through reading, and through listening to your inner self. The methods have been known for centuries; not only centuries as you think of them, but for the lifetime of this earth as you know it, and even before — when the poles were reversed and when there were other stars in the sky and when the planets were not the planets that you know.

You may take a break.

(Terry B.: "Where did you get the oregano, and in what form did you sniff it?")

It was in the Indies and it was dry.

(One of the subjects discussed at break concerned the degree of "permanence" of the physical human form.)

In our own sessions I have explained something that I haven't mentioned in class, and it is this: For every moment of time that you seem to exist in this universe, you do not exist in it. The atoms and molecules have a pulsating nature that you do not usually perceive, so what seems to you to be a continuous atom or molecule is, instead, a series of pulsations that you cannot keep track of.

Physical matter is not permanent. You only perceive it as continuous; your perceptive mechanisms are not equipped to detect the pulsations. Now, I am speaking to our friend over here (Art O., an engineer) because he may perhaps have a comprehension of what I am trying to explain, because of his background.

(Art O.: "Are these pulses extremely fast in our terms?")

They are indeed. In certain conditions however, the inner self, abandoning its usual reliance upon the physical senses, is aware of these periods that would seem to you to be negations.

Your consciousness fluctuates in the same way. It is here and then it is not here, but the physical self focuses upon only those moments of physical reality. Because consciousness fluctuates however, other portions of your self have memory of those times when it is not focused in "physical reality," and this is also a portion of your entire existence.

This isn't half as complicated as it sounds. Whether or not you remember your dreams, for example, a certain portion of you, under hypnosis, could remember every dream that you ever had in your life. So a certain portion of you remembers those nonmoments when you are not focused in physical reality, when your existence is in another dimension of actuality entirely and you are perceiving what I will call, in your term of reference, nonintervals. I like the term nonintervals better than nonmoments.

(Art O.: "Is this noninterval a moment of this existence?")

It is indeed, in this existence; and also these nonintervals are moments in other dimensions of reality.

(Jim H.: "Might this be compared to the rotating light in a lighthouse?")

It may, if you like the analogy.

(Art O.: "The analogy I get is of an electromagnetic wave, a carrier wave, and it's rectified. The intervals are the positive pulses and the nonintervals are the negative pulses.")

This is why I was talking to you.

(Art O.: "Are there more than two pulses?")

There are, and the whole self is aware of all of these realities. With no unkindness meant, you all know yourselves and your weaknesses and failures, so why should you suppose that the self you know is the only self that you are? Surely, it has occurred to you that you have abilities you are not using, that other realities connected with your innermost existence aren't being expressed in the existence you know of.

(To Art O.): I want you to think about the implications of what I have said concerning nonintervals.

(Jim H.: "Would a noninterval be a positive interval to another aspect of our existence?")

It is, and they would not perceive your existence here, for to them it would be a noninterval.

(Jim H.: "Could this be the key to the simultaneous existence of all of our lives, the key to nontime?")

Yes, indeed. And some evening I will tell you that you should change your conception of the word "lives." This is the first hint I have given, either in our private sessions or in class, of some rather important material. But think of what you mean when you use the word lives, and see how limited the term is.

I am going to end our session, but I have a comment. I have said this before: You are as dead now as you will ever be. Now if you understand that remark and think about it, you will understand much that is behind what I have said this evening.

(Art O.: "Then we are as alive now as we have ever been?")

That is correct — except that in the life in which you are now involved, you are not focusing upon the full potential of your vitality.

(Janice S.: "Was there a continent of Mu?")

There was. Now, I tell you to remember your dreams. In your context I will tell you again not only to remember your dreams, but to learn to come awake in the middle of them and realize that you can manipulate within them. You form them. They are yours, not something thrust upon you in which you are powerless.

(Janice S.: "We are using our existence as the dream?")

What I have said applies to what you just said. In one context what you call physical reality is a dream, but in a larger context it is a dream that you have created. When you realize that you form it you come into the memory of your whole self.

And when you realize that you form the events of your life in the same way, you will learn to take hold of your entire consciousness in whatever aspect it shows itself in this life. Through all of this you must realize that you are not powerless. Remember, also, that this life is a dimension of experience and reality even if it is, in contrast, a dream in a higher level of reality in which you have your larger consciousness.

ESP CLASS SESSION:
TUESDAY, JANUARY 12, 1971

(The first part of the session concerned a class member and her reluctance to look deeper within herself.)

Very nicely in class, she personifies the feelings that each of you have to some degree, involving your inner self. . . . She shows her feelings in an exaggerated fashion for you to look at, and so when she speaks it is not only for herself but for everyone in this room, including Ruburt.

(To the member): You have, indeed, been performing a useful service in class, but I expect to see it changed. For when you begin to look within yourself you will set the others a fine example, and so you shall.

(During break Jane read excerpts from some material concerning Gnosticism. This was followed by a discussion of the data Seth introduced in last week's class session, concerning the pulsating nature of atoms and molecules — and this in turn led to the consideration of possible origins for the so-called flying saucer phenomena.)

One small note: In some respects these pulsations represent what happens in some of your flying saucer incidents, for you do not have a vehicle such as the one you think you perceive. I am speaking of only certain cases, where you have visitors from other realities.

What happens is that you have an attempt to exchange camouflage realities. The beings entering your plane cannot appear within it as themselves. Since their atomic structure is not the same as yours, distortions must occur in order to make any contact possible. Thus you are greeted with a certain set of sense data. You then try to figure out what is happening but the sense data, you see, means that the event is already distorted to some degree. The physical vehicles that are often perceived are your interpretation of the event that is actually occurring.

Our friend back here *(Paul W.)* could well appear, you see, as a UFO in another aspect of reality, and frighten the inhabitants. You forget that consciousness is the only true vehicle. No part of your consciousness is imprisoned within you. It materializes in one aspect or another. I use the word "materializes" because it makes sense to you, but it is distortive since it predisposes an appearance within matter. Yet all realities, as you know, are not physical.

It is theoretically possible, for example, for any of you to disperse your consciousness and become a part of any object in the room — or to fly apart, to disperse yourself out into space — without leaving your sense of identity. This is not practical in your terms, yet many of you do it to gain refreshment while you are sleeping. Consciousness by its very characteristics carries the burden of perception. This is the kind of consciousness you are used to thinking of. You cannot imagine it without perception in your terms; and yet consciousness can be vital and alive without your idea of perception. The last part of that sentence is important.

(To Art O.): Now, my dear scientific friend over there: Atoms and molecules, minute as they may appear to you, also carry their burden of consciousness and responsibility. Yet there is a portion of consciousness that can joyfully perceive in a manner that is not dictated by its nature; it can playfully perceive as a creative aspect of its being, without responsibility. In one manner of speaking the very air about you sings with its own joyful consciousness. It does not know the same kind of burden of consciousness that often oppresses you. *(Speaking generally):* You are so frightened of death, in your terms, that you dare not turn your consciousness off for one second; for you fear that if you do, indeed, who will be there to turn it back on again?

(Art O.: "Is the whole entity involved in this dispersion of consciousness, or just the portion of it we know now?")

It is the way that galaxies form. It is the way that the universe expands, and it is the way that entities form. Now, that is your answer. Chew that one over for a while.

I am pleased because you are thinking this evening, all of you — that is what I want you to do. Ideas have no reality unless you make them your own. Make friends or enemies of them. Fight with them or love them but use and experience them, not only with your intellect but with your feelings.

(Bert C. spoke of relating to oneself and to others.)

Until you are honest with yourself and become consciously aware of yourself, you cannot honestly relate with others; you will project upon them your own fears and prejudices. You cannot afford to help them because you have too many insecurities within yourself. Now, you form the physical reality that you know, individually and *en masse*. To change your world you must change your thoughts. You must become consciously aware of what you tell yourself is true every moment of the day, for that is the reality that you project outward.

(Bert C.: "It sounds like a life-long task just to work out the first half of that, before you can begin to relate to others.")

It is, indeed. However, telepathy does exist. Others are aware, then, to a large extent of what you are thinking and feeling.

(Bert C.: "My true feelings, despite what I might project consciously?")

The true feelings do not necessarily imply the violent or aggressive feelings. They also imply the feelings of love and acceptance that are buried beneath your own fears, and those you are terrified of expressing in physical reality.

(*Bert C.: "I think I understand then, that all of these different levels of my consciousness are being communicated — not only by me consciously, but also telepathically."*)

That is true. When you project your ideas outward, you often behave as if they were not yours but belonged to another. Therefore it behooves you to understand what your ideas and feelings are, and not to be frightened of them.

(*Jim H. told of finding a man asleep at his work. Jim explained his ideas and emotions concerning the incident, and wanted to know how he could change them.*)

You can indeed change them, but do not deny the part of you that wanted to wring the other man's neck. You were so frightened of the thought that you immediately inhibited it. Let us consider. You are terrified of the idea that evil is more powerful than good, that one stray violent thought of yours was more important and powerful than the vitality of good. At least you were aware of the thought. Now say the following happened, that in your terms you progressed to the point where you were no longer aware of the feeling —

(*Jim H.: "You don't just automatically think good things about this fellow, and repress the negative thoughts without becoming aware of what you felt."*)

Of course, so your muscles tensed, your adrenalin production increased. You wanted to wring his neck but you said, "God bless you, my fine young fellow. May you live a long and merry life."

Telepathically, our fine young fellow knew exactly what you were feeling. You were out of contact with your feelings. At this point of your spiritual progression, you only imagined that you wished him good. The muscles were already contracted in your body because you did not admit your true feelings.

Now three weeks later we have another encounter. Our poor ignorant workman again falls asleep at his chores. Our good minister comes by. He sees the idle one upon the floor snoozing, and he thinks, "I would like to kick you in the you-know-where." But then, "Oh no, I cannot think such an unchristian thought. Violence is wrong." So before he even admits to himself what he feels, hiding any acknowledgement of aggression, he bends down and says, "My good man, may you live long and heartily. God bless your life." He pats himself upon the back and thinks, "I am growing more spiritual day by day."

In the meantime, his muscles have contracted ten times because they could not be put into activity, as the thought behind them was denied. Our poor man is again subconsciously aware of the intent, but only to some degree.

Three months later you have had a really bad day. You are mad at life in general, and now you find our friend upon the floor again; this time, perhaps, he is asleep at a somewhat more important chore that you wanted done. *(Humorously):* Now far be it from me to accuse you of such an act, even in a fantasy, but this time you are out of your mind. Again, it behooves you to deny your true feelings in order to be spiritual — which is not true spirituality — and you say again, "God bless you, may you go in peace."

This time the psychic safety valve has had too much. The nicest thing that could happen would be that you suddenly blew your stack and kicked him. The worst thing that could happen would be that once again you restrain the acknowledgement of the pent up, perfectly natural aggression that is now ready to explode — so you send out a thought-form out of all proportion to any of the events that have transpired. The thought-form causes your friend severe harm; and all of this because you were afraid that one stray aggressive thought of yours was more powerful than the vitality that resides in each of you.

(Jim H.: "In the beginning, before we compounded the frustration and the emotional charges, would you have recommended an action like saying, 'Come on, this is wrong. I've probably done this sort of thing myself, but it really bugs me. We have to get up and get to work here.' Would being honest with him at that level have prevented these charges?")

Yes. The most important thing, however, is to acknowledge the feeling as legitimate, with its own realm of existence, to admit it as a part of yourself. Then choose how you want to deal with it. You do not make others the brunt of your anger; anger is merely a method of communication.

(Jim H.: "I don't want to direct the brunt of my anger at either of us. One, I don't want to kick him. Two, I don't want to hurt myself in some way.")

Originally you were not angry enough to kick him. The thought existed, but it wasn't strong enough to bring about the physical reaction even if you had fully admitted it. Do you follow me?

(*Jim H.: "Yes. I want to learn how to handle such feelings, without trying to repress them."*)

You should first of all admit that the feelings exist as a part of yourself, at the ego level. Whenever you close your feelings off from yourself you are, in your terms, less alive. Then, as far as is possible, communicate those feelings verbally in whatever way you choose. Use anger as a method of communication. Often it will lead to results that you do not think of, and beneficial ones.

You certainly understand that I am doing with your case the same thing that I have done with others, so please do not be offended. I do not want any of you, you see, to use these ideas as superficial bandages for your bleeding psyches. . . . So you are not as bad as I pegged you. You might be inclined in the direction I have indicated, but then so is everyone else in the room, including Ruburt.

(*Jim H.: "Now would you define bad in that context?"*)

I do not define bad. When I use the term it is according to your own definition. You have an idea that good is gentle and bad is violent. This is because in your mind violence and destruction are the same thing. By this analogy, you see, the soft voice is the holy voice and the loud voice is the wicked one, and a strong desire is the bad desire and a weak desire the good one. You become afraid of projecting ideas or desires outward, for in the back of your mind you think that what is powerful is evil.

Instead, I am telling you that the universe is a good universe. It knows its own vitality, and that vitality is within you. You can encourage it freely. Your own nature is a good nature and you can trust it. Because something is difficult does not mean it is good.

(*Jim H.: "The first night I was here you said, 'We will see more of you.' You were quite definitive about it. I've often wondered, why the certainty?"*)

Because I knew why you had come here, and I knew your wife would come also. I am not saying there is no free will. I am simply making a statement about this realm of probabilities.

(*Jim H.: "To me that implies a prior knowledge of our lives."*)

It does indeed, in your terms, but that knowledge is also available to you. Now we cannot cover one topic clearly in a single evening, much less one hundred and one topics. In reference, however, to one remark you made earlier: You have in almost all of your lives been strongly involved in what you would call religious endeavors. Your remaining lives were just as religiously involved in opposite endeavors, in your terms, but we will go into that later. The holy soul turned inside out is some fleshpot, let's put it that way.

You have always been involved with questions concerning good and evil, and you had two existences in two civilizations in Egypt. In one of these your friend over here *(Bert C.)* was involved. It is too late to go into that incarnation this evening and besides neither of you are ready to benefit from it yet. It is not a fascinating story to be told only for your enjoyment, but it will help when you can understand it.

I am much more concerned with the reaction of all of you to the material that Ruburt read this evening *(on Gnosticism)*. Now if it seems to you that one class member is monopolizing a session, then remember what I have said before: The questions spoken by one are the unspoken questions of many.

It has seemed to many of you that you have been tinged by evil, from birth. *(To Jim H.):* In one of your past lives you not only heartily believed this, but taught it.

As Ruburt would put it, your sidekick over here *(Jim's wife, Jean)* did not go along with your ideas at all in that life. She was a male at that time, however, and you were a female and a priestess. So was your friend *(Bert C.).* As a male in that life she had an expanding effect upon your personality, but you were very given to ritual and a belief in magic acts, and to the idea that existence in itself was evil and wrong. You were indeed a member of the sect now called Gnostic.

(Gnosticism was a selected system of religion and philosophy, uniting features of Platonism, orientalism, Christianity, and dualism. It embraced pre-Christian times and later, and took several forms. In all of them its central doctrine held that knowledge — gnosis — was the means of salvation from the tyranny of matter, more than philosophy or faith.

(Jim H.: "Is that why I react so strongly against Gnosticism now, because I've gone beyond that point?")

Not only that, but because you sense in yourself still some sympathy toward the beliefs. While you are freeing yourself you recognize within your psyche a leaning in that direction, and so you lash out whenever you hear such ideas, not realizing that you lash out against yourself.

(Kathy B.: "Is that why I have a similar reaction to this Gnostic literature?")

You were at that time a male and a friend of his. Now almost all who come to these classes have at one time or another been engaged in such endeavors. You have all been a part of other classes, though not necessarily with me. Because of your long interest, certain aspects will hit many of you very strongly. Association operates not only within one life, but between lives in your terms. Words and phrases spoken now will trigger your memories, and those memories will become alive if you allow them to.

(To Art O.): Even our African god over there can remember his past lives if he will only allow himself to do so.

(Art O.: "Is that life the reason why I like African music now?")

It is one of the reasons. The other reason has to do with another life in which you were musically inclined.

Now I am going to bid you all a fond good evening.

(To Mary M.): I have one message for our friend over here, however, and it is quite simple. When you do not know what to do, relax and tell yourself that other portions of yourself do know; they will take over. Give yourself some rest. Remind yourself that in many ways you are a very successful person as you are. Success does not necessarily involve great intellect or great position or great wealth; it has to do with inner integrity. Remember that.

I bid you all, now, a fond good evening.

ESP CLASS SESSION:
TUESDAY, FEBRUARY 9, 1971

(This session also contained the very interesting material that Seth gave concerning his own perceptions while he is addressing a group of people; that data is quoted in the 575th session, in Chapter Nineteen.)

Now I do have something to say to this one *(Sue W.)*, and that one *(Jim H.)*, and to some extent to all of you. There is no need to justify your existence. You do not need to write or preach to justify yourselves, for instance. Being is its own justification. Only when you realize this can you begin to utilize your freedom. Otherwise you try too hard.

This also applies to our friend Ruburt. If you become too determined to justify your existence then you will begin to close out areas of your life. Only those areas that mean safe justification to you will have meaning, and the others will begin to disappear. You do not have to justify in any terms.

Now if you would each, for ten minutes a day, open yourselves to your own reality there would be no question of self-justification, for you would realize the miraculous nature of your own identity. I have said this before in class: You are as dead now, and as alive, as you will ever be. In life you can be as dead as you think any corpse is — even, by contrast, far deader.

When I come here to speak I focus my energy, but not toward this room as a destination, for in your terms this room does not exist to me. In your terms, this room does not even exist to you. You pretend to agree that it does; we meet in no place of space or time. The true meetings that take place here have nothing to do with the room or the people that you think you are. You know that you hallucinate the room, that you are as much in trance here as you ever are when you are in psychological time. I simply want you to realize that if this life is a trance, then you can turn the direction of your consciousness to perceive greater realities that presently exist. You can be aware of your own greater identity, even as I am. You sit within the miracle of yourselves and ask for signs. It is your inner eyes I would open.

As you know yourselves, you only accept those suggestions, ideas and hang-ups that suit your purposes at this time. You are not, therefore, at the mercy of any neurosis from a past life, nor are there any fears from your present lives that you cannot conquer. I have not said that you will necessarily conquer them, but it is within your ability to do so.

The decision is your own according to your understanding. You cannot be hounded from one level of reality to another by a fear that you do not understand. You cannot be threatened in this life by fears from your early childhood, or by so-called past existences, unless you so thoroughly believe in the nature of fear that you allow yourselves to be conquered by it. Each of your personalities are free to accept and develop, from the miraculous banks of reality, those experiences and emotions that you want, and to reject those you do not want.

Let me give you a more concrete example that each of you can use in your own way. Suppose the worst, that in this life you have the following background: You are poor, you are of a minority race, you are not intellectual, you are a woman, you have a severe physical defect and you are no beauty. Now you set these challenges for yourself in a so-called past life. This does not mean that you cannot use all of your courage and resolution to solve these problems. You set them in the hope that you will solve them. You did not set them like millstones about your neck, hoping ahead of time that you would drown.

All you have to do is realize your own freedom. You form the reality that you know, not esoterically, not symbolically, not philosophically. Some great oversoul doesn't form it for you — you cannot put the burden there, either. You have in the past, collectively and individually, blamed a god or a fate for the nature of your personal realities — those aspects, indeed that you did not like.

The personality is given the greatest gift of all; you get exactly what you want to get. You create from nothing the experience that is your own. If you do not like your experience, then look within yourself and change it. But realize also that you are responsible for your joys and triumphs, and that the energy to create any of these realities comes from the inner self. What you do with it is up to the individual personality.

(During break class members discussed fate and predestination.)

Some evening I would like our lady over here to talk to me about predestination.

(Bernice M.: "I would like you to talk to me about it.")

You are not "programmed." Nothing happens because it must happen. Every thought that you have now changes reality. Not only reality as you know it, but all reality. No act of yours predisposes a future self to act in a particular manner. There are banks of activity from which you can draw or choose not to draw.

(Bernice M.: "Do we make instantaneous decisions? For example, I was thinking of the Los Angeles earthquake today. A man walked out into the street and was killed by a falling brick. What made this one person in the entire building walk out?")

This particular individual was quite aware of what would occur, on what you would call an unconscious basis. He was not predestined to die. He chose both the time, in your terms, and the method, for reasons of his own.

(Bernice M.: "Regardless of who chose, it was destined that he die.")

It was not predestined. He chose. No one chose for him.

(Bernice M.: "But he had made the decision before.")

Before when?

(Bernice M.: "Before he was killed.")

He knew that he was ready to go on to other spheres of activity. Unconsciously, he looked about for the means and chose those immediately available. This particular individual, three days earlier, had made the plan. There was no predestination involved. Because a tree branch falls, this does not mean that it was destined to fall in either the particular manner of its fall nor in the timing of the fall. There is a great difference between free choice and predestination.

(Jim H.: "Didn't you say earlier, referring to the woman who was born in a minority race, that her challenges had been set up by a previous personality, in our terms?")

By the whole self.

(Jim H.: "The decision was made when that previous personality had returned to the whole self for a period of reevaluation?")

You must realize, again, that we are speaking of divisions for convenience's sake, where none really exists. At the same "time," so to speak, that this personality is born into a minority race, in a completely different era it may be born rich, secure and aristocratic. It is searching out different methods of experience and expansion. Do you follow me?

(Jim H.: "I understand. I thought you probably meant the challenges had been set up by the whole self.")

Indeed. Remember, this is your entire identity of which we are speaking. It is only you who are presently aware of but one portion of it; and this portion you insist upon calling yourself. You are the self who makes these decisions.

(Bert C.: "What recourse would the poor individual who was born with all of these seemingly insurmountable handicaps have, were she to say consciously, at the ego level, 'I just don't want any of this. I would have much preferred to have been born aristocratic'?")

The inner self realizes, however, that potentials are present that would not necessarily be present under other circumstances — abilities that can not only help the present personality but other individuals, and even society at large.

Your main point of contention is brought about by the emotional barriers that are caused by the difference in terms. It is as if you choose to work for a day in the slums. It would be ridiculous for you to choose to do this, and then say to yourself, "Why did I choose to work in the slums? I would prefer to work on Fifth Avenue." You know the reason, and your entire identity knows the reason. You hide it from the present self simply to insure the fact that the present reality is not a pretended one.

A rich man who tries to be poor for a day to learn what poverty is learns little, because he cannot forget the wealth that is available to him. Though he eats the same poor fare as the poor man, and lives in the same poor house for a day — or for a year or five years — he knows he has his mansion to return to. So you hide these things from yourself so that you can relate. You forget your home so that you can return to it enriched.

Consciousness is not made up of balances so much as it is made up of exquisite imbalances, and the focus of awareness is to some degree the result of this state of excitability. In this state all elements are never known because new ones are always being created. I am not speaking of physical elements, but of the psychological characteristics of consciousness, for even those continually merge and change.

You are not now what you were ten minutes earlier. You are not the same being physically, psychologically, spiritually, or psychically, and ten minutes later you will be different again. To deny this is to try to force consciousness into some rigid form from which it cannot ever be freed, to apply rules to it that make a very neat psychological landscape.

(Now Seth's voice really began to boom out.)

Now I would like you again to realize the energy that is available. If Ruburt can use it, you can each use it in your own way. I want you to open up those barriers that you have erected within yourselves; this voice is only used as a symbol of the energy and the strength that is available to each of you, as you utilize those abilities that are your heritage.

You should hear your own echo of my voice as a symbol of your own energy and joy. Forget the cringing selves that you sometimes are and remember, instead, the magic essence of your own being that sings even now through your fingertips. That is the reality which you are seeking. Experience it fully. Do you need an old dead thing like me to tell you what life is? I should be ashamed.

Now, I bid you a fond good evening, and those blessings that are mine to give, I give you. Travel in peace and joy and safety, in your bodies and out.

ABOUT THE AUTHOR

Jane Roberts (May 8, 1929 – September 5, 1984) grew up in Saratoga Springs, New York where she attended Skidmore College. Jane was a prolific writer in a variety of genres including poetry, short stories, children's literature, fiction, and non-fiction. Her international best-selling non-fiction books include *Seth Speaks, The Nature of Personal Reality, The Nature of the Psyche,* and *The Individual and the Nature of Mass Events.* Her enormously popular novels include *The Education of Oversoul Seven, The Further Education of Oversoul Seven,* and *Oversoul Seven and the Museum of Time* (now published as *The Oversoul Seven Trilogy*). Yale University Library maintains a collection of Jane's writings, journals, poetry, and audio and video recordings that were donated after her death by her husband, Robert F. Butts.

INDEX

Meta particles, 303
Middleton, Patty, 365, 267, 270, 272, 274, 277, 290
Milford (Pa.) science fiction conference, 34
Millenius, 348
Mind
    intuition by, 234
    matter created by, 40, 242
Minneapolis, 67
Mohammedanism, 337, 340–341
Molecules
    condensation of consciousness into, 25
    consciousness of, 11, 118, 233, 416
    coordinate points and, 67
    pulsating nature of, 412
Moment point, nature of, 21
Moods, cycle of, 102
Mossman, Tam, 149
Mother, anima and, 192
Mu, continent of, 414
Multidimensional God, see God
Multidimensional personality, xxi, 9, 10, 31, 50, 52, 153, 348, 365
    awareness of realities by, 201–203
    conscious utilization of, 25
    consciousness of, 52
    as maintained by God, 207
    many lives of, 53
    materialization of self by, 51
    nature of, 10–15, 31–32
    as real you, 52
    reincarnational personalities and, 165–166, 190–192
    in state of becoming, 50
    understood by all, 324
Mystic consciousness, 209

Nature, attitude of human race toward, 177–178
Negative webs of probabilities, 231
Nonintervals (nonmoments), 413
Nonviolence, Lumanian, 214–215, 223–224
Nostradamus, 328

Objects
    as manifestations of selves, 17

as symbols, 60–62, 256–257, 383–384
Odors, visual reality of, 266
Open channels, 15
Operant conditioning, 265
Opposites, theology of, 161–162, 343
Oral traditions, 242
Oregano, 351, 410, 412
Original sin, 58
Ouija board, xi
Out-of-body experiences, 281–282
    Christ's, 367
    death and, 120, 127, 129–130, 133
    entry into other realities during, 245–246
    Jane's, xiv, 62
    other bodies in, 257
    See also Astral travel
Outer ego, 9
    camouflage by, 12
Over-population, 177–178
Oversoul, 423

Pain, reason for, 301–302
Painting
    Jane on, 326
    of Jane speaking for Seth, 165
    Lumanian, 221–222
    Rob's 1954, 320, 322
    Seth on, 73, 150, 156–157
    of Seth, xvi, 73
    of Speakers, 312
Parents, choice of, 59
Past, the
    alteration of, 232
    and the future, 90
    as now, 408, 411
Paul (Saul), 330–332, 339–347, 372, 377
Peace, love of, 174
Pendulum, use of, to gain information, 150
Perception
    by consciousness, 415–416
    creation and, 26–28
    after death, 141–143
    differing systems of, 239–241
    by soul (entity), 70–76
    See also ESP

Truth, nature of, 375, 398
Turkey, 352
Turning the other cheek, 171–172
Twins, 182

UFOs, 415
Unconscious
  choice of death by, 423
  as conscious, 191
  formation of physical body by, 9,
    18
  psychologists' use of term, 79
  Seth as dramatization of, xx
  See also Subconscious
Universe
  as idea construction, xi–xii, 79
  source of, 200–201
Utah, 67

Van Elver (artist), 156, 157
Violence
  early civilization opposed to,
    214–216, 222–223
  thoughts of, 417–419

War, 178, 214
  hatred of, 174
Watkins, Carl, 20, 170, 174, 175, 177,
  312
Watkins, Sue, 20, 170, 174, 175, 177,
  370–378, 382–388
  on Seth, 384–388
West Coast (of U.S.), 67
White holes, 379
Willy (cat), 7, 162, 167–168, 174, 287,
  314
"Withers, Frank," 157
Words as symbols, 60–61, 62

Yahoshua, 312–313

Zealots, 349, 350, 372, 373, 374, 332,
  333, 347

New Seth Books, Online Seth Courses
Seth Conferences & Workshops

"THE EARLY SESSIONS" – BY JANE ROBERTS

"The Early Sessions" are the first 510 sessions dictated by Seth during the first six years of his relationship with Jane Roberts and her husband, Robert F. Butts. Published in nine volumes, these new Seth books offer fresh insights from Seth on a vast array of topics.

"THE PERSONAL SESSIONS" – BY JANE ROBERTS

"The Personal Sessions," originally referred to as "the deleted sessions," are Seth-dictated sessions that Jane Roberts and Robert F. Butts considered to be of a highly personal nature, and therefore kept separate from the main body of the Seth material.

THE SETH AUDIO COLLECTION

These audios consist of rare recordings of Seth speaking through Jane Roberts during her classes in Elmira, New York in the 1970s, and recorded by her student, Rick Stack. This collection represents the best of Seth's comments gleaned from over 120 class sessions.

ONLINE SETH COURSES

This in-home learning experience offers an intensive immersion into some of the most important concepts presented in the Seth material. (Includes live online interactive webinars with instructor Rick Stack.)

SETH CONFERENCES & WORKSHOPS

These gatherings offer a unique opportunity to meet people of like mind, increase your understanding of both inner and outer reality, and enhance your ability to create your ideal life.

For further information, contact New Awareness Network, Inc.
(516) 869-9108 between 9:00 A.M. – 5:00 P.M. ET
sumari@sethcenter.com, or visit our websites:
www.sethcenter.com
www.sethlearningcenter.org
www.sethconference.org

ALSO BY JANE ROBERTS

The Nature of Personal Reality. Seth explains how the conscious mind directs unconscious activity, and has at its command all the powers of the inner self. Included in this book are excellent exercises for applying these theories to any life situation.

The Individual and the Nature of Mass Events. Extending the idea that we create our own reality, Seth explores the connection between personal beliefs and world events.

The Magical Approach. Seth reveals the true, magical nature of our deepest levels of being, and discusses how we can live our lives spontaneously, creatively, and according to our own natural rhythms.

The Oversoul Seven Trilogy. The adventures of Oversoul Seven are an intriguing fantasy, a mind-altering exploration of our being, and a vibrant celebration of life.

The "Unknown" Reality, Volumes One and *Two*. Exploring "probable realities" and the interdependence of multiple selves, Seth explains how understanding unknown dimensions can change the world as we know it.

The Nature of the Psyche. Seth reveals a startling new concept of self, answering questions about the secret language of love, our inner reality that exists apart from time, the real origins and incredible powers of dreams, human sexuality, and how we choose our physical death.

Dreams, "Evolution," and Value Fulfillment, Volumes One and *Two*. These books answer crucial questions about the entire significance of Seth's system of thought as he takes us on an odyssey to identify the origins of our universe and our species.

The Way Toward Health. Woven through the poignant story of Jane Roberts' final days are Seth's teachings about self-healing and the mind's effect upon physical health.

This book is co-published by Amber-Allen Publishing and
New World Library. To contact either company, or for information
about our other products, please call or visit us online.

Amber-Allen Publishing is dedicated to bringing a message
of love and inspiration to all who seek a higher
purpose and meaning in life.

For information about other bestselling titles from
Amber-Allen Publishing, please call or visit us online.

(800) 624-8855
www.amberallen.com

New World Library is dedicated to publishing books and audios
that help improve the quality of our lives.

For a catalog of our fine books and audios, contact:

New World Library
14 Pamaron Way
Novato, California 94949

Phone: (415) 884-2100 or (800) 972-6657
Catalog requests: Ext. 50
Orders: Ext. 52
Fax 415-884-2199

www.newworldlibrary.com

ALSO FROM AMBER-ALLEN PUBLISHING

The Four Agreements by don Miguel Ruiz with Janet Mills. Based on ancient Toltec wisdom, The Four Agreements offer a powerful code of conduct that can rapidly transform our lives to a new experience of freedom, true happiness, and love. (Available in paperback, illustrated book, ebook, audiobook, and Spanish.)

The Four Agreements Companion Book by don Miguel Ruiz with Janet Mills. This companion book offers additional insights, practice ideas, questions and answers about applying The Four Agreements, and true stories from people who have already changed their lives. (Available in paperback, ebook, and Spanish.)

The Mastery of Love by don Miguel Ruiz with Janet Mills. Using insightful stories to bring his message to life, don Miguel Ruiz shows us how to heal our emotional wounds, recover the freedom and joy that are our birthright, and restore the spirit of playfulness that is vital to loving relationships. (Available in paperback, ebook, audiobook, and Spanish.)

The Circle of Fire by don Miguel Ruiz with Janet Mills. This beautiful collection of prayers (including the popular *Circle of Fire Prayer*), guided meditations, and powerful prose, will inspire and transform your life. (Available in paperback, ebook, and Spanish as *Oraciones.*)

The Voice of Knowledge by don Miguel Ruiz with Janet Mills. In this life-altering book, don Miguel Ruiz reminds us of a profound and simple truth: the only way to end our emotional suffering and restore our joy in living is to stop believing in lies — mainly about ourselves. (Available in paperback, ebook, audiobook, and Spanish.)

The Fifth Agreement by don Miguel Ruiz and don Jose Ruiz with Janet Mills. Ruiz joins his son to encourage us to see the truth, to recover our authenticity, and to change the message we deliver to ourselves and to everyone around us. (Available in paperback, ebook, audiobook, and Spanish.)